Ideology

Ideology

A Multidisciplinary Approach

Teun A. van Dijk

SAGE Publications
London • Thousand Oaks • New Delhi

First published 1998

SAGE Publications Ltd
6 Bonhill Street
London EC2A 4PU

SAGE Publications Inc
2455 Teller Road
Thousand Oaks, California 91320

SAGE Publications India Pvt Ltd
32, M-Block Market
Greater Kailash – I
New Delhi 110 048

British Library Cataloguing in Publication data

A catalogue record for this book is available from the British
Library.

ISBN 0 7619 5654 9
ISBN 0 7619 5655 7 (pbk)

Library of Congress catalog record available

Typeset by Photoprint, Torquay
Printed in Great Britain by The Cromwell Press, Trowbridge,
Wiltshire

Contents

Preface

Most scholars have a number of dream projects in mind: topics they have always wanted to investigate and write about, but for various reasons never did. I have many such unrealized academic dreams. For many years, an innovative study on the relations between ideology and discourse has been one of them.

Ideology has been dealt with in literally thousands of books and articles, but (as many other authors also conclude) its definition is as elusive and confused as ever. So, to write a book that would specifically deal with the complex relations between ideology and discourse is more than a challenge: it is pure hubris, especially since such a book should of course begin with a proper theory of ideology. How could I possibly contribute anything new and interesting given such an enormous literature?

Not surprisingly, therefore, it soon turned out that the theoretical component of such a study would itself be a major undertaking. One single book would barely be enough to explore the many issues, concepts and disciplines involved in the analysis of ideology, let alone the relations between discourse and ideology.

Nevertheless, I accepted the challenge, and this book is the first instalment of this major enterprise. It discusses some of the fundamental concepts of such a new, multidisciplinary theory of ideology, and sketches the overall outline of the ways ideology is expressed and reproduced by discourse. The overall theoretical framework for my approach to ideology may be summarized by the triangle formed by the concepts Cognition, Society and Discourse. That is, first, the status, internal organization and mental functions of ideologies need to be studied in terms of social cognition. Second, the conditions and functions of ideologies are obviously not only cognitive but also social, political, cultural and historical. And third, ideologies are formed, changed and reproduced largely through socially situated discourse and communication.

Instead of simply adding results from psychology, the social sciences and discourse studies, however, these three central concepts have to be reformulated and integrated into one theoretical framework. Discourse should be explicitly related to the structures and strategies of the personal and social mind, as well as to those of social situations, social interactions and societal structures. In the same way, also cognition should be linked with both discourse and society, thus serving as the necessary interface by which social structure can be explicitly related to discourse structure.

The vast majority of studies of ideology (whether Marxist or non-Marxist) are rooted in the social sciences and pay extensive attention to ideologies in relation to class, dominant groups, social movements, power, the political economy or, more recently, to gender and culture. They have paid less attention to the cognitive and the discursive dimensions of ideologies, however. Indeed, classical work hardly analyses the details of the 'ideas', 'beliefs' or 'consciousness' assumed to constitute an ideology. Even most contemporary approaches ignore the advances in current cognitive science, and, vice versa, most cognitive science is barely interested in questions of the mental structures and functions of ideologies. This is why I pay more attention to this cognitive dimension of the theory, while emphasizing that ideologies may well be located in the mind but that this does not mean that they are therefore less social.

Though usually of later vintage, extant work on discourse and ideology does of course emphasize the important role of text and talk in the (re)production of ideologies. To my knowledge, however, among the many studies of ideology, some of which also deal with language or discourse, there is not a single one that details *how exactly* ideology shapes text and talk, and conversely, how it is formed, acquired or changed by discourse and communication.

As part of the more social and political component of the theory, and establishing an explicit link with my previous big project, this book will occasionally use racism and racist ideologies as an illustration of the theoretical argument. This does not mean, however, that I offer a fully fledged account of racist ideologies, which would need to be accounted for in a separate monograph. However, whereas throughout the book my comments on ideology, racism and discourse will be rather general, Chapter 28 offers a concrete case study of a recent text about race relations in the USA, namely, Dinesh D'Souza's book *The End of Racism*.

A muldisciplinary theory of ideology can be accomplished only by reducing its complexity. I am not a psychologist, a sociologist or a political scientist. This means that my overall perspective and organizing conceptualizations will often be those of discourse and discourse analysis. There are worse biases, given the fundamental role of discourse in the formation and expression of ideology as social cognition and in the reproduction of ideologies in society. At the same time, it is obvious that this book cannot do, redo or undo the relevant substantial work that has already been done in the social sciences.

As suggested, this book is the first result of a bigger project. It sketches the overall framework of the theory. In later studies I hope to detail each of its main components, namely, those of social cognition, social interaction and societal structures, as well as the structures of discourse involved in the expression and reproduction of ideology. These studies will also feature concrete empirical studies of the relations between discourse, cognition and society, as well as more detailed reviews of the relevant literature.

I may disappoint some of the readers whose notion of discourse is exclusively associated with the more literary, philosophical or postmodern notions of 'discourse' or 'text'. After more than thirty years, the study of discourse has become a multidisciplinary field, featuring sometimes highly explicit and detailed theories of structures and functions of text and talk. Unfortunately, many fashionable approaches that currently refer to 'text' or 'discourse' ignore these advances, and for that reason offer an unsuitable basis for a theory of ideology.

Even in a theoretical book like this, I highly value accessibility for scholars and students from different disciplines. This means that esoteric jargon will be avoided, and theoretical terms only introduced and explained where necessary. Many of the notions dealt with in this book have been discussed in sometimes rather technical earlier studies. In order to be able to construct an integrated theoretical framework, many details had to be ignored in favour of the overall outline of the theory. I hope to be able to pay attention to these details in the following studies in this series.

There is another way in which this book differs from much other work on ideology: it barely looks back. Many studies, as is customary in philosophy and sociology (and much less in, e.g., psychology and linguistics), are commentaries (on commentaries) on the classics, from the French *philosophes* and Marx/Engels to Lukács, Gramsci, Althusser, Foucault and Habermas. (For detail, see the excellent introductions and historical overviews by Larrain, Eagleton and Billig, among others.)

In this book I want to go beyond such a history and philosophy of ideology, and integrate new ideas of contemporary discourse studies, linguistics, cognitive science, political science and new developments in the other social sciences. In other words, in order not to get entangled in endless debates with the classics, I have left such debates to the many other authors who engage in them. Instead, I present a systematic, analytical study, in which the old debates and current other studies of ideology play a role only in the background, in the footnotes and in the references. This of course does *not* mean that I think most earlier work on ideology is irrelevant. On the contrary, there are many studies whose theories, concepts and empirical results are also suitable for my own project. However, in the first, theoretical book of this project, I prefer to focus on the overall framework and present that as clearly and analytically as possible, without extensive comments on, discussions with, or references to the vast amount of earlier work. Moreover, in order to keep the already extensive bibliography within normal proportions, most references will be to books and not to articles. In the next volumes I hope to enter more explicitly into a debate with other approaches to ideology.

Since this book will, I hope, be followed by others in this project on discourse and ideology, I welcome the comments of readers. They may help me improve the theory in these next studies.

Acknowledgements

Finally, I am glad to be able to acknowledge the comments on an earlier version of this book by Michael Billig, Terry Eagleton, Philomena Essed and Ruth Wodak. I am especially grateful for the extensive comments by Martha Augoustinos and Luisa Martín Rojo. Some of them kindly disagreed with the overall perspective, others with details of my discussion. I have tried to argue as clearly as possible where some of these discrepancies are inherent to the choices I have made in this book, and in other cases gladly corrected my errors and filled various gaps. Otherwise the usual formula applies: any remaining errors are of course mine.

Teun A. van Dijk

1

Introduction

The fuzzy life of 'ideology'

It's almost a routine. Studies of ideology often begin with a remark about the vagueness of the notion and the resulting theoretical confusion of its analysis, as I did in the Preface. Indeed, of all essentially contested and controversial concepts in the social sciences and the humanities, that of 'ideology' may well come out near the top of the list. One historical and political – and, yes, ideological – reason for this special status may be that 'ideology' is one of these notions that have divided Marxists and non-Marxists, as well as 'critical' scholars and 'uncritical' ones – obviously divisions that are themselves ideological.

Still, as a general concept, ideology is hardly more vague than similar Big Terms in the social sciences and the humanities. In many respects, the same holds for such notions as 'society', 'group', 'action', 'power', 'discourse', 'mind' and 'knowledge', among many others. These notions defy precise definition and seem to happily live the fuzzy life inherent in such catch-all terms that denote complex sets of phenomena and that are the preferred toys of philosophers and scholars in the humanities and the social sciences. Where 'ideology' differs from these other general notions, however, is that its commonsense usage is generally pejorative.

Definitions generally are hardly adequate to capture all the complexities of such notions. Indeed, such fundamental notions are the objects of inquiry for theories and whole disciplines. Definitions cannot be expected to summarize all the insights accumulated in such bodies of knowledge – even if there were no controversies over the meaning of the central concepts of such disciplines. In sum, as with many similar notions, and apart from its uses in everyday discourse, the various versions of the concept of ideology are simply the scholarly constructs of competing theories. That is, at least with this word, it is as Alice was told in Wonderland: we define what the word means. Of course, presuming that 'we' have the power to do so.

Traditional approaches

Despite the controversies and the many different approaches to the concept of ideology, the historical terms of the debate remain remarkably similar. We are routinely brought back to the eighteenth century, when Destutt de Tracy in France proposed a 'science of ideas' to be called *idéologie*, a science which, incidentally, never made it, unless we take philosophy (or psychology?) as its current representative.[1] With equal predictability, we will then meet Marx, of course, usually in the company of Engels, and then their followers (neo- or not) in our century, among whom Lukács, Gramsci and Althusser play a prominent role. Similarly, on the non-Marxist side, we are bound to encounter a sequence of sociologists and philosophers, of whom Durkheim and Mannheim are merely the most famous.[2]

As is customary in sociology and philosophy, these and other classics still appear so prominently in most current discussions of ideology that it is hard to find more analytical and sophisticated studies that integrate new concepts and insights of contemporary approaches in the humanities and the social sciences.

The remnants of the classical debates are also crystallized in the everyday, commonsense uses of the notion of 'ideology', namely, taken as a system of wrong, false, distorted or otherwise misguided beliefs, typically associated with our social or political opponents. For many in the West – laypersons, politicians and scholars alike – communism was (based on) such an ideology. It was often seen as the prototype of an ideology.[3] The legacy of Marx and Engels, to whom this negative, critical concept of ideology is usually attributed, is thus posthumously discredited by the very notion they introduced themselves.

At the same time, this negative meaning and uses of the everyday concept of ideology shows what most earlier analysts also emphasized, namely, that ideologies express or conceal one's social or political position, perspective or interests: few of 'us' (in the West or elsewhere) describe our own belief systems or convictions as 'ideologies'. On the contrary, Ours is the Truth, Theirs is the Ideology. Capitalism, the Market, or Christianity, even when 'we' are no fans of them, are 'ours' and therefore not usually described as ideologies in everyday discourse.

We see that as residues of scholarly debates, commonsense conceptions of the notion of 'ideology' capture in a nutshell many of the main tenets of the classical tradition: (a) ideologies are false beliefs; (b) ideologies conceal real social relations and serve to deceive others; (c) ideologies are beliefs others have; and (d) ideologies presuppose the socially or politically self-serving nature of the definition of truth and falsity.

The critical element of the notion of ideology in this tradition is usually associated with various notions of power and dominance. Following Marx/Engels, ideologies were first of all defined as the prevailing ideas of an age.[4] According to the political economy of these philosophers, these dominant ideas were associated with those of the ruling class. They are part of the 'superstructure' and hence determined by the economic or 'material' base of society. Because the ruling class, however defined, controls the means of production, including the means of the (re)production of ideas – most notably those of politics, the media, literature and education – they are also able to make their ideologies more or less accepted by the ruled as the undisputed knowledge of the 'natural' ways things are.

Later debates in this Marxist tradition, however, questioned the economic determinism of the classical definitions of ideology. Ideas, laws, philosophy, literature, and hence also ideologies, may in part develop autonomously with respect to the material base, and may even exercise their influence, top-down, on that economic infrastructure.[5] With Gramsci, these relations between ideology and society were conceptualized in terms of 'hegemony'. Thus, instead of the imposition of dominant ideologies by a ruling class, hegemony more subtly works through the management of the mind of the citizens, for example by persuasively constructing a consensus about the social order.

It is especially this neo-Marxist view and its variants that have inspired many debates on ideologies at least until the demise of Communism around 1990, when the terms of the debate changed again. Many of these approaches are now merging with a broader critical concept of ideology, for instance in the field of cultural studies.[6] Yet, whether as dominant or hegemonic ideologies, contemporary versions of the Marxist idea of the combined socio-economic and symbolic power of elite groups remain alive in many current approaches to ideology. In my own account of the role of the elites in the reproduction of racism, we shall encounter a special version of that idea.

In ongoing dialogue with (and often in opposition to) the Marxist strand of the tradition, sociologists and philosophers have continued to debate, with increasing sophistication, the social and political dimensions of knowledge, truth and scholarship itself. For a long time, their insights into society were precisely self-defined as non-ideological, and hence as truthful and scientific. Both politically and in a scholarly context, Marxism was no exception. Above the fray of politics, and unbound by social or economic interests, thus, most scholars considered themselves a *freischwebende Intelligenz*, that is, beyond the pale of self-serving falsehood, and only interested in the disinterested search for the truth – only to be accused by more critical others of engaging in precisely what they wanted to avoid in the first place, namely, an ideology. This ideology of science, which tries to conceal its interests and wants its own beliefs to be accepted as truth by those who recognize its power and dominance, is thus hardly different from other ideologies that are developed to achieve hegemony, to legitimate power or to conceal inequality – if only in the domain of knowledge. It is at this crucial point where the philosophy and sociology of ideology and the philosophy and sociology of science overlap.

It is only in a later stage, in the second part of the twentieth century, that more inclusive and less pejorative notions of ideologies develop. Here, ideologies are usually defined as political or social systems of ideas, values or prescriptions of groups or other collectivities, and have the function of organizing or legitimating the actions of the group.[7] Most later work on political belief systems is rooted in this more general concept of ideology.[8] It is at this point where my own exploration will start. Yet, it will be emphasized that also the notion of a 'belief system' is still much too

general, and in need of further analysis. This is one of the reasons why this
study also intends to continue (the few) psychological approaches to
ideology.[9]

In this informal summary of some main strands of the classic debate about
ideology, most notions, including the more controversial ones, are as
familiar as the names associated with them. Although many are not very
precise, as may be expected for such fundamental terms, these are the
notions that are being used, and that have influenced the foundations of
virtually all social sciences. Most studies of ideology, instead of going
beyond the classics, keep repeating, reformulating and reinterpreting this
Master Narrative of the Story of Ideology. Therefore, I feel delightfully free
to presuppose this history to be known and to explore new ways of
addressing the old problems, and at the same time perhaps create some
interesting new problems.

A framework for a multidisciplinary theory of ideology

The philosophy and sociology of science tell us that old theories and
approaches are seldom discredited because they are explicitly proven false
or inadequate. Rather, other ideas become accepted that seem to be more
attractive for whatever reason, sometimes because they provide a better
account of the 'facts', or because they focus on other, more interesting facts.
Therefore, for the same strategic reason that I presuppose the history of the
study of ideology to be generally known, it will not be my aim to discredit,
attack or debate the multitude of such classical approaches. Such a dispute
would precisely look back and remain entangled in the same frameworks of
discussion and thought (see, however, some of the endnotes for comments
on the relevant literature). Of course, this book cannot start from scratch, and
will use and integrate those classical ideas about ideology that remain
relevant in a new approach.

My main purpose, then, is to look ahead, to find alternative theoretical
frameworks, to explore and incorporate other disciplines, and especially to
work towards a comprehensive *theory* of ideology. Among other things,
such a theory would describe and explain the following:

- the general status of ideology as a cognitive and social system
- the differences between ideologies and other (systems of) 'ideas'
- the components and internal organization of ideologies
- the relations between ideologies and other shared social representations
- the relations between ideologies and values
- the relations between ideologies and social structures
- the relations between ideologies and groups and their interests
- the institutional embedding of ideologies
- the relations between ideology and power and dominance
- how ideologies are acquired, used and changed
- how ideologies are reproduced

- how ideologies are expressed in social practices in general
- how ideologies are expressed and reproduced by discourse.

Obviously, this is a research agenda that could keep several hundreds of scholars busy well into the next millennium, so my aims have to be more modest, and I shall therefore focus on only some aspects of such a theory.

I need not do so merely within the confines of the disciplines that have up to now dominated the debate, namely, philosophy, sociology and (in part) political science. Since I continue to talk about ideology, some of the more familiar notions, also from these disciplines, will appear again in my own approach. However, where necessary, they will be framed and formulated in a novel way, and related to concepts and theoretical developments that hitherto have received scant attention from the leading ideologues of the study of ideology. That is, a theory of ideology first of all needs to be multidisciplinary.

Yet, we all have our limitations, interests and preferred ways of thinking, and my approach will therefore be located in the conceptual and disciplinary triangle that relates *cognition*, *society* and *discourse*. There are worse sites of inquiry when dealing with the notion of ideology. First, even among those who deny it, ideologies are at least implicitly taken as some kind of 'system of ideas', and hence belong to the symbolic field of thought and belief, that is, to what psychologists call 'cognition'. Second, ideologies are undoubtedly social, and often (though not always) associated with group interests, conflicts or struggle. They may be used to legitimate or oppose power and dominance, or symbolize social problems and contradictions. They may involve social collectivities such as classes and other groups, as well as institutions, organization and other parts of social structure.[10] Hence the pervasive interest of sociologists and political scientists in the notion of ideology. And third, many contemporary approaches to ideology associate (or even identify) the concept with language use or discourse, if only to account for the way ideologies are typically expressed and reproduced in society.[11] Concealment, legitimation, manipulation and related notions that are seen as the prime functions of ideologies in society are mostly discursive (or more broadly semiotic) social practices. Of course, as we shall see, this does *not* mean that ideologies are expressed only by discourse, but merely that discourse has a specific role, among other social practices, in the reproduction of ideologies.

Having staked out this very broad and multidisciplinary field of inquiry, it is my contention that precisely the complex *relationships* involved here – namely, those between cognition, society and discourse – are needed in an explicit theory of ideology. To say that ideologies are systems of 'ideas' and hence in need of a psychological approach will be an interesting suggestion only if we realize at the same time that these 'ideas' are *also* social (and political and cultural), and that we therefore need to account for them in terms of the study of social representations and their functions for *social cognition.*[12]

And conversely, if ideologies are part of social structure and somehow exhibit or even control the relationships of power and dominance between groups (classes, social formations, organizations, etc.), such a sociological approach will similarly be relevant only if we realize that ideologies characterize the 'mental' dimension of society, groups or institutions. Combined then, these mutual relationships locate my theory first of all in a joint psychological–sociological account of the *social mind in its social (political, cultural) context.*

However, this still leaves us at a level of mental or social abstractions that have no empirical grounds. We need to 'see' ideologies expressed or lived by social actors, and 'at work' in concrete social situations, that is, in everyday *social practices.* Many of these practices would do as a domain of empirical research. Thus, forms of everyday discrimination against women and minorities may be studied as manifestations of sexist and racist ideologies. However, although we may well assume that such discrimination is largely ideologically based, it does not as such 'articulate' these ideologies themselves – at least not as explicitly as the discourses that explain, defend, legitimate, motivate or otherwise 'formulate' fragments of the 'underlying' ideologies.

In other words, although discourses are not the only ideologically based social practices, they certainly are the most crucial ones in the formulation of ideologies in their social reproduction. Language use, text, talk and communication (together subsumed here under the overall term of 'discourse') are needed and used by group members to learn, acquire, change, confirm, articulate, as well as to persuasively convey ideologies to other ingroup members, to inculcate them in novices, defend them against (or conceal them from) outgroup members or to propagate them among those who are (as yet) the infidels. In sum, if we want to know what ideologies actually look like, how they work, and how they are created, changed and reproduced, we need to look closely at their *discursive manifestations.*

Note that such a discourse analysis itself is multiply related to a cognitive and a social account. Discourse meanings, inferences, intentions and many other properties and processes of the mind are intimately linked with an adequate account of text and talk. At the same time, it has become the standard view in discourse studies that discourses are forms of social action and interaction, situated in social contexts of which the participants are not merely speakers/writers and hearers/readers, but also social actors who are members of groups and cultures. Discourse rules and norms are socially shared. The conditions, functions and effects of discourse are social, and discourse competence is socially acquired. In sum, discourse and its mental dimensions (such as its meanings) are multiply embedded in social situations and social structures. And conversely, social representations, social relations and social structures are often constituted, constructed, validated, normalized, evaluated and legitimated in and by text and talk.

Having sketched this rich conceptual triangle of discourse–cognition–society, we have a unique framework to precisely articulate the relationships that also are needed in the theoretical account of ideology. Of course, this is a complex project, or rather a vast paradigm for research, of which one scholar can only design the general outline and study some smaller fragments.

Aims of this study

This book aims to contribute to such a necessarily collective enterprise. In order to be able to emphasize what has often been neglected, my contribution will focus on the structures and strategies of discourse, social cognition and their mutual relationships, as well as on their social embedding – and less on societal (class) structure, or on those institutional, cultural and political dimensions of ideology that have received primary attention in earlier work. Of course, such an emphasis does not imply that the socio-political study of ideology is less fundamental.

Preparing the more specific studies of ideology and its relations to cognition, society and discourse, this book, then, primarily aims to do some of the theoretical groundwork. It does so by examining a number of theoretical concepts that may be needed (or rejected) in such a framework. This also allows me to position my own approach and conceptual analysis in relation to current and past approaches: even new theories have historical backgrounds, and at least need to spell out which extant ideas deserve to be further elaborated and which ones are theoretically less fruitful. Thus, instead of reviewing again the history of such classical notions as 'ruling ideas', 'false consciousness', 'hegemony' or 'legitimation', I undertake a conceptual analysis of these and related notions in my new framework, and will either propose to redefine them or to leave them as history.

Obviously, such theoretical and conceptual groundwork has its own limitations. Many of the notions discussed in this study have been the object of impressive philosophical and social scientific treatises. Some of them (like 'knowledge' or 'group') are the object of whole (sub)disciplines. I am unable to redo or undo all this previous work. However, I discuss some of it briefly in a new perspective and try to relate it somewhat more explicitly to the new notion of ideology I shall develop in this and the following studies.

Even where earlier studies are relevant for my enterprise, their main problem seems to be the lack of theoretical explicitness. Most crucially lacking is a theory of the internal components, structures or organization of ideologies. Very few of the large number of studies about ideologies ever get down to the mundane job of describing what *they actually look like*. In the same way, although most studies discuss the *functions* of ideologies for groups, group members, society and culture, there is not much work that spells out the details of such social or cognitive functions and that explains ideological structures in terms of such functions. Thus, if ideologies are being developed to 'legitimate' power or social inequality, what is the precise nature of these legitimation processes and practices? And finally, if ideologies are expressed and reproduced, if not constituted, by discourse, similar questions may be asked – how does this happen, what discourse structures are involved and how *exactly* are these related to the social context? In sum, although much classical and current work on ideology is interesting and relevant also for our own discussion, their analyses usually remain at a level of abstraction that defies detailed inquiry. It is the aim of this book to design some of the elements of a research programme that will try to answer such fundamental questions.

The new concept of ideology

To do this, I intend to develop a new notion of ideology that serves as the interface between social structure and social cognition. In that framework, ideologies may be very succinctly defined as the *basis of the social representations shared by members of a group*. This means that ideologies allow people, as group members, to organize the multitude of social beliefs about what is the case, good or bad, right or wrong, *for them*, and to act accordingly.

Ideologies may also influence what is accepted as true or false, especially when such beliefs are found to be relevant for the group. In that latter, epistemological sense, ideologies may also form the basis of specific arguments for, and explanations of, specific social arrangements, or indeed influence a specific understanding of the world in general. Note, though, that ideologies in this framework are not simply a 'world view' of a group, but rather the principles that form the *basis* of such beliefs. Here we enter the perennial debate about the relations between ideology and knowledge, which we also need to examine in some detail.

In most (but not all) cases, ideologies are self-serving and a function of the material and symbolic interests of the group. Among these interests, power over other groups (or resistance against the domination by other groups) may have a central role and hence function as a major condition and purpose for the development of ideologies. Ideologies thus operate both at the overall, global level of social structure, for instance as the socially shared mental 'monitor' of social competition, conflict, struggle and inequality, and at the local level of situated social practices in everyday life.

The core of this new concept of ideology is not an arbitrary invention that would take us too far from earlier scholarly as well as commonsense notions of ideology. If that were to have been the case, we should have had to invent a new term altogether. Several current definitions of ideology share important elements with my own. Many authors would agree that an ideology is something like a shared framework of social beliefs that organize and coordinate the social interpretations and practices of groups and their members, and in particular also power and other relations between groups.

Thus, to quote just one of many such definitions by an influential scholar, Stuart Hall defines ideology as follows:

> By ideology I mean the mental frameworks – the languages, the concepts, categories, imagery of thought, and the systems of representation – which different classes and social groups deploy in order to make sense of, figure out and render intelligible the way society works. (Hall, 1996: 26)

We see that many elements of my own approach already appear here: a mental framework of beliefs about society and the cognitive and social functions of such a framework for groups. Given his other work, Stuart Hall would probably have no objection if we were to add to his definition that ideologies are not limited to making sense of society, but that they also serve to regulate social practices. In the explanation of his definition, he explicitly refers to the role of ideologies in the stabilization (and one might add, the challenge) of particular forms of power and dominance.

The aim of this book, then, is to go beyond such definitions, and actually spell out what exactly these 'mental frameworks' are and how exactly (members of) social groups 'make sense' of, communicate and otherwise interact in society on the basis of such frameworks. That is, we need not only a definition, but also a detailed *theory* of ideology.

The cognitive versus the social?

One possible objection to the cognitive definition of ideology in terms of the basis of the social representations shared by a group may be that this approach is too 'idealist'. As will become clear later in this book, such a critique would be misguided. Ideologies are not merely defined in cognitive terms, but also in terms of social groups, group relations, institutions, at the macro-level and in terms of social practices at the micro-level. It will be emphasized that ideologies are constructed, used and changed by social actors as group members in specific, often discursive, social practices. They are not individual, idealistic constructs, but the social constructs shared by a group.

However, it will also be stressed that for a theoretically useful theory of ideology, we should analytically distinguish between these socially shared mental representations, on the one hand, and the social practices that are (partly) controlled by them, or by which they are constructed. Such a distinction is as useful as that between grammars or discourse rules and actual language use. Hence, although a theory of ideology has an important cognitive component, such a theory would not be complete without an equally crucial social component. This does not imply, however, that the theory of ideology, as is the case for traditional Marxist approaches, should be 'materialist' in the sense that it is rooted (only) in the socio-economic base of society.

In sum, and more generally for my work, I precisely advocate a productive integration of the cognitive and the social, the individual and the collective. That both discourse and ideology are social constructs and accomplishments should by now be a truism, and it also informs the approach in this book. Much contemporary discourse analysis is socially (or rather 'interactively') oriented and ignores the crucial cognitive dimension of language use and social practices. This book will therefore focus on cognition (and discourse) rather than on the (more familiar) social dimensions of ideologies, but that does not mean that these are less important. No adequate theory of discourse or ideology can be developed without examining the role of socio-cultural knowledge and other shared beliefs that provide the 'common ground' of all discourse and social interaction. My point is that these 'representations' are *both* social *and* mental.

More specifically, an exclusively social or 'interactionist' theory of discourse or ideology is unable to describe in detail how exactly societal structures (groups, power, institutions, etc.) and even social interaction and contexts condition the actual production and understanding of discourse, and indeed the very participation of social actors in social interaction. If language users share knowledge, rules or 'methods' then these should *also* be made explicit in cognitive terms. The 'intermediate' representations and processes involved in these complex and detailed relationships between society and discourse are not and should not be ignored, or mystified. We are able to explain such relationships only if we know how language users actually go about writing or talking, reading or understanding, and indeed interacting, that is, by thinking and by 'making sense' of what they and their co-participants do. This does *not* mean that discourse (or ideology) is reduced to individual persons, nor to their minds. But text and talk of language users cannot be explained without at least a serious cognitive analysis of the minds of such language users, and especially how such minds shape and are shaped by discourse and other social practices in context.

Obviously, cognitive science does not provide the full story about the representation and processes that are involved in language use and the development and the uses of ideologies. Cognitive science is unfortunately not interested very much in social representations and ideologies, nor in social issues more generally. With some notable exceptions, most current social discourse analysis in turn ignores cognition, for example, because it is afraid of psychologism, cognitivism, mentalism or individualism. None of these -isms needs to be feared as long as one knows that discourse and ideology are social phenomena and as long as one embeds cognition in social contexts and society. That people think, and share their beliefs, is part of that social life of language and ideology, and analysing thinking and believing, in detail and explicitly, is also a task of the socially minded scholar. Theoretically, then, there is no alternative but to integrate a social and a cognitive analysis in the study of ideology, as will be extensively argued throughout this book. Ignoring either the social or the cognitive dimension of ideology will imply unwarranted reduction. This book, and also my other work on discourse, emphatically rejects such reductionism.

A critical approach

Apart from being multidisciplinary, and attempting to formulate a more explicit theory of ideology within the discourse–cognition–society triangle, my work on ideology also aims to be *critical*, in the sense of articulating an explicit position of scholarly dissent in relationships of societal dominance and inequality.[13] Contrary to traditional critical approaches, however, this does *not* mean that the definition of ideology is limited to a concept that sees ideology only as an instrument of domination. There are good theoretical and empirical reasons to assume that there are also ideologies of opposition or resistance,[14] or ideologies of competition between equally powerful groups, or ideologies that only promote the internal cohesion of a group, or ideologies about the survival of humankind. This implies that, as such, ideologies in my approach are not inherently negative, nor limited to social structures of domination.

Does this more general conception of ideology take away the critical edge of the enterprise, as is sometimes suggested, or prevent ideological critique? Of course it does not. No more than that the use of the general concept of 'power' precludes a critical analysis of power *abuse*, as well as solidarity with the forms of counter-power we call resistance. The same is true for the general concept of 'legitimation'. Again, ideologies may be critically examined when (unjustly) legitimating power abuse or domination, but that does not mean that all legitimation, as such, is negative. Most forms of applied ethics will accept the legitimation of resistance against domination. It would be rather arbitrary to use the notion of ideology only for the belief systems we do not accept. What about the ideological belief systems we are indifferent about – would we have to declare them non-ideological because we have not made up our mind about them? Obviously, as will be argued in more detail later, this cannot be a fruitful criterion for the use of a theoretical concept. Thus, ideologies will only be (generally) defined in terms of their contents and structures, as well as in terms of their cognitive and social functions.

Such a general notion is perfectly compatible with a critical analysis of 'bad' ideologies such as those of class domination, racism or sexism, that is, of ideologies that deny, conceal, legitimate or monitor social inequality. A general concept of ideology not only provides a more solid framework for a critical approach, but also allows comparison among different kinds of ideologies, the changes of ideologies from systems of resistance to systems of domination (or vice versa), and a more coherent and complete study of the embedding of ideologies in social cognition as well as in social structure. In this sense, my study explicitly continues but also tries to renew the tradition of critical theory in the social sciences and the humanities initiated by the Frankfurt School sixty years ago.[15]

My previous major project was a study of the ways racism is reproduced by discourse. In order to establish a link with this work, and at the same time to have a more specific example, several chapters will make some comments on *racist ideologies*. These examples are merely illustrative – a fully fledged theory of racist ideologies would require a separate monograph, with its own theoretical framework and especially a serious empirical study of the ways racist ideologies manifest themselves, for instance in discourse.[16]

Organization of this study

The discussion of some of the key topics of a theory of ideology will be organized as follows. It starts with what I consider to be the core of such a theory, namely, the account of what ideologies 'are', where we can 'find' them, what they look like, what their components are and how they are related to other phenomena of the same kind. This will bring us to the study of ideology as the foundation of social cognition, and of the relations between ideologies and other mental representations, such as values, attitudes, opinions, knowledge and mental models of events. At the same time, such an analysis allows us to spell out the cognitive functions of ideologies. Having established such a framework, I am able to discuss more explicitly a number of classical concepts associated with the notion of ideology, such as (false) consciousness, truth and falsity, common sense and (in)consistency, among others.

Next, such an account of ideology in terms of social cognition will be located in a social context. That is, we need to spell out first of all what it means exactly that social cognition in general, and ideologies in particular, are socially shared, and indeed *who* or *which groups* have them, and especially also *why*. This brings us to the analysis of the fundamental social functions of ideologies. Such functions will probably also shed further light on the elusive problem of the internal structures of ideologies. Similar questions may be asked about the discursive manifestations of ideologies in their social contexts. Which contexts, situations, participants, institutions, groups and group relations, or other micro or macro social structures are involved in this 'practical accomplishment' of ideologies in discourse, and hence in the everyday enactment and reproduction of ideologies? Which relationships of power, dominance, resistance, competition or conflict constrain or occasion such ideologies? This framework allows us finally to discuss in somewhat more detail the many social concepts traditionally associated with ideology, such as those of power, domination, elites, institutions, groups and communities.

Since these social embeddings and functions are obviously the reason why people develop and use ideologies in the first place, I might have started with a discussion of these social notions. In many respects this would have been theoretically more adequate. However, given the orientation of traditional research, we know much more about these social dimensions of ideology, so that I may first focus on the less familiar study of the cognitive core and then locate these in their social contexts and highlight their discursive reproduction. In other words, I first want to know what ideologies 'are', that is, what they look like, so as to better be able to study their role and function in society.

Finally, the multidisciplinary triangle requires analysis of the ways in which socially shared ideologies manifest themselves in a specific but crucial type of social practice, namely, discourse. That is, I need to briefly indicate how ideologically based social representations shared by a group influence the actual, situated text and talk of individual social actors. And conversely, it should be spelled out how ideologies in turn are constituted, changed, challenged and reproduced by discourse. One of the powerful features of such a discourse analytical approach is the theoretical sophistication of contemporary accounts of the detailed structures of text and talk. Such an analysis allows us, among other things, to focus on the relations between discourse structures on the one hand, and the structures of ideologies on the other hand. At the same time, together with the socio-cognitive account, this discourse approach will be needed to discuss some more or less 'discursive' notions of traditional approaches, such as persuasion, manipulation, legitimation, concealment, and other things social actors 'do' with ideologically based talk and text. In other words, we here deal with the many central aspects and conditions that define the reproduction of ideologies.

The various cognitive notions discussed in Part I are discussed in theoretical terms, without specific reference to empirical (experimental or other) evidence. Apart from defining one major part of the theory of ideology, these cognitive notions will, however, be 'applied' in Part III, in the analysis of the processes of discourse production and comprehension. This means that part of the empirical evidence of cognitive concepts may be sought in the way they explain processes of language use. That is, apart from indexing social context, discourse structures may themselves feature indications of underlying, mental representations. Their analysis may thus yield rich evidence for such representations and mental processing, and thus complement evidence usually obtained in laboratory experiments. In the later, empirical discourse studies planned in this project we hope to do just that: show how ideologies and other social representations control discourse structures, and vice versa. Part III provides the theoretical framework for this empirical study of these relationships.

The order of the main parts of this book is merely a research strategy and says nothing about the order, causation, primacy or hierarchy of discourse or cognition over society, or vice versa. It does not imply, for instance, that ideologies as forms of social representations are 'first' in the mind before they are 'in' society, or that 'internal' structures of phenomena need to be studied before their 'external' functions. I assume that such (discursive or ideological) structures will often develop as a function of their uses and functions in society. Nor do I suggest that microstructures of everyday situated interaction should be studied before (or instead of) their macrosocial constraints, such as group relations or institutional context.

Cognition, discourse and society are related in extremely complex ways, in which influence and dependence are usually bidirectional, multilevel, and both cognitive as well as social. In that perspective, then, there is no point in affirming that ideologies are first or primarily or 'really' cognitive or social. They are essentially and crucially *both*. That does not mean, however, that we need to talk about everything at the same time, or that we cannot make analytical distinctions between different dimensions, levels or orders of phenomena, even in an integrated, multidisciplinary study. On the contrary, understanding of these analytically established structures and functions at various levels of description and explanation is a necessary condition for the development of a *theory* of ideology.

It should be emphasized that the chapters of this study can do no more than provide a first analysis of some of the key topics and the overall framework of a new theory of ideology. Subsequent studies, for instance about ideology and its detailed relations to the structures of cognition, society and discourse, will then have to develop these notions with more theoretical precision and on the basis of empirical data.

Part I

COGNITION

2

Ideas and Beliefs

Ideas

Whatever else ideologies are, they have always been associated with socially shared *ideas*. First, such ideas were seen as the object of a new science of ideology, as proposed in the wake of the philosophical movement of the French Enlightenment. Later, ideologies acquired their negative connotation as systems of the dominant ideas of the ruling class. Or they were defined as the false ideas of the working class's being misguided about the conditions of its existence. As a more sophisticated version of such 'false consciousness', ideologies were later described in terms of the persuasive, hegemonic ideas being accepted by dominated groups as part of their common sense about the nature of society and their place in it. And finally, beyond the confines of an analysis of class struggle, ideologies have been viewed more generally as any system of self-serving, mythical or otherwise deceptive ideas defined in contrast with the true ideas of 'our' science, history, culture, institution or party.

Whereas several of these defining notions will be dealt with later, let me first examine what exactly these 'ideas' are. The notion of 'idea' is one among many in the history of the study of ideology that hardly are specified in more detail than the everyday, commonsense meanings of these terms. If we assume for a moment that ideas (apart from being abstractions or social constructions) are at least *also* things of the mind, and that therefore psychology should tell us something about them, a relevant literature review would be disappointing. Modern psychology books do not talk about ideas, at least not explicitly and not in these terms: the term does not appear in the subject index of most current books in cognitive psychology. So let me begin by analysing some of its everyday meanings:

1 Ideas are objects or processes in/of the mind.
2 Ideas are the products of thinking or thought.
3 Ideas are part of knowledge.
4 Ideas may be personal or socially shared.

5   More specifically, ideas are new, original interesting thoughts and about
    important issues.

Many standard expressions and other forms of everyday talk provide the
evidence for such conceptual meanings. People talk about ideas they have
been 'walking around' with without as yet speaking about them, as ideas that
are developing in their 'heads' or 'minds', as having or not 'having' an idea
(sometimes meaning that they know or don't know something, as in 'I have
no idea'), but also as the ideas (shared by the members) of a group, a
movement, philosophers, a revolution, and so on. Thus, people may 'come
up' with an idea, or an idea may 'come up' with them. Conversely, we may
claim to have 'given' her that idea, or 'put that idea in her head'.

Often, the concept of an 'idea', whether of a person or a group, is not
merely identified with any trivial products of 'thought' one may have, but
with more original ones – the expression 'I have an idea' therefore means
something like 'I have a new, original, thought.' And the hapless scholar
being accused of 'not having any ideas' is thereby damned as being someone
who has no original scholarly thought. Therefore, a 'system of ideas' is
sometimes simply equated with socio-cultural, philosophical, artistic or
scientific thought or theories, as is most obviously the case in the 'history of
ideas'.[1]

On the other hand, people may have 'wrong ideas', and are then accused
of ethically doubtful or socially unacceptable beliefs, and similar connota-
tions seem to be at work when warning people not to 'get any ideas'.

These and many other colloquial uses of the concept of 'idea' clearly
signal that whereas psychology spurns the mundane notion of 'idea', the
commonsense uses focus on ideas as a specific category of (products of)
thinking, namely, fresh, original, new and sometimes unacceptable thoughts,
both in everyday life, as well as entertained by people hired to do so, such as
philosophers and other scholars, writers and artists, and indeed by 'ideologues' in the more political realm. These ideas may be expressed by the
person who has them, conveyed to others, shared by others and a whole
group; they may be further developed, influenced and manipulated. Once
shared, ideas may thus become part of the public domain, and thereby
acquire a more social or cultural dimension.

Minds

This relative vagueness of the concept of 'idea' may have kept psychologists
from adopting it in their theoretical vocabulary (using instead several
notions that are barely less precise, as we shall see), but its intuitive
meanings clearly suggest that ideas are constructs or products of thinking,
that is, of the *mind*, whether or not they are socially or culturally shared.
Thus, if ideologies have anything to do with ideas, then at least one of their
dimensions should be accounted for by the theories being developed in the
new cross-discipline now commonly called 'cognitive science', featuring

cognitive individual and social psychology, cognitive sociology, cognitive linguistics, philosophy, logic and artificial intelligence.

Mind versus body?

This will also be my first step: whatever else they are, ideologies are sets of specific ideas and hence 'mental' objects. Although trivial for most cognitive scientists, such a first step is not without controversy for some social and discursively oriented psychologists and social scientists. For them, talking about the 'mind' is like talking about the 'soul' some centuries ago, namely, a remnant of scholarly or religious myths, in this case of the old Cartesian dualism separating 'mind' from 'body'.[2]

This book will not waste many words on this controversy. The modern study of cognition assumes no such dualism. As far as psychological and neuroscientific insights go, the mind is a specific property of the brain-in-the-body. As with most psychologists, I abstract from the neurological basis of these 'mental' properties of the brain and conduct my analysis at another level of description and explanation. The dominant (and often contested) metaphor of what such a mind does is that of 'information processing'. Though limited for several reasons, the metaphor has proved quite successful in accounting for at least some aspects of the typical things people are able to do due to their minds: perceiving, understanding, thinking, remembering, speaking and interacting. We shall later see that such brain-based minds of persons also have a social dimension, being the product or construct of social interaction, in their acquisition, development and uses.[3]

However, this biological basis of the mind does not mean that talking about and analysing the mind and its properties needs a *reduction* to the neurobiology or, further down, to the biochemistry or the physics of neurons or brain cells. No more so than that talking about action requires analysis of muscle movements (and further down to the molecular and atomic properties of nerve and muscle tissue). And no more than that a discussion of discourse is pointless unless based on references to our articulatory or auditory organs, air waves, the chemistry of ink or the electromagnetic properties of computer disks.

That is, all these attempts at reduction that occasionally plague scholarly inquiry are usually no more than a form of sometimes well-intentioned but naive fundamentalism. They ignore both the commonsense and the scholarly need to understand and theorize about reality at different *levels* or *dimensions* of observation, experience and thinking, including about abstractions and things which that same mind construes for us as-if-they-were real, such as ideas, actions, persons, groups and society itself.

In that sense the mind is a product of itself. And a very handy construct at that, multiply used in everyday life, as well as in all scholarly endeavours. Thus, when we need to talk about things like ideas, it is simply quite convenient to do so in terms of properties of the concept of mind, whether minds 'really' exist or not. Reification here simply is no more than an inevitable but useful product of our understanding, as long as it allows us to describe, explain and otherwise account for events and phenomena we want to understand. Minds, thus understood, are both the 'means of production' as well as the 'product' of mental activities like thought. This is what analysis and theorizing are all about.

It is also in this sense that we accept to be 'mentalist', as long as that term is *not* meant to imply that, conversely, all phenomena that have a mental dimension are 'in fact' or 'really' *only* things of the mind. Persons, actors, actions, interactions, situations, groups and societies as a whole may be mental constructs or have mental dimensions at some level of analysis, but obviously a theory of such constructs needs to go beyond a 'mental' analysis and move to another level of commonsense thinking and theorizing which we call 'social'.

That I used several paragraphs to discuss the very relevance of the notion, and hence of a theory, of mind is merely because, as suggested, there are still scholars who for various, sometimes somewhat (neo)behaviourist reasons assume that minds can be dispensed with, that all allegedly mental things are but a widespread, commonsense and psychological illusion, and that all relevant mental notions could and should better be accounted for in terms of what people observably do or accomplish, especially jointly, in social situations. Since this point of view, which may be defended in more or less radical versions, also touches upon a theory of ideology, we will have to deal with those 'interactionist' – as one may call them – ideas (*sic!*) later.[4] Note, though, that my critique of anti-mentalist discursive psychology does not imply that I disagree with much of its criticism of contemporary mainstream psychology, such as its neglect of the socially situated and discursive dimensions of the development and uses of 'mental' objects.

Beliefs

Although informally perfectly acceptable as a concept that may be used to theorize about ideologies, I shall nevertheless abandon the notion of 'idea'. Not only because it is too general or too vague, but also because it has associations that I do not want to take along in my discussion: for example, that ideas are often seen as new or original thoughts. Instead I shall use another general notion of psychology, namely, that of *beliefs*.

Knowledge and beliefs

Many of the things that have been said above about ideas also apply to beliefs. They are also products or properties of thinking, and therefore also associated with the mind. Anything that can be thought is here taken as a belief. However, I use the term as a technical term. This means that some commonsense meanings of the term will not be included in the concept. For instance, in everyday language, the concept of 'belief' is mostly used as being opposed to that of 'knowledge'. Beliefs in that sense are subjective, and may hence be wrong, unfounded or misguided. Knowledge, on the other hand, is (the product of) thought that is found to be true.

We shall have to come back to this distinction, because it has been crucial in the history of the study of ideology. At the moment, however, all products of thinking will be declared to be beliefs. In other words, beliefs are the building blocks of the mind. Knowledge in that case is merely a specific category of beliefs, namely, those beliefs 'we' (as a group, community, culture, instance or institution) take to be 'true beliefs', according to certain grounds or (truth) criteria. These criteria establish that the beliefs (for us) are valid, correct, certified, generally held, or otherwise meet socially shared standards of truthfulness. Obviously, these criteria are socially, culturally and historically variable, and so is the knowledge based on them. This also means that beliefs in this technical sense are not merely subjective or even unfounded or untrue products of thought, or beliefs (like religious ones) that are only accepted as 'true' by a specific group of people, but also include what we call knowledge. The epistemology and psychology of these beliefs, as constituents of ideologies, will be one of the aims of the rest of this part of this study.[5]

Judgements and opinions

Similarly, beliefs are not thoughts that are limited to what exists, or what is (or may be) true or false. They may also pertain to evaluations, that is, to what we think (find) to be good or bad, nice or ugly, permitted or forbidden, acceptable or unacceptable, and so on – the products of *judgements* based on values or norms. Such beliefs are commonly called *opinions*, to which I shall turn later, because ideologies prominently feature such opinions. The distinction between knowledge and opinion goes back to the classical distinction between *epistémê* and *doxa*, made by Plato, defined as systematic (scientific, philosophical) knowledge, and (possibly erroneous) popular belief, respectively.

Whatever their differences, I shall provisionally subsume knowledge and opinions under the general category of beliefs. Thus, that a specific drug has a specific chemical formula is a belief (which we may hold to be true), and so is the belief (which we may or may not hold to be true or defensible or appropriate) that such a drug is good or bad for our health, or the belief that drugs should, or should not, be prohibited, or the belief that the prohibition of drugs, and not drugs themselves, wreaks social havoc. In sum, also the ethics and aesthetics of the products of judgement are part of a general theory of beliefs. Obviously, this is merely a first delimitation of the concept of 'belief' we use: specific cognitive theories provide the details of such (still very vague) approximations. I hold such cognitive theories of beliefs to be as necessary for a theory of ideology as theories of power, group or class in more traditional approaches to ideology.

However, this first approximation towards the notion of 'belief' does not mean that there are no complications. First, we may assume that people have beliefs that are not the product of conscious thought. In the same way as grammars of natural language are a form of largely implicit knowledge, people may also have many beliefs they are not aware of, and that have been acquired without much conscious processing. This means that I do not limit 'thought' to conscious mental processes, although people may usually become or be made aware of the beliefs they hold.

Second, we need a lower and an upper limit on beliefs. A religion might be described as a 'belief', but in such cases one should rather speak of a *belief system*. This means that we need some notion of a 'basic belief' of which more complex beliefs or belief systems may be composed. Ignoring a vast philosophical discussion here, I shall simply define a basic belief as any product of thought that cannot be decomposed into more than one belief (see below for further discussion). Traditionally, such a belief is described by a proposition consisting of one (n-place) predicate and *n* arguments, possibly modified by a number of modalities. Note, though, that this is a logico-philosophical definition, and not a cognitive one. The cognitive character-ization may be in terms of the ways beliefs are represented, that is, in terms of relations between nodes in a mental network, or more substantially as any elementary thought that may be (found or made) true or false or with which one may agree or disagree. That is, the concept of 'table' is not a belief, whereas the thoughts expressed by the English sentences, 'This is a table', 'The table is red', 'The flowers are on the table', and 'The flowers should be on the table', would be beliefs. This is admittedly quite elementary, but it will have to do for our discussion until we deal more explicitly with mental structures.

Emotions

There is a class of 'mental' objects that may or may not be beliefs, depending on one's theoretical position, namely, affect or emotion. Under one analysis, emotions are not mental at all, but constitute a separate realm. Feeling angry or jealous, in that case, is not a belief, but at most a 'state of mind', or even a 'state of body' – for example, the tendency to hit or hate someone. However, whatever emotions *are* exactly, and granted that they are not merely of, or based on, the mind, they do have obvious mental (thought, belief) dimensions as well. Feeling angry or worried about genocide in Bosnia implies or presupposes the belief that there is genocide in Bosnia, and usually also that genocide is wrong. In this respect, emotions may involve the (mental) interpretations of our 'state of mind' or 'state of body'. That is, an emotion usually has an object (though this may be very vague), namely, what we are moved about, and if we know what that is, emotions and beliefs need to be closely related. Hence, at some level of analysis, also emotions or affect belong to the realm of beliefs. This will again be crucial for a theory of ideology, because many ideologies are ﹀ seen to embody affect, as is the case for 'ideologies of hate' such as racism, or 'ideologies of love' such as some religions, or the 'ideologies of anger' that fuel resistance or revolutions. Of course, this is still highly impressionistic, so further conceptual analysis will be necessary.[6]

Beliefs and cognition

Within this huge field of 'belief research', then, I shall first of all focus on the cognitive and social psychology of beliefs, and later deal with their discursive and social dimensions. In psychology the analysis of beliefs as products of thinking, as we have seen, locates them in the mind, and more particularly in what is called 'memory'.[7] Memory, in this technical sense, is nothing but a theoretical construct of the 'cognitive' part or dimension of the mind, that is, the theoretical location where information is stored and processed. In that sense, beliefs may be defined as units of information and information processing, just as much as they may be seen as the products of thinking, or indeed as the (mental) conditions and consequences of discourse and social interaction. It all depends on the level, the scope and the nature of the theory. Modern cognitive psychology has adopted the useful (but limited) metaphor of information processing, without, however, implying that our minds function like computers.

I won't go into the details of the properties of human information processing, such as those involved in perception, interpretation and storage of sense data, or the activation and uses of earlier stored units of information. I shall simply assume that beliefs are units or representations that result from and are involved in the processes of information processing taking place 'in' memory. In sum, the mind, or memory, is a storehouse of beliefs, and at the same time is defined by the mechanisms (processes, strategies, mental activities) that produce or process such beliefs. Thus, beliefs may be constructed, stored, reactivated, organized in larger units, and such processes take place in the accomplishment of all cognitive tasks (which in turn are usually part of social action and interaction).

This does not mean that *all* of the mind or memory is filled with beliefs as we want to define them. Memory may also feature information of a structural nature (such as the composition of a sentence or a story) that is not, in my sense, a belief. Besides such more abstract knowledge or competence, we 'have' abilities like knowing how to walk, eat, or ride a bike, and these are again not beliefs as intended. Beliefs apparently need some kind of 'content' or 'object'. They must be *about* things. We believe *that* something is truthful, graceful or hateful, whether or not such 'objects of thought' correspond to something which we hold to be 'real' in the world. We also have beliefs about 'unreal' or mental objects, such as fantasies, dreams, goals or theories. Thus, for us, both 'thinking that' and 'thinking of' involves beliefs.

Propositions

When described, beliefs usually are assigned a format of the kind 'X is (or has the property) P', or 'X and Y are related by relation P'. Now, this is quite similar to the kind of format we know from philosophy and logic, and which we call *propositions*. It is therefore quite common to describe mental units such as beliefs in terms of propositions. This does not mean of course that we actually do have propositions in memory, the mind, let alone in the brain, but only that our theoretical language in which we speak about the mind uses the concept of proposition in order to describe and analyse beliefs in terms of a propositional format. If we had a more useful format, we would probably soon dump the notion of proposition, since it has all kinds of drawbacks – it was especially designed to account for the analysis of what people 'pro-pose', that is, of statements and arguments in natural language.

Although widely used in semantics for the description of (meanings of) discourse, propositions as we know them are not exactly flexible instruments to account for all structures of meaning. The same is true for the description of beliefs. As we shall see later, meanings are a type of belief, namely, the specific belief(s) associated with expressions (utterances) in natural languages. Yet, with all its limitations, I shall occasionally use this propositional format to describe the contents and the structures of beliefs. The advantage of such usage is that propositions can again be expressed in natural language, so that we can use natural language to talk about the contents and the structures of beliefs.

Thus if we have the belief that the genocide in Bosnia should be stopped, such a belief may be propositionally described as follows:

1   Must (X (stop, (commits (Y, Z(genocide)))))

or similar variants, depending on the kind of 'logic' of beliefs we adopt. Many aspects of this belief are not part of this proposition – for example, our knowledge about genocide, about who is responsible for the genocide (in order for that person or group to be stopped), that the 'must' here is a moral or political obligation, and that X is probably a powerful agent (person, group or state), that the action of stopping X committing genocide needs to be taken now or as soon as possible, and so on. That is, both as to content, and to structure, a belief may be quite complex. In principle, however, all these aspects may again be represented propositionally, so that most beliefs are in fact a *complex cluster of more elementary propositions*, or simply a 'propositional complex'.

This abstract language to describe mental objects such as beliefs is not always necessary for more informal or higher-level theorizing, so I shall use it sparingly. That is, many beliefs can simply be described more informally with our natural language expressing such propositional complexes, such as:

2   The genocide in Bosnia must be stopped.

3   Someone should prevent the genocide in Bosnia.
4   The massive killings of innocent people in Bosnia must be halted.

These examples also show something we shall later encounter in more detail: that natural language expressions of 'underlying' mental beliefs may take many forms and variations. These may depend on the variable properties of the context, such as participants and their roles, goals, setting, shared knowledge, and so on. That is, language use or discourse do not merely express beliefs, but also are forms of action and interaction, and these properties also influence the structures of sentences. We should merely be aware of the fact that the sentences in 2–4 are merely *expressions* of beliefs and not the beliefs themselves.

Networks

Although propositions are quite common to represent units of the mind like beliefs, there are of course alternatives, some of which are suggested to be closer to the neural, network structure of the brain.[8] Thus, we may represent a belief as a collection of nodes related by paths or more specifically as graphs with edges and nodes, and so on. The node 'genocide' may thus be connected with the node 'Bosnia', whereas the latter node may again be related to the nodes 'country', 'ex-Yugoslavia' and 'Muslims', whereas the node 'genocide' may be related to such nodes as, 'mass killing', 'innocent people', 'Holocaust', 'ethnic groups' or 'ethnic cleansing'. Such representations of beliefs in terms of graphs, or further 'down' as neural networks, show more clearly than propositions that the 'content' of a belief may be complex, and that beliefs may be related to many other beliefs (such as, 'Bosnia is a country in former Yugoslavia', etc.). A network may then be equivalent to a list or organized schemata of propositions, but it shows the relevant relationships between the concepts of these propositions more clearly. Moreover each link between nodes (where each node represents, e.g., a neuron or cluster of neurons) may be given a certain weight or strength of its connection depending on how often it has been activated or used. Each belief could then be defined (at least at one level of representation) as the complex state in which the brain is when the relevant links have been established or computed. According to such a connectionist approach, thus, beliefs or complex belief structures are not simply located at one specific location of the brain, but rather represented as a distributed network of nodes and their positively or negatively weighted links. In this book, however, we shall not further explore these different modes of representation and mental activity. Instead, we conduct our analysis at a more abstract, macro-level of mental representation and operation, in which somewhat easier to handle, 'symbolic' instruments such as propositions can be used.

Further problems in the definition of 'belief'

Thus, I shall provisionally use propositions to represent beliefs. It should be borne in mind, however, that since we can only write or talk about propositions by expressing them in a natural language (or other sign system), the beliefs they describe are conceptualized in terms of (the meanings of) that natural language. This linguistic bias obscures the fact that beliefs may be complex mental structures of which only some concepts are captured by the propositions as expressed in sentences of a specific language. In other words, beliefs (and the propositions we use to describe them) should not be confused with their contextually or linguistically variable expressions. Whether or how at least some concepts or beliefs are formed or structured as a function of their verbal expression in a specific language, is a famous but different problem.

The theoretical ambiguity of the notion of belief also appears in the possibility of describing beliefs at different *levels of abstraction*, as we also know from the theory of semantic macrostructures in discourse. That is, we may at a very high level of abstraction characterize a large cluster of beliefs about the present situation in Bosnia as a 'civil war' or as 'genocide'. Such concepts and the propositions formed by them are, however, some kind of high-level 'summaries' of a large number of more specific, more detailed, or lower-level beliefs, for instance about battles (and their details), about rape, murder, arson, and many other acts that, together, define a civil war or genocide.

This raises the question whether we may or should speak of *basic beliefs*, that is, beliefs that do not 'summarize' more specific beliefs. This question is related to the nature of thought and perception, for example, of (basic) events, actions or properties. In the same Bosnia example, thus, we may observe or think of people who shoot (at) others, and maybe we might 'decompose' such a perception of or thought about the act into a sequence of components, such as 'taking the gun', 'raising the gun', 'pulling the trigger', and so on. However, there seems to be a culturally conventional, basic level, below which events and actions are no longer decomposed as 'natural' units in everyday perception, propositions and descriptions. Thus, we do not usually decompose and conceptualize the – theoretically infinite – movement of 'raising the gun' in increasingly smaller parts of the movement. That is, we may be able to actually 'see' very small movements, but they are no longer culturally coded in a separate concept.[9] We may assume that such conceptually driven (and probably culturally variable) perception and thought also provides the basic level of the formation of beliefs. Most of our beliefs about Bosnia will be at a much higher level of conceptualization than this basic level, which is usually limited to personal experiences and direct observation in specific contexts. For later recall, use and description, such very low-level beliefs will usually no longer be accessible; they tend to be subsumed by higher-level beliefs. We shall later see that this also is true for discursive descriptions, which, depending on context, genre and various other constraints, may be fairly low-level (detailed, specific) or more or less high-level.

That is, beliefs, whether described as propositions or networks or in terms of other languages of (mental) representation, obviously do not come alone.

Simple beliefs may be combined to compound beliefs (such as, 'If the leaders of large countries do not decide to do so, the genocide in Bosnia will not be stopped'). They may cluster with large numbers of other beliefs, and thus form the complex belief clusters we call knowledge or attitudes. Thus, all we know about the situation in Bosnia is such a cluster of beliefs, and all we know and think about genocide or how to prevent it, is another cluster of beliefs.

Another issue involved in the characterization of beliefs is their relationship to the external world. As mental objects of some kind, they are often taken to 'represent' some 'fact' in the real world. Depending on our ontology, however, such a representation–relation may have a more passive or more active nature. If we assume facts to exist independently of the mind, as would typically be the case for the facts (events, processes) of nature, beliefs would rather be mental stand-ins (models, symbols, icons, images, etc.) of the facts. On the other hand, we may also take a more active view of beliefs, and define them in terms of socially based, mental constructs that constitute the 'facts', typically so of social and cultural 'reality'.

I take this latter, *constructive* view of beliefs – representing the world, even the facts of nature, involves interpretation and understanding of that world in terms of socially acquired conceptual categories. In that sense beliefs constitute the world-for-us. This obviously does not mean that the natural or social world does not exist independently of our beliefs, but only that people structure, understand and experience it (directly or through instruments) in terms of their beliefs. Nor does it mean that people's commonsense experiences of the out-thereness of their perceived and lived world is misguided, but only that such experiences themselves are mental representations. What happened in Bosnia was all too real. But conceptualizing 'what happened' as a 'civil war' is obviously a mental as well as socio-cultural or political construct.

In this sense, then, beliefs may still be described as being *about* the objects, properties, events, actions or situations of this 'external' world, as long as we realize that such an experience presupposes a socio-culturally controlled 'projection' of beliefs. And for the same reason it still makes (common as well as theoretical) sense to talk about *true* and *false* beliefs, depending on whether or not their representation corresponds to the 'projection rules' or truth criteria accepted within a given culture.

Apart from thus associating mental representations with the intersubjectivity of culture and society, such a constructive cognitive approach also easily explains imaginary, fictional or abstract beliefs, lies, plans, expectations, hopes, illusions, as well as personal or social biases in the perception and understanding of the world. Obviously, this is what we need in a theory of ideology.

This brief account of beliefs and their propositional or other forms of representation also suggests that even for such a fundamental notion in the cognitive and social sciences as 'belief' our theoretical frameworks are as yet quite primitive. It is one of these notions we all use quite frequently, but when pressed to define exactly what they mean, most scholars probably will soon give up. Because of their conceptual discreteness, propositions expressed in some natural language at least have the advantage (and sometimes the disadvantage) of 'freezing' vast networks of conceptual nodes into a relatively simple format. Obviously, this is also fundamental for everyday communication, since it is usually impossible (and mostly contextually irrelevant) to conceptualize and express *all* we believe about some situation.

Ideologies as beliefs

The reason I have talked about ideas, beliefs, compound beliefs and finally about clusters of beliefs as constructs of the mind, is obviously that ideologies are just that: clusters of beliefs in our minds.[10] That is, one way to describe and analyse ideologies is in terms of a cognitive psychology of the internal structures, relations, processing or other 'mental manipulation' of (some kind of) beliefs. This is not merely a psychological trick to explain away or reduce ideologies to memory units, but quite close to our commonsense notion of ideologies as 'systems of ideas', such as feminism, socialism, racism, anti-racism or environmentalism. That is, we know that feminists, socialists, and so on 'hold' or 'stand for' a number of beliefs, beliefs about what is true or false (about gender or class relations), and what they 'find' good or bad (about these relations) and what should be done about it.

Again, to account for ideologies in terms of beliefs and belief systems, and hence as properties of the mind, does of course not imply that ideologies are *only* mental, nor that their analysis should stop there. It has been stressed already that ideologies are *also* socially shared and related to societal structures, an obvious insight which, however, needs a different theoretical analysis. Similarly, beliefs are not only personal, nor do they always spontaneously 'emerge' as products of the individual mind. Rather, many of them are socially acquired, constructed and changed – for example, through social practices and interaction in general, and through discourse and communication in particular. This means that besides their mental dimensions, they have social dimensions, neither of which can and should be reduced to the other. The point of any explicit theoretical analysis is to distinguish between the different (mental, social, cultural) dimensions of ideas and ideologies, and then to establish relationships among them.[11]

Many contemporary approaches to ideology emphasize that ideologies are not merely systems of beliefs, but also feature such phenomena as symbols, rituals and discourse.[12] It may be readily agreed that such phenomena are often part of ideological systems and practices in a broader sense. However, it is theoretically more useful to distinguish between ideologies as such, that is, socially shared beliefs of a specific type, on the one hand, and their *expression* or *enactment* in symbols, rituals, discourse or other social and cultural practices, on the other hand.

Of course, this again raises the broader question about the relations between language and thought, and whether beliefs – as defined here – presuppose language (or other forms of semiotic expression) in order to be conceptualized. This more general question, however, is beyond the scope of this book. With most psychologists I shall simply assume that (although of course the mind, and hence our beliefs, is largely also acquired by language use) specific beliefs do not themselves require a natural language in order to be formed and used in thinking.[13]

In Part III, we shall find that discourse analysis provides 'empirical' evidence for the theoretical relevance of the cognitive notions introduced in this and the following chapters. That is, although theoretical analysis of belief systems and other mental representations may be a valid aim in itself, a multidisciplinary theory of ideology studies such beliefs primarily in order to describe and explain social practices in general, and discourse in particular.

Cognitive analysis but no reductionist cognitivism

In this chapter, we have begun to analyse some of the 'mental' aspects of ideologies, and we shall continue that analysis in the other chapters of this first part. That is, against reductionist theses that aim to redefine ideas, beliefs or ideologies only in terms of social interaction or discourse, I claim that the mind needs analysis in its own terms. But against cognitivist reductions that claim that all social interaction and discourse, as well as social structures, are 'really' constructs and hence products of the human mind, I shall similarly take a social position and claim that beliefs and ideologies also have an important social dimension that requires analysis in its own terms.

Thus, trying to make explicit both the commonsense notion of ideology, as well as the traditional concept of ideology in philosophy and sociology, a cognitive approach may spell out in somewhat more detail the components, contents and structures of ideologies. At the same time, it makes explicit the relations of ideologies, as systems of specific beliefs, with other types of beliefs, such as attitudes, knowledge and opinions. Doing so, I am sketching the first part of a multidisciplinary framework, and designing the relevant theoretical concepts that allow us to talk about ideologies and their embedding in cognition in a somewhat more sophisticated way than has been done before in traditional work on ideology. This will be the task of the other chapters in this part of this study.

3

Social Beliefs

Personal versus social beliefs

We have seen that ideologies first of all may be defined in terms of beliefs and that such beliefs may be organized in various ways. In several disciplines, and especially in the study of political cognition, 'belief systems' have been the standard way to talk about ideologies.[1]

One of the problems with a general term such as 'belief system' is that it is too comprehensive to describe the specific sets of beliefs which I want to call ideological. As we have seen, everything people think may be called beliefs, and we therefore need to make further distinctions. Thus, the beliefs expressed in the following sentences are not typical for what we usually call ideological beliefs:

1. Water freezes at 0 degrees centigrade.
2. Amsterdam is the capital of the Netherlands.
3. Last month I lectured in Valparaiso.
4. I like ice-cream.
5. Krzysztof is my neighbour.
6. There was a young girl of Nic'ragua / Who smiled as she rode on a jaguar.

That is, we know or believe many things in everyday life that hardly fall under the broad term of ideological beliefs, where the latter category comprises beliefs that somehow have to do with a special ideological 'position' or with group interests. Among such 'non-ideological' beliefs is knowledge about undisputed facts, as in 1 and 2, past experiences as in 3, personal preferences as in 4, mundane facts of everyday life as in 5, and fictional or literary 'facts' as in the first two lines of the limerick in 6.[2] Note though that, as usual for isolated examples, we should add a provision like 'under standard interpretation'. It would not be too difficult to construct a context or text in which even these beliefs may be ideologically based. This is especially the case for 'undisputed facts', a commonsense category that itself is based on a specific field of knowledge and truth criteria. Such beliefs may be challenged (and sanctioned as 'ideological') by others, as Galileo Galilei found out several centuries ago in his dispute with the Catholic Church.

Episodic and social memory

In order to make our next theoretical step in the analysis of ideologies, we therefore need to make a distinction between different kinds of beliefs. In psychology such a differentiation may be associated with different regions, parts or functions of memory, such as episodic and semantic memory. Episodic memory is the part of memory where beliefs are stored about concrete episodes (facts, events, situations, etc.) we have witnessed or participated in ourselves, or about which we have information through discourse from others. That is, episodic memory stores our personal experiences, and might therefore also be called 'personal memory'. Examples 3, 4 and 5 above are examples of personal beliefs as stored in episodic memory.[3]

Note that such terms as 'episodic' or 'personal' memory are merely theoretical constructs to account for different kinds of mental processes and representations and their functions. As explained in the previous chapter, such theoretical domains of memory need not correspond for instance to different regions of the brain (although they might – as observed for instance by selective memory loss of personal experiences, resulting from brain lesions). This is more generally true for the cognitive notions used in this chapter and this book: they do not pretend to reflect the neurological or biological properties of the brain, which would require a very different level and kind of theorizing.[4]

There are also beliefs we typically share with many others, for instance most other members of a group, organization or whole culture, and which therefore may simply be called *social* (or *sociocultural*) *beliefs*. Our vast 'knowledge about the world' is constituted by such socially and culturally shared beliefs. These are usually located in what cognitive psychology calls 'semantic memory'. However, we shall speak of *social memory*, since not all of this knowledge has to do with the general meanings of words, and hence need not be called 'semantic' in any standard meaning of that term. Examples 1 and 2 above are typical instances of such socially shared beliefs.[5]

Ideologies, as I shall discuss in more detail later, typically belong to the realm of social beliefs, and are therefore located in social memory. Thus, if ideologies are belief systems, we need to be at least a bit more specific and say that they are *social belief systems*.

That is, the theory being developed here emphasizes that there is no such thing as a purely individual or personal ideology.[6] Ideologies are essentially social, that is, shared by members of *groups* or collectivities of people.[7] Later (Chapter 15) we shall discuss this social basis of ideologies in more detail, and try to find out what kind of groups typically develop ideologies. Thus, intuitively, the people waiting at a bus stop are not the kind of 'group' which we normally assume to share the same ideology because of the mere fact that they are waiting for the bus together. Of course, they may accidentally share an ideology, but not *as* would-be bus passengers. On the other hand, people participating in a demonstration are a more likely collectivity to share an ideology, namely, the very ideology that in fact led them to participate in the demonstration in the first place. Even more so, members of action groups, political parties or socio-economic classes seem to be the people who typically might be expected to share an ideology. For our cognitive analysis here, thus, it is sufficient to know that ideologies are shared (as well as acquired and used) by social groups or collectivities.

Although ideologies are a property of social groups, individual members may of course 'have' or 'participate in' an ideology *as* group members. That is, they may personally endorse, accept or use a group ideology in their everyday practices. In this respect, ideologies are like natural languages. Languages such as English, Chinese or Kiswahili are also (knowledge) systems that are essentially social and shared by the members of a group – the speakers of those languages. But that does not mean that the members of such a speech community do not know and use the language individually. In a similar way, I shall say that ideologies are to be defined as ideologies-of-groups that may be individually (and as we shall see, variably) *used* by the members of the group. This way of formulating the *shared* nature of ideologies emphasizes the group-based, societal dimension of ideologies, while at the same time accounting for the role of ideologies in the (variable) practices of social members in everyday life. Both theoretically and empirically, this relationship is crucial, since we are able to actually observe ideologies 'at work' only in these social practices, as is also the case for the manifestations of language systems or grammars.

It should also be stressed that as soon as we talk about ideologies or other beliefs as being socially shared, this involves a mode of generalization and abstraction. This does not mean that, as individuals, social members all have identical copies of such beliefs and ideologies. Rather, it will be assumed that each member may have a personal *version* of the shared belief or ideology, a version that is obviously a function of individual socialization or ideological development. Some people may only have a rudimentary (and perhaps rather incoherent) personal version of the ideology, whereas others ('the ideologues') have a much more detailed and consistent one. This notion of personal versions of ideologies also accounts for the frequently found individual differences (and even contradictions) in the expression of ideologies in empirical research.[8] This does of course not imply that therefore there are no shared, social beliefs or ideologies, no more than that individually variable knowledge and uses of language implies that there are no grammars. The point is only that as soon as we talk about groups and their knowledge or ideologies, we abstract from such individual differences.

The distinction between personal and social beliefs is handy for many cognitive and social reasons. Probably the most compelling reason to make this distinction is that social beliefs may be assumed by group members to be *known* to most of the other group members. In discourse this means that social beliefs may be *presupposed* by the speaker, and need not be explicitly asserted as new information. In that respect discourse is like the proverbial tip of the iceberg: most of its implied or presupposed meanings remain 'hidden' (mentally speaking). Many of the facts of everyday life are thus routinely presupposed in talk and text, for instance that Bosnia is a country in former Yugoslavia, what genocides are, what civil war is, and so on. Cultures are typically characterized (also) by such bodies of shared beliefs. As we shall see in detail later, the same is true for the shared and taken-for-granted (often commonsense) beliefs that define the ideology of a group.

Socio-culturally shared beliefs have a number of further characteristics. For instance, as briefly suggested above, most of these beliefs have a *general* or *abstract* nature. That is, they are mostly not about concrete facts, but about general properties of facts. If we know what a civil war is, we know about civil wars and their properties in general, and we may apply such knowledge when observing or speaking about all possible civil wars. Distinctions between specific civil wars are thus abstracted from. In logical terms, we may say that episodic knowledge consists of beliefs that can be described by propositions that have constants, referring to particulars, whereas social knowledge consists of beliefs that may be represented with propositions with variables. This is not surprising, because the very fact that beliefs are socially shared implies that they are used in many different situations.

Particular versus general beliefs

At this point, however, the common distinction between personal/episodic and social/general beliefs meets its first hitch. For instance, the civil war in Bosnia is on the one hand a specific event (or a collection of events), but knowledge about it is not merely personal, but widely shared, and hence social, and at the same time not abstract or general. It is defined by a particular location, time period, participants and actions. Because, as I did above, we talk about 'the' civil war in Bosnia, the use of the definite article presupposes that there actually is or was such a civil war, and that we know that recipients know it. The question then is whether this kind of knowledge is episodic (personal, particular) or rather social, or maybe both? Do we need a further distinction in the 'system of beliefs' in memory?

Such a further distinction may indeed be useful. This means that *both* for personal and social beliefs we may further distinguish between *particular* (episodic, context-bound) and *general* (abstract, context-free) beliefs.

Thus, beliefs about the civil war in Bosnia would be an example of particular social beliefs which may be shared and presupposed like any other social knowledge of a more general or abstract kind, such as the knowledge we have about civil wars in general. Another term that may be used to refer to such shared social knowledge about particular people and events would be 'historical knowledge'. The important point is here to remind ourselves of the fact that not all social beliefs are general, abstract or context-free. In the same way as personal knowledge in episodic memory represents people's personal experiences, we may thus say that historical knowledge is about specific 'collective' experiences of a group, society or culture. The Holocaust may be prototypical of such a collective group experience – and its shared representation in social memory.

On the other hand, in my personal knowledge systems, I may have knowledge about concrete personal experiences, such as the fact that my friend Ruth went abroad yesterday, but also more general or abstract knowledge of a personal nature, such as the fact that Ruth is a friend of mine, that my neighbour is also a professor, that I always do my shopping on Saturday morning, and so on. That is, I do have personal knowledge that is not about concrete, particular events, but represents a more general state of affairs (e.g. friendship), habitual events, or personal properties. The notion of 'self' may be defined in terms of this abstract, personal knowledge. In all these cases, this knowledge does not apply to unique events, actions or situations, but to many instances of them in my personal life.

Such general personal beliefs may monitor my specific social practices in a similar way to that of more general, socially shared beliefs. But they are still personal knowledge, because I may not generally assume that most other people in my group or culture share these beliefs with me. In a strict sense, even when family members, friends or acquaintances (or when I am famous, many others) may know some of these beliefs, my own personal beliefs are strictly speaking individual: they define me as a unique person, and their description would fill an autobiography.

Ideologies as general social beliefs

Having made these distinctions, ideologies may be assumed to be constituted by *socially shared, general beliefs*. That is, they do not feature beliefs about specific, historical events. Our specific, historical knowledge and opinions about the civil war in Bosnia may well be influenced by ideologies (e.g. those of nationalism, pacifism, and so on), but they are not themselves part of such a more general and abstract ideology. Similarly, although my personal beliefs may also be influenced by ideologies, they are not socially shared by a group and hence, as such, are not part of ideologies.

Again, we may compare this definition with that of language: my personal language use is of course controlled by a socially shared grammar and rules of discourse, but it is not properly part of such abstract knowledge of the language. Of course, we may define a language empirically in terms of the set of its actual manifestations in language use, but this is hardly the case for the socially shared, abstract systems of rules of the grammar. In that respect, ideologies should rather be compared to grammars than to language defined in terms of the infinite set of its 'uses'.

For the moment, we shall ignore these personal beliefs and individual 'uses' of ideologies, but later we need to show how they may be influenced by social beliefs. This link between the social and the personal is crucial, because most social practices, and hence most discourse, are by definition accomplished by one or a few individual persons in particular contexts. That is, if we ever want to explain that social practices or discourses are ideological, or that ideologies are reproduced by them, we need to establish the theoretical relationships between the social and the personal, the general and the particular, the group and its members, and the abstract system and its specific instances or uses.

Knowledge and opinions

Having made a distinction between personal and social beliefs and their corresponding domains or functions of memory, let us now further examine the kinds of belief that define the social mind.

We have earlier seen that ideologies are often assumed to tell groups and their members what is good or bad, wrong or right. That is, ideologies feature *evaluative beliefs* or *opinions*. More specifically, since ideologies by definition are social and shared, they feature the *social opinions* of a group. And because social beliefs are often general and abstract, so are these social opinions, for instance the general opinions feminists have about gender inequality. In fact, as we shall see in more detail below, the social opinions that constitute an ideology are so general and abstract that they organize clusters of domain-specific social opinions of a group, namely, *attitudes*. Thus, general opinions about gender inequality in a feminist ideology may be assumed to underlie a large number of more specific feminist attitudes about, for example, discrimination and harassment on the job, unequal political power, and so on.

Given the distinctions made above between social and personal beliefs, we may further assume that this distinction also applies to opinions: besides the social opinions we share with other group members, we also have personal opinions, which are stored in episodic memory. We shall see later that such personal opinions may of course be influenced by the social opinions of the groups individuals identify with. Obviously, also these personal opinions may be general ('I love ice-cream', 'I like my neighbour') or specific, that is, evaluations of specific personal experiences ('I enjoyed teaching in Valparaiso last month').

There are many other cognitive and discursive ways to characterize opinions. One typical (though not exclusive) property is that opinions vary contextually, or within a group or community. An opinion thus presupposes that there are possible *alternative opinions*. It does not make sense to apply truth criteria to a social opinion: 'We don't want any more immigrants' is a xenophobic opinion that is neither true nor false, but a belief with which one may *agree* or not, or that allows us to judge the opinion holder. Opinions are typically entertained or expressed from a specific position or perspective, by a person or a group, or in a specific situation, and are therefore also called *points of view*. Opinions are not beliefs that tell us something about the world, but rather about people who have them, or about the relations (judgements) people have to the world.

Attempts to define the notion of opinion, as we see, bring in another major type of socially shared belief, namely, *knowledge*. Whereas opinions define what we like or dislike, what is good or bad for us, or what must or should not be done, knowledge is defined in terms of what (we think) is the case, what is true or false. Whereas opinions, as evaluative beliefs, presuppose a judgement based on socially shared values and norms, our socio-cultural knowledge consists of socially shared *factual beliefs* based on socially acknowledged truth criteria. These truth criteria or rules of evidence may be those of everyday common sense (dependable perception, reliable communication, or valid inference), those of science, those of religion, or any other evaluation basis, depending on the social domain, group or culture for which truth or factuality must be socially established.

Factual beliefs may be true or false. Thus, the proposition 'The Hague is the capital of the Netherlands' is a factual belief, although it happens to be false.[9] It does not imply an evaluation, and its truth value can be established by 'objective', generally accepted, truth criteria. When describing people who entertain a factual belief that we think is false, we typically do so with the verb 'believe': 'Larry believes that The Hague is the capital of the Netherlands.' On the other hand, knowledge is true factual belief, and the socio-cultural knowledge we deal with here consists of socially or culturally shared factual beliefs that are true according to (similarly socio-culturally shared) truth criteria. Similarly, at the interpersonal level, we say that someone 'knows' something if we think that what he or she (factually) believes is true. In other words, both at the interpersonal and the social level of analysis, knowledge is closely associated with *sharing* factual beliefs and sharing the criteria for the establishment of the truth of such beliefs. This is only a first approximation, and we shall come back to the definition of knowledge and its relations to other beliefs (including ideologies).

The distinction between knowledge and opinion is very old, and goes back to the opposition between, respectively, *epistême* and *doxa* in classical Greek. Relevant for this chapter is that we find it theoretically useful to distinguish between socially shared evaluative beliefs or opinions (and attitudes), on the one hand, and socially shared factual beliefs, or knowledge, on the other hand. Whereas social opinions are based on values and hence on the moral order of society, factual beliefs draw on what we may call its 'epistemic order', that is, the underlying system that features the basic truth criteria for beliefs about the world.

This distinction is deeply embedded also in our commonsense thinking and judgements about the world. Social members routinely distinguish between beliefs or statements about the objects or events of the world, and those that involve their personal or social relations or positioning ('attitude') with respect to the properties of these objects or events, for example as being desirable or undesirable. For instance, people distinguish what they *know* about abortion from what they *think* about it. They know that knowledge may be culturally shared ('we all' know what abortion is), but that opinions usually vary between different persons or groups ('we' are Pro-Choice, but 'they' are Pro-Life in the abortion debate). They know that, in discourse, cultural knowledge is often presupposed, whereas opinions usually need to be defended.

Despite these (and other, more formal and philosophical) criteria, the distinction between knowledge and opinions is very hard to make explicit. What for some people or in some contexts is called 'knowledge', may be an 'opinion' for others or in other contexts. We might say that opinions are represented by propositions that feature evaluative predicates, that is, predicates that presuppose values, whereas factual beliefs do not. For many examples such a criterion would apply nicely, but for other cases the distinction between evaluative and non-evaluative predicates is not that clear.

Thus, the belief 'Amsterdam is the capital of the Netherlands' is obviously factual, and 'Amsterdam is a beautiful city' is clearly an opinion. But that does not mean that 'being the capital of' cannot be used evaluatively, as in the accusation 'Amsterdam is the capital of drugs.' Similarly, we may use the apparently factual predicate 'is a village' as part of an evaluative proposition, as in 'Amsterdam is only a village, when compared with New York.' We may factually conclude from a verdict that Henry is (was convicted as) a thief, and still have no opinion about Henry, but at the same time entertain the opinion that Harry is a thief because he stole some of my ideas. Many predicates may thus have a more factual or descriptive and a more evaluative meaning or use, as is the case for 'big', 'heavy' or 'dangerous'.

The same is true for socially shared beliefs, and hence for the distinction between socio-cultural knowledge and social opinions or attitudes. Thus, smoking may generally be found to be 'dangerous for your health', and the belief that this is the case may be qualified as a factual social belief, which can be proven to be true by generally accepted truth criteria, such as scientific experiments or statistical evidence, for instance as established by the Attorney General in the USA. At the same time, there are variable social opinions about smoking, even about its 'alleged' danger. Feminists will claim that gender inequality is a fact, and adduce statistics to prove it, whereas many conservative men (and some women) may disagree. In other words, at some level of analysis, the distinction between social knowledge and social opinion is not that clear. It is at this point also that ideology may be involved in the distinction.

Epistemological approaches

Also the intricate accounts of knowledge and beliefs in contemporary epistemology offer little assistance in establishing clear-cut theoretical criteria for the distinction between knowledge and opinions. The ingenuity of theorists as well as ordinary language users nearly always provides counter-examples to most formal accounts. Thus, knowledge (of a person A) is traditionally defined in terms of the conditions (a) *p* is true, and (b) A believes that p. But this allows for the possibility that A may just have a lucky guess (as during a multiple choice test), and correctly believe that p, so that we also need to add a third condition (c) A is justified in believing p. Such justification should be based on the truth criteria mentioned above.

One problem with such abstract philosophical definitions is that they tend to ignore the social and discursive contexts of truth conditions, criteria and justification. That is, the actual *use* of a statement type like 'Chandra knows that p' does not presuppose that p is true, but that the *speaker* (also) believes that p, and believes that there is enough evidence for p. That is, the problem of the conditions of Chandra's knowledge reverts back to the problem of the knowledge of the speaker, so that we are back at square A. This means that social issues of intersubjectivity and consensus become involved here. The same is true for the acceptance of the truth criteria by which someone is thought to be justified in her or his beliefs, criteria that are historically and culturally variable. In our contemporary culture, such criteria may ultimately be those of 'science', but these are also known to offer no ultimate 'foundation'. In sum, somehow always social and cultural criteria of knowledge (and hence of opinion) become part of a more empirically warranted account of knowledge and beliefs. Abstraction from such social contexts, and trying to find a context-free definition of knowledge, thus seems to create more problems than it solves.

Hence, in this tripartite cognitive–social–discursive approach, we do not deal with 'abstract' knowledge, but with mundane talk and thought about real personal or social knowledge, according to which A is said to 'know p' if A believes p and also the speaker, or a whole community, believe that p. This of course makes knowledge relative, but there is no way to escape such relativism. True, the speaker and the whole knowledge-community may be in error about p (and there are many historical instances where this was the case), but in order to decide that such is the case another speaker-knower (from outside the community) needs to establish this error in the first place, so that knowledge is again made relative to *that* speaker-knower, and so on. In other words, for beliefs of people to be promoted to the status of (true) knowledge, we have no practical or theoretical means to escape the consensus of some belief community by whose criteria A's beliefs are deemed to be true. Moreover, such a philosophical approach does not offer an account of the difference between factual and evaluative beliefs – by which criteria other than social ones are we able to establish that 'Henry is a thief' is true?

Cultural versus group beliefs

Therefore, in order to solve some of the theoretical puzzles of the distinction between knowledge and opinion, let me make a further distinction, a distinction we also will need in the further definition of ideology, namely, that between *cultural beliefs* (or societal, or simply 'common' beliefs) and *group beliefs*. Although both the notion of 'culture' and that of 'group' are themselves fundamentally ill-defined (see Chapter 15), the point of the distinction is to differentiate between general, taken-for-granted beliefs of a whole society or culture, and the more specific, often partisan, beliefs of various social groups within such an overall culture. As we shall see in more detail below, ideologies typically belong to the second type of beliefs. We shall assume that ideologies form the foundation of such group beliefs.

One of the more specific reasons why we need this distinction is the following. As suggested above, some groups in society have beliefs which they qualify as knowledge, whereas others (other group members) qualify these beliefs either as false factual beliefs or simply as opinions. If such is the case, the very epistemological as well as cognitive theory of knowledge becomes a precarious undertaking. We would need to assume a relativist theory of knowledge, according to which all knowledge is relative to a group or culture. Any belief 'we' (members of our group) would hold to be true, and which is shared by everyone in our group, could in principle be challenged by others as false or as an opinion.

We shall further explore these relations between beliefs, knowledge and opinions in Chapter 11, and here only make some overall assumptions about the furniture and architecture of the social mind as a theoretical construct. In earlier versions of this theory, it was postulated that ideologies are the basis of the social mind. Although this explains how ideologies organize people's attitudes, this would also predict that *all* knowledge, as one major part of social cognition, is ideologically controlled. Whereas this is undoubtedly the case for many types of knowledge, especially knowledge about the social world and knowledge that involves different interests or goals, this is not a very plausible assumption. Moreover, if all our knowledge is ideological, the notion of ideology loses much of its explanatory power. People have vast amounts of everyday, commonsense knowledge about the world that neither seems to be contested nor is obviously ideological. How then should a basic ideological system control or organize some parts of our socio-cultural knowledge and not other parts?

I therefore decided to put the original architecture on its head, or, if you like, back on its feet. Instead of defining ideologies as the basis of all social cognition, we will now assume that general, cultural knowledge is the basis of all group-specific beliefs, including ideologies. Such cultural knowledge, or cultural common-ground, may be defined as the (fuzzy) set of those beliefs that are shared by (virtually) all competent members of a culture, and that are held to be true by those members by similarly shared criteria of truth. This is also why we may simply call this the repertory of 'common knowledge' of a culture. It is this knowledge that all new members of a culture have to learn (e.g. during socialization, formal education, through the media, etc.) in order to become competent members. As suggested above, this is the kind of knowledge that in most social situations – for example, in interaction and discourse – may be presupposed, and which is called 'knowledge' by all members. This knowledge consists of all uncontested, commonsense beliefs, as well as of those specialized (e.g. scientific) beliefs that have been 'adopted by the culture' as a whole, for instance our knowledge that the earth is round and not flat and turns around the sun (despite our everyday perception to the contrary). It should be emphasized that this notion of cultural knowledge refers to a collective, social phenomenon. It says something about beliefs shared by a cultural community, and not about the knowledge of all individual members. Children, the mentally disabled, cultural newcomers and others who are not (yet) fully competent may only partly share this cultural knowledge. That is, full cultural competence of each member may be measured by the amount of cultural knowledge acquired, at least passively or implicitly (not all knowledge may always be accessible actively).

Contrary to this kind of cultural knowledge, different groups may have beliefs that for them also constitute uncontested knowledge, in the same way as cultural knowledge is accepted by the whole cultural community. This group-knowledge may be verified by truth criteria that are either generally cultural, but differently applied, or by group-specific criteria. Typical examples are the kinds of knowledge as they are generally accepted within the sciences, the professions, religions or political groups. Interestingly, most of these knowledges build on general cultural knowledge, because otherwise inter-group understanding, communication and interaction would hardly be possible. Some knowledge partly extends or substitutes commonsense cultural knowledge, as is typically the case for scientific, technical or professional knowledge. In these cases also the truth criteria for verification may be much stricter or elaborate. Conversely, religions may share knowledge (e.g. about God) and may adopt truth criteria (such as faith) that are not shared outside the religious group. And finally, different socio-political groups may have specific knowledge about society and its groups that is not (yet) common knowledge – for instance feminist insights in gender inequality, or ecological insights into forms of pollution. As suggested, some of these insights (whether scientific, religious or social) may be adopted by the whole cultural community. Even some specialized truth criteria of one group (such as statistical evidence, the use of specialized machines, etc.) may become adopted as a truth criterion by the whole cultural community. And vice versa, what in one historical period was culturally shared, common knowledge may be abolished by the cultural community as a whole and later only be maintained by epistemically 'deviant' groups.

The distinction between cultural and group knowledge is recursive and can be applied both to whole cultures, as well as to subcultures. That is, at a historical, cross-cultural or universal level of description and explanation, what is cultural knowledge for one culture, may appear to be specific group-knowledge at a higher level. Cultural conflicts as well as difficulties of cross-cultural communication and interaction bear witness to this form of relativity. The same reasoning would then leave open the possibility of a stock of 'universal' knowledge, that is, beliefs that are shared by the competent members of all cultures. Again, many commonsense and every-day beliefs (about people, their bodies, about the weather, nature and basic social relations) would be candidates for such a stock of everyday knowledge. It is hard to imagine cultures that would not have shared beliefs about mothers and their children, about men versus women, about young versus old people, about the parts of the body, about edible food, and so on.

Similarly, the culture versus group distinction also applies at lower levels, that is, within cultures. Groups and their knowledge are often characterized in terms of subcultures, within which specific groups may again be distinguished with their own knowledge system. Similarly, groups or sub-cultures need not be part of one culture, but may be constituted over cultural boundaries, as is the case for professionals, scholars and members of different religions or political ideologies.

Neither cultural nor group knowledge is a well-defined concept. They are essentially fuzzy, in the sense that there is no effective procedure to establish for each culture or group what beliefs they collectively share (or indeed which are only shared by part of the group). Yet, the notions are far from arbitrary, and a quite reliable test (and there are others) is *presupposition* in discourse. Cultural knowledge may be presupposed in all types of discourse by all competent (adult, sane, etc.) members, except of course in all didactic and pedagogical discourse that serves to teach such knowledge. The same is true for group knowledge, which may be presupposed by all group members in all their discourses (except of course in didactic or initiation discourse, or in discourses directed at other groups, such as propaganda).

It will be assumed that general cultural knowledge (whatever its further structures, functions, acquisition and change) must be the foundation of social cognition. All specific group beliefs as well as the very interaction, communication and mutual understanding of members of different groups presuppose such cultural knowledge.

Cultural knowledge is therefore also the basis of all evaluative beliefs, including socially shared opinions, attitudes and ideologies, as we shall see in more detail below. For instance, different groups may have different opinions about abortion, nuclear energy or state control over the market, but such different opinions presuppose general (as well as specific group) knowledge about what abortion, nuclear energy, the state or the market is. Prejudices against, say, Turks thus presuppose that we know at least that Turks are a people and not a brand of ice-cream or sportswear, although (as some research shows) we may know very little else about Turks than that they are a 'foreign' people. In other words, opinion differences still need a common ground consisting of a cultural basis of knowledge.

The concept of cultural common ground is most obvious for shared knowledge. However, we may wonder whether it also applies to other kinds of beliefs, such as opinions. Since opinions, nearly by definition, are the kinds of beliefs people may disagree about, this does not seem very likely at first sight. Yet, in the same way as we have a general epistemic order, there may be a culturally shared moral order, featuring the uncontested opinions –

as well as the principles of moral judgement, that is, cultural values – of a given culture. Just as specific societies have laws as well as a constitution, thus, cultures have a moral basis which again monitors interaction, communication and discourse across group boundaries. Again, such moral principles should be uncontested and presupposed in all evaluative talk, action and interaction. They are also the basis for judgements about and sanctions against moral deviance by individual members of a culture.

In the same way as specific group knowledge presupposes cultural knowledge, group opinions and their underlying norms and values should presuppose the culturally shared moral order. And the same top-down or bottom-up dynamic may be at work here. What the norms, values and opinions of a specific group are may gradually become culturally shared by a whole culture, and vice versa. What once was a culturally shared norm or opinion may later become characteristic for a specific group. For instance, whereas Christian religion may once have been constitutive of the moral order of much of Western culture, it has now been reduced to that of a specific religious group. And the basic normative system of human rights which once was specific to groups of philosophers in the eighteenth century is now largely accepted throughout Western (and other) cultures.

The overall architecture of the social mind we have now constructed is one which has a general cultural basis of common factual and evaluative beliefs. This cultural common ground is acquired and accepted by virtually all members, and presupposed in all discourse and other interaction. It is on this basis that different groups may develop specific knowledge and opinions, and may compete for epistemic or doxastic hegemony, or indeed even for (partial) acceptance in the general common ground for the culture(s) in which they participate.

The same is specifically true for ideological competition and struggle. Whereas it was earlier assumed that ideologies are the basis of social beliefs, and we added that these were the social beliefs of a specific group, we meant just that – ideologies will be defined as the basis of social group cognition. In this case, it is perfectly acceptable to have them control both the opinions or attitudes of the group, as well as their knowledge, because specific group knowledge may very well be related to the interests or other properties of the group, and be involved in competition, struggle or domination.

This way of organizing the social mind also implies that as soon as social beliefs enter the set of general cultural beliefs, they by definition are no longer ideological *for that culture*, but simply basic knowledge or opinions that are shared by everyone, taken for granted, and uncontested. Of course, another culture (or the same culture in a later period) may of course again deem such beliefs to be ideological. In other words, ideologies always presuppose specificity for a group or culture, and hence competition, confrontation, or at least evaluative comparison at a higher level or from a point of view outside the group or the culture.

This also elegantly solves the *relativity* problem for knowledge and other beliefs. If we assume that there is no absolute knowledge, and hence no ultimate truth criteria, we still do not need to be relativist with respect to a given culture – knowledge may well be accepted as true within a given culture, given the truth criteria of that culture. This may even be the case within each group, whose members will claim that *their* beliefs are true, whereas those of other beliefs are false factual beliefs or merely evaluative opinions. When dealing with the relation between knowledge and ideology in more detail (Chapter 11), I shall elaborate this point.

Types of beliefs

Before I continue my analysis of the contents and organization of the social mind, let me recapitulate the kinds of social beliefs and distinctions we have encountered so far:

- personal versus socially shared beliefs
- specific versus general or abstract beliefs
- specific social beliefs or historical beliefs
- factual versus evaluative beliefs (opinions, attitudes)
- truth criteria versus evaluation criteria (norms, values)
- true factual beliefs (knowledge) versus false factual beliefs (errors, illusions)
- cultural beliefs (common ground) versus group beliefs.

These distinctions also imply, thus, that beliefs in general should be described as group beliefs (G-beliefs) and cultural beliefs (C-beliefs), and the same is true for knowledge and opinions. Usually, when we speak about knowledge, we mean C-knowledge, and not G-knowledge. The latter type of knowledge is accepted only by one or several groups and is often simply called 'beliefs' (e.g. 'They believe that God exists', 'They believe that the market will solve all social problems'), or opinions, illusions, myths, fiction, fallacies, and so on, by other groups. Ideologies, as we shall see, are the general, social beliefs that are the basis of G-beliefs. And cultural beliefs form the common ground of (virtually) all social beliefs of (virtually) all groups of a given culture.

At the same time, these distinctions provide a framework for the social dimension of the classical opposition between *objective* and *subjective* (or intersubjective) knowledge and beliefs. If objective knowledge consists of those beliefs that are shared by everyone, and can be shown to be true by the truth criteria of a community, then such objectivity may also be C-objectivity or G-objectivity, depending on whether they are shared by one or more groups or the whole culture. As with knowledge, when we speak about objectivity, we usually mean C-objectivity. Subjective beliefs are all those beliefs that are associated with a specific person, group or culture, and which are not accepted by all members, all groups or all cultures, respectively, depending on the perspective or scope of the description.

These distinctions are not merely the fruit of cognitive or philosophical speculation, but rather specific hypotheses about the organization of memory in general, and social memory in particular. They are necessary in order to define ideology, and to solve the well-known problem of the differences between knowledge and ideology. Moreover, they are used in describing and explaining different discourse structures. Knowledge and opinions are expressed and sustained in different ways in discourse, and require different forms of 'evidence'.[10]

We have also seen that in natural language and commonsense discourse the notions 'belief', 'knowledge' and 'opinion' may be used differently than we did above. On the other hand, we have tried to make explicit some of the implications of the everyday uses of such terms. Instead of the cognitive distinctions made above for social beliefs, we may make similar distinctions in the discourses that express or construct such social beliefs. Instead of 'beliefs', we might then account for different types of discourse in terms of the different types of descriptions they give of the social world.[11]

As we have argued before, there are many reasons why we do not adopt this kind of discursivist reduction. In this case, for instance, although the cognitive distinctions should be shown to be relevant for discourse description, language users are not always able to make explicit their knowledge of different forms of social beliefs. More generally, then, *it is important to distinguish carefully between beliefs and the expression of beliefs in discourse*. The latter are also a function of the constraints of the context, including personal beliefs or experiences, and not only of the underlying structure of social memory.

It has been assumed above that factual beliefs may be said to be true or false, as are the propositions that represent them. However, it might be argued that truth values only apply to actual statements or expressions of beliefs, that is, in discourse, and only in the pragmatic context of assertions. 'Is The Hague the capital of the Netherlands?' expresses a factual belief, but there is no point in calling this belief 'true' or 'false' – indeed, the question presupposes that the speaker does not know whether the belief 'that The Hague is the capital of the Netherlands' is true or false. At most, the belief may be said to be *possibly true*, given the presupposed knowledge that The Hague is a city in the Netherlands, and the seat of the Dutch government and parliament. Such a possibility may also be expressed by modal expressions such as 'maybe', 'perhaps', and so on, which also express doubt about the truth of a belief. In other words, factual beliefs are not just true or false, but also possibly true or false. In formal terms, they are not just propositions, but propositional functions, which may be turned into actual (true or false) propositions in contextualized discourse, and if they are asserted. In sum, if we continue to speak about true and false beliefs, the social mind may feature factual beliefs of which the truth status is unknown. We shall come back to the discourse manifestations of social cognition in Part III.

In sum, both personal and social opinions imply *differences of opinion*, that is, my opinions (versus those of others), on the one hand, and our group's opinions (versus those of other groups), on the other.

Attitudes

I shall use the term *attitude* to denote general, socially shared, evaluative beliefs (opinions) of groups. Or rather, I shall reserve the notion of attitude to refer to specific, organized, *clusters* of socially shared beliefs, such as the (often complex) attitudes about nuclear energy, abortion or immigration. This means that, contrary to the sometimes confused usage in social psychology, personal opinions are *not* called attitudes, whether or not they are particular or general. Individuals may of course 'participate in' or share a social attitude, as they also may share in social knowledge or know a language. I shall for the moment leave open the possibility that the notion of attitude may also apply to clusters of socially shared *particular* opinions, for example about *this* civil war in Bosnia and not just about civil wars in general. Although social opinions and hence attitudes typically vary between groups, we might also speak of cultural attitudes if a cluster of social opinions is shared by a whole culture, as might typically be the case for cultures defined by one religion.[12]

Why the 'attitude' concept cannot be dispensed with

Some social psychologists have criticized the traditional notion of attitude on more fundamental, anti-cognitivist grounds. They dispute that people 'have' something like attitudes in the first place, and that such attitudes control people's actions or discourse. According to these critics, opinions or attitudes do not 'exist' at all, at least not as 'fixed' mental representations. They emphasize that opinions (like the mind in general) are social constructions. Moreover, these scholars emphasize that opinions should be defined in terms of their discursive formulation. For them, opinions vary with the context in which language-users rhetorically engage in debate or other interaction with other participants. Instead of attitudes, discursive 'repertoires' are proposed to account for such variations in the formulation of opinions. And if attitudes should 'exist' mentally at all, they should rather be dynamically represented as some kind of rhetorical structure, or as an argument.[13]

As has been emphasized before, there are many arguments why this position is theoretically untenable. A detailed discussion of this issue is beyond the scope of this book, so a few succinct arguments will have to suffice here to reject this approach to attitudes.

(a) In more general terms, it has already been shown that a reformulation of cognition in terms of discourse is a form of interactionist (if not behaviourist) reduction that fails to describe and to explain fundamental properties of both thinking and discourse. If all 'non-observable' mental entities would need to be dispensed with, we would also have to throw out beliefs in general, including knowledge, rules, and of course discourse meaning, among many other cognitive notions. Moreover, interaction and discourse structures themselves are abstract and hence unobservable. The same is true for other practical and theoretical 'unobservables', such as groups, power, inequality, institutions, society and culture, which we also postulate (in a social theory) in order to be able to describe and explain people's activities ('behaviour'), among other things. In sum, if 'observability' were a criterion, neither commonsense nor theoretical analysis of action, discourse or society would be possible, no more than an analysis of people's minds.

(b) To abolish the 'mind' as a practical and theoretical notion for everyday and scholarly observation and explanation, and without providing a serious alternative, is not only counterintuitive, but also inconsistent with all available evidence. That minds are obviously (also) social constructs does not mean that they do not 'exist', as a specific and complex property of people's brains. An interactionist, discursivist or constructivist reduction of the mind is unable to explain what people do when they think, believe, have opinions, remember, and so on.

(c) Opinions (and hence attitudes as socially shared opinions) also underlie other social practices than discourse, as is the case for prejudices in relation to acts of discrimination. To reduce prejudice to (say) verbal 'repertoires' (whatever these are exactly) is to deny that discrimination may be 'based on' prejudice, or to deny that prejudices, for all practical, social and theoretical purposes, 'exist' independently of discriminatory behaviour. Moreover, such social opinions and attitudes are gradually acquired and may change, and hence are not 'fixed', although, at the level of the group, they should remain relatively stable across several contexts of their application.

(d) Both for common sense, and theoretically, people or groups are assumed to 'have' opinions and other beliefs also when they do not always express them in talk, or in other social practices for that matter.

(e) That people usually tailor the precise formulation or *expression* of an opinion to the constraints of different contexts, does not imply that the underlying personal opinion itself may not, for all practical purposes, be the same in different situations. We know that persuasion and rhetoric may fail, and that people often 'do not change their opinion'. This is especially the case for socially shared opinions, which by definition can only be shared when they are not different from one local context to the next, and hence from person to person.

(f) The reduction of opinions to their *ad hoc* formulation is inconsistent with a basic condition of social interaction and social groups: that social members may share a 'common ground' of beliefs. Paradoxically, radical social constructionism that denies mental beliefs is inconsistent with its own social claims, and reduces beliefs (and ideologies and culture) to the solipsism of interacting individuals in unique contexts.

(g) Of course, *personal* opinions (whether shared with a group or not) may – but need not – adapt to specific social situations or contexts. But this does not entail that therefore they are not mentally represented. As I shall show later, people represent their personal and local knowledge and opinions about an event in mental models (see Chapter 7). It is this representation of (personal) opinions in models that explains contextual variation, and also provides a solid ground for the explication of *both* discourse and other social practices in which such opinions are expressed. Mental model theory elegantly explains all objections against the postulation of socially shared attitudes, and does not have the numerous problems inherent in reductive 'discursivism'. Thus mental models allow for shared social opinions or attitudes to be relatively stable (although they may change in time), while at the same time providing for individual and contextual variation and uniqueness.

(h) And finally, alternative proposals, such as 'repertoires' or 'rhetorical mental structures' are either left undefined as to their precise structure and status, or in fact also boil down to something (unobservable!) people 'have'. They are a form of knowledge or belief, and hence mental. After all, we can hardly assume that repertoires are floating in the air or in people's mouths. If they allow people to talk or understand talk and text, we have no alternative but to locate them in the minds of people, as is the case for grammars, discourse rules, norms, and indeed knowledge and other beliefs.

The critique of the classical notion of attitude is correct in concluding that (besides many other flaws) traditional social psychology largely ignored the crucially discursive and social nature of attitude construction and manifestations, and underplayed the contextual variation of attitude expression. However, this is no reason to throw out the baby with the bath water, to deny that opinions and attitudes do not 'exist', to claim that they are merely mentalist 'reifications' and that where relevant they exist only as discursive formulations.

Denying the existence of attitudes because they are 'unobservable' would in this case be as silly as affirming such existence, simply because there would not be any direct evidence for either claim. This is the case for *all* properties of the mind. They are being postulated, practically and theoretically, because they are real in their consequences: they explain how and why people can 'meaningfully' and 'purposefully' act and talk. They explain very powerful commonsense self-observations: people know they think, they know they know things, and they know they 'have' opinions, whether or not they express them, and even if they express them differently in different situations. People know that often they agree with others, and may thus share opinions as members of a group. The 'silent majority' is defined in terms of such a community of people sharing the same or similar attitudes, even if they do not always express them. There is no more 'reification' involved here than in the commonsense and theoretical assumption that people have contextually variable knowledge as well as more general sociocultural knowledge that may be (variably) used in different contexts.

In sum, in a more explicit theoretical framework which describes their precise status, their internal organization, their cognitive and social functions, 'attitudes' remain a useful concept. To reduce opinion clusters on, for example, immigration or nuclear energy, to forms or repertoires of talk, is to confuse levels of description and explanation, to ignore that manifestations of human activities may have explanatory underlying structures, and to challenge commonsense observations, without providing a theoretically sound alternative. It is like saying that feeling hungry does not 'exist' because we can't see that, and that such a feeling should in fact be described only in terms of people ingesting lots of food. We know that people are hungry (also when they are not eating) because they are able to tell us, in the same way as they are able to tell us that they feel bad about being hungry, or that they have the opinion that poverty is due to the riches of the rich. Opinions, thus, are not less real than hunger, and should not be reduced to their manifestations in discourse or social practices.

Concluding this brief and incomplete argument, we find no grounds to abolish the notion of attitude. On the contrary, especially also in a theory of ideology, such a notion, when properly analysed, is crucial. It accounts for the 'common ground' of socially shared opinions of groups of people and for the ways these allow group members to interact, to coordinate and to organize their social practices, even in different contexts. What we *do* need, however, and what was another major shortcoming of much traditional attitude research, is a much more detailed analysis of their internal organization. Similarly, we need to examine in more detail how socially shared opinions or attitudes are linked with personal ones and in different contexts. And of course, we should spell out the social situations and social structures in which social groups develop and change their attitudes, and especially how they do so exactly. And finally, yes, we must account for the ways both social and personal, general and specific opinions are being expressed and formulated in text and talk. These are some of the tasks of the next chapters.

Social representations

So far, I have used the general notion of belief in order to describe personal versus social beliefs, specific versus general beliefs, factual versus evaluative beliefs and group versus cultural beliefs. As systems of knowledge and attitudes, these beliefs are organized in many ways, for instance by schema-like structures such as scripts, scenarios, frames or other organizational patterns of memory. In order to have a general concept that specifically applies to *organized clusters of socially shared beliefs* (knowledge, attitudes, ideologies, etc.) as located in social memory, I shall henceforth use the term *social representation*, of which social beliefs are the constituent elements.

The concept of 'social representation' has been used in social psychology and the other social sciences in many different ways.[14] Here, however, the term 'social representations' (SR) will only apply to organized clusters of socially shared beliefs. Thus, knowledge scripts and attitudes are both examples of social representations, and so are ideologies. The next chapter will deal with the internal structure and further properties of these social representations. One crucial dimension of a cognitive approach is not only to describe the structures of mental representations, but especially also the *processes* or *strategies* of their social acquisition, use and change.

Habitus

Especially in sociology, another term used to denote socially shared representations is *habitus*, usually defined in terms of 'structured dispositions' for social practices that are partly autonomous and partly a function of societal structures.[15] As I have done with the notion of ideology, habitus is sometimes compared with a generative grammar in order to emphasize the creative, active use social actors make of such dispositions. I shall not further use this notion, because cognitively it is only very loosely defined. It certainly is less explicit than the notion of (a system of) social representations, or social cognition, used in this chapter. Moreover, the concept of 'disposition' in the definition of this concept is psychologically inadequate, if not circular, because it defines cognitive structures in terms of their 'output' (such as social practices) which precisely need to be explained in terms of other, cognitive representations. For instance, prejudice as a social habitus should not be described as a 'tendency to discriminate', but be analysed in terms of mental structures in such a way that discrimination, verbal derogation, disclaimers ('We are not racist, but . . .'), as well as many other manifestations of prejudice can be explained.

Social cognition

I shall henceforth use the term *social cognition* to refer to the combination of socially shared mental representations and these processes of their use in social contexts. This usage is different from one of the uses of the term 'social cognition' in current social psychology, where it often refers to the more individualistic, information-processing approach to social memory prevalent in the USA, as distinct from (mostly) European approaches to social representations, social identity, social categorization and intergroup relations.

In this book, I advocate an integration of these (and other) approaches to social cognition. That is, on the one hand, it should be recognized that the mental representations and processes of social beliefs and actions need to be described in explicit detail, whereas on the other hand social cognition, and especially ideology, can fully be understood only in terms of their social functions for social actors as group members in social situations.[16]

That much current work on social memory representations and processes largely uses the prevalent information-processing metaphor of cognitive psychology is no problem as long as we know it is merely a metaphor, and as long as detailed processing theories provide insights that alternative approaches do not provide. Also, as suggested, the use of this metaphor does not at all commit us to an individualistic approach to the human mind, as long as we know that the mind is socially constituted and used, and hence mental representations should also be described in terms of their functions for group members and whole groups.

Ideologies: a cognitive definition

The ideas developed above, based partly on current psychology, partly extending them, provide the conceptual instruments for a provisional cognitive description of the nature and status of ideologies. In the following chapter I shall add further details, especially also about the social dimensions of ideologies. In other words, we now only pretend to sketch part of the overall theoretical picture.

We have discovered, above, that ideologies cannot simply be called 'belief systems', because there are many types of belief that are not ideological in the usual sense, nor in the sense we would like to reserve for the concept of 'ideology'. We need to locate ideologies in the social mind, because they are not individual, contextualized, ad hoc beliefs, but socially shared by collectivities of some kind. Finally, we identified those socially shared beliefs that need to be kept outside the control of specific ideologies, namely, all culturally shared social beliefs, including especially the epistemic common ground of a culture.

The closest we got to the notion of ideology, thus, was to define them in terms of the social beliefs shared by specific social collectivities or 'groups', where the notion of 'group' needs to be defined later. This would mean that an ideology is the set of factual and evaluative beliefs – that is, the knowledge and the opinions – of a group. Depending on how we define groups later, this is indeed quite close to the notion that is used most often in commonsense and scholarly approaches to ideology, as we have seen before.

This means that this chapter has given a first answer to the basic question about the 'nature' of ideologies: They are not metaphysical or otherwise vaguely localized systems 'of' or 'in' society or groups or classes, but a specific type of (basic) mental representations shared by the members of groups, and hence firmly located in the minds of people. Thus, ideologies are not 'above' or 'between' people, groups or society, but part of the minds of its members. Again, this does *not* mean that they are therefore *individual* or *only* mental. On the contrary, just like languages, ideologies are as much social as they are mental. It is this integrated socio-cognitive analysis that characterizes my approach to ideology. In a more social and critical analysis, I shall later have to examine the social, political and cultural conditions, consequences and functions of ideologies thus defined – for example, in terms of the values, identities, relations, aims, positions and power of social collectivities of specific kinds.

Ideologies as the foundation of group beliefs

I shall, however, further limit the concept of ideology in order to make it even more specific as a theoretically viable notion and suggest that ideologies are the *foundation* of the social beliefs shared by a social group. In other words, a bit like the axioms of a formal system, ideologies consist of those general and abstract social beliefs, shared by a group, that control or organize the more specific knowledge and opinions (attitudes) of a group. Formally, this would mean that the propositions that constitute an ideology should be derivable from the variable knowledge and opinions about various domains of social life. For instance, if ethnic prejudices pertain to human rights, immigration, integration, education, housing, access to resources, and so on, of minorities or immigrants, then the ideological beliefs would be formed by such general propositions as 'We are fundamentally different from them', 'We are superior to them', 'They are a threat to us', 'They do not respect our norms and principles', 'We are tolerant', and so on. Later we shall see how such propositions are organized in ideological schemas.

As may be expected, such basic ideological beliefs must be both general and abstract, and also very relevant for a group. They typically would not deal with details of everyday social life, but apply to fundamental dimensions of the group and its relations to other groups. As we shall see later, they must be functional for the group as a whole, and reflect the conditions of its existence and reproduction.

In an earlier version of my theory, I limited ideologies to the foundations of evaluative beliefs.[17] The reason for this decision was that ideologies generally apply to what is most characteristic of a group, namely, its opinions about itself and other groups. However, once we have relegated all forms of commonsense and general knowledge to the cultural basis of the social mind, ideologies may also be taken as the basis of group knowledge. This would mean that they do not only embody the specific values but also the truth criteria of a group. For instance, Christians share the basic ideological belief that God exists. Feminists typically assume that women do not have an equal share in society's resources. And ecologists have basic knowledge about pollution and the relations between humans and nature. Some of these general beliefs that originally were characteristic of special groups, with 'special interests', have become part of the general cultural common ground.

That ideologies control group opinions or attitudes, seems obvious. Shared opinions must be important for the interaction, coordination and reproduction of the group, and these judgements require values and general principles that are typically variable across groups. They define competition, struggle and inequality. Is this also true for specific group knowledge? Provisionally I shall assume that this is the case: if factual beliefs are shared by a group, then they are socially relevant enough to get an ideological foundation. Also, the truth criteria in that case should be group specific, because otherwise the beliefs would probably be part of the common cultural ground. Thus, procedures of proof, evidence and acceptance of beliefs in scientific discourse and communication, are very different from those of politics, religion, corporate business or the mass media, or indeed from those in everyday life.

However, even within this much more specific scope, it may seem odd to call all specific group knowledge ideologically based. This may be true for religions, or even for action groups, where religious and political ideologies determine how the world is understood, and where group interests may be involved. But what about, say, the medical knowledge of doctors, the legal knowledge of lawyers, or of our own scholarly knowledge? In some cases there may not even be any competition, conflict or struggle from outside the group. Yet, professional knowledge, as many studies and everyday experiences show, is a symbolic resource for professional, elite power. It is a resource that is carefully protected, and serves the interests of the group. Hence, it is plausible that the nature of that knowledge itself, and the ways it is acquired, changed, validated and used, is also profoundly ideological. Thus, medical knowledge of the body, which may seem scientifically 'true', not only competes with religious and commonsense knowledges, but also embodies the typical truth criteria and other principles and hence the ideology (or ideologies) of the medical profession. Such knowledge may be used and abused, it may be applied in order to control people, and it most certainly is a fundamental condition for the reproduction of the profession.[18] Thus, although perhaps less relevant for each detailed piece of professional knowledge, it seems likely that also professional knowledge as a whole is internally and functionally characterized by underlying ideological principles.

It has already been suggested that as soon as the basic evaluation criteria of a group, and hence its social beliefs, are increasingly adopted by society as a whole, the group specificity of such social beliefs is lost, so that they are no longer ideological in our strict sense, but simply part of the cultural common ground. Of course, this does not mean that such a cultural common ground itself may not be declared 'ideological' at an universal level of description and evaluation. As is increasingly clear in the contemporary world, also whole cultures may clash, compete and hence have interests, so that their shared common ground and its basis principles of evaluation may again be ideological in comparison with those of other cultures. In other words, if knowledge and other social beliefs are relative, so are ideologies.

If a general culture consists of generally accepted, uncontested beliefs, which in fact define the shared common sense of its members, then we might be tempted to call precisely such beliefs ideological. Ideologies have often been declared really influential if nobody notices them, and if they define common sense. This may be true, but it is inconsistent with the theory that links ideologies with groups, group interests, group relations, struggle, domination or specific world views. That is, we are only able to understand and analyse common cultural ground as ideological if we have possible alternatives, other examples, other cultures, conflicts between cultures, or when a specific group within a society or culture challenges the social beliefs of the common ground. In other words, again, the relativity principle applies: common cultural ground can only be called ideological at a higher, comparative, universal or historical level of analysis. If all members of a culture believe, for example, in the existence of God, then such a religious belief is no longer ideological, but simply shared knowledge, *within that culture*. That is, there are no groups within that culture that disagree, contest or otherwise provide an alternative view of society in that respect.

On the other hand, if specific common-ground beliefs in fact are in the interest of a specific dominant group (e.g. beliefs about the properties and roles of women until not too long ago) and yet taken for granted, tacitly accepted and uncontested by the other groups, then we already distinguish between different groups (e.g. men and women) and their different interests, so that in that case such common-ground beliefs would in fact be beliefs that are those of one group, as imposed on society or culture as a whole.

This suggests that parts of common ground may be ideological anyway, but again this is true only with respect to a comparative or higher level, in which we are able to distinguish different groups and conflicting interests in such a society or culture. From within a totally homogeneous culture, no conflicts of interests of any common-ground beliefs can even be perceived or thought. As soon as one social group realizes that the common ground is in fact not in the interests of all, then a set of common beliefs will be declared ideological, and attached to a specific dominant group (e.g. whites, men). In the same way as group beliefs may become cultural beliefs in many ways (usually by power, hegemony, inculcation, and so on), also the reverse may be true, when individuals form a group that challenges generally accepted social beliefs, develops opposed beliefs and hence its own ideology of resistance.

These social constraints on ideology formation need to be attended to later. It is, however, interesting that even within a cognitive account of ideology, we need to postulate a social and cultural basis. In a social sense, this requires social interaction, sharing, social situations, organization and often also institutionalization. In the 'purely' cognitive sense (if there is such a thing) talking about the 'social mind' means first of all that cognitive representations are not limited to individuals but in some sense distributed among 'many minds'. This presupposes information exchange – for example through perception, discourse or interaction – which again brings in the social dimension. Secondly, and more interestingly, we assume that the very mental contents, architecture and organization of the social mind shared by group members reflect social and cultural constraints. We are unable to define 'knowledge' without having recourse to social or cultural conditions, and the same is true for attitudes and ideologies. Thus, if we talk about a cultural common ground of generally shared beliefs than this is not just a socio-cultural account, but also tells us something about the very foundation of the mind, of social memory and how other beliefs, including social ones, are grounded and organized. Similarly, also the more specific group beliefs that members of different social groups develop, share and use, are differentiated only with respect to both this general common ground and to the social beliefs of other groups.

We now have a first impression of the cognitive status and 'location' of ideologies. The next crucial step is to examine what such ideologies actually look like, how they are organized, and how they related to the social beliefs (group knowledge and attitudes) of which they form the foundations.

4

Structures and Strategies

Modes of description

If there is anything a theory of ideology must provide, then, it is an account of the *structures* of ideologies. Few topics in earlier approaches to ideology have been ignored so consistently as the simple question: If there are ideologies, then what do they look like? No sophisticated structuralism was necessary to spell out the typical components, the building blocks of ideologies, and how these are combined in various patterns. Yet, this seldom happened, so that ideologies usually remained in an analytical limbo, somewhere between 'systems of ideas' and 'social interests', where everybody could project into them what they wanted.

For contemporary psychology, linguistics and discourse analysis, as well as for some of the social sciences, such questions of structure are routine – describing, analysing and explaining phenomena first of all means that we should specify their structures and their functions. Such analyses may be *static-structuralist*, or *dynamic-processual*. The first, as we know it from modern grammars, specifies the structural components or units, as well as the principles (rules, norms or other regularities) of their composition in larger units. The more dynamic approach, familiar in psychology, microsociology and conversation analysis, spells out the actual processes, moves or strategies, that is, the mental or interactional dynamics of construction, for instance as an account of how social actors or language users go about, online, 'doing' or 'making' such structural units as mental representations, actions or discourses.

Structural versus strategic analysis

I shall henceforth refer to these alternative modes of description as the structural and the strategic approach. The first analyses objects as finished products, the latter characterizes the ways in which such objects are gradually built up or interpreted. These approaches may be seen as fundamentally different, as true alternatives, or as complementary ways of accounting for the same phenomena, depending on one's philosophy of language, discourse, interaction or cognition. The more strategic approach would then seem to account more adequately for what social actors, thinkers or language users are actually *doing* in concrete situations, whereas the structural approach would be more abstract and context-free, and rather account for what social actors know , or what the *product* or *result* is of their strategic thinking or action.[1]

At the moment, both in psychology, as well as in conversation analysis and the social sciences, the more dynamic, strategic approach is more popular after the earlier, structuralist phase. Yet, as suggested, such approaches are in fact complementary. First of all, both are abstract, both operate with abstract categories, and both operate with some kind of rules. Even when analysing the dynamics of cognitive processes or social interaction, we operate at various levels of abstraction, with theoretical constructs accounting for what is being observed. Thus, conversation analysts may do so in terms of actions, turns, moves and their sequencing in talk, whereas psychologists operate with cognitive units such as concepts, propositions, mental representations or networks, and the strategies of their mental manipulation in production and understanding. And neither cognitive psychologists nor those who analyse interaction and conversation operate at the various physical, physiological or auditory levels of 'reality'. That is, any abstract account of construction processes or strategies presupposes some kind of components or structural units known and used by information processors as social actors.

That is, also a strategic approach assumes that speakers know what structures are more or less well formed, and what rules or other structural principles are available to them as (mental and social) resources when engaged in strategic construction. In that respect, thus, the structural and the strategic approach are complementary approaches to the description of the various phenomena of cognition and interaction.

Similar remarks may be made for other, more complex social structures, such as groups, organizations, group relationships, and whole societies, which also may be structurally accounted for in terms of their conceptual building blocks and the principles of their construction, on the one hand, or the strategic processes of their actual operation, construction, reproduction, formation or change, on the other hand.

Abstract versus practical competence

There is, however, one difference between these two approaches that is more fundamental. Structural approaches tend to be more abstract and context-free, in the sense of characterizing ideal types or general patterns, and tend to ignore variations, 'deviations' and 'errors'. Modern structural and generative grammars and earlier psycholinguistics usually take such an approach. Under the influence of new directions in cognitive psychology, socio-linguistics and conversation analysis, such abstract normativity was relinquished for an account that focused on the on-line, ongoing processes or strategies of what actors are actually thinking, saying or doing, including individual, contextual variations and 'errors'.

Instead of the neatly separated levels of grammars or other structural theories (e.g. those of argumentation and narration), and the theoretical distinction between 'langue' and 'parole' or between 'competence' and 'performance', the dynamic approach emphasizes that people think, speak and act strategically. This means, among other things, that they follow various goals, operate or act at various levels of production or understanding at the same time and, while doing so, make mistakes, have lapses of memory, get confused, or take short-cuts. Despite such 'imperfection', they are usually able to repair these and to re-interpret the data at hand. In sum, they are clearly competent in managing this bewildering amount of tasks to accomplish rather successfully, though not perfectly, what they set out to do, namely, understand something, say something or do something in a specific context, often jointly with other people. In that respect, the strategies of text comprehension are not much different from those of conversation and interaction. Both require an abstract or normative competence, as well as a more practical competence or ability.

Dynamic processes of thinking and acting are possible only when people also know and share more abstract rules and structures. They often know what sentences, sentence sequences, actions or interactions are more or less well formed, acceptable or understandable. Such knowledge and judgements are not merely displayed in ongoing discourse. Sometimes they may also be applied in a more abstract, context-free fashion, because their knowledge is not limited to one situation or to one token, but necessarily more general, and hence abstract. This allows them to adequately produce and interpret a potentially infinite number and variety of different perceptions, discourses or actions. In sum, although the structural and strategic approaches have a different flavour and focus on rather different aspects of thought, discourse and interaction, they always presuppose each other, and a fully fledged account should integrate them both.

Structures and strategies of social cognition

It is against this general background that we also should approach the question of the structures of ideology, defined as the underlying frameworks of the socially shared beliefs of group members, as explained in the previous chapter. Such ideologies are abstract, and hence a more 'structuralist' approach seems more appropriate. Unlike discourse and action, ideologies, as we understand them, are not locally produced in the sense of shaped by each specific social context, by a single speaker and utterance (see Chapter 22 for this concept of context). They do not vary from one moment to the next, and are not strategically adapted to individual recipients. On the contrary, given their social, group-based functions, they must be relatively *stable* and a *context-free* resource for many group members in many situations. Again, in that sense, ideologies are like grammars, defined as abstract systems of knowledge (rules) that enable all competent speakers of a language community to communicate in many different contexts.

On the other hand, ideologies are of course *context-sensitive* if we use a broader concept of 'context', including the relevant dimensions of social

structure, such as groups and institutions, social relations of power, historical development, and so on. Given the earlier definitions, ideologies are
formed and changed as a function of such (broader) social 'contexts',
although such changes are usually rather slow. To avoid further confusion, I
shall not use this broader, commonsense notion of 'context', and instead use
the sociological term 'social structure', or else the term social 'macro-
context' to denote the properties of the social structure that are specifically
relevant for a specific ideology.

That ideologies themselves are relatively stable does *not* mean that the
expressions and *uses* of ideologies are not variable, strategic and context-
sensitive. On the contrary, the theory will precisely need to spell out how
such expressions of ideologies are adapted by individual social actors and
strategically tailored to the situation at hand. So much so, that they may even
seem to be non-existent in a particular situation. To wit, sexist men will not
continuously make sexist remarks in all situations. Thus, whereas *expressions* of ideologies in social practices will be variably occasioned and
contextually managed, we assume that ideologies themselves, as well as
other shared social representations, need to be relatively stable.

Such stability is necessary in light of the cognitive and social functions
ideologies have for the many different members of a group in different
situations. Ingroup co-operation, continuity and reliability of action and
judgement and many other properties of successful group membership and
social practices would be impossible without at least a minimum of stability.
In the same way as language users would be unable to speak and understand
their language without a more or less stable grammar, group members would
be unable to accomplish their daily practices and social judgements without
more or less stable social representations such as knowledge, attitudes and
ideologies, of which abstract ideologies are necessarily the most stable
socio-cognitive constructs.

On the other hand, even such more or less stable representations need to
be acquired, changed or abolished by groups and their members, and such
processes of change, though slow, of course need an account of a more
dynamic nature. That is, all structures, also those of ideologies, eventually
also need an account of their active *construction* (formation or change) by
group members in social contexts.

Schemata

Whereas structural analysis is a well-known and quite sophisticated procedure in linguistics and discourse analysis, the structural account of cognition
in general, and of social cognition in particular, remains at a relatively
modest level of theoretical sophistication. We have seen that the overall
architecture of the mind is a fairly simplistic construct, with some overall
distinctions between short-term and long-term memory, and between episodic and semantic memory. Beliefs may be represented in (similarly

simplified) propositions or networks, and belief-clusters may in turn be organized by various schemata.

This schematic approach is a relatively plain counterpart of structural analysis in linguistics, and usually lacks the more dynamic dimension needed to account for the construction, uses or changes of such schemata. Thus, if we want to explain how people perceive objects, scenes or events, how they produce or understand sentences and stories, the knowledge they have to do so is assumed to be organized in such schematic patterns. People have ideal, abstract or prototypical schemata for the structures of a chair, an event, a story, people, groups as well as social structures. It has become standard practice in psychology to specify and distinguish event-schemata, people-schemata and story-schemata, among others.[2]

Such schemata of naive, commonsense knowledge usually consist of a number of characteristic *categories* (such as the complication and the resolution in a story), that may be combined in a specific order and hierarchy, and allowing for variable terminal elements. Typically, as is the case in the generative grammar of sentences, such structures are represented in tree-like (directed) graphs, consisting of a top node, several edges and a number of lower-level nodes representing subordinate (included) categories.

Note that what is being described here is not real-world objects, but our socially shared, conventional and cultural *knowledge* about such objects, that is, mental structures or representations. It need not be emphasized again that these structures are merely abstract, theoretical accounts of the organization of socio-cultural knowledge. Yet, although many alternatives could be imagined, they should not be arbitrary; they need to account for empirical phenomena of actual understanding, discourse and action. Some knowledge structures better account for how people go about perceiving, speaking and acting than others. For instance, a hierarchical structure may better explain differences in availability or accessibility of certain top- or high-level categories than structures that are not organized that way.

However, an account of the organization of the mind that is closer to a neural model of the brain might provide alternative theoretical accounts that are based on (neural) nodes or pathways that are in various stages of readiness or excitation. Theoretically, these may be no more than notational variants if their descriptive and explanatory power in the account of information processing, thinking, speaking or understanding is the same. That is, at lower, more detailed levels of processing, neural models of representation and processing may be more relevant, whereas at the higher, more complex level, other representational formats for knowledge, such as abstract schemata, may be theoretically more useful.[3]

The same may be true for actual *processing* of schemata – at a fairly high and complex level, people process information linearly, as is the case in the understanding of words and sentences or the execution of actions. However, as soon as we want to account for the full complexity of such tasks at all levels, we must assume that processing needs to be 'massively parallel' as the preferred phrase of connectionist theories goes. If we add all the levels that account for, for example, discourse production and understanding (phonetic, phonological, lexical, syntactic, semantic, stylistic, interactional, pragmatic, contextual, etc.), the number of structures being processed in relation to such beliefs is so high that we must assume that these processes operate in parallel. Unfortunately, we know as yet very little about the details of such parallel, neural processing and 'representation' when applied to belief systems.

Scripts

Structural descriptions of social representations may also take a more dynamic form, especially when they aim to render the structures of events and actions. Thus, the notion of *script* has been widely used to account for the knowledge people have about the stereotypical events of their culture, such as celebrating a birthday, an initiation ritual, going to the supermarket, or participating in a university class, among myriad other well-known events.[4] As the script-metaphor suggests, such knowledge is represented in terms of a setting, time, location and a sequence of events and actions and the typical or optional actors that participate in them, like students and professors in classes, and pilots, flight attendants and passengers in air travel. Of course, we may imagine other types of structures, as long as they are able to account adequately for the actual mental and social activities of people.

It should be emphasized again that such knowledge is general and abstract. In order to be applicable in the very large number of possible situations people may be involved in, we must either assume that such structures themselves are infinitely variable (in a way similar to that in which the rules of a grammar allow the structural specification of an infinite number of possible sentences), or that the abstract schemata are being used by flexible *strategies*, which may tailor them to each particular situation. There are also intermediate solutions, where schemata or scripts are assumed to be built up of smaller structural units (in the way that 'paying' is a sequence of basic actions that may be found in most economic interactions, like buying a product, or paying for a ticket in the movies) that may be combined and hence vary in a more flexible way.[5] But even then, actual variation is practically infinite, given the (theoretically) infinite ways of accomplishing these component basic actions. So, any account, whether a more structural or a more strategic one, has or needs to be complemented with flexible rules or strategies that adapt structural categories or units to their variable uses by different people in different situations. This is as true for the production and comprehension of sentences, as it is true for everyday conversations, complex institutional dialogues, or for more or less complex social acts such as going to the movies, managing a firm or governing a country.

The main point in all these cases is (a) that we need to assume socio-culturally shared and mentally represented knowledge, (b) that such knowledge needs to be organized so that it can be effectively acquired, accessed and changed, and (c) that such knowledge needs (internal or external) strategic means for its variable and effective uses by individual users in concrete situations. Later we shall see that we need to add a number of social properties of knowledge – it is not acquired, used and changed in abstract situations, but in social situations by social actors, as well as in institutions, organizations and whole cultures.

Organizing evaluations

With all their theoretical limitations (most schema theories are not exactly examples of formal explicitness and conceptual sophistication), these various approaches to the account of the structures and strategic uses of knowledge have been relatively successful. It is not surprising, therefore, that similar schema-theoretic roads have been followed in social psychology.[6] Thus, if people have schemata or scripts for storms, stores, stories and storytelling they probably also have them for people, groups, intergroup relations, domination, organizations, governments and democracy. The same is true for the myriad of communicative events that describe or constitute such social objects, such as conversations, negotiations, parliamentary debates, impression management as well as corporate management.

The theoretical task then consists in spelling out these various structures as well as the strategies of their usage. This is easier said than done. One question is whether it is likely that all or at least many of these mental representations have the same or similar categories or whether their overall structures are at least the same or similar, if only because of obvious reasons of cognitive economy. Intuitively, we may assume that there are considerable differences: our beliefs about chairs, chairpersons and chairing a meeting probably do not have the same internal organization. Yet, chairs may have structures that are at least comparable to many other objects, chairpersons are not very different from other people or roles, and chairing a meeting is not essentially different from many other forms of interaction. So, we may have object-schemata, person-schemata, role-schemata, and interaction-schemata, and similar schemata (or scripts, or scenarios, etc.) maybe developed for groups, relations of domination, organizations, civil wars, democracy or, indeed, ideologies.

However, there are some complications. What has been said, above, especially applies to the organization of knowledge, but does it also apply to the organization of opinions, attitudes and judgements? We may postulate person-schemata and group-schemata, and maybe scripts for parliamentary sessions and civil wars, but how do we organize the opinions and attitudes we have about such social objects or events?

Despite a number of modest attempts,[7] few detailed representation formats have been provided for evaluative structures. In fact, we do not even know whether such evaluations should be represented separately from our knowledge about the objects of judgement. If people have a group-schema about, say, Turks, does this mean that such a schema should also feature the opinions and the prejudices people may have about Turks?

For instance, a simple network could have 'Turks' as a node, and this node would be related to nodes that specify our knowledge about Turkey as a country, about Turkish as a language, about Turkish society and culture and so on, but that central node would also be related to nodes representing our evaluation of Turks as a people (or about the Turkish language, culture, religion, etc.). If many or most of the important (or central) nodes of the Turk-schema or Turk-network were negative, then this would represent a prejudice. Such a simple, integrated approach, where factual and evaluative beliefs are represented in one group-schema, meets a number of criteria for cognitive organization, namely, those of simplicity and economy. The question is whether it works – does such a schema account for prejudiced discourse and interaction, and does it explain discrimination, among many other forms of biased perception and interaction?

Attitude structures

Although at present we don't have a clear answer to such questions, we may however take a different theoretical approach and assume that in the same way as factual and evaluative beliefs can be distinguished, we may also distinguish between factual belief structures, on the one hand, and evaluative belief structures on the other hand. At the moment, this is merely an analytical distinction: it may very well be that in the mind (in the brain) these form one network. But, following the common sense of social members, we may provisionally distinguish between cultural knowledge, on the one hand, and group knowledge and group attitudes on the other hand.

One argument for this separation, apart from differences in social practices and discourse, is that knowledge is socio-culturally based on different methods of assessment and verification, namely, truth criteria such as observation, reliable sources, argumentation, proof or experimentation. Opinions are constructed and combined along very different methods of assessment, and following different criteria, such as values, group goals and interests, and social group relations. To establish where Turks come from in the world, what language they speak, or what religion they have, among other things, requires 'information' from newspapers, textbooks, atlases, everyday conversation and observation, as well as inferences from other knowledge, for instance about languages, religions, Islam, politics or the Mediterranean. When expressing such knowledge, as such, language users presuppose that others have similar beliefs (truthful or not) and that the methods to establish the truth of such beliefs or to settle disputes are socio-culturally shared.

However, prejudices about Turks are developed and used, and probably organized in quite a different way. First of all, as empirical evidence shows, people may have negative attitudes about Turks even without having any knowledge about them. Indeed, experiments and everyday experiences show that some people even express prejudices about non-existent peoples! And although most people who have prejudices about other groups usually have at least *some* knowledge about such groups, knowledge often prevents stereotyping and prejudices. The development of prejudice precisely avoids the methods and reliability criteria of knowledge, such as repeated observation, inference, proof, reliable sources, and relations with other knowledge; hence, obviously, their role as forms of pre-judgement. Generalizations are made from one or two observations, fallacies made in argumentation, unreliable sources are used, if at all, and so on.[8]

Even more importantly, apart from such 'fallible' information processing and judgement (which characterizes much thinking in general), what counts in the construction of prejudices are the goals, the interests and the values of the group. That is, if the group is Christian, and if Islam is defined as different, opposed to, or even as a threat to Christianity, and hence to Us, then Turks, like most other Muslims, may be negatively represented on the relevant category of religion. The same may happen for appearance, origin, employment, language, habits or perceived personal traits. In other words, besides the relevant knowledge categories for groups, group members may bring to bear a number of categories that are (for them) essential in the evaluation of other groups. One of these categories may be appearance, so that, for white people, anybody who is not white (and having other features of 'European' appearance) may be categorized as essentially different, deviant or dangerous on that dimension. Whether such basic categories have historical or even biological foundations is irrelevant. What counts is their socio-cultural construction and reproduction. People may learn and unlearn that differences of appearance are crucial in categorizing and especially in judging others.

The point then is that in general the structures of evaluative social representations such as attitudes (and as we shall see, of ideologies) are probably organized in a way that reflects or facilitates their social (group-based) functions, their social construction, and their social uses in everyday social practices. If skin colour is relevant to categorize and judge negatively other groups in order to be able to discriminate against them or oppress them, then such a real (or indeed imaginary) characteristic may become a category of the evaluative schema that defines (ethnic) attitudes in general and prejudices in particular.

Traditional approaches in the social psychology of attitudes follow some of these arguments in their assumption that attitudes always consist of three components: a cognitive, an evaluative and an emotional one.[9] Obviously, a three-component assumption does not tell us much about detailed structure or organization, only about the nature of the beliefs involved in attitudes. I have further argued that, whatever the 'real' organization of beliefs in the brain–mind, I prefer to keep factual beliefs apart from evaluative beliefs, and hence distinguish between knowledge and attitudes. As defined, the latter are only evaluative.

Finally, since emotions (when not confused with evaluations) are strictly personal and contextual, they cannot be part of socially shared, abstract group attitudes. They may, however, become triggered and mingled with the actual uses of attitudes in concrete situations by individual members. I may now be angry (or desperate) about a political decision, an emotion that may be triggered by activating or constructing a negative opinion in the current context. But a group cannot be continuously 'angry', in the strict sense of being angrily aroused. Socially shared, continuous 'affect', such as hate or anger, is not, in my view, an emotion, but a form of strong evaluation (which may of course be expressed in the language of emotions). It is highly unlikely that there are groups all of whose members are constantly emotionally aroused about some issue, but as is the case for ethnic prejudices, they may well share and maintain a negative evaluation about other groups.

Following a more fruitful way of cognitive inquiry into the more detailed organization of evaluative belief clusters, I assume that group members develop schemata or other abstract structures for the organization of social judgement. Such attitude-schemata for groups, thus, will feature those general categories that have developed as a function of the goals, interests as well as the social and cultural contexts of group perception and social practices. In some socio-historical situations this may be skin colour (as with prejudices of whites against blacks), religion (as in anti-semitism), gender (as in sexism), political ideology (as in anti-communism), and so on. Thus, whatever is relevant for evaluation, and the practices legitimated in terms of a negative (or positive) evaluation, may thus be selected as a category of the group-attitude-schema.

These schemata may be different for different types of group relationships, namely, those based on origin, ethnicity, gender, age, class, profession, and so on, but the same principles will be at work in the construction of attitudes. Note again that although it is plausible that both knowledge and attitudes usually operate in the conduct of discourse and other social practices, attitudes are distinct from knowledge, and so are their internal structures. Categories in attitudes may be used that have no basis in knowledge at all, but that are simply useful for negative judgement. The same is true for the order or relevance of such categories in the schema. Thus, in ethnocentric and racist attitudes, the appearance of other group members (even when 'objectively' barely different from that of our own group) may take the highest position in the category, and the same may be true for language, religion, socio-economic status, occupation, habits or attributed personal 'character' (e.g. being lazy or criminal).

Interestingly, and as we shall see in more detail later, the selection and ordering of categories of judgement are obviously not arbitrary, but a function of the social position, goals, resources, activities and other interests of the group that shares such an attitude. For the unemployed 'They take away our jobs' may become a prominent judgement of a prejudiced attitude, so that the socio-economic position of the other group becomes crucial. This process not only plays a role in relations of domination, but also of resistance. Thus, for linguistic minorities, the language of the linguistically dominant group will be a major category of judgement.

What seems rather straightforward for the organization of social opinions about other people and groups – the construction of evaluative group schemata consisting of variable hierarchies of social categorizations – is less obvious for attitudes about social issues and problems, such as abortion, nuclear energy or pollution. Although here also groups of people are involved about whom we may develop opinions, such attitudes rather focus on right or wrong social practices, or even about properties of objects or nature. Semantically such 'problems' may be construed (by different groups) as implying some kind of norm violation, if not as a threat, but such semantic contents are not readily reduced to abstract, general categories that allow the description of large classes of attitudes. And yet, given the typically organized nature of the mind, it is highly unlikely that such attitudes merely consist of *lists* of propositions representing opinions about what people like or dislike.

My theoretical approach tries to go beyond the traditional approaches to the structures of opinions in social psychology, such as consistency and balance theories. What we find here is an account of the mutual relations between (sets of) propositions and the dynamics of their acceptance or rejection by individuals. Thus, adopting mutually inconsistent opinions may create 'cognitive dissonance', which people try to resolve by strategically adapting their opinions. Similarly, we may find further analysis of opinion propositions in evaluative 'molecules' whose development and change may mutually influence each other. If, for instance, I like John but disapprove of nuclear energy, than what happens when I also know that my friend John does approve of nuclear energy? Would this make John less likable and/or nuclear energy less detestable, or do I apply other useful strategies to combine the inconsistent 'valences' of my opinions?[10]

These traditional questions about the acquisition, organization and change of opinions and attitudes remain relevant today. However, they address somewhat different dimensions from those I am interested in. First, they do not distinguish between personal and social opinions, nor indeed between opinions and attitudes. Secondly, they focus on the individual 'management' of opinions in specific contexts and situations, rather than on general, complex and socially shared attitudes. Thirdly, they do not answer the question about the overall organization of such attitudes, and the relations of such an organization with the social dimensions of the groups that entertain them. However, such questions are still relevant as soon as we need to examine the ways concrete opinions are produced by individuals in specific contexts, possibly as a result of mutually 'inconsistent' attitudes. These strategies of opinion management and the representation of opinions in mental models (see Chapter 7) need to be dealt with separately.

From this discussion, we may provisionally conclude that evaluative social representations, such as attitudes, have their own 'logic', that is, their own, socially based schematic organization and categories, which are a function of the symbolic or material interests of the group. I shall later examine in more detail what these 'interests' are.

The argument I have been pursuing in this chapter suggests that if all social representations have their specific structural categories and organizational principles, this should also be so for the very foundation of such social representations, that is, for ideologies. This hypothesis will be explored in the next chapter.

5

Structures of Ideologies

Searching for a format

Given the assumption that social representations such as knowledge and attitudes of groups are organized by a non-trivial structure, it is plausible also that ideologies are not merely a list of basic beliefs. The acquisition, the changes and the uses of ideologies in social practices suggest that we should try to find schemata or other structural patterns that are typical for ideological systems. Since we have no a priori or theoretically obvious format for such structures, we have to build such schemata from scratch and find evidence that suggests how ideologies may be organized.[1]

One heuristic option is to assume that the structures of ideologies are similar to those of other social representations. For instance, if scripts organize our knowledge about stereotypical events, do ideologies also have such a script-like nature?[2] This assumption may be rejected without much hesitation: whatever we know about ideologies, they do not in any way reflect the stereotypical structures of events. First, ideologies are much more general and abstract, and do not merely apply to specific (types) of cultural events, such as shopping or going to the movies. Second, ideologies not only apply to events, but also to situations, processes, groups, group relations and other facts. Indeed, given the fundamental nature of ideologies and their assumed role in the management of social representations of groups and group relations, they should somehow reflect how groups and their members view a specific issue or domain of society. Third, ideologies do not merely control knowledge but also opinions about events, and such opinions do not represent event structures. Scripts, therefore, do not constitute a likely candidate for the kind of organization we would expect ideologies to have.

Since attitudes are clusters of socially shared, evaluative beliefs, it is therefore more plausible to examine whether ideologies have the structural features of attitudes. Such an assumption would probably also make it easier to link ideologies with attitudes, for instance when we assume that ideologies organize attitudes, or that they assign some form of coherence to the clusters of attitudes that are governed by the same ideology.

Especially since we as yet have no definite idea about what attitudes look like in general, our question about the similarity of attitude structures and ideological structures might well be moot. So, let's take a few examples of attitudes and see whether their possible structures suggest a more general format that also may be relevant for ideologies. For instance, there is good

evidence that at least some groups of people have attitudes about immigration, abortion and nuclear energy. Thus, a (prejudiced, nationalist or racist)
attitude about immigration may feature the following evaluative beliefs,
among many others:

1   Too many people come to our country.
2   Our country already has too many people.
3   Immigrants only come here to live off welfare.
4   Most immigrants are economic refugees.
5   Immigrants require scarce housing and jobs.
6   Immigrants face growing resentment in the inner cities.
7   The government must send back illegal immigrants.
8   Immigration has to be restricted to 'real' refugees only.

These evaluative beliefs, which are routinely expressed in both elite and
popular discourse about immigration, together define the (negative) attitude
about immigration.[3] However, as presented, it merely seems to have the
structure of a list of beliefs. If there is structure here, it is at most an
argumentative one: opinions 1 to 6 may be interpreted as arguments that
support the normative political conclusions 7 or 8.

At another level of abstraction, attitudes may be structured by the basic
categories of *problem* and *solution*, where the problem category is recursive.
Immigration is conceived of as a set of problems that result from immigration: overpopulation, lack of housing and work, growing resentment, and so
on. The solution category, what must be done to solve the problem, in this
case coincides with the main normative conclusion of the other opinions.[4]
This specific example does not imply, incidentally, that *all* ideologies and
attitudes have a problem/solution structure. However, many ideologies,
especially of dominated and dissident groups, organize around basic beliefs
about what is wrong, and about what should be done about it.

If we were to disregard the general nature of the beliefs (this attitude
exists in most European countries as well as in North America), it could
even be organized as a *story*, with an orientation such as 'Our country did
not have many problems and not many immigrants'; complication: 'Suddenly many immigrants came to the country, and caused a lot of social and
economic problems'; resolution: 'Restrict the number of immigrants.'[5]

Finally, some further structure may be assigned to this attitude by
applying a *group-schema* to it, in which immigrants are characterized by, for
example, the following categories and their (here highly simplified) belief
contents typical for a prejudiced attitude:[6]

- *Origin*: Third World;
- *Appearance*: mostly people of colour (unlike Us);
- *Socio-economic characteristics*: they are poor and want to become
  rich;
- *Cultural characteristics*: they speak other languages, are often Muslims,
  and have strange habits;

- *Personal characteristics*: they are illegals/criminals, cannot be trusted, don't want to work hard, etc.

We see that attitudes may be organized in different ways: in terms of an implicit argument, in terms of problem/solution categories or the related categories of stories, and finally in terms of a group schema.

Further analysis, however, suggests that these structures can only be very tentative. First, the most articulate structure, namely, the group schema, defines an attitude about immigrants rather than about immigration, although these attitudes are of course closely related. Second, narrative and argumentative structures characterize the *discourse* in which these beliefs may be used, but not the beliefs themselves.[7]

The problem/solution category seems more promising, since it is very abstract and general, and reflects the fact that attitudes are usually developed for social issues or problems, as seen by a specific group. For the groups who share them, the same is true for evaluative beliefs about nuclear energy or abortion. Yet, this structure is so general that it has little organizational significance, since it does not say more than that a social issue is a problem for the members of the group, and that these members also have a solution for it.

Do ideologies have a problem/solution structure? Many ideologies indeed seem to have something like that. Thus, whereas racism typically defines immigrants, foreigners, minorities or others as the reason for most social and economic problems, and withholding 'our' scarce resources (residence, citizenship, housing, employment, equal rights, etc.) as the solution, similar simple analyses may be made for anti-racism (problem: racism; solution: equality, diversity, etc.), feminism (problem: male chauvinism; solution: equal rights, etc.), and environmentalism (problem: pollution; solution: stop polluting). Other ideologies, such as liberalism, do not seem to have such a clear problem/solution structure, although originally it may have had such an organization as an opposition ideology against feudalism.

In sum, where attitudes seem to represent a problem or a social conflict, they may well have at least some structural features that we also find in ideologies. This is of course hardly surprising since ideologies are most likely to represent (real or imaginary) problems and conflicts of interests of – or between – social groups. As is obvious from the example of immigration, there is therefore also a strong polarization between Us and Them, as representatives of the groups involved in such a conflict. Similar observations hold for the attitudes about nuclear energy and abortion.

Very tentatively, these examples provide us some suggestions for at least some ideas about the format of ideologies: problem/solution, conflict and group polarization. Let us analyse these potential categories of ideological structure in more detail.

Group conflict

Although ideologies may have some features that we also encounter in more specific attitudes, we need to explore a bit further to come up with a format that is general enough to fit all ideologies, and specific enough to be non-trivial and functionally useful in the cognitive management of ideologies as well as in their acquisition and applications.

Instead of starting with the organization of social representations in general, we may also inquire whether the structure of ideologies is a function of their role in society. We have already seen that often social conflicts between groups with different interests are involved. We also know from most traditional approaches that ideologies are typically used as foundations for domination and resistance; that is, they represent social struggle. Moreover, ideologies are also intuitively functioning as self-serving principles involved in the explanation of the world in general (as in religious ideologies) and of the social and economic worlds in particular (such as conservatism or capitalism). Finally, ideologies have a normative dimension, and summarize what group members should do or not do: for example resist oppression, stop pollution, or prevent abortion.

If we assume that many if not most ideologies are a socio-cognitive representation of the basic evaluative and self-serving beliefs of group members about social struggle and group conflicts, it may be most fruitful to study this fundamental feature in more detail in order to find out the most effective format that might organize such beliefs. Crucial for such a representation is how group members see themselves and how they see Others.

Thus, typical for a racist ideology is that we are representing Us as superior, and Them as inferior, and that as a consequence we (should) have preferential access to society's scarce resources (for an empirical case study of such a racist ideology, see Chapter 28). This is even the case when racist groups claim Us and Them to be equal but different, and hence advocate separation of the 'races', because also in that case no equal access to scarce social resources is usually permitted. A similar basic representational format may be postulated for male chauvinists and their opinions about gender relations. Feminist ideologies are not merely the mirror-image of sexist ideologies, but represent Them (men) as oppressing Us, and themselves as engaged in resistance against gender inequality. Religious ideologies represent Us as (good) believers and Them as (bad) non-believers (infidels, heathens, etc.). And finally, environmental ideologies represent Them as polluters, and Us as those who resist pollution and defend nature and the rights of animals, for instance. More generally, conservatives see themselves as defending traditional social relationships and moral values against Them (progressives, etc.) who want to change these in favour of social equality.

Recall that these highly simplified ideological representations are not, as such, true or false, although each group will of course tend to believe its own ideological beliefs to be true or justified. Thus, we may agree that prejudices based on racist or sexist ideologies are wrong or otherwise misguided, and hence defined in negative terms, but this evaluation of course only holds on the basis of an anti-sexist or anti-racist ideology.

The very general polarization schema defined by the opposition between Us and Them suggests that groups and group conflicts are involved, and that groups build an ideological image of themselves and others, in such a way that (generally) We are represented positively, and They come out negatively. Positive self-presentation and negative other-presentation seems to be a fundamental property of ideologies. Associated with such polarized representations about Us and Them, are representations of social arrangements, that is, the kinds of things we find better (equality, a clean environment) or those which we believe others stand for (inequality, a polluted environment, a free market). At this very abstract level these social arrangements are specifications of more general *values*.

Thus, if 'freedom' is a general, socio-cultural value, then 'freedom of the market' is one of the things a capitalist ideology will represent as something We stand for; feminists will translate this general value in terms of the freedom of women (freedom from oppression and inequality, freedom of choice, and so on); and environmentalists will interpret the value as freedom from pollution, and so on. We shall focus on the nature of values later, but they obviously play a fundamental role in ideologies. This is not surprising when ideologies are taken to be the basis of group beliefs.

In sum, ideologies are representations of who we are, what we stand for, what our values are, and what our relationships are with other groups, in particular our enemies or opponents, that is, those who oppose what we stand for, threaten our interests and prevent us from equal access to social resources and human rights (residence, citizenship, employment, housing, status and respect, and so on). In other words, an ideology is a self-serving schema for the representation of Us and Them as social groups. This means that ideologies probably have the format of a group schema, or at least the format of a group schema that reflects Our fundamental social, economic, political or cultural interests.

Such an assumption is plausible when we think of the various social functions of ideologies, to which we shall return in more detail later. Thus, ideologies may be used to legitimate or obscure power abuse, or conversely they may be used to resist or denounce domination and inequality. Ideologies thus are needed to organize our social practices in such a way that they serve our best interests, and prevent others from hurting such interests.

These various more or less intuitive conceptions of the nature and functions of ideology, and the assumption that ideologies may be represented as group schemata, suggest the following categories for a tentative format of the structure of ideologies:

- *Membership*: Who are we? Where are we from? What do we look like? Who belongs to us? Who can become a member of our group?
- *Activities*: What do we do? What is expected of us? Why are we here?
- *Goals*: Why do we do this? What do we want to realize?

- *Values/norms*: What are our main values? How do we evaluate ourselves and others? What should (not) be done?
- *Position and group-relations*: What is our social position? Who are our enemies, our opponents? Who are like us, and who are different?
- *Resources*: What are the essential social resources that our group has or needs to have?

These categories and the basic questions they stand for seem to be the fundamental *co-ordinates of social groups*, and the conditions of their existence and reproduction. Together they define both the *identity* as well as the *interests* of the group. Thus, if ideologies are primarily representations of the basic properties of groups, then this schema should be a serious candidate for the organization of ideological beliefs.

This schema seems fairly generally applicable to all ideological groups, whether based on more or less inherent characteristics (gender, ethnicity, age, etc.), on what we do (as for professional ideologies), our goals (as for ideologies of action groups), norms and values (as for conservatives versus progressives; religious and non-religious people), our relations with others (superiors versus subordinates), and the typical resources we do or do not have (rich versus poor; employed versus unemployed; homeless versus those who have a home). That is, each category may be needed to define all groups, but groups may also be identified specifically by one particular category.

This may also explain why there are differences between membership, activity, goal, etc. ideologies. Thus, feminism is typically a goal ideology, that is, defined by the hierarchically most important belief of the ideology, namely, to arrive at full equality for women and men. Similarly, the ideology of black nationalism is a membership ideology when it is limited to questions of appearance and 'racial pride' (as old slogans about 'black is beautiful' and 'négritude' imply), and a position or resistance ideology when it focuses on self-determination and black empowerment. Capitalism on the other hand would rather be a resource ideology, aiming to ensure freedom of enterprise and freedom of the market. In other words, the categorial structure of ideologies also allows a *typology* of ideologies, as well as the possibility of changing hierarchies in the representation of ideological beliefs.

Each category of this ideological format functions as the organizing pattern of a number of basic evaluative beliefs. Note though that these beliefs are by definition ideological. Thus, journalists in their professional (activity) ideology, may represent themselves essentially as gathering and bringing the news, for instance. They do this, they would say, in order to inform the public and more generally to serve as a watchdog of society. Obviously, these are ideological goals, because we know that many journalists hardly do this. That is, such a goal is at most a benchmark or a property of an ideal type: how journalists would like to be. The same is true for their (professional) values, such as truth, reliability, fairness, and so on. The specific resource of journalists, access to which must be guaranteed as a condition for the existence or the activities of the group, would be information or the freedom of the press (as it is freedom of the market for managers, and freedom of research for scholars, and freedom from discrimination for feminists and anti-racists).

It should be emphasized that this abstract categorial schema is merely a theoretical construct that may be used to organize and explain the basic evaluative beliefs of group members. This schema, as such, does not tell us yet how ideologies are acquired, used or changed, how they manifest themselves in social practices, and how they reproduce themselves in society. It is also a social representation. This means that it characterizes groups, at a macro-level. Individuals members on some dimension may not identify with the group, and hence not share the ideology of the group. Socially this usually implies that they are considered as dissidents, traitors, deviants, or otherwise as group members who no longer 'belong' to the group, and may hence be excluded, marginalized or otherwise punished. I shall return to these and other social conditions and consequences of ideological group memberships later.

Note that, at the moment, the schema primarily serves as an organizing framework for ideological beliefs. That is, its function here is cognitive. Yet, as suggested, each of its categories is rooted also in social structure, that is in group membership criteria, social activities and goals, group relationships, social values and social resources. This will later allow us to define ideologies precisely as the socio-cognitive interface between the (mental) social representations shared by the group, and the social identity, activities, organization, and so on, of the group and its members.

Later I also need to analyse how this abstract schema, designed as an organizational pattern for ideological beliefs, can be empirically founded. That is, we should see it not just as a theoretical construct, but as a schema that actually does play a role in the acquisition, changes and uses of ideologies. One of the ways to assess the empirical nature of the schema is to make a systematic study of social practices, and especially of discourses that express ideological beliefs. If these expressed beliefs and their inferences appear to be organized according to the ideological schema, then we have some evidence that the schema is indeed a socio-cognitive device used by social groups and their members to organize their basic beliefs.

There is an interesting implication of choosing a group schema as a format for the structure of ideologies, namely, the obvious relation it has with *group identity*. If ideologies monitor the way people *as group members* interpret and act in their social world, they also function as the basis of their social identity. Structurally this would suggest that the first category (membership) is not the only one that defines identity, although it seems to organize beliefs about what we 'essentially' are (white, black, men, women, poor or rich). However, it is obvious that the whole schema, all categories together, defines group identity: what people do, their goals, their values, their relations to other groups, and their resources for survival or social

Cognition

existence also are part of their identity. The first category in that case defines only a fragment of group membership: a number of more or less inherent or relatively permanent properties (such as origin, appearance, gender, religion, language or other cultural specifics) that define primary group membership criteria, as well as conditions of inclusion and exclusion (for details about social identity, see Chapter 12).

Also, it should be stressed from the outset, as will be developed in more detail later, that social actors are obviously members of many social groups, and that therefore they have *multiple, sometimes conflicting identities* and hence share a mixture of ideologies. Discourses and social practices in concrete contexts will show such complex combinations, conflicts and sometimes inconsistencies. The same is true, cognitively, for people's attitudes, models and opinions, which may be monitored by different ideologies, of which the unique combination may be personal or limited to sub-groups (such as the sub-group of US middle-class black women journalists). Obviously, empirical research needs to take such complex interactions into account in order to be able to describe ideological social practices and discourse (for an illustration of how several ideologies interact, see Chapter 28).[8]

Contents

The same is true for the contents of the respective categories of the schema. What we now have is an abstract framework. Ideologies, however, are content-specific, and further empirical work is necessary to spell out the actual group beliefs that are organized by these categories. This will also allow us to link the ideologies with the more specific attitudes that are in turn controlled by these ideologies. I shall therefore be brief about the contents of ideologies.

At an elementary level of analysis, ideologies consist of clusters of basic social beliefs organized by the schematic categories proposed above. Although these beliefs may in principle be about anything that relates to the social experiences and practices of social groups and their members, they will mostly be about conflicts of interests between groups, typically so in relations of competition, domination and resistance. That is, ideologies usually organize attitudes which in turn control those social practices of the group and its members that are somehow *relevant* to the interests or identity of groups, and are related to membership criteria (inclusion and exclusion), activities, goals, values, relations to other groups, and resources. Since these beliefs are often evaluative, they presuppose socio-cultural values, such as truth, co-operation, equality, freedom and autonomy, among many others (see Chapter 6). Thus managers may hold the ideological belief that they want to be free from state intervention, and feminists that they want to have equal rights as men, among many other ideological beliefs.

In sum, the contents of group ideologies pertain to what, for each group, is the preferred social and moral order, whether or not such an order is seen as just or unjust. Yet, although it may seem as if some groups may develop ideologies which 'cynically' acknowledge that they are not 'just' for other groups, the fundamental social role of positive self-images for most groups will usually entail that groups develop an ideology which they see as ethically good or defensible. Thus, whereas (at least some) proponents of a neo-liberal ideology may recognize that 'liberalization' and other market policies may make the rich richer and the poor poorer, it is likely that the underlying ideology maintains that freedom of the market will eventually benefit all. In that respect, we may generally assume that group ideologies cannot be 'cynical', but always imply positive self-presentation. One possible exception that needs to be further explored may be ideologies of some dominated groups, a 'false consciousness' that may result from manipulative hegemony, in which the own group is represented as negative in relation to dominant groups, as would be the case for forms of interiorized racism.

Ideologies develop as a functional consequence of the conflicts of interest that emerge from goals, preferences or rights that are seen as mutually incompatible. Groups may want to claim, defend, legitimate, explain, or otherwise manage such interests against other groups in society, while at the same time rallying their own members behind such claims so as to make sure that attitudes of individual members, and social practices based on them, co-ordinate and facilitate the realization of ideological goals. In the remaining chapters, I shall further examine such ideological 'contents', and especially their social conditions, consequences and functions in the management of social interpretations, practices and discourse.

6

Values

Introduction

Values play a central role in the construction of ideologies. Together with ideologies they are the benchmark of social and cultural evaluation. Like knowledge and attitudes, they are located in the memory domain of social beliefs. That is, we do not take values as social or sociological abstractions, but as shared mental objects of social cognition.

Unlike group beliefs, values have a broader, cultural base. Together with culturally shared knowledge, they are part of the cultural common ground. Whatever the ideological differences between groups, few people in the same culture have very different value systems – truth, equality, happiness, and so on, seem to be generally, if not universally shared as criteria of action and at least as ideal goals to strive for. Of course, there are cultural differences. Some values may not even exist in another culture, or may have different implications in another culture. Also, the hierarchy of the importance or relevance of values may be different from culture to culture. Whereas in one culture honesty may be fundamental, another culture may emphasize modesty. For these reasons, cultural clashes and conflicts of values, also in communication, are notorious, as is especially clear in variations in politeness, deference or directness of text and talk, among many other differences.[1]

Values are shared and known, and applied by social members in a large variety of practices and contexts. Obviously, they form the basis of all processes of evaluation, and hence for opinions, attitudes and ideologies. Thus, if ideologies are the basis of group beliefs, and if values are in turn broader and more fundamental, values must be the basis of the evaluative systems of a culture as a whole. Indeed, values are the pillars of the moral order of societies.

This fundamental socio-cultural status of values also precludes their reduction to individuals. These may share, adopt or reject the values of their group, but we would not say that personal goals or ideals are values.

Value systems

Despite the frequent use of the notion of value in the social sciences and politics, they are fairly elusive. Usually, and unlike beliefs, they are described in isolated terms, such as truth, intelligence or beauty, or in terms of concepts for which English does not have a single word, such as 'enjoying a good life'. If they are basic building blocks of the evaluations that are involved in social opinions, as attributes that are predicated of any socially relevant object (people, events, actions, situations, etc.), then they might well be atomic concepts. Indeed, truth or beauty hardly seem decomposable in more elementary concepts, unless these would be good and bad, so that 'beauty' would be 'good appearance', for instance, whereas honesty would be one type of 'good character'.

This attempt at analysis also suggests that values seem to be organized by the fundamental dimensions of everyday life experiences and observation as well as for social action and organization. Thus, we have attitudes that describe positive properties of the mind (intelligence, smartness, erudition and wisdom), whereas others characterize what we value most about bodies: health, beauty, and so on. Similarly we have a series of values for judgements about personal 'character', such as honesty, integrity, modesty, kindness, openness, patience and so on.

The same is true for actions, which also need to be evaluated routinely, and hence require a complex set of values, such as resolution, decisiveness, speed or efficiency. Interaction requires evaluation by means of a series of social values, such as politeness, tolerance, co-operation, helpfulness or altruism, among many others. As elsewhere, the opposed concepts by definition denote negative evaluations of people, that is, what people generally would not want to be or do, or be accused of: impoliteness, intolerance and egocentrism. Many of the interaction values mentioned here of course also apply to discourse, as is obviously true for politeness and co-operation.

What is true for action and interaction, also applies to more complex social structures, social relations, organizations and whole societies. This means that democracy, freedom, equality, independence or autonomy are such fundamental societal values. Given the nature of ideologies as basic systems of group beliefs, we may assume that these typical societal values play a special role in them, as is indeed the case – virtually all major social and political ideologies will emphasize one or more of these societal values.

In sum, if we draw an intuitive picture of the personal and social world, each fundamental dimension (mind, body, character, action, interaction, society) of observation and evaluation has its own special values. Some of these values may be very general and apply across these dimensions, as is true for good and bad, ugly and beautiful.

Finally, the interpersonal and social scope of cultural values probably does not exhaust the system – we also have values to qualify nature or animals, either in very general terms of beauty, but, as is obvious in environmental ideologies, also in terms of cleanliness, being unspoiled, and so on. The same is true for all objects of our senses, so that for our taste alone we have a long series of values: sweetness, delicateness or smoothness, obviously also culturally variable.

These examples also show that many values are *historical*: They were once 'invented' as being positive properties of mind, action or society 'we' would have to strive for. This 'terminal' aspect of ideologies also suggests that they are motivational and goal-oriented; that is, they qualify 'ideal' end-states or results of human endeavours.

Values and ideologies

Theoretically, then, values monitor the evaluative dimensions of ideologies and attitudes. That is, basic social opinions are constituted from values when applied to specific domains and issues in society. Thus, if journalists value truth and reliability of reporting, then this is an ideological specification of the cultural value of truth and reliability. The same is true for the selection of the value of equality by feminists, minority groups or anti-racists in the construction of their egalitarian ideologies.

Obviously the selection and construction process by which values are incorporated in ideologies is again self-serving. It should fit the various interests of the group, such as their membership, activities, goals, relations to other groups and resources. In other words, general cultural values may be 'appropriated' by a group, as is typically the case with freedom in neo-liberal and conservative ideologies. This is also why the values category itself was added to the ideology schema proposed in the previous chapter: The values selected as primordial for each group constitute the selected benchmark for their identity and self-evaluation, the evaluation of their activities and goals, and especially their evaluations of other groups, underlying goals and judgements of interaction.

Also negatively, values may be used for self-enhancement, as when white racists feel superior to non-whites. This superiority feeling is a summary of a biased comparison process in which We are seen as more intelligent, more efficient, harder working or more democratic than They are. That is, for all values that are especially relevant to us, we self-evaluate Us as better. At most we may grant them superiority on values that are less relevant for us, such as musicality, being good in sports or hospitality.

As we have seen for the example of freedom before, different or even opposed social groups may select the same value, but invest it with very different ideological content. Managers ideologically 'incorporate' (pun intended) the value of freedom as 'freedom of the market' or 'freedom from state intervention', as a self-serving ideological goal that guarantees their power and interests. Journalists similarly want to secure their power, interests and resources by emphasizing the freedom of the press, or the freedom of information, obviously primarily for themselves. On the other hand, liberation movements, feminism, and other dominated groups focus on freedom as a guarantee for equality, independence, autonomy and access to scarce social resources, and generally as, 'freedom from oppression'.

We see that the positive values that define the moral order of a society or culture are used by all groups not only as a criterion of evaluation, but also as a basis for the legitimation of their own interests or goals. For dominant groups, such ideological value-integration obviously will be used to legitimate their domination, and for dominated group to legitimate their opposition, dissidence or resistance (see Chapter 26). That is, the fundamental legitimacy of any ideological group presupposes that it remains part of the cultural moral order. Few racists openly defend inequality (see, however, Chapter 28), but will self-present themselves as emphasizing the relevance of nationalism and their own freedom (from being 'mixed' with others). When seen by many others as flouting the principle of equality, thus, blatant racists are therefore usually marginalized. Hence the prominent role of denials of racism: whatever one may have against minorities, it will never be self-defined as racism. Thus, once a fundamental value (such as equality or democracy) is generally accepted in a society, such values can no longer be simply 'rejected' by groups without losing their credibility, respect or societal legitimacy.

The differential ideological incorporation of values by different groups also suggests that values, as cognitive representations, are not limited to non-ambiguous concepts. 'Freedom' thus means something rather different for a corporate manager than it does for a union representative. The same is true for most groups and most values, as complex 'big' values such as 'democracy' show. Theoretically, it would therefore probably be more adequate to speak of value-complexes. Thus the freedom-complex would feature, for example, the following components of the desirable goal described with the concept of 'freedom': (1) we can do what we want to do; (2) nobody is limiting our actions, etc.

Values are not merely integrated into ideologies, but govern social beliefs more generally. Also group attitudes of specific social domains may use values as benchmarks for evaluation, justification and legitimation. For instance, one of the evaluative arguments used in the rejection of immigration is that the country is 'full'. For rather fundamental social, cultural (and probably biological) reasons, 'overpopulation' (and, implicitly, ethnic mixing) are here used as negative values in the application of xenophobic ideologies to the domain of immigration.

7

Mental Models

From the social to the personal

One fundamental lack of all traditional and contemporary approaches to the theory of ideology is that they do not account for the relation between the social and the personal in the accomplishment of social practices. We have seen that ideologies, like knowledge, attitudes and values are *social* representations, shared by the members of groups. At the same time, each serious theory of ideology needs to describe and explain how such social representations are constructed and used by individual group members in and by their social practices in general, and their discourse in particular.

We also know from both research and experience that these social practices of individuals are not always 'in line' with group ideologies. Apart from the variable constraints of context, there are personal idiosyncrasies, different personal histories and different personal experiences, among many other factors that may affect the variable 'expression' of ideologies in action by members as individuals. An empirical theory of ideology that would systematically describe and explain ideological practices also needs to account for such differences, variation, dissidence and contradictions. Though ideologies are shared with others, people make individual use of them, as they do with their knowledge of the language or the attitudes of their group or culture. Since also these personal and contextual uses and variation have general properties, they need to be part of a theory of ideology. In other words, such a theory must describe and explain also how ideologies are actually used or applied.

Such a theory at the same time explains the opposite process, namely, how ideologies are gradually acquired, developed and changed in and by situated social practices, and especially by discourse. Since social beliefs are not innate, we must assume that they are gradually acquired by social perception, interaction, and especially in communicative events. However, these specific events vary individually and contextually, so we have the problem of how a 'unified' group ideology may develop from such highly variable experiences and practices. Apparently, a process of normalization and unification is at work, that enables general, abstract beliefs to be shared by many or most members of groups, again much in the same way as natural languages are learned by language users interacting with each other in many different situations.

In the discussion of social representations in general, I have already suggested that besides the social and abstract account of such representations, we need to realize that although they are shared at the group level, this does not mean that all group members have identical 'copies' of the representations. Rather, we must assume that because of obvious individual differences of 'ideological socialization' in the group, each member has her or his own personal 'version' of the ideology. Obviously, this personal version must be close enough to the abstract group ideology for members to be able to function appropriately as competent group members. Again, comparison with the social and shared nature of grammars and individual knowledge of a language is instructive here.

It should be stressed that personal 'versions' of ideologies are still to be seen as social representations. In the memory theory used here this means that such personal versions of ideologies are part of social memory, and not of personal (episodic) memory. Despite the idiosyncratic nature of some of the features of this personal version of ideologies (mostly they will be less complete than the group-level ideology), their overall form is general and abstract, and largely socially shared. In that respect they should be clearly distinguished from the *individual uses* of ideologies in specific *contexts* as a basis for individual social practices and discourse. It is this last aspect of the relation between ideology and its manifestation in social practices that is the topic of this chapter.

Mental models

Theoretically, therefore, what we need is an *interface* between socially shared representations and personal practices, that is, a theoretical device that enables us to connect social (semantic) memory with personal (episodic) memory and their respective representations. Since the early 1980s, cognitive psychology has with considerable theoretical and empirical success developed such a theoretical construct, namely, that of a *mental model*.[1]

Mental models are representations in personal memory of events or, as the term 'episodic memory' suggests, of episodes. Thus, when witnessing, participating in or hearing/reading about a car accident, people construct a model of such an event. Obviously, this model is subjective: it represents the personal experience and interpretation of the event by the participant. Thus, what people know personally about such an event, as well as their perspective on and opinion about the event, is represented in their subjective, individual models of the event. For discourse this means that the model is being constructed for the event the discourse is *about*.

In a theory of discourse production and comprehension, to which I shall turn later, the notion of a model is especially attractive, since it accounts for the (personal, subjective) *interpretation* of the discourse by language users. Indeed, we may now simply say that to understand a discourse ultimately (and via a number of complex processes) consists in the construction of a model. Conversely, in discourse production, the model is precisely the starting point for text and talk: it is the personal knowledge, experience or opinion about an event that is being used as 'input' to the discourse production processes. That is, models also account for the traditional notion of intention and plan. This means that because they are more or less independent with respect to discourse meanings, models also explain personal variation and biases of discourse or their interpretation. As we know intuitively, we may construct an interpretation of the text that may be partly at odds with the meaning of the text, or indeed with that of the intentions of the speaker or writer.

As suggested, models are essentially personal and subjective. They embody personal interpretations and experiences of actions, events and discourse about such episodes, and this is true for all social practices. This personal dimension may be the result of earlier experiences (old models that are being activated or updated) that constitute the personal history of each person, as well as other, more general or abstract personal representations (personality, personal opinions, and so on).

People are engaged in the ongoing interpretation of the episodes of their everyday lives from the moment they wake up until they fall asleep (or lose consciousness). Such interpretations should be seen as contextually relevant constructions of such episodes in mental models stored in episodic memory. These models also account for the familiar notion of an *experience*. That is, it is not the 'real' episodes themselves that play a role in our lives, but rather their personal interpretation or construction as models, that is the way episodes are experienced. We may therefore call this particular class of models *experience models*. It comes as no surprise that such experience models are built around the central category of self, which gives the orientation and the perspective to the model, and which defines the essentially subjective nature of experience models. This means that also representations of our future actions, that is, *plans*, are a type of experience models, although these will generally be less specific than the ways we represent actually 'lived' experiences.

Besides the subjectivity of everyday understanding of our environment, experience models finally also account for the notion of consciousness. Being conscious means (among other things) that we are aware of ourselves as well as our environment, and are actively constructing interpretations of ourselves and that environment.[2]

People do not only build models of episodes in which they are engaged themselves, but also models of those episodes they witness and especially those they hear and read *about*. In order to be able to distinguish them from episodic models about personal experiences, I shall here call them *description models*, in order to emphasize that we know the episodes through (discursive) description. Since we may also talk about our personal experiences, and typically do so in personal stories, the sets of experience and description models obviously overlap. Other episodes we *only* know about vicariously, that is through discourse, typically so for many of the episodes reported in the mass media. As suggested above, description models (earlier called 'situation models'), are needed as a basis for text production and comprehension. It is plausible, however, that description models are shaped after our experience models, because we tend to understand unfamiliar episodes in light of those we know personally.

As is the case for all models, also models of events talked or written about feature specifications of more general knowledge about such events. Thus, a model of an event during the civil war in Bosnia is not just built from the unique, specific and new information we get from the media, but also from an 'application' of general knowledge about civil wars, armies, killing, ethnic relations and Yugoslavia. It is in this way that social representations are 'concretized' in models, and social memory related to episodic memory and subjective representations. As we shall see later, such episodic models that interpret discourse, will be fundamental in relating ideologies to discourse structures.

To avoid terminological confusion, I shall henceforth use the term *episodic model* (or *mental model* or simply *model*) to denote any kind of model in episodic memory, that is, a subjective representation of an episode. As explained above, I use the term *experience model* (or simply 'experience') for those episodic models that represent personal participation in or observation of episodes in our own lives. More generally the term *event model* will be used to denote any kind of model that interprets events or situations (personal or otherwise) referred to by discourse. I also make this distinction here because the current psychological literature rather confusingly deals with different kinds of models, without explicitly distinguishing them, and because the various notions of model will be needed below in showing how ideology monitors social practices. Note finally that all models may represent both small actions and events (like eating an apple), compound or sequences of events (like meetings) as well as large and complex episodes such as vacations or civil wars. In other words, episodic memory consists of sets and systems of hierarchically organized models. Part of that system, that of our experience models, defines our autobiographical 'past'.

Event schemata

Although no general theoretical proposal has as yet been made about the structure of these models, we may assume that these structures must be able to manage effectively the interpretation of events, a process that people are engaged in many hundreds of times a day. This suggests that also here a handy schema might be at work, or a number of categories and rules or strategies to construct such patterns for each situation.

Such a schema is hardly obscure, and has been proposed in different guises, for instance in the theory of social episodes,[3] as well as in the functional semantics of propositions. Since people not only represent events in models, but also routinely talk about them, for example, in everyday stories, it is not surprising that the categories of these models somehow also appear in grammatical and discursive structures: setting (location, time), circumstances, participants (and their various action roles: agent, patient, experiencer, object, etc.), and finally an action or event.[4] Indeed, we may argue conversely, that once we have introduced the notion of model and its typical event (or action and situation) schemata, these schematic structures may be seen as the cognitive basis and explanation of discourse structures. In other words: the structures that organize the way events are understood will also influence the ways such events are talked about.

Context models

There is one particular type of event that has a crucial influence on discourse and its structures, namely, the communicative event or situation in which the current discourse is being produced and/or received. The mental models of such communicative events will be called *context models*. Since context models represent part of our personal experiences, namely, the one in which we are engaged when communicating, context models are merely a specific type of experience models. That is, also context models are personal, subjective and possibly biased, and hence represent the personally variable interpretations and opinions of communicative events. We routinely tell stories about them by later activating such context models.

Context models also have the same structure as experience models, namely, that of a setting (time, location), circumstances, participants and their various roles, and finally a communicative action (see Chapter 22 for details). Crucial in context models is the participant category of self as a speaker/writer or hearer/reader. It is this self-category that defines the subjectivity of discourse, monitors perspective and point of view, and organizes many other subjective features of text and talk.[5]

Context models are also special because they act in turn as the interface between event models and discourse. They tell the speech participants who they are, as what they participate in this event, and a lot of other relevant information and opinions about the present social situation of talk or text. The pragmatic constraints that influence discourse meaning and form are represented in this context model, such as the conditions for speech acts (usually knowledge about what I and my interlocutor know, want or do), conditions of politeness (such as social status or power), institutional circumstances, group membership, mutual knowledge, opinions about each other, as well as the goals and intentions of the communicative event, and so on.

That is, instead of merely abstractly spelling out these many 'pragmatic' constraints of contexts, or vaguely referring to the role of context, we now have a rather concrete proposal for a more explicit cognitive representation of such contexts. At the same time, context models explain how our personal knowledge about people, actions, events or situations, as represented in event models, will be expressed in discourse as a function of the information in this context model. That is, context models also operate as the crucial, but hitherto theoretically elusive, control system in discourse processing.

Whereas our knowledge about an event, as represented in experience or event models, may be relatively stable across contexts, context models typically represent the changing, ongoing nature of text production/ comprehension and especially of face-to-face talk. Participants continually update and change their interpretation of the current situation and represent this in their context models, which in turn will send their information to the system of (linguistic) formulation or interpretation. Conversely, during the interpretation of discourse, our context models (including for instance our assumptions about the credibility of the writer or speaker) may of course affect the way we represent the events talked or written about, that is, our event models. In that respect, event models are not only a function of more general knowledge of the world, but also a function of the mental representation of the context in which they were constructed – the same story in a tabloid may be interpreted in a different way (be assigned a different event model) than when it is published in a serious broadsheet newspaper.

Thus, whereas event models may be described as the basis for the *semantics* of discourse, context models are the basis for their *pragmatics*, that is, their speech acts, politeness moves, variable lexical or syntactic style, rhetorical figures of persuasion, and any other feature of discourse that signals or 'indexes' part of the context, such as choice of dialect or sociolect, pronunciation, formality or informality, familiarity and intimacy, both in intonation as well as in lexical selection, and so on. In sum, all properties of discourse that are contextually variable are by definition monitored by these 'pragmatic' context models. (For simplicity, I use the notion of 'pragmatic' here in the broad sense it has in much contemporary work in this area, although I personally favour a stricter use of the term, namely, as applying only to the speech act or illocutionary dimensions of discourse; see Chapter 21 for details.)

Linking the social and the personal

We have now construed one side of the interface that links ideologies to concrete social practices and discourse, namely, the ways individual social members represent events, actions or situations in models, and how they manifest, enact or accomplish these in actual acts and discourse. Details of the (psycholinguistic) processes involved in the 'formulation' of model information in words, phrases, sentences and texts, or conversely in the interpretation of these verbal structures in terms of underlying models, will be ignored here. They are beyond the scope of this book, but I shall later have to say some more about them when I discuss the ways ideologies are expressed in discourse.

The next step in the theory is to link individual models with social representations, because this is the important barrier we need to cross, namely, how to get from the personal or individual to the shared and social, and vice versa. The enormous advantage of a cognitive component in a theory of ideology (and the same is true for a theory of discourse and social interaction) is that this missing link can be defined (also) in cognitive terms.

In this case, this relationship is established by the fact that models obviously not only consist of purely personal and individual beliefs, but also of situated instances of social beliefs. Thus, when being involved in a car accident we not only know about our personal experiences, or about the colour or the make of our car, and the unique circumstances of this accident, but in order to construct the model, we also need socially shared knowledge about cars, accidents, roads, and so forth, in general. In other words, relevant elements of social representations, such as scripts, will be activated and instantiated into knowledge that fits the present model. For instance, general knowledge that cars usually have four wheels may become relevant to construct that *this* car also has four wheels, and so on. Such general knowledge may of course be adapted to the unique circumstances represented in a model (e.g. to represent cars with three wheels). The same is true for the construction of context models: we need general knowledge about people, speakers, communicative events, discourse genres, politeness or social relations in order to be able to construct an adequate model of the present communicative event.

Note that this relationship of instantiation and contextual 'application' and adaptation between social representations and models also may be defined in the other direction, and thus explain the very acquisition and change of knowledge, attitudes and ideologies. That is, once constructed for specific events, these models may be abstracted from and generalized, and thus be transformed into scripts or other structures of socially shared representations. Formally, this process consists in the change from constants into variables in the propositions that represent the beliefs in the models and the social representations.

More empirically, this process may be described as follows: having repeatedly observed or read or heard about specific events, social members are able to make generalized inferences, and thus construct beliefs that are relevant for many different situations, so that the beliefs become useful for their social status as socially shared knowledge.[6]

Such inference processes need not even be accomplished only mentally: discourse itself is capable of making such generalized, abstract statements. Social members thus exhibit and at the same time practice their ability to switch from unique, personal representations of event *tokens*, to the socially shared, general representations of event *types*. This also means that social learning need not be limited to the 'empirical' generalization and abstraction from experiences, that is, from models.[7] People may also acquire social representations directly, by interpreting generic or abstract sentences and discourses, as is typically the case in pedagogical or explanatory text and talk. Also, social members already *have* vast prior knowledge, and may use this directly by making inferences that may produce new knowledge from existing social knowledge.

Evaluative beliefs

Models not only feature unique personal knowledge about events, but also opinions about them. When observing, participating in, or reading about a car accident, people may at the same time construct evaluative beliefs about the (other) driver or about the ('terrible') accident as a whole. These opinions will become a natural part of the model, as also when we read about 'ethnic cleansing' in Bosnia, or about our interlocutor in a conversation. Hence, both event models of discourse, and context models, feature personal opinions about the people, objects or events represented in the model.

As is true for personal and social knowledge, also these opinions need not merely be personal. Also evaluative beliefs may instantiate socially shared beliefs, that is attitudes, for instance about car accidents, traffic or civil wars. The same processes of activation, instantiation and adaptation are at work here, and again in both directions – Personal opinions may be seen to be shared by others, and thus are generalized as social beliefs and attitudes. The acquisition and change of social representations may similarly be based on the generalization and abstraction of opinions in personal models.[8]

Such acquisition need not only be 'empirical', that is, based on personal experiences, but may also be directly inferred from generalized opinions in opinion discourse, for instance in editorials in the newspaper, or group-based evaluations of other group members in conversations. The most dramatic example of the latter process is the familiar acquisition of prejudices. These may be based on a single or a few personal experiences that are 'over-generalized' as general beliefs, or they may directly be derived from prejudiced propositions in discriminatory text and talk.

Individuals are members of various social groups. If each such group has an ideology, individuals share in several ideologies at the same time. When constructing their models, this also means that general beliefs of more than one ideology may be 'applied' in the model. If these ideologies are mutually inconsistent, this may give rise to models that seem to be inconsistent. Thus, a person may interpret or write a news story, observe or participate in a social event as a woman, as black, as a journalist, as an American, as a Christian, as young and as a Democrat, among other identities. The resulting model may show a unique and seemingly chaotic combination of beliefs derived from the ideologies with which that person identifies. This is true both for the models of the events written about, as well as for the context model that represents the unique communicative event. In many situations, thus, people will select or prefer one or more of their present social 'identities' to be dominant in the present context model. Thus, the black woman journalist will often, because of professional constraints and expectations, bring to bear, in the current context model of her news writing, professional attitudes and ideologies rather than her identity as a black woman. The detailed structure of context models thus provides an explanation for the ways ideologies indirectly 'map' onto communicative events.

The same will be true for the discourse based on such a model, which in addition may be further constrained and modified by the context model: The black female journalist may well have a personal opinion about news events, but her editor or readers may not approve of her actually mentioning those. This means that in the later chapters, I need to investigate a large number of conditions, processes, strategies and contexts that are relevant in the complex expression and accomplishment of ideologies in interaction, text and talk.

Finally, ideologies and the attitudes based on them not only influence the formation of contextually variable personal opinions in models, but may also operate in *selective activation* of 'old' models (previous experiences), for instance in storytelling, news reporting or recall of news. One obvious way in which this happens is that people tend to activate (recall) those models whose opinions are consistent with those of the group attitudes they share. Propositions in such attitudes may thus operate as a powerful search cue. This is well known from empirical work on racism, in which many white people typically recall negative stories about immigrants, stories that are consistent with ethnic prejudices. These stories may function as 'evidence' in prejudiced arguments: 'You read about that in the paper every day.' Conversely, they may 'forget' or otherwise suppress stories that confirm negative propositions about their own group. More generally, people may selectively search for models as 'confirming evidence' in everyday 'hypothesis testing'.[9]

Conclusions

With the introduction of models in a theory of ideology, I now have established the necessary links between ideologies and the actual social practices that construct or implement such ideologies, roughly in this order from 'deep' cultural beliefs, via group beliefs to their manifestations in social practices (and vice versa) (see Figure 7.1).

Figure 7.1 shows first that ideologies must be based on a system of cultural common ground, featuring shared general knowledge and attitudes and their underlying principles, such as values and cultural truth criteria. Groups select from this cultural base specific beliefs and evaluation criteria, and construe these, together with other basic principles of their group, as systems of specific group beliefs that are organized by underlying ideologies. These representations of the social mind monitor the formation of the social dimension of personal mental models in episodic memory. Models that are controlled by group beliefs may be called ideologically 'biased'. The

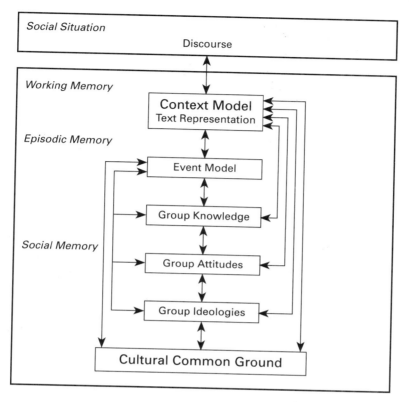

Figure 7.1

personal dimension of these mental models is monitored by old mental models (earlier experiences) as well as by general representations (personal knowledge, self, personality) of individuals. Finally, under the constraint of context models, these personal event models and experience models may be expressed in discourse or enacted in other social practices.

We have also seen that because of the nature of discourse, also shortcuts are possible. That is, whereas ideologies are theoretically linked to discourse only in the indirect way described above, discourse may also directly express fragments of attitudes and ideologies. And vice versa, ideologies are not merely learned and changed because of personal experiences, but may also be constructed, at least partially, directly from ideological statements in discourse. Political and religious conversions are sometimes of this nature. Propaganda precisely has the function of directly affecting the attitudes and ideologies of social members, even when 'examples' or 'illustrations' may be given as persuasive 'evidence' for the validity of general beliefs. This possibility of a direct link between discourse and ideology also explains the familiar strategies of manipulation, as well as the classical notion of false consciousness. Since discourse need not be limited to the expression of personal experiences, and hence to concrete social and economic conditions of social members, ideologies may also be acquired more directly, that is, through argumentation and other persuasive means to communicate ideological beliefs.

However, most ideologies that control everyday life are gradually acquired on the basis of a large number of personal experiences and discourses, and hence do have their 'empirical roots' in personal models. It may be assumed that such ideologies are also less easy to manipulate, because they need to be consistent with prevalent experience models. However, for all situations where social members have fewer, biased or incomplete personal experiences (models), it will be much easier to manufacture ideologies that have no 'grounding', but which members acquire as a result of propaganda by elites who control the means of public discourse. I shall examine these and other social conditions of the acquisition and change of ideologies and their relations with discourse in later chapters. Important for now is that we have the theoretical instruments to describe such processes, and especially to analyse what 'goes on' between social practices, discourse and ideologies.

Another essential implication of the mental-model theory presented here is that it explains the fundamental aspect of situational or contextual *variation*, and hence the possibility of *change*. Ideologies and other social representations are general and abstract, and more or less permanent. However, we have also witnessed that in specific actions and discourse, there may be considerable personal and contextual variation in the expression or 'uses' of ideologies. Indeed, because of these considerable personal variations, empirical studies of ideology (especially in political science) sometimes conclude that there are no general group ideologies at all.

In the present framework, we are able to account both for the frequent observation that many group members in many situations *do* act and talk more or less in the same way, while on the other hand accounting for the uniqueness of all individual actions and discourse, as it is based on personal models. Since models incorporate instances of social beliefs, while also featuring personal knowledge and opinions, their expression in discourse and action may very well have the chaotic and contradictory nature that is so often observed, in discourse studies as well as in social or political surveys.[10] Moreover, individuals are members of various social groups, each with their own ideology, and as individuals they may, depending on context constraints, draw on several ideologies at the same time, thereby also possibly exhibiting contradictions that express conflicting interests between these groups. I shall return to this issue of variation and consistency in the next chapter.

Thus, whereas ideologies are themselves the interface between the 'social mind' shared by group members, on the one hand, and social structure, on the other hand, models are in turn the interface between the social and the individual, and hence between the general and the particular, and between shared representations and the actual practices that generate or manifest them in concrete social and personal situations. Without this last interface, we are unable to describe the cognitive basis of (unique) social practices and discourse, or (with the exception of discourse of a generic nature) to explain how these are monitored by ideologies.

8

Consistency

Consistency versus variation

One problem that has often come up in discussions about ideology is whether ideological beliefs form a *consistent* system. Both traditional work in political psychology as well as in discursive and rhetorical psychology suggests that ideologies are hardly consistent. Both in their actions and in their text and talk, people show many inconsistencies and dilemmas, and these do not seem to presuppose neatly consistent underlying systems.[1]

The problem with these observations is that while they are undeniably correct, they do not allow firm conclusions about the structures or the contents of ideologies. This is not only true because such studies rarely have an explicit concept of ideological structures in the first place, but rather because they confuse situational, contextually bound *expressions* or uses of ideologies with the ideologies themselves.

We may compare this inconsistency argument with that in linguistics about the role of grammar. If we examine people's spontaneous talk, we may observe that they do not exactly always follow the rules of abstract sentence grammars. To conclude from such personal, contextually variable uses of a language system that there is no grammar (or that the grammar is incoherent) is of course hardly persuasive.

Now, if we apply the same argument to the domain of ideologies, where people not only 'follow' one but possibly many different ideologies, depending on their various group memberships, the conclusion is even less persuasive. That is, we not only need to account for such variation, but also, and perhaps more importantly for the many situations in which social members *do* follow their ideological orientation. That is, ideologies should not be studied merely for isolated contexts or single group members, but across contexts and for many group members. If such comparisons never or seldom allow any ideological continuity, then we would have to give up the very notion of ideology as a monitoring underlying system. In that case we do have to explain, though, how social members are able to interpret the various social practices in terms of what usually are called ideologies, such as 'He is a conservative', 'He is a racist', 'She is a feminist', or 'She is an environmentalist', and so on.

Coherence and consistency

Although we may argue that variable ideological expression does not, as such, entail the inconsistency of underlying ideologies, the opposite conclusion need not be true either. Forms of ideological continuity of social practices do not as such imply ideological consistency, at least not in a strict logical sense.[2] At the very least, we need to assume that if there is some 'order' in ideologies they are at most psycho-logically consistent. Indeed, ideologies are cognitively and socially constructed, naive basic 'theories' of social life, and especially about groups and their relations to other groups. That many members will only acquire and use sometimes incomplete and inconsistent fragments of such ideologies seems obvious, and has already been accounted for (see also below).

What about the ideology at the social level, however – that is, as a shared ideology of a group? Again, the comparison with the acquisition of grammars is instructive here. There is no doubt that people learn their mother tongue in highly disparate, variable social contexts, and observing the language use of many (especially less educated) members, one might conclude that their grammar is hardly complete or perfect. Yet, for their daily lives they manage quite well in communicating.

The same is true, at the level of individual members, for the sometimes fragmentary ideologies members acquire as a result of discourse and social interaction. But at a more abstract level, grammars and other forms of knowledge should also be considered at the level of a whole community. Some people in the community know the 'official' grammar better than others, and formal education precisely involves the teaching of such grammars to the young. Ideological teaching may not, as such, be a subject in most schools, but both in socialization as well as in formal education and the later uses of mass media and everyday conversations or other discourses, there are many examples of inculcation or 'ideological learning'. There are many situations in which members are able to compare their experiences (models), including their opinions, as well as their attitudes, with those of other social members.

That is, the evaluative system of individual members gets 'normalized' with respect to the social beliefs of the group, community and culture as a whole. As is the case for grammar, people may well not have active knowledge about the precise contents or structures of such ideologies, but, in the evaluation of their own social practices and those of other social members, they should in general be quite competent in making the 'right' evaluations, and follow the ideological principles that are in the interests of the group. This is the case despite the fact that people may be manipulated to adopt 'inconsistent' ideological principles when they lack adequate information or personal experiences to draw on.

As basic group beliefs, ideologies are not merely based on the experiences of a few members, but grounded in the socially and historically developed, accumulated and (discursively) transmitted experiences of the whole group, now and in the past. Such collective experiences will be a powerful corrective to fully inconsistent and incomplete ideologies. Intra-group discourse will provide the experiences, the evidence, the arguments, the situations, and so on, that are necessary for the whole *group* to develop its group ideology, even when individual *members* do so imperfectly or quite variably as a result of their specific social position or as a consequence of the influence of other ideologies. For large, institutionalized or otherwise organized groups, there will be special ideological institutions (training, lectures, seminars, media and propaganda) that may spell out the details of such ideologies, as is the case for religions (Churches), political parties, unions, non-governmental organizations (like Greenpeace), or large social movements such as the women's movement, as we shall see in more detail later.[3]

The crucial point here is that although not all individual members need to be able to explicitly formulate the ideologies of the groups of which they are members, groups as a whole may still develop complex and more or less coherent group ideologies. Such groups will have leaders or other elite group members (the ideologues) who know and teach or transmit such an ideology to new members. If most group members were to have highly fragmentary or incoherent ideologies, they would be unable to organize their relevant group attitudes and form the models that are necessary for their everyday practices as group members.

In sum, given various social constraints on groups and group relations, and the collective and historical experiences of their members, we may therefore provisionally conclude that, *at the level of the group*, ideologies should be fairly stable and coherent.

Conditions of variation

Situational and personal variation is easy to explain while maintaining the notion of an underlying ideology that is more or less coherent. Let us examine some of the conditions of such variation.

The first reason is that ideologies are not always immediately linked to discourse, but usually indirectly, that is, via more detailed knowledge, attitudes and personal episodic models. That is, in their everyday lives, social members rather operate at the 'meso-level' of group beliefs, rather than at the high, abstract level of ideologies. For instance, they may be aware of and apply opinions on immigration or unemployment rather than abstract ideological principles of a racist (or anti-racist) ideology, although the latter may sometimes be made explicit in accounts and argumentations, and appear more often in the discourse of the elites.

Second, ideologies, as well as attitudes and knowledge, are socially shared, and hence 'context-free' in the sense of being stable across different, specific social situations at the micro-level. In these everyday contexts and practices, people deal with more concrete events, people and situations, as represented in mental models. These models are strategically adapted to the situation at hand, and this means that sometimes the expression of an ideologically 'correct' opinion may be less appropriate for reasons of politeness, positive self-presentation and commonsense interests – racist shopkeepers would soon be broke if they were to openly derogate their black customers, for instance.

Moreover, since social members are members of several groups, they'll bring to bear several ideologies in their models of everyday events, so that the models may become seemingly incoherent. The same is true for their practices and discourses. People may adhere both to more or less human-itarian and democratic principles, but at the same time not apply them to certain social relations: for example, those of gender, age or ethnicity. The use of various ideologies in one situation (and in laboratory experiments the same is true for simulated situations) thus results in sometimes complex models which exhibit apparently incoherent opinions in discourse, typically expressed in disclaimers such as 'I am not a racist, but . . .', 'I am all for equality of women, but . . .'. Personal experiences and biographies, local circumstances and interpersonal relations will further contribute to the complexity of such models and the discourses based on them. Indeed, many of these observations have already been made, in other terms, in classical studies on *cognitive dissonance*,[4] which we are now able to reformulate in terms of model structures and relations between models and social repre-sentations. Hence, as suggested before, conclusions about the contents and structures of ideologies need to be based on comparisons of many events in which variable properties of discourse are explained in terms of such constraints.

In other words, variability of ideological expression is explained by the complex interplay of several ideologies and their contextually specific uses, whereas the continuity of ideological opinions can be explained in terms of socially shared ideologies that are rather stable and context-free. No need therefore to assume that ideologies are sets of mutually incoherent proposi-tions. If such were the case, people would in principle *always* express themselves incoherently, also across situations, and there is no evidence for that. On the contrary, we know from work on racism (and sexism, etc.) that talk on ethnic (or gender) relations rather consistently has recourse, in variable contexts, to similar basic norms, values, principles, ideological propositions and more specific attitudes. Unless personal and social circum-stances change dramatically, or when being targeted by persuasive dis-course, someone advocating liberal immigration rules today, will not be for strict ones tomorrow.[5]

That is, the 'normal' situation is that of individual variability, and the situation that especially needs to be explained is precisely the fact that many different people in many different situations still appear to use very similar ideological opinions. It is ideological conformity and consensus that are remarkable, and much less that different people with different experiences have differences of opinion. On the other hand, if such conformity is mainly explained in terms of the identical social or economic situation of a group, then individual variation and dissent are the phenomena that need to be explained.

Change

Of course, ideologies may change, but this takes time, in particular because they are socially shared, and groups need much time to change their basic ideologies because such changes need much public discourse and debate. And precisely during such periods of ideological formation and change, other (opposed) ideologies may become more relevant in the control of action and discourse, and more personal variation will be the result. For instance, after the demise of state socialism and communism around 1990, which also affected the Left in general, leftist ideologies entered a state of transition as well, whereas neo-liberal market ideologies have become not only more dominant but virtually hegemonic. As a result, even in more or less progressive media, socialist discourse has become 'unfashionable'. I shall come back to these social and political conditions of changing ideologies later.[6]

Conclusion

From these arguments it may be concluded that ideologies 'ideally' reflect the goals and the interests of the group, and do so optimally when these interests are coherently translated into a set of basic beliefs shared within the group. Such coherence facilitates the organization of new attitudes about specific issues and the co-ordination of social practices by different members in different situations. That is, coherence is a condition of continuity and reproduction. As a theoretical hypothesis it explains members' experiences, observations and expressions of such continuity.

Variations and contradictions in the enactment or expression of such ideologies are perfectly compatible with this hypothesis if we assume that such manifestations are explained by multiple ideological allegiances of social actors, both at the level of attitudes, as well as at the level of specific, contextual and personal, models of events, which in turn monitor discourse and other social practices. As is generally the case for social representations, including knowledge (including knowledge of the language or about inter-action), social members are experts in adapting these shared representations to their personal needs and contextual constraints.

It is also at this level that systematic variation and 'deviation' may give rise to attitudinal and finally to *ideological change*, as soon as enough members, and especially leaders who control public discourse, are able to persuasively communicate such alternative systems of judgement to other group members. Changes in feminist and socialist ideologies are well-known examples of such transformations. In this way, ideologies, despite their relatively stable nature, may with some delay flexibly change as a consequence of (a) changing social interests and (b) the everyday experiences of group members, and of course (c) persuasive ideological discourse. These and other conditions for ideological continuity and change will be discussed in later chapters.

9

Consciousness

Introduction

When dealing with the cognitive dimension of ideologies, another issue needs to be addressed, namely, that of consciousness. In the first place, this notion has been part of the history of the study of ideologies since Marx and Engels, mostly in the form of 'false consciousness'. Second, we may ask whether social group members have, experience or use their ideologies more or less consciously, or whether these belief systems are acquired, used and changed more or less 'unconsciously' or, in other terms, 'implicitly'.

False consciousness

The traditional notion of 'consciousness' (German: *Bewußtsein*) plays a central role in the traditional accounts of ideologies, especially in combination with its negative modifier 'false'.[1] This phrase then usually refers to group ideologies that do not reflect the 'objective' socio-economic interests of a group. Thus, workers or poor people may develop an ideology that is rather in the interests of, respectively, the ruling class, the elites, the company they work for, or the owners or the managers of that company.

Such a 'false' or misguided ideology may be the result of a mixture of ignorance, indifference, manipulation, compliance or concern for short-term interests (e.g. not to lose one's job, getting a pay-rise) at the expense of long-term, structural interests, such as ownership of the means of production, or at least shared planning and decision making. The contemporary 'alienation' of the working class in times of the hegemony of liberal market ideologies is a well-known example in point: large segments of the working-class no longer vote socialist nor even social-democratic. Having obtained a minimum of job security and income, they adopt more or less conservative market ideologies or forms of liberal individualism.

The social dimensions of this problem will be dealt with later (see Chapter 11). Here, I focus on the cognitive aspect of this classical issue in the theory of ideology. What, indeed, *is* consciousness exactly? In the description of the issue in the previous paragraph, I have freely replaced false consciousness by false ideologies. That is, consciousness is obviously taken as a 'state of mind', in this case of sets of beliefs. More specifically, since the 'consciousness' of whole groups or classes is involved, these beliefs must be socially shared. Hence, the most adequate translation of the term in my framework would simply be that of social representation. This comprises not only basic ideologies of the group, but also their attitudes and knowledge. The advantage of such a broad definition of this vague term is that not only value systems and judgements may be involved, but also knowledge.

Indeed, the concept of false consciousness is also used in order to denote ignorance of the 'real' social facts, for instance about the interests of specific social arrangements, policies or practices. Again, such ignorance may result from widespread indifference and apathy, which may again result from oppression or partial satisfaction with the status quo. Or it may more actively be inculcated through biased information or by other forms of ideological manipulation by dominant groups. In that case ideology as false consciousness of dominated group A in fact implies the acceptance of a hegemonic ideology of dominant group B, for instance as those beliefs that misrepresent social inequality as the allegedly natural or immutable nature of the current social and moral order. In other words, the notion of 'false' here also implies conceptions about truth and falsity of beliefs and ideologies about social life, to be discussed in Chapter 11.

In sum, my analysis of the traditional notion of 'false consciousness' proposes to make the notion of 'consciousness' more explicit, first of all, by using the term 'social representation', including knowledge as well as (evaluative) attitudes and ideologies. Second, the notion of 'false' may be assigned two different meanings: (1) wrong, partial, incomplete, biased or otherwise misguided factual beliefs (which presupposes that there is 'correct' or 'true' knowledge; see Chapter 11), and (2) evaluative beliefs that lead to judgements and social practices that are not in the interest of the own group, and may be in the interest of a dominant group. After this conceptual clarification of a classic notion, I later study in more detail which discursive conditions and what social situations may bring about such non-self-serving social representations.

Having somewhat clarified the notion of (false) consciousness, we remain with the empirical question whether the main (Marxist) theses of ideological domination and inculcation and the construction of 'misguided' ideologies by dominated groups is correct in the first place. That is, first of all, there may not be just one 'dominant' (class) ideology in the first place, but a complex structure of elite ideologies that may mutually compete for control or hegemony.[2]

Second, although it is plausible that when the ideological elites have control over the means of ideological production (especially politics, education and the media) their social representations about society may be quite influential, this does not entail that dominated groups will actually adopt such representations. Whereas such ideological influence may be plausible in situations in which no alternative knowledge and opinion sources are available or accessible, and if dominant attitudes do not obviously clash with the immediate interests of dominated groups and their members (typically so in racist ideologies), such inculcation is much less obvious when group

members are able to observe directly the contradictions between the inculcated ideologies and attitudes and their everyday experiences. Indeed, if
such were the case, social and individual resistance and change would be
difficult or even impossible. These issues will be dealt with in more detail
when I study the social dimensions of ideologies.[3]

Consciousness as awareness

A related problem of the definition of (false) consciousness, and hence of
ideologies, is whether people who 'have' them are actually 'aware' of them.
We already have seen in the previous chapter that this is not necessarily the
case. Social members are barely aware of many of the social representations
they have, and of the ways these control their social practices and evaluations. As we shall see later for the notion of 'common sense', ideologies
may be or seem so 'natural' that people don't even realize they have them.
As is the case for knowledge of natural language (people's shared competence), ideologies often are simply part of everyday life, and taken for
granted.[4]

While this is true and probably applies to many ideologies, it is hardly a
property of all ideologies. Some ideologies are explicitly 'invented' in the
appropriate historical and social circumstances and explicitly propagated
among group members. Especially for dominated groups, thus, it is crucial
that the ideology be made and kept conscious, and there are many organizational practices that will make sure that such is the case: media messages,
party or group meetings, socialization events, initiation rites, propaganda,
and so on, will make sure that members learn to be aware of the ideological
basis of their group membership.[5]

Unlike much implicit grammatical knowledge, some ideologies may
partially be made explicit in everyday discourse, for example when people
defend their own ideologies or attack others. Parts of the arguments in such
debates will be based on ideological principles that may need to be
formulated explicitly as premises of an argumentation. This means that
language users of the ideological group get frequent 'exercise' in acquiring
the group ideology.

Whereas oppositional ideologies by definition will tend to be more
explicit and conscious among group members, dominant ideologies will
precisely tend to be implicit and denied, or felt to be 'natural' by their
members. Such group members may indeed be unaware of their ideologies
(typically so of male chauvinism, racism, etc.) until they are challenged by
members of the other group.

Although the notion of 'consciousness' may be clear in it its everyday
sense, it is theoretically hardly explicit. Being conscious of, being aware of
or realizing something, first of all, is a 'state of mind'. For instance, it may
mean that active processes of thinking, mental arguing or simply information search have access to specific information. If so, people are able to use
such information in arguments, or for further processes of inference.

In other words, there are many types or grades of 'consciousness' between totally explicit awareness and knowledge on the one hand, and largely implicit knowledge and 'mere' use as 'lived experience' on the other hand. This distinction is socially often associated with that between 'ideologues' and the 'masses', a distinction we need to analyse as part of the social analysis of ideologies.

Cognitively, the distinction means that at least some group members – and for each group this fraction may be different in size – not only share the ideology but also explicitly know its major tenets, and are able to talk about them as such, and even argue for them as such. It has been frequently observed that such explicit ideological self-awareness is rare, and usually limited to leaders, opinion-leaders and other elites. These are also those who have the function to formulate and persuasively inculcate the relevant ideological beliefs among group members – for example via propaganda – or who are able to explain relevant everyday events in terms of the ideology.[6]

On the other hand, such explicit knowledge of ideological beliefs may be limited to only a few basic beliefs, or only be accessible in their more specific form, for instance as opinions in particular attitudes. For instance, people may be unable to spell out general racist or ethnocentric principles as such, but they very well know that they disapprove of liberal immigration or of preferential job and housing allocation to minorities or refugees. That is, in that situation, their knowledge is still explicit, general and social, and may be expressed as such: 'We in our community think that . . .'. Another intermediate stage of awareness is when group members have such attitudes on some issues, but not on other relevant ones. For instance, they may share a prejudiced attitude on immigration, but have (as yet) no ethnic attitude on education or language use.

Finally, largely implicit are those ideological opinions that only exist at the level of models of concrete events: for example when someone does not want a foreign neighbour, but does not generalize or rationalize this explicitly in terms of group attitudes ('We don't want foreign neighbours because . . .'). Social interests in this case are completely translated and integrated into personal interests. I surmise, though, that such totally implicit knowledge and attitudes are rare in most contemporary societies, where most members have access to the mass media: in such a situation people quickly learn to legitimate their personal opinions in terms of the shared attitudes of the group. Systematic discourse analysis of ideological text and talk provides insight into these various levels or grades of ideological awareness.

Also, I later need to demonstrate whether and how such awareness may be enhanced (or suppressed) by communication: for example by party or group propaganda, teaching, seminars, meetings, media and so on. The fact that many ideological groups organize various forms of 'consciousness raising' or 'awareness training' suggests that such forms of ideological explication may be an important organizational feature of ideological groups, especially for dominated groups or social movements.

The contemporary uses of the notion of consciousness in cognitive science are quite different from the traditional meaning of (false) consciousness. In current debates the concept of consciousness applies to the complex problem of how we can explain how brains can be associated with the (self-) consciousness of minds. In many respects this problem boils down again to the eternal problem of brain–mind identity and difference. Once it is accepted that, at some level of analysis, brains also have mind-like qualities, we at the same time explain the elusive notion of consciousness – for example, in terms of knowledge of self, knowledge about the present context, and especially in terms of ongoing mental processes like thinking (including the ability of people to be able to think about themselves and their own thinking). It is this kind of consciousness that especially characterizes the ongoing construction of mental models of experience (see Chapter 7).

With our contemporary knowledge about the brain and the mind, there does not seem to be an additional property of either of them that needs special explication in terms of consciousness or awareness. An operating human mind is by definition 'conscious' when people know about themselves, their ongoing activities and their ongoing thoughts. Then there is the distinction between 'conscious' and 'automatic' processing of information. This suggests that consciousness and mind cannot simply be identified – processing in the first case involves self-awareness of short-term memory processes, or as knowledge of what one is now doing. In Chapter 7 it was proposed to represent at least part of this knowledge in experience and context models, which therefore may also be seen as the kind of overall mental monitor sometimes associated with awareness. Of course, this does not solve all problems related to the notion of consciousness, but for my discussion it should do.[7]

Awareness and denial

Finally, we need to realize that more-or-less explicit knowledge of ideological beliefs of group members who positively identify with a group usually implies positive acceptance of such beliefs. This also means positive self-presentation and description of such beliefs. It is well known for instance that virtually all racists will deny that they are racists, and many of them seem to reject racist ideologies when described as such.[8] However, when not described as racist, but, for example, as nationalist, or as 'normal' or 'natural' beliefs in favour of the own group, then the same ideological beliefs may well be perfectly acceptable. In other words, knowledge and acceptance of ideologies and their derived opinions by group members usually implies acceptance of ideologies-as-described-by-the-group-itself.

The converse is true for the rejection or change of (other) ideologies, as is the case for anti-communism and anti-racism, which are based on other-description of ideologies. Such opposite ideologies may again be reflected in the argumentative, explanatory or legitimating discourse of group members sharing the ideologies thus criticized, for instance in well-known disclaimers such as 'I am not a racist, but . . .', or 'I am not a sexist, but . . .', and so on. Indeed, given the negative meaning of the concept of ideology in everyday usage, groups and their members may deny that they have an ideology in the first place. Thus, being in favour of market-freedom will seldom be self-described by its adherents as a belief that characterizes a 'capitalist' ideology, or even as a 'liberal' ideology. Similarly, Christians or Muslims will not usually self-describe themselves as adherents of religious ideologies. At most, terms such as 'philosophy', 'principles', 'convictions' or simply 'belief(s)' will be acceptable as self-descriptions of ideologies.

I shall later investigate such strategies of self-description, denial and legitimation in the expression and defence of ideologies in more detail. For my present discussion such examples only show that people are aware of conflicting ideologies, that they know that their expression of specific opinions may be 'heard as' expressions of a normatively unacceptable ideology, and that they usually self-represent and defend their own ideologies in positive terms.

10

Common Sense

The meanings of 'common sense'

Related to the notions of consciousness and awareness is another socio-cognitive notion that plays a central role in contemporary discussions of ideology, namely, *common sense*. This notion has roots in different philosophical and sociological traditions.

First of all, it is often associated with Antonio Gramsci's contributions to the theory of ideology, and especially with the concept of hegemony.[1] As soon as groups and their members accept a dominant ideology as a reflection of their own goals, desires or interests, or as a representation of a natural or otherwise legitimate social order, their ideologies may turn into beliefs that are taken for granted or simply common sense. Ideological dominance and hegemony is 'perfect' when dominated groups are unable to distinguish between their own interests and attitudes and those of dominant groups. In that case, they may not even be able to see conflicting ideologies (even when in their own best interests) as viable or acceptable alternatives. I shall later come back to the social dimensions of such forms of ideological compliance.

Another main source of the notion of common sense may be found in phenomenological microsociology and ethnomethodology, for example as inspired by Alfred Schütz.[2] Here common sense is simply defined in terms of the implicit social knowledge that group members *take for granted* in their everyday social practices. This members' knowledge is essentially shared lay-knowledge, and should be distinguished from elite or theoretical formulations or explications of knowledge. Indeed, compared with explicit, scientific knowledge, commonsense knowledge may sometimes be described as wrong, biased, misguided or otherwise unfounded. However, outside such a critical account of common sense, it should be emphasized that whatever the truth-status of commonsense beliefs, they are usually true and accepted by the people who hold them, and will therefore be at the basis of their everyday experiences and interactions, that is, their *practical* accomplishments. In other words, for group members they are true 'for all practical purposes'.

Describing and explaining such mundane practices, therefore, also requires making explicit the similarly mundane beliefs (methods, rules, etc.) that group members take for granted. This means that their actions, including their discourses, will be described from their own point of view, and possibly in terms of the notions and categories they use themselves. Indeed, using the theoretical categories of the sociologist may fully misrepresent the ways members understand and accomplish everyday activities. In other words, a theoretical account of common sense and what is taken for granted in interaction, at the same time becomes a methodological principle, namely, to study social reality as much as possible from the point of view, and in terms of, the social actors themselves.

One important implication of the notion of taken-for-granted knowledge for the study of discourse is that such knowledge tends to be presupposed. That is, such beliefs are not explicitly stated, but incorporated without challenge in new statements about social reality, because language users may assume that the recipients have similar beliefs, and indeed similar, recognizable 'methods' to organize everyday interaction in general, and conversation in particular. This link between common sense, knowledge and discourse will be explored in more detail later (Chapter 11).

For my discussion, these various notions of common sense, and especially the Gramscian and the ethnomethodological ones, also suggest elements for a theory of ideology. For this reason, contemporary studies of ideologies tend to emphasize the implicit, taken-for-granted, common-sense nature of ideologies as 'lived experiences' in the everyday lives of groups and their members.[3] In light of the discussion about consciousness and awareness in the previous chapter, this conception of ideology identifies ideologies with the non-conscious, unaware mode of ideological practices. People simply go about their everyday business and spontaneously see and judge social reality and events in terms of a belief system that is normal and unproblematical, and which they assume is shared by other group members. Only in situations of complications, challenges or other deviations from the accepted system of knowledge, may group members be (made) aware of the problematic nature of their commonsense or ideological beliefs. In such situations, however, they may have similarly commonsense 'methods' to deal with problems and try to resolve them for the situation at hand.

What is common sense?

Given my earlier discussion, this account of common sense and ideology explains only part of the facts. Where the notion of common sense is relevant, I first of all need to make it explicit. As so many 'mental' terms in the philosophy of ideology, and the microsociology of everyday life, this notion was until recently seldom made explicit beyond a characterization in terms of mundane, taken-for-granted beliefs. But we have seen that there are many kinds of belief in the realm of cognition or memory, so I need to specify which ones can be seen as commonsense beliefs.

Our proposal for definition will again be straightforward – common sense is just another term for the set of social beliefs. Like the latter, it is social, shared by members of a group or community, and involves knowledge as

well as opinions.[4] In those respects, common sense is a modern variant of
the notion of consciousness discussed in the previous chapter.

One dimension of common sense, however, absent in the intuitive notion
of consciousness is its argumentative nature. Common sense is typically
referred to, especially in everyday (commonsense!) uses of the term, when
arguments are said to be based on common sense.

In other words, unlike sociologists, who take common sense as the shared
knowledge underlying all mundane interaction, the commonsense meaning
of common sense usually involves discourse: arguments, accounts, explanations, defences and legitimation.[5] More specifically, it connotes that such
knowledge is direct, immediate, unreflected, untheoretical and unscientific,
but based on or derived from everyday observation or experiences. Common
sense in this sense is an implicit, naive 'theory' of the world.[6]

More critically, this same explanation may therefore imply that common
sense is essentially unreliable, possibly biased by social prejudices and
illusions, if not the result of manipulation. In both cases, common sense is
also associated, at least implicitly, with popular or lower-class cognition, as
what 'common people' think and find.

We see that common sense has many meanings and various critical
interpretations, which need analytically be kept apart. Hence, we first keep
its basic meaning, that is, as social representations, in order to account for
taken-for-granted knowledge, but add that this may also include taken-for-
granted other beliefs, such as socially shared opinions (and prejudices).
'They take away our jobs', is a typical example of such commonsense,
prejudiced opinions.

Next, the argumentative and discursive role of common sense needs to be
represented differently, in terms of the ways social representations (knowledge and attitudes) are activated, used and contextually adapted in communicative events, that is, as part of specific models. A commonsense
argument, then, is an argument based on a common sense model, that is, a
model of which much of the knowledge and opinions is largely shared by
others. The same is true for commonsense descriptions, accounts and
explanations. Such accounts are typically founded on 'what we all know' on
'what everybody says', (consensus), or on commonsense truth criteria ('I
have seen it myself').

Third, the dimension of common sense as being immediate, unreflected
and untheoretical may simply be described in terms of the type of social
representations being shared within a group (expert versus lay knowledge,
etc.), and also in terms of the more or less unproblematic processing of
social knowledge. Models are directly formed from instantiations of general,
shared knowledge, and not by independent, critical examination of the
'facts', nor by more complicated thinking or reasoning. Hence also the elitist
association of common sense with what is taken-for-granted by the uneducated 'masses'. This need not always be a negative implication: common
sense is also positively valued as an antidote against scientific sophistication,
jargon, and needlessly complex explications of what 'ordinary' common

sense will tell us more directly and more transparently. In this sense, common sense positively reflects what is 'obvious' and 'for all to see', against the pretensions of fancy scholarship. When used in this sense, it may also be a tenet of anti-intellectualism.[7]

And finally, this sociological dimension – who indeed 'has' common sense, and who uses it – needs to be described on the basis of a sociology of knowledge and a study of discourses (and especially argumentations and explanations) by various groups and their members. In sum, a theory of common sense examines its structures and status as social representations, its processes or strategies in thinking and its uses in social practices and discourse, and its uses by specific social groups.

In this cognitive section, we may for instance examine in which respect common sense, as represented in social representations, is being used in the formation of models: in interpretations of events, as personal instantiations of social knowledge and other beliefs, as being strategic (fast but not perfect) and, as we shall see later, as being largely implicit, that is, as not explicitly commented upon in discourse.[8] One, more romantic association of common sense as mode of thought, may be put to rest from the start: in many contemporary, mass-mediated societies with virtual universal literacy and high education levels, there is hardly such a thing as 'pure' common sense, in the sense of shared, unreflected, untheoretical knowledge, based only on our experiences. Precisely one of the reasons why Serge Moscovici and French social psychology introduced the very notion of social representations was to emphasize the 'popular' integration of scientific theories.[9] The best known case of this phenomenon is the now common use of notions from psychoanalytical theories.

Similarly, elites who have special access to the media, and hence indirectly to the minds of the public at large, will routinely describe and explain events in terms of implicit or explicit scholarly theories, and this will obviously also influence the social representations and explanations of other group members. It follows that although everyday perception and understanding may well be based on personal experiences and on a more or less unreflected application of commonsense knowledge in the construction of models, these socially shared representations also involve more or less simplified versions of scholarly knowledge. The same is true for truth criteria, inferences and argumentation. Accounts and explanations have become largely acceptable only when based on truth criteria that are themselves socially and culturally variable versions of more philosophical or scholarly ways of arguing and thinking. Asking the opinion of a sorcerer, examining entrails or the lines of one's hand, or looking at the stars, among many other remnants of old popular criteria of truth, have been largely discredited as superstition. In sum, in most modern societies, there is no 'pure and popular', scientifically uncontaminated, common sense, but rather a gradual difference with explicit, scientific, methods of observation, thinking, proof and truth criteria.

More generally, we may conclude that the difference between group beliefs and cultural beliefs is relevant for a theory of common sense, and most of what we have said above also applies here. That is, specific group knowledges and opinions may slowly be integrated in (or excluded from) the cultural common ground. Common sense is then more or less what we try to conceptualize with the term 'cultural beliefs', that is, the knowledge and opinions, as well as the evaluation criteria, that are common to all or most members of a culture. Like common sense, these cultural beliefs are also used as the basis for specific group beliefs, and also function as the general base of presupposed beliefs in all accounts, explanations and arguments.

Ideologies as common sense

The same applies to the identification of ideologies as forms of common sense. Depending on context and social group, ideologies may be more or less known and used explicitly in the conduct of everyday life. Thus, we may distinguish between the explicit treatises of the 'ideologues' and the ideological 'commonsense' reasoning of other group members, but should be aware that these different modes of thinking and discourse mutually influence each other. History has shown that much of what once counted as 'scientific knowledge' (e.g. about women or blacks) may now be rejected as unfounded, if not prejudiced 'common sense'.[10]

That many everyday actions are being accomplished routinely, and seemingly unreflectedly, does not mean that members are unable to make explicit at least some of the knowledge and other beliefs that are implied or presupposed by their practices and discourses. Misunderstanding, conflicts, challenges and various factors of the context may give rise to various modes of 'explication', in the double sense of the term: as making explicit, and as explanation or account.

Both the social representations on which such explications are based, as well as the nature of the explications themselves, namely, as valid and acceptable arguments, may be more or less explicit and more or less imbued with widely shared, popular versions of scientific knowledge. This may be true more often and more explicitly among members of specific (elite) groups, but my point is that because of general education and the media, such philosophical and scientific influences on 'common sense' may be fairly widespread among many ideological groups.

Thus, most members of environmental groups have a fair amount of more or less technical knowledge about the nature, the causes and the consequences of pollution. Feminists may have extensive knowledge and attitudes about gender relations, and their arguments may be based not only on the shared immediate experiences of all or most women, but also on scholarly research or intellectual argument.

Concluding we should emphasize that if common sense is identified with the *general* beliefs of a culture, and if ideologies as the foundation of *specific* group beliefs are based on such a cultural common ground, *ideologies themselves are not a form of common sense*. Indeed, the very 'common' in common sense implies that such 'sense' is being shared, and hence rather cultural than group bound. Moreover, ideologies are usually much less taken for granted than are general cultural beliefs, because they are often more explicitly taught within the group and contested and hence defended across group boundaries. People are usually more explicitly and consciously Christian, socialist or feminist than 'Western'. Only in cross-cultural conflicts are people made aware of the common sense of their own culture. In other words, ideologies as defined here should not typically be identified with common sense, but rather with uncommon sense or non-sense.

11

Knowledge and Truth

Ideology versus knowledge

In many classical approaches as well as in most commonsense and political conceptions, ideologies are typically described as false, wrong, misguided, and as such opposed to true – and especially scientific – *knowledge*. Full discussion of the issues involved here would require a monograph by itself. So I shall only briefly summarize some major tenets and take a position that fits the theory presented in this book, elaborating the suggestions made in Chapter 3.[1]

The critical opposition of ideology and knowledge goes back at least to Marx and Engels and their conception of 'false consciousness', which implies that in specific situations and under the influence of ruling class manipulation, the working class may have misguided beliefs about the material conditions of its existence. Dominant ideologies in that case are an instrument of the ruling class which serves to conceal its power and the real socio-economic conditions of the working class. Throughout the history of political economy and sociology, similar distinctions were made, usually opposing ideology to scientific knowledge, that is, (with Durkheim) the 'sociological facts' established by social science. Until today, as we have seen before, ideology is thus characterized in terms of common sense, as beliefs that are taken for granted, and in general with naive views of everyday life that may be at variance with the knowledge produced by 'objective' scholarship.

It is hardly surprising that these views have also met with considerable critique. Thus, it has been pointed out that the history of science clearly shows how much scientific knowledge and methods themselves may be based on ideologies that are in the interest of the elites, if only in the interest of scholars themselves. From a different, ethnomethodological, point of view, commonsense knowledge of social members has received a more positive evaluation in terms of the practical basis of social practices, and as a viable means by which members manage their everyday lives.[2]

Against the background of this briefly summarized history of the opposition between ideology and knowledge, we should finally examine the role of knowledge in the conception of ideology presented in the preceding chapters. It was assumed that ideologies form the 'axiomatic' base of the social beliefs of a group. These social beliefs may be factual or evaluative. For the evaluative beliefs (opinions, attitudes) of a group, which may be typically contested by other groups, it is rather easy to accept that they are ideological. But what about their knowledge? How can knowledge be ideological, and still be called 'knowledge', that is, 'true belief', in the first place, instead of being characterized as 'mere' group belief (in the everyday sense of that term) or as 'opinion'. Or should we assume that, since all knowledge criteria are historically and culturally variable, also all knowledge is relative and hence possibly 'ideological'? Let us examine these questions in more detail, and reformulate some tentative answers within the theoretical framework presented in this book.

For various theoretical reasons, it was assumed that ideologies essentially involve values and therefore monitor the evaluative beliefs of groups, that is, attitudes. One question that may be raised in that case is whether ideologies may also influence non-evaluative, factual knowledge, or even whether more generally we should adopt the view that *all* knowledge is ultimately ideologically based. We might call this the ideological relativism thesis, following the more general view that all knowledge is socially and culturally relative, given the historically and culturally variable nature of truth criteria that form the basis of such knowledge. Let us examine whether this thesis can be defended within the framework of this book.

The nature of knowledge

Both in everyday life as well as in epistemology, knowledge is usually defined as justified true belief. Thus, in common sense language use, we may adequately say that we *know* that p if we believe that p and if we have good reasons, evidence or proof that p is true. That is, if called into question, knowledge statements may have to be justified, for example in terms of culturally accepted truth criteria, such as personal observation, reliable sources (media, experts, etc.), logical inference, common sense or consensus ('Everybody knows that . . .'). Similarly, again in everyday discourse, we attribute knowledge to others, rather than mere beliefs, if what others believe is true according to us, that is, if someone else shares our knowledge. On the other hand, we use the word 'belief' to denote those of our own beliefs for which we have no, or insufficient, evidence, or those of others which we know to be false or about which we have insufficient evidence.

Epistemology provides further conditions for (rather marginal) cases of (lack of) justification, for example when someone believes something that happens to be true, but has the wrong (non-justified) reasons for doing so. I won't go into these and other complications of the contemporary philosophy of knowledge. Similarly, I shall ignore the ontological intricacies of truth and truth conditions regarding 'what is the case'. That is, I shall not further analyse the question whether truth or 'facts' may exist independently of human perception and conceptual understanding. Nor whether physical facts do exist whether or not we know them, whereas social facts are always

constructed, and hence cognitively and socially relative. In the commonsense world, things and facts are simply assumed to exist whether we know
them or not. Linguistic or cognitive relativism or constructionism are not
characteristic of lay epistemics.[3]

We have seen that knowledge presupposes truth criteria, that is, grounds
for justification, whether they are commonsense criteria in everyday life and
hence a basis for the cultural common ground, or scientific ones in the
specific group beliefs of scholarship. We have also seen that these criteria
are historically, socially and culturally variable – what in one period, group
or culture is accepted as reliable evidence of true knowledge, may be
rejected as unacceptable in others. In other words, at the meta-level of a
theory or philosophy of knowledge, as well as in a social and cognitive
approach, knowledge is by definition relative, given the changing nature of
knowledge criteria.

In the practical, everyday world of each period, group, society or culture,
such relativism would be disastrous. Whether 'objectively' valid in some
cases or not, people need to be able to say that some things are true and
others are false, and that there is knowledge on the one hand, and (mere)
beliefs on the other. That is, they take the existence of most objects and the
truth of many facts of their everyday cultural and natural worlds for granted,
and will allow variable types of doubt or ignorance about other things. They
therefore distinguish between knowledge and beliefs, and between objectivity and subjectivity, where subjectivity is defined in terms of personal or
group beliefs that are unfounded according to us (our group) or according to
the commonsense truth criteria of the shared culture. Whether epistemologically or sociologically naive or not, such distinctions work 'for all
practical purposes', both for lay people, as well as for the 'professionals of
truth', such as journalists, lawyers and scholars.

Ideological relativism?

Does this (simplified) account of knowledge also allow us to decide about
the nature of the relations between ideology and knowledge? This first of all
depends on our basic theory of ideology. If ideology is the axiomatic basis
of the mental representations shared by social groups, and if ideologies vary
as a function of the various interests (membership, activities, values,
position, resources) of each group, the ideological relativism thesis implies
that what group members know is a function of their ideology.

Obviously, in its strong form this thesis cannot be defended. There is no
doubt that most of the knowledge of most groups is shared by other groups.
Or rather, most knowledge is generally, and socio-culturally defined and –
except for some realms of professional or expert knowledge – not in terms of
specific groups. Indeed, all intergroup communication and interaction, and
even ideological conflict, presupposes a vast domain of shared knowledge.
Moreover, most of this knowledge is undisputed and taken for granted, as

explained above. Thus, most people in contemporary Western culture know what trees, tables, cars, computers and myriad other things are, and presuppose such tremendous amount of knowledge in their everyday discourse. As we have argued in Chapter 3, most knowledge that people of different groups have is part of the cultural common ground and hence undisputed and taken for granted. Thus, the first conclusion is that, given a group-based definition of ideology, the strong form of the thesis of ideological relativism (namely, that all knowledge is ideological) cannot be defended without changing both the commonsense and the theoretical meanings of the concepts of 'knowledge' and 'ideology'.

But what about the weak version of the thesis? Is specific group knowledge ideologically based? The sociologically and politically informed answer to this question would undoubtedly be affirmative, possibly referring to a long history of ideologically based 'scientific facts' (for instance about poor people, women, blacks or gays) that obviously were in the interest of some group, namely, the white male middle class and its scholars. Many other examples can be mentioned in which what is defined or presented as knowledge are in fact false beliefs, half-truths or one-sided true beliefs that favour specific groups, and that are directed against others.

Note that this argument not only applies to false or incomplete beliefs, but also to true beliefs. Nothing, indeed, can be as persuasive as the social facts being marshalled by the civil rights movement or the women's movement when it comes to criticizing discrimination and claiming their rights, as both critical scholarly research as well as fundamental litigation have shown. That is, minorities or dissident groups will focus on, and highlight their own truths, and such knowledge could thus, at least in one sense, also be called ideological.

If these arguments are correct, we must conclude that the weak version of the ideological relativism thesis is correct: some knowledge in society is a function of the ideological position or power of groups. This is especially the case when such knowledge pertains to the social position of the group itself, or if it is related to the social issues that define the ideological opinions of the group. Thus, depending on one's view about smoking, different beliefs about smoking may be focused on, emphasized, concealed or denied. Many examples may be given from public debates about smoking, as well as about immigration, abortion or nuclear energy. Some of these beliefs may even be true (according to culturally accepted truth criteria) and hence qualify as common knowledge, but even then they may still be called partisan in the context of the other beliefs and attitudes of a group. Their 'facts' may thus not be Ours.

Knowledge or opinion?

One possible objection against this conclusion is that group-dependent knowledge is not knowledge at all, but *opinion*, so that the argument about ideological knowledge would be pointless, if not a contradiction.[4] This argument may be supported by commonsense uses of the concept of 'knowledge'. Groups that are in conflict and participate in an ideological debate would not readily grant that what the others believe constitutes knowledge, but will claim that such beliefs are mere opinions. For example, research on patterns of discrimination and ethnic beliefs may confirm the everyday experiences of minorities in the Netherlands, namely, that racism is endemic in Dutch society. However, such a conclusion is challenged by most Dutch (including most social scientists) as being merely an opinion, and in fact hardly more than a typical anti-racist accusation. That is, facts may be denied if seen to support the ideological position of the others, even if such facts are the result of research that has been carried out according to generally accepted scientific methods which in other research would never be challenged.

Note incidentally that the concept of 'opinion' used in such accusations has a broader sense than used in this book, where it only means an 'evaluative belief'. In everyday language use 'opinion' is sometimes also used as referring to 'factual' beliefs that (others think) are false. In the rest of this chapter, I shall often use the broader, commonsense notion of 'opinion', in order to have a word that denotes all beliefs that are not true and hence part of knowledge but are evaluative beliefs or false factual beliefs.

We now are facing a dilemma. If at least some knowledge is ideological, it will in many everyday situations be challenged as not being knowledge at all, but merely opinion. Such judgements presuppose the general definition of knowledge, that is, that beliefs are only accepted as true if *we* (also) accept them as true. In this case, 'we' may be simply (most of) the other members of a culture, society or group, or a scholar or other outsider judging the beliefs of such a culture, society or group. In other words, if factual beliefs are defined as opinions as soon as they are understood to be ideological (at least by the others), then we are back to square A, that is, that ideologies typically monitor evaluative beliefs only, and not knowledge. In fact, we would then only have general cultural knowledge, and not specific group knowledge. Following this argument, we would again have to conclude that knowledge is not ideological, simply because the cultural meaning of knowledge presupposes non-partisan belief: as soon as (even true) knowledge is socially expressed by an ideological group, it will be degraded to (mere) belief by the others.

But also this conclusion is problematical. Indeed, each side in an ideological debate may firmly believe and even be able to prove that their beliefs are true. If not, I would have to recognize that my own books on racism feature mere opinions and not knowledge that results from careful, empirical and theoretical research. Indeed, I would further claim that given such scientific criteria and my results, I 'know' some 'facts' about racism in the Netherlands, whereas those who simply deny such 'facts' (according to me) are expressing merely an opinion that is obviously based on nationalist, ethnocentric or racist ideologies, and not on reliable experience or scientific research.

The problem of this (very realistic) last example is that most people in society may firmly believe something, while a few others believe the opposite. Theories of knowledge in terms of consensus, common sense or shared cultural beliefs, would in that case be in trouble – critical, dissident knowledge of a few would then be defined as an opinion by a (vast) majority. Indeed, many people have burnt on the stake for that reason, and the problems of Galilei with the Catholic Church have only recently been resolved, after more than three centuries. Contemporary social movements and action groups have their own stories about the difficulty of getting their beliefs accepted as knowledge, and not rejected as mere ideological opinions.

There is another aspect involved in the ideological struggle about knowledge and truth, namely, meaning. That is, different social groups of course share a vast amount of socio-cultural knowledge, as well as many truth criteria. This allows members of different groups to understand each other, to argue and sometimes even to persuade each other. However, given their different interests, some concepts may be defined in a different way in different groups. Thus, in the ideological debate about racism in the Netherlands, it may well be accepted (given the role of – some – social scholarship in such debates) that more than sixty per cent of Dutch employers state that they prefer white men over women and minorities. This statistical 'fact' may be granted (and thus statistics admitted as a truth criterion), though seldom highlighted, in a debate with anti-racists. But the difference of opinion begins where one group considers this fact as proof of racism, whereas the other group simply does not want to call this fact a form of racism at all, but at most a form of prejudice, misguided beliefs or resentment. Indeed, the other group may define 'racism' only in terms of ideologies of racial superiority, and as characteristic of the extreme Right.

In other words, 'racism' never applies to 'people like us', so that *any* evidence of racism that might be applicable to 'our people' is automatically disqualified as being ideologically biased, and an unjust accusation. In other words, it is not the knowledge or its basis here that is rejected as an opinion, but rather the meaning and application of a concept. And since there is no 'objective proof' for the correct use of one specific meaning of the words that deal with social structures and relations, any use that may not be in our own interests may be rejected as incorrect or biased, that is, as an expression of an opinion, so that also its truth criteria do not apply in the same way. Indeed, many of these terms are generally seen as involving value judgements anyway, and not as descriptors of objective facts or properties, as is also true for words like discrimination, democracy, conservative, progressive, dangerous, healthy, and so on.

We might therefore further specify that any belief, including factual beliefs, that implies a value judgement, thereby may become an evaluative belief or opinion for others. Thus, the concept of racism may truthfully describe the ethnic situation in the Netherlands. But for both racists and anti-racists alike, the term has a negative implication, so that its use tends to be seen as a value judgement. Similarly, the statement that some country is not democratic may well be intended and used as a factual statement, but given the fact that it may imply a value judgement, it may also be interpreted as an opinion, and hence as an accusation. Even obvious descriptive terms, such as woman or child, may thus in some contexts be intended or understood as implying a positive or negative value judgement, and hence as the expression of an opinion instead of a factual belief.

This analysis shows something else, namely, the ideological basis of the core of much (social) knowledge, such as the very concepts that define such knowledge. Indeed, if 'racism' has the broad conceptual meaning it has for anti-racists, others may think exclusively of aggressive, extremist, right-wing racism, or only about explicit racist ideologies, when using this term. That is, as soon as part of a concept, when applied to our people, is seen to be inconsistent with our interests, people also adapt their knowledge and the language used on the basis of it. Similarly, most feminists will probably tend to define 'sexual harassment' in broad terms, whereas many men (and some women) may find this exaggerated and would accept only overt, blatant and very aggressive forms of sexual violence in such terms. In other words, each group may also have its own concepts and language use, and these would be ideological as soon as dimensions are added to, or deleted from, the concept so as to accommodate the interests of the group.

In sum, one way in which ideologies control knowledge is the way they monitor conceptual structures and hence word meanings. The question then becomes: who should define such concepts and meanings? This question brings us to the relations between knowledge and power.

Knowledge and power

An analysis of the role of ideology in the study of knowledge not only involves an abstract epistemology or cognitive science, but also many social dimensions that have to do with the establishment of truth, truth criteria and what counts as knowledge in society.[5] Power is one of these dimensions. Let us therefore examine whether such a perspective may resolve the dilemma between the thesis that says that at least some knowledge is ideologically based and the thesis that claims that all ideologically based knowledge should be called opinion, so that knowledge by definition is non-ideological.

There are several ways to tackle this issue. The first is to change the definition of knowledge. Instead of saying that knowledge is 'justified true belief', we may say that knowledge for a given culture or society can never be more than 'justified belief', whether or not it is objectively true, or whether or not knowledgeable others now or later think it is true or false. That is, the combined pragmatic-semantic definition is thus reduced to a pure pragmatic one, which in fact claims that knowledge is based on the power of the consensus, that is, on the kind of truth criteria accepted within the epistemic community. Thus, for the Dutch community, the dominant consensus is that the Netherlands is not a racist country, and that those who claim otherwise are not expressing knowledge, but an ideological or otherwise misguided opinion.

This solution is also in line with discourse analytical, microsociological and ethnographic thinking, which emphasizes the role of knowledge as being generally presupposed and taken for granted within a society or culture. It also is consistent with a historical and political approach, which would claim that what counts as knowledge in any period or community is determined by who has the definitional or other truth-determining power in society, such as public opinion, the church, the media or science. This argument will also correctly predict that if specific minorities, dissidents or individuals express beliefs they hold (and even prove) to be true, these will either not be believed, or their knowledge will be disqualified as mere opinion, or they will be prevented from expressing their beliefs in the first place. Of course, it may well be that such 'deviants' later may prove to have been right, and hence (from an outside point of view) to have expressed knowledge, but that does not mean that they were right for the epistemic community.

Given this power over the definition of truth and knowledge, one may claim that such a consensus is itself ideological while being in the interest of the community as a whole. But such a position would be inconsistent with the specific definition defended here – ideologies are defined for groups and presuppose different (and often conflicting) group interests *within* the same community. Of course, if we were to see a whole community (culture, society) as such a group, this would constitute the boundary case of what I define as an ideological group (see Part II), and indeed the ultimate form of ideology, namely, that of the consensus, and a culmination of hegemony if such a consensus could be established by the elites. The interests defended in that case are indeed those of the community as a whole, and defended against any deviant individual or subgroup. Although such a position may be defended, it would in fact collapse the notion of ideology with that of societal norms or culture, and it would mean that we are unable to use it in a more specific inter-group sense.

So, if we maintain the definition of ideology in terms of interests of different groups within a community, the next question is whether we allow the definition of knowledge to be group-dependent as well. That is, not only within the community as a whole, but also within its various ideological groups, knowledge would then be defined as justified belief, whether or not it is true, or whether or not other groups or 'independent' truth instances would qualify such beliefs as opinions. Again, such a position would correctly predict the use of the notion of knowledge within groups, as long as it can be justified with the truth criteria accepted within that group.

Obviously, much of the general socio-cultural knowledge holding within the group may be shared with other groups, and the same may be true for most truth criteria. But especially the beliefs and truth criteria that are related to the interests of the group, or the special issues that are relevant for the group, might well be specific, and hence ideologically based – again, whether or not they are 'objectively' true or false. Thus, the specific knowledge of women about sexual harassment, of feminists about gender inequality, of anti-racists about racism, or of ecologists about pollution, constitute relevant examples.[6] Again, in these cases such knowledge may well be objectively true (given an independent truth instance), but it may be rejected as opinions, lies, or fantasies by those who oppose such groups.

Conversely, their opponents may firmly believe – and never see as mere opinion – things about gender, immigrants or pollution that are objectively false. That is, what counts is what the group members believe and what, within their own system of verification, they believe to be justified – whether or not such truth criteria are themselves biased. A typical example is knowledge about ethnic relations. Dominant majority group members may feel that any knowledge and epistemic criteria in this case as defined by minority groups will be biased. This is, for instance, the case for those (many) white journalists who do not take minority sources and their statements seriously. In other words, the basis of credibility judgements themselves may be partisan, and hence ideological. This also explains why specific group knowledge of one group will often be rejected as mere opinions by opposing groups. Indeed, very often the very ideological conflict itself may not only be about socio-economic conditions or resources, but about truth criteria themselves.

Since many ideologies are constituted by fundamental opinions about Us and Them, we must assume that not only the basis of attitudes are evaluative beliefs, but also those of specific group knowledge. That is, although within the ideological group, knowledge is still distinct from opinion, the knowledge criteria themselves are self-serving and value-oriented. For instance, such criteria may involve (value) judgements about who is a reliable source, what is relevant information, what perceptions can be trusted, or what data can be depended on. Thus, Christians may admit God as one of the instances of truth, and anti-racists the everyday experiences of minorities in a racist society.

Concluding remark

Concluding this succinct discussion of the role of knowledge and truth in a theory of ideology, we thus find again that ideologies in general monitor group attitudes – that is, evaluative beliefs – but that also specific factual beliefs may be defined as knowledge within the group. That is, ideologies essentially control group specific *judgements* about what is good and bad, and also about what is true or false *for us*.[7] This may also include parts of the meanings of specific concepts (such as 'racism'). This does *not* mean that, from an independent point of view, *all* group knowledge is ideological, since each group obviously shares knowledge with other groups. Nor does it mean that all truth criteria are ideological, since each group must be able to argue in such a way (using general truth criteria) that others can be persuaded of their position.

Ideological knowledge control, however, does consist in selecting concepts and truth criteria that may be specific to a group, and may involve attributing special credibility to specific truth instances, such as God, Science, the Party or the Union. This also means that again within the group itself such partisan knowledge is not found to be 'ideological' (and hence misguided) at all, but knowledge like any other kind of knowledge. But since group values, principles and other basic beliefs are involved that reflect the interest of the group, our (outside) description of course would generally take such knowledge and its truth criteria to be ideological, as defined.

12

Identity

What is identity?

Ideologies consist of a fundamental schema of which the first category defines the membership criteria of a group. Together with the contents of the other categories, such criteria define the social identity of a group. This means that whenever a group has developed an ideology, such an ideology at the same time also defines the basis for the group's identity. The question is what this implies exactly. Does it mean that group members can only be considered group members, and hence partake in a group's ideology when they actually identify themselves as group members? What exactly 'is' such an identity, and the process of 'identification' in the first place?

Again, my approach to such questions is socio-cognitive: identity is both a personal and a social construct, that is, a mental representation. I briefly discuss this element in the theory of ideology precisely because it may be situated at the boundaries of a theory of social identity, a theory of social cognition and a sociological theory of group membership.[1]

In their representation of self, people construct themselves as being a member of several categories and groups (women, ethnic minorities, US citizens, journalists, environmentalists, etc.). This self-representation (or self-schema) is located in episodic (personal) memory. It is a gradually constructed abstraction from personal experiences (models) of events.[2]

Since such models usually feature representations of social interaction, as well as interpretations of discourse, both experiences and their inferred self-representations are at the same time socially (and jointly) constructed. Part of our self-representation is inferred from the ways others (other group members, members of other groups) see, define and treat us. When experiences are shared with others, abstracted personal experiences, and hence self, may partly merge with the self-representation of the group. A feminist may thus feel herself to be a feminist in more or less the same way as other feminists do, and, in that respect, self of an individual feminist may be partly constructed with the elements of the socially shared self-schema of feminists as a group. The more the feminist construction of self corresponds to the socially communicated and shared group schema, the more an individual woman will 'identify' with feminism.

This does not mean, of course, that such a weak or strong group identification needs to be dominant in specific events and situations. A feminist journalist, when gathering or writing news stories, may well primarily identify as a journalist (and hence adopt ideologically based journalistic attitudes, including the opinions and models derived from those) and only secondarily as a feminist, and the converse will be true if that same woman participates in feminist action.

In other words, group identities may be more or less abstract and context-free, in the same way as all social representations are. Similarly, social members may share in several social identities that are more or less stable across personal contexts, and thus defining a personal self, but in concrete situations some of these identities may become more salient than others. Thus, in each situation, the salience, hierarchy or relevance of group identification will monitor the actual social practices (e.g. the action priorities or 'motivation') of social actors. Unless we admit a theoretically doubtful notion such as 'situational identity', thus, we should distinguish between relatively context-free personal identity (which may be a composition of various social identities) or personal self, on the one hand, and the actual, situated practices of social actors that may be seen as manifestations of (some aspects of) personal identity.

People may 'objectively' be members of groups (and be seen by others as group members) and still not identify with their groups. Such well-known forms of dissociation, which most dramatically may occur for inherent-identity groups (young, old, men, women, whites, blacks, etc.), but also for professional groups, probably implies that such 'members' do not share the ideology of the group either. Indeed, they may, for a number of reasons, rather identify with opposed groups and their goals and values. Derogative words such as 'traitor', 'renegade', 'dissident', 'Uncle Tom' and so forth show what kind of reactions and sanctions group members may face when denying or leaving their own group. It also explains why anti-racists are sometimes considered to be more of a problem in white society than racists – they share the ideology of the others that 'our' society is racist, and thus threaten the positive self-definition of 'us' as the dominant group (see Chapter 28). Treason is, either literally or at least symbolically, a capital offence for many groups, as is the case for sedition, defection, and becoming an 'infidel'. Conversely, strong identification and co-operation will usually be positively valued in terms of solidarity, allegiance and fidelity. All this applies not only to social practices, but also to ideologies and the forms of 'mental' solidarity with groups represented in self-representations that may be assumed to be at the basis of such social practices.

Personal and group identity

These arguments suggest first that we need to distinguish between social or group identity and personal identity. The latter takes the two forms informally described above: (1) a mental representation as (personal) self as a unique human being with its own, personal experiences and biography – as

represented in accumulated mental models, and the abstract self-concept
derived from it, often in interaction with others; and (2) a mental representation of (social) self as a collection of group memberships, and the identification processes that are related to such membership representations. These
identification processes may be assumed to depend on a comparison between
personal and social self. If the membership criteria, activities, goals, norms,
values, position or resources of the group are in line with (at least consistent
with) those of the personal self construct, identification may be more or less
strong. If not, a process of dissociation may take place, including association
with other groups.

For a theory of ideology, this of course has implications for the ways
individuals identify with group ideologies and attitudes. When membership
is largely ideological (as for political parties, Churches, etc.), such ideological dissent usually implies leaving the group altogether when one's dissent-
ing opinions are inconsistent with those of the group as a whole. For
professional ideologies this is much more difficult because they are closely
related to goals and interests of everyday professional practices. It is difficult
to 'be' a professor and at the same time not 'feel' like one, and if professional ideologies represent the aims, values, norms and social resources
of the professional group members, ideological dissociation is seldom in
one's personal interest. Of course, there may be other considerations, other
ideologies and values, which may be accepted as more valid, despite one's
group membership. Thus, occasionally professors may espouse student
ideologies.

Ideology as group identity?

All these processes account for personal variation and the complexity of the
manifestations of group ideologies in everyday life. However, it should be
recalled again that ideologies are essentially shared and hence need to
be defined at group level. The same is true for the social or collective
'identity' of the group as a group. Usually, identity is taken in an individualistic fashion, in terms of representations and identification processes of
group members. However, in the same way as groups may be said to
share knowledge, attitudes and an ideology, we may assume that they share
a social representation that defines their identity or 'social self' as a
group.[3]

My attempt to bring some clarity to the multitude of notions related to the
field of ideology suggests that, at least at the cognitive level of description,
social (group) identity probably collapses with a *group self-schema*. And
since I have taken such a schema as the most likely candidate for the format
of a group ideology, we need to conclude that group identity collapses with
group *ideology*.[4] Given the way I have analysed social ideologies, this is not
entirely improbable, since the relevant categories precisely define what
'identifies' the group, especially also in relation to other groups. That is, the

ideological group self-schema should represent precisely those fundamental beliefs that are generally shared (acquired, used, reproduced) at the group level, and answer such fundamental questions such as 'Who are we?', 'Where do we come from?', 'Who belongs to us?', 'What do we (usually) do, and why?', 'What are our goals and values?', and so on.[5] The theoretical (general, ideological) answers to such questions are therefore continuously taught and repeated in social encounters, symbolic interaction, and other group activities. It is this that is inculcated, sometimes explicitly (in didactic situations or in times of crisis), and often implicitly, in the many group-relevant social practices of the group, its institutions and its members.

On the other hand, there are a number of arguments that plead against equating group identity with ideology. Thus, if the cognitive dimension of group identity is defined in terms of the specific social representations shared by the group, the notion of group identity is more inclusive than that of ideology. After all, ideology was more strictly defined as the 'axiomatic' basis of the shared social representations of a group. That means that ideologies form at most the basis of group identity, that is, the fundamental propositions that pertain to more or less stable evaluations about 'our' group's membership criteria, activities, goals, norms and values, social resources and especially our position in society and the relations with special other groups.

Just like personal identity, social identities may change. Whereas some basic (ideological) principles may remain more or less identical over a relatively long period of time, the more specific social representations, such as attitudes, may adapt strategically to social and political change. Thus, although the peace movement might of course keep its basic pacifist ideological principles, specific attitudes about different forms of disarmament, the deployment of nuclear arms, and other issues may depend more directly on the political situation, including the changing attitudes of opponents, or the realization of one's major goals.[6]

Such changes of group attitudes more generally pose the question about the nature of social identity. If social identity is defined in terms of shared social representations, and if these may continually change, also the very notion of identity should be more a dynamic than a static notion. But if social group identity is in turn a crucial defining property of social movements and other groups in the first place, then the very notions of movement and group need to be much more dynamic. As we shall see in more detail in our discussion about groups, in Chapter 15, this would mean that a group is not merely a more or less stable collectivity of people, but also or rather defined in terms of a permanently changing set of cognitions and their concomitant practices. Identity then becomes a *process* in which such a collectivity is engaged, rather than a property. For that reason the term *identification* would probably be more satisfactory than the more static term 'identity'. Just like persons, groups may thus be permanently engaged in a 'search' for their identity, as a function of social structures as well as changes.

Social identity as collective 'feeling'?

Social identity is often associated also with more *affective* or *emotional* dimensions. Although these concepts open the well-known Pandora-box of emotion theory, and raise the old question whether emotions are (also) cognitive and not (merely) physiologically based, we should not run away from such theoretical problems. The point is that if emotions necessarily have a physiological basis, they need to be strictly personal, since groups obviously have no bodies. But, similarly, groups have no minds, and we still speak about socially shared mental representations. Thus, what does it mean that group members may share 'emotions' as distinct from sharing (strong) evaluative beliefs?

If emotions are (also) defined in terms of bodily arousal of some kind, then a 'shared' emotion would imply that group members would be constantly aroused. Thus, if feminists are 'angry' about male chauvinism, does that mean that all individual women who identify themselves as feminists constantly 'feel' angry. Of course not. However, individual feminists may be (more) likely to become angry at specific moments of expressions of male chauvinism. But *that* is not the same as saying that feminists as a group (permanently) 'share anger', in the strict sense of an emotion.

Rather, I would suggest, such an expression does not denote emotion at all, but strong negative beliefs. Indeed, while holding such strong negative beliefs, some feminists may never actually feel angry about social inequality of the *group*, although again they may become angry about personal experiences of such inequality. The same is true, more generally, for *feelings* of social identification. One may 'feel' strongly about one's membership of a group, but again such a 'feeling', I propose, is a set of evaluative social representations (e.g. attitudes about equal pay, abortion, etc. for feminists), rather than an ongoing emotion shared by all or most members of the group.

In other words, the frequently observed emotional attachment of members to a social group may not be, as such, an alternative to the cognitive definition of group membership given above. This does not mean that individual group members may not tend to be (more) emotional in their personal (but group-related experiences). However, it does mean that such emotions, as such, cannot be actually 'shared'. They may be known, respected, talked about, and in that way they are 'shared'. But there is no such thing, it appears, as a 'collective emotion' of a more or less permanent nature. This again does not mean that, at a specific moment, a collectivity of people may not have more or less the same emotion, for instance when demonstrators are angry during a demonstration. But that is not the same thing as a shared, collective feeling of a group, a feeling that exists also beyond such specific 'emotional' moments.

Other means of social identification

However, unlike ideologies, social identities need not, as such, be limited to the cognitive realm. Group identity may also be defined, at least partly, in terms the characteristic social practices of group members, including collective action. Indeed, members of a social movement might identify as much with the 'ideas' shared by the group, as with such typical group activities as demonstrations, strikes, meetings or rituals. Initiation rituals may indeed be a major criterion of group membership and hence of (feelings of) identification. The same is true for group-identifying symbols, such as uniforms, flags, badges and many others. Again, theoretically one might see both social practices and these symbols as expressions or manifestations of a more abstract, 'underlying' group identity, as we have done for ideologies.

However, the personal and social processes of identification and sharing are not limited to such abstract, cognitive representations. In order to avoid reduction of group identity to specific actions or ad hoc symbols, we might require that the practices and symbols involved should also have a more permanent, general or routine nature. Indeed, uniforms and flags typically have a more permanent character. And group identification with, for example, demonstrations seems more likely when such demonstrations are more or less characteristic of the group, and not when they occur just once or twice. An apparent exception to this rule are prominent historical events that contribute to group identity, such as the Russian Revolution for communists or the March to Washington for the civil rights movement. Thus, also many nationalist movements tend to search for famous historical events, historical figures, monuments, places as symbols of group identity. Precisely given their historical nature, they have become preserved as parts of collective memory, and hence again qualify as a criterion for identification.[7]

These well-known examples suggest again that group identity does not seem to be limited to shared mental representations, but involves a complex array of typical or routine practices, collective action, dress, objects, settings, buildings (like churches), monuments, prominent historical events, heroes and heroines and other symbols. At the same time, a more cognitive approach would in that case emphasize that it is not so much the symbolic actions and objects themselves that are criteria for identification, as rather their collective social construction, that is, again some form of shared representation. It is not the material form or substance of the cross that defines Christian identity, but the complex, interpreted 'story' that the cross symbolizes and that Christians share. In other words, where group activities may suggest that identification is based on collective action or relevant objects, further analysis suggests that precisely the 'symbolic' nature of such phenomena requires at least also a cognitive analysis in terms of the socially shared interpretations assigned to such collective actions and symbolic objects.

This conclusion does not imply that all criteria of social identification are 'merely' mental. Apart from the actual social discourses and other practices in which group members may engage, as well as objects, settings and other properties of collective events, also various kinds of *social structure and organization* may be involved in identification. Thus group identity may also depend on official membership activities, such as asking and paying fees, electing officials and leaders, institutionalizing a movement, and so on. We shall deal with these (more) social dimensions of groups in Chapter 15, but it should be emphasized here that the cognitive dimensions of 'feeling' that one is a group member, as well as the shared processes of group identification, may also be related to social practices, organization and institutionalization. Indeed, you may really feel you are a member as soon as you get your membership card. Not surprisingly, one lexical manifestation of the relation between group identity, ideology and institutionalized membership is obvious in such expressions as whether people are 'card-carrying' members of a movement or not.

There is one major problem when we extend the notion of social identity towards the vast world of social practices, symbols and organization – it would make the notion of identity as comprehensive and vague as that of *culture*. In that case, social identity might even collapse with that of group-culture. That is, in the same ways as members of a larger national or ethnic culture would identify with their culture, a similar process would exist for social groups. Since the notion of social identity has no fixed meaning, we might simply adopt such a broad definition, but somehow we seem to be overextending the notion in this way. We would probably also hesitate to extend the notion of personal identity to all actions, dress, personal objects, and so on, of a person, although also here, it would simply depend on whether one opts for a broader or a more specific view of identity. Characteristic actions, ways of speaking or dress could of course be taken to define a person's identity.

The conclusion from this discussion should be that, as is the case for ideology, social identity is a very fuzzy notion, and it simply depends on the theorist whether a strict or broad perspective is taken. I tend to opt for the stricter and more precise definition. That is, in the same way as we distinguish between ideologies as such, on the one hand, and the many manifestations of ideology in discourse, interaction and ideological symbols, on the other, we may thus restrict social identity as such to a shared core of social self-definition, that is, to a set of social representations that members consider typical for their group. The social practices, symbols, settings or forms of organization that are typical for a group and with which members identify, would in that case be the *contextually variable manifestations of social identity*. In line with the subjective nature of 'feelings of belonging' or 'commitment' with respect to a group, such a socio-cognitive definition would also explain that it is not so much a social practice, symbol, setting or organization itself that is part of a social identity, but rather their meaning or interpretation for the group.[8]

This definition of social identity as a socially shared mental construct also allows for individual variations of interpretation, historical changes in the meaning of the 'external' manifestations of social identity, as well as for processes of socialization of members at the individual level and group formation at the social level. Indeed, different groups may be associated with the same type of social activities, objects, symbols, settings or organization forms, but attach totally different meanings (social representations) to them, and thus construct a different kind of social identity. In that sense, social identity is as intersubjective as personal identity is a subjective construction, although both constructs are obviously also a function of social interaction and negotiation, and of the attribution of identity by other people and other groups, respectively.

Finally, this socio-cognitive approach to the analysis of social identity also allows a systematic relationship with the role of *discourse* in the construction of social identity.[9] An important part of the formation and reproduction of social groups may indeed have a discursive nature. Social groups in general, and social movements in particular, are constituted by various forms of *intragroup discourse*, such as meetings, teaching, calls for solidarity, and other discourses that define the ongoing activities, the reproduction, and the unity of the group. On the other hand, social group identity is especially also construed by *intergroup discourse* in which groups and their members engage for reasons of self-presentation, self-defence, legitimation, persuasion, recruiting, and so on. Although it was suggested above that I prefer to distinguish between social identity itself and the social practices, including discourse, based on such an identity, it is obvious that group discourse is a rich source for the analysis of 'underlying' social identities.

13

Social Cognition

The relevance of social cognition

Having completed the first part of the theoretical framework for the study of ideology, let me take stock of the relevance of the cognitive component in such a theory, and then discuss some open problems and further prospects.

The main arguments that have given rise to a cognitive component have been the following:

1   Whatever else ideologies are, or whatever social conditions and functions they have, they are first of all systems of beliefs. The nature of these belief systems, as well as their relations with other mental objects and processes, (also) need to be studied in a cognitive framework.
2   Ignoring such cognitive dimensions of ideologies, and merely analysing them in terms of social practices, social formations, or social structures, provides incomplete insight into ideologies, and constitutes an improper reduction of complex social phenomena, and hence an inadequate theory.
3   Ideologies are socially acquired, shared, used and changed by group members, and hence are a special type of socially shared mental representations.
4   Ideologies are reproduced through their everyday uses by social members in the accomplishment of social practices in general, and of discourse in particular. Such uses not only have social foundations but also cognitive ones, such as the personal experiences, knowledge and opinions of social members. In order to relate the social dimension of ideologies with their personal uses, only a cognitive theory is able to provide the necessary interface.

Beyond 'belief systems'

We have seen that ideologies are not just any set or system of ideas or beliefs, because in that case they would simply coincide with cognition in general. Nor should ideologies be reduced to the social knowledge, attitudes or 'worldviews' individual people have. Rather, ideologies form the 'axiomatic' *basis* of the shared social representations of a group and its members. That is, they are *both* mental *and* social phenomena.

It is this integrated socio-cognitive aspect of ideologies that is the core of the theory presented in this book. Though traditionally associated with mental notions such as 'ideas', 'beliefs', 'consciousness', 'common sense' and related notions, these mental dimensions of ideologies have rarely been analysed in any detail in most philosophical and sociological studies of ideology. Similarly, the psychological work on ideologies has paid attention to 'belief systems', but these were hardly analysed as such, but rather used as an independent or dependent variable in the explanation of social or political 'behaviour'. The same is true for socio-historical studies about the ideas or ideologies of specific groups or periods, although such studies obviously provide an interesting empirical basis for further analysis of underlying ideological systems.

In this framework, a cognitive analysis first establishes the nature of the theoretical components of ideologies, namely, specific beliefs. Theoretically, such beliefs are traditionally represented as propositions, although other formats might be envisaged as long as they are able to account for the general and abstract nature of ideologies.

That ideologies are not merely the 'beliefs' of a group may also be concluded from the following list of different kinds of beliefs people may have:

1 knowledge (factual beliefs) of individual persons about particulars (people, objects, events, etc.)
2 knowledge of individual persons about categories or classes of particulars and their properties
3 opinions (evaluative beliefs) of individual persons about particulars (people, objects, events, etc.)
4 opinions of individual persons about categories or classes of particulars and their properties
5 knowledge of social groups about particulars (people, objects, events, etc.)
6 knowledge of social groups about categories or classes of particulars and their properties
7 opinions of social groups about particulars (people, objects, events, etc.)
8 opinions of social groups about categories or classes of particulars and their properties
9 social beliefs of a whole culture (cultural common ground)
10 norms, values and truth criteria as the basis of the cultural common ground.

Ideologies as social representations

Against the background of a critique of traditional approaches to ideology, it was first decided to limit ideologies to *socially shared representations* of a *general* and *abstract* kind. That is, ideologies are of the same family as socially shared knowledge and social attitudes. Ideologies are not individual and not represented like specific, episodic memories, or as personal opinions. This is also why the comparison between ideology and language (or grammar) is so instructive. Both are abstract social systems shared by groups and used to accomplish everyday social practices, namely acting and communicating, respectively.

This group-based nature of ideologies and the social beliefs they control explains how and why social attitudes may be organized as coherently structured sets of group opinions. Since we typically may disagree about opinions and different groups may have different or conflicting goals or interests, it is not surprising that the ideologies that underlie such opinions are associated with groups.

For other social beliefs, such as knowledge, this appeared to be less straightforward, simply because knowledge that is associated with a group is often described as a partisan opinion. For that reason, we distinguished between general, taken for granted, consensual knowledge of a culture, on the one hand, and the factual beliefs of a group, on the other hand. These beliefs group members (with their own truth criteria) may call knowledge, but others may see them as 'mere' beliefs or opinions. It is this specific group 'knowledge' that is controlled by group ideologies. In other words, knowledge is always by definition relative, that is, described as 'true' relative to a group or to a whole culture, according to the truth criteria of that group or culture.

Since ideologies represent the 'axioms' of social group beliefs they are relatively permanent. Even less than attitudes and group knowledge, and certainly less than personal beliefs, they do not change overnight. Given their position in the system, their change would involve the change of a vast part of the social representations of most members of a social group, and such a change usually takes a lot of time.

The structure of ideologies

Once ideologies are defined as the foundation of group representations, we need to examine their internal structures. What kind of abstract social beliefs are involved here, and how are these organized? As everywhere in the cognitive system, effective processing and uses in social practices requires organization, for instance by abstract schemata consisting of a number of categories. That is, if people have to learn, use and eventually change many ideologies in their lives, at least as many as the groups they belong to, then it is likely that they acquire and use a special ideological schema to do so.

Since no such schema is available from other domains of cognition, I provisionally proposed a schema featuring categories that would represent the essential social dimensions of a group, namely, membership, activities, goals, values, relations to other groups and resources. This tentative schema should be used to represent the fundamental opinions group members have about themselves, as well as about their position in society. In other words, a group self-schema is the core of all ideologies. Thus, racism as an ideology is first about who We (white people, Europeans, etc.) are, what we look like, where we come from, what we stand for, what our values and resources are, that is, what our interests are, and how they relate to those of a specific other group, namely, non-whites.

The familiar polarized nature of the expression of ideologies, as Us and Them, reflects the position (or group relations) category of such an underlying structure. This schema also explains the essential group-based, and self-serving nature of many ideologies, as representing not only the interests of a group, but also its social position and perspective on any social issue that is relevant for it. This relevance is again measured in relation to the fundamental beliefs of each category, such as membership, goals or resources. Any social event or arrangement that may be at odds with these essential group interests will thus be judged negatively, and such negative judgements are used as the basis for negative social action, such as discrimination.

From social representations to personal models

Finally, precisely in order to be able to relate such abstract and fundamental forms of social cognition to the particularities and realities of situated action and discourse, another interface is necessary to translate and connect social opinions with the personal ones of individual social actors. After all, although ideologies as such are social and shared, they are actually *used* and reproduced by individual group members and in specific social practices. Therefore, the important notion of a mental model was used to act as this interface between the social and the personal. Models represent specific events and actions, and hence account for unique experiences in specific contexts, but at the same time they embody instantiated ('applied') versions of social knowledge and opinions as they are derived from knowledge and attitudes. That is, via the more specific social opinions of attitudes (e.g. about affirmative action), individual group members may form their own personal opinions, as represented in models, about concrete instances of affirmative action, and act upon (speak about) such opinions. Various kinds of model form the basis of action, text and talk, and thus provide the interface that allows ideologies to be expressed and reproduced.

With this, admittedly still sketchy, framework we at least have a coherent theoretical 'chain' that links social structures, including groups and group relations (e.g. of domination), via ideologies to other social representations, and the latter again with models, which finally provide the missing link with discourse and action. And conversely, we now have the means to describe and explain how ideologies – and social relations – may be produced by discourse and interaction and their cognitive consequences.

Relevance of the theoretical framework

The framework also allows us a somewhat more explicit discussion of a number of classical issues in the philosophy of ideology, such as the truth–falsity debate, or whether a critical concept of ideology should be restricted to ideologies of domination. I have provisionally answered both questions negatively: ideologies are not primarily about what is true or false, but about how people represent their beliefs about themselves and about the social world, truthfully or not. The criterion is not truth but relevance (self-serving social functions, interests). In other words, and somewhat loosely, we may say that we need a pragmatics of use of ideology rather than a semantics of truth. The same is true for the restriction to the use of ideologies to reproduce power abuse and domination.

Obviously, ideologies are often developed and used to sustain and legitimate domination, and such uses invite critical analysis. But the interesting and theoretically much more attractive thing to do is to match domination with resistance, and ideologies with counter-ideologies, for example sexism with feminism, racism with anti-racism. I have argued that there is no good theoretical reason why the second parts of these pairs should not also be ideologies. That may require some conceptual adjustment with respect to the traditional notion of ideology, but it surely is a more adequate approach, while at the same time not blunting the critical dimensions of the traditional (Marxist, neo-Marxist) approaches.

In sum, adding a powerful cognitive dimension to the philosophical and sociological tradition, and relating both to a more concrete discourse analytical approach, allows us to design an analytical framework that one day may lead to a proper 'theory' of ideology. This will allow us to both describe and explain in detail how *exactly* members of specific groups speak, write and act ideologically. Instead of the more global, macro approaches to ideologies in terms of belief systems, hegemony or social formations, this approach spells out the structures, the everyday uses, the cognitive and social functions, the acquisition and the changes of ideologies within such a broader societal context.

Other approaches

Interestingly, precisely also in the social and critical approaches to discourse and ideology, ideologies have been rife.[1] Instead of self-critically examining which theories, concepts and methods are most adequate and effective, the dominant ideology in the study of ideology says that cognitive science is at the wrong (scientistic, positivistic) side of the fence. Linguistics, at least among linguists who have become critical analysts of ideology, is more acceptable, if only as a useful instrument, or because the social dimensions of language can be emphasized. But among the philosophers and sociologists, both were irrelevant or suspect, or simply unknown or ignored.

Those who are justly opposing the limitations of much contemporary psychology, have thrown out the cognitive child with the bath water, although, just like discourse and language, cognition or mental representations can be as 'social' as any concept in the social sciences.

The price that has been paid for this ignorance or ideological exclusion is that analysis of the way social group members actually go about talking or acting ideologically has been reduced to an account that fails to link social structures with cognitive structures and again with discourse structures. Apart from the misguided accusation of individualism, cognitive approaches are also rejected because of the thesis that these are mentalist, and hence opposed to the 'materialism' required in the (Neo)Marxist paradigm, or the 'interactionism' that governs much current work in ethnomethodology or discursive 'psychology'.

In interactionism, the mind is either seen as a figment of the dualist (mind versus body) imagination, or as irrelevant because what counts, socially, for social members, is what is 'observably' being displayed. This neo-behaviourist misconception is hardly much more sophisticated than the old version of behaviourism that has marred psychology and the social sciences for decades. Yet, at the same time, obviously mental concepts for hardly observable things like meanings, understanding, rules, and so on, keep appearing, unanalysed, in such interactionist approaches, as if 'displays' of meanings or understandings are more observable than these meanings or understandings themselves. Yes, in common sense they are, and as such are used as evidence ('I have seen this myself', 'I have heard this myself'), simply because the socially shared concepts that govern perception are taken for granted in commonsense observation. But, if common sense should be used as evidence, then we should *also* use the commonsense acceptance of the obvious presence of meanings, intentions, knowledge and opinions as properties that people 'have in mind'.

And why discourse expressions, action, social practices, social or economic conditions, interest or power are more 'materialist' than meanings and understanding, has been accepted by fiat instead of by investigation. Any adequate epistemology will tell us that *all* these things are both socially and mentally constructed – actions or discourses cannot be observed any more, and are no more material, than meanings, knowledge, opinions, values or ideologies. No interactionist or materialist discourse analyst or sociologist goes down to the level of physical or biological body movements to describe social action. Given the concepts and knowledge of our culture, social actions are themselves conceptual constructs paired with these physical observables of the movement of body and mouth. Their understanding by group members is no more immediate than 'underlying' meanings, as frequent observations of ambiguity or vagueness of discourse or action also show.

That is, *both* the social and the cognitive notions are abstract constructs of everyday understanding, action and mind, as well as of their non-naive theories. None of them is more or less 'material', 'observable' or otherwise more relevant because being socially 'displayed'. Understanding what people 'observably' do or say, is *also* an interpretation of both lay participants and scholars. That such interpretations are being acquired, used, changed, negotiated in social situations and in social interactions, is obvious (and a good reason to criticize psychologists who in turn ignore *that* dimension), but does not mean that therefore cognition is irrelevant.

On the contrary, all these interpretations and the knowledge and opinions on which they are based, are themselves both mental and social, depending on the scope or the level of theory and analysis. Discourse is the most obvious example in point, while obviously involving mental representations (meanings, knowledge, abstract structures at many levels), and at the same time being a form of social, political or cultural action. In sum, social and cognitive analyses of discourse and ideology that mutually ignore each other are doomed to produce incomplete, reductive or plainly misguided theories and analyses.

This conclusion does not imply that we should blindly accept all theories, methods or philosophies of contemporary cognitive psychology and cognitive science, nor the mainstream orientation in cognitively inspired social cognition research in social psychology. Overall, this research has been justly criticized for its fundamental lack of accounting for the social dimensions of the mind, its individualism and its mentalist reduction.[2] Similarly, mainstream social psychology has ignored the fundamental role of discourse in the construction of the social mind. On the other hand, from a theoretical point of view, both social cognition research as well as research on social representations may be criticized for the simplicity and the vagueness of their analysis of mental structures and processes. And finally, virtually all psychology (except the study of political cognition) has ignored the fundamental role of ideology in the control of social representations and social interaction.

Open problems

Of course, also the framework presented here is hardly complete. The schema designed to represent ideological structures is very tentative, and I am not sure it allows representation of all types of ideologies, especially those (like environmentalism) which seem to focus more on nature than on groups, or vast ones, such as communism or religious systems, which have the whole world as their scope. Also, the schema may be too simplistic. Complex sets of ideological beliefs may need more structure than that of a simple schema, although the routine application of ideological principles in everyday life probably does not allow a very complex structure either.

Next, it was assumed that ideologies organize and monitor more specific group knowledge and attitudes. But we have only the faintest idea how that happens (or how, conversely, ideologies are derived from specific social beliefs). The lack of sophisticated theories for the structures of social representations in general, especially also of attitudes, is another problem. Much empirical work on concrete expressions of ideologies in discourse may be necessary to reconstruct such 'underlying' social representations.

Many of these problems are related to our fragmentary knowledge about the organization, the contents and the processing of social beliefs in general. Some of these traditional problems, such as those that pitch stability and continuity of attitudes or ideologies against often-observed variation, contradictions and dilemmas, have in my opinion been theoretically resolved with the introduction of event and context models in episodic memory. These models also explain the classical cleft between the macro and the micro, the social and the personal, and provide the interface between ideologies and social practices. I consider this element in a general theory of ideology as crucial and as one of the major new ideas this study would like to propose.

Other problems remain, however. Some of these can be resolved by empirical work, not only in the laboratory, but especially also by detailed analyses of manifestations of ideologies in discourse and social practices. However, it is unlikely that problems of mental structure and organization can simply be solved by more or better observation. At present there is little hope that neurological (brain) research will soon deliver the underlying building blocks that will explain the internal organization of social representations. This means that we need to satisfy ourselves with the more abstract, higher-level analysis in terms of cognition.

As is the case for all 'non-observables', theoretical cognitive modelling is the crucial answer, and will allow us to find more elegant ways to account for the 'data' (discourse, social action, social organization, social processes, etc.) at hand. Notions such as 'models', 'scripts', 'schemata' and 'social representation' precisely are the result of such theoretical endeavours. The same is true for my attempt to devise a more detailed theoretical concept of ideology as the basic framework of social representations.

Besides the fundamental problems of mental architecture and organization, a socio-cognitive theory of ideology needs to account for actual acquisition, uses and change. A major role in such a theory is again played by mental models that serve as the interface between ideologies and other social representations, on the one hand, and everyday experiences and practices, and especially discourse, on the other hand. That is, models form the missing link of a cognitive theory of the actual acquisition, uses, implementations and changes of ideologies. They explain how social members produce and understand action and discourse and how in turn such processes are linked with socially shared beliefs, and hence with ideologies.

However, we still have limited insight into the ways contextualized personal experiences and practices are being shared, normalized and accepted at the 'aggregate' level of groups. Discourse and (mass) communication again play a fundamental role here, but we should not forget that accounting for discourse production and understanding is a description of what social members do, and not what whole groups do. Sharing beliefs interactively is one thing, but sharing beliefs throughout a group is another, hardly less complex phenomenon, especially if we do not want to reduce such sharing to a mere accumulation of individual learning and interaction.

In order to solve some of the problems mentioned above, we therefore need to take a closer look at the social dimensions of ideologies, and then examine how the combined cognitive and social approach can be validated by detailed discourse analysis.

Part II

SOCIETY

14

Ideology and Society

Relating the cognitive and the social

Whereas the first part of this book has made a strong plea for the incorporation of a cognitive component in a multidisciplinary theory of ideology, no such plea is necessary in this second part for a social approach to ideology. All traditional approaches agree that ideologies are social, if only by their multiple social conditions and functions.[1] Even in my cognitive approach, this social dimension has been emphasized. Ideologies are not merely sets of beliefs, but socially shared beliefs of groups. These beliefs are acquired, used and changed in social situations, and on the basis of the social interests of groups and social relations between groups in complex social structures.

It is the task of this second part to spell out some of these social dimensions of ideologies, and to show *why* social actors and groups develop and use ideologies in the first place. Also, we need to study how ideologies are socially 'invented' and reproduced in society. One crucial component in this process of reproduction is discourse, which we therefore need to study separately in the next part, but which as a form of social interaction is obviously part of the social component of the theory of ideology.

Many traditional and new issues need to be dealt with in this social framework. Besides the expression of ideologies in discursive interaction, we must investigate what kind of *groups* are or may be involved in the development of ideologies. Second, *group relations*, and especially those of power and dominance, and their role in the development of ideologies, must be investigated. The relevance of 'classes' should be assessed as part of such a broader analysis of group relations. Third, the *institutional* and *organizational* dimension of ideologies and their reproduction, such as the role of politics, education and the media, should be part of a social analysis. And finally, at the highest or most abstract level, we should explore the role of *culture* in the development and reproduction of ideologies.

Again, each of these topics would require a monograph by itself, and many of these have already been written. However, my approach is more modest. I shall again presuppose most classical work on the social dimensions of ideologies to be known, and set up this part as an integrated component of a new multidisciplinary framework, which I hope will be detailed in later theoretical and empirical studies. Also, as suggested before, I shall not repeat the classical debates, but only examine whether some of the issues involved will be relevant for my approach or not. For instance, whether ideologies are essentially 'dominant' ideologies or not, is a topic that will be touched upon only briefly: I have already indicated that I advocate a broader concept of ideology.

Organizing the social account of ideology

Ideally, this part of the book might be set up so that we start with the micro-level of ideological interaction and gradually extend our scope to more embracing social structures and processes. However, since we deal with the fundamental, discursive and interactional, dimension of ideological reproduction separately in the next part, this part will generally operate on more abstract meso- and macro-levels of social structure and culture. Instead of beginning with the discursive expression and mundane accomplishment of ideology, this part therefore offers another aspect of the basis and the context for the study of such discourse, as was also the case for the previous part. That is, the study of ideological text and talk will later be framed in a combined cognitive and social account of a theoretical basis that needs to be established first. If we later want to find out what 'social members' or 'group members' do or say in a social context, we first need to examine what ideological membership, groups, group relations, interests, power or dominance mean.

Such a decision is partly arbitrary, and an argument could be construed for a different order of analysis. This way of framing the approach also involves the debate about the micro–macro link that has raged in modern sociology. Obviously, I can't discuss let alone solve all the problems that have been brought up in this debate. However, the cognitive and discursive components offer interfaces that have been lacking in this (missing) link. Indeed, as has been argued before (Chapter 7), the link between groups and individual persons as social actors or group members, as well as the link between socially shared cognitions (including ideologies) and actual social practices of such actors, also has an important cognitive dimension. It is only in their minds that social actors are able to combine their own, unique, personal and contextual constraints on ideological practices, with their socially shared knowledge and opinions about their group membership, about group relations and about social structure.

The society–cognition–discourse link

There can be little doubt, then, that the missing link (also) needs to be cognitive. Without their socially shared beliefs social actors cannot possibly know and interactionally accomplish their group membership, which is a crucial condition for the existence of groups and organizations in the first place. Thus, even in this chapter we should never forget that it is not the group, nor the organization, nor any other abstract societal structure that directly conditions, influences or constrains ideological practices, but the ways social members subjectively represent, understand or interpret them. This not only explains the details of the production of discourse and action, but at the same time allows for the necessary individual variation, deviance, opposition, dissidence and change, also, of ideologies and other social structures.

This does *not* mean that societal structures, groups, power or economic conditions *only* exist in the minds of social actors. It has already been observed that the 'existence' of such social structures is a human construction, and hence a mental as well as a social and practical accomplishment. In commonsense as well as in theoretical accounts, social structures and conditions are also postulated to exist independently of the mind, not so much epistemologically, but simply analytically and sociologically. They represent another realm of existence, and another level and scope of analysis, just as physical, chemical, biochemical, biological, physiological, neurological or cognitive 'realities' exist both as objects of theoretical analysis and as part of people's mundane experiences.

Thus, social structures and processes 'exist' both for all practical purposes and as objects of sociological analysis. They become relevant for interaction and discourse, however, through the cognitive interface of social actors. Thus, racism, racist organizations and racist reporting 'exist' for social actors just as well as their concrete manifestations in everyday racist discourse and actions. Recognizing the fundamental role of cognition, and especially of social cognition in such a multidisciplinary account of ideology, does *not* mean therefore that we 'reduce' the social to the 'cognitive'.

On the contrary, it is theoretically most fruitful to recognize the 'existence' of both, but then to design a theory that *integrates* these different dimensions or levels of social reality. In the same way, then, that I have included a 'social' component in the mind, I now emphasize the important cognitive dimensions of society. Ideologies, just like knowledge, public opinion, languages and values, and other socially shared mental phenomena, may then be studied in a sociological study, even when such a study will focus more on their 'expression' in typical social 'objects' such as action, groups or organizations. After the study of social cognition in the previous part, we thus encounter a cognitive sociology in the present part.[2] The sociology of knowledge is merely one of the subdisciplines within such a framework, of which also the sociology of ideology is an inherent part.

Social functions of ideologies

One of the major tasks of such a sociology of ideology is to explain not only the structures of ideologies as postulated in the previous chapters, but especially also to account for the *functions* of ideologies in society. Virtually no short definition of ideology will fail to mention that ideologies typically serve to legitimate power and inequality. Similarly, ideologies are assumed to conceal, hide or otherwise obfuscate the truth, reality or indeed the 'objective, material conditions of existence' or the interests of social formations.

Besides such more negative functions of ideology, we may add that ideologies positively serve to empower dominated groups, to create solidarity, to organize struggle and to sustain opposition. And both at the negative and the positive side, ideologies serve to protect interests and resources, whether these are unjust privileges, or minimal conditions of existence. More neutrally and more generally, then, ideologies simply serve groups and their members in the organization and management of their goals, social practices and their whole daily social life. All these functions are social, and the concepts involved in their description largely sociological. Indeed, they are essentially conditions for the existence and the reproduction of groups, or for the collective management of the relationships between groups, rather than functions that only serve individuals. Besides the cognitive functions of ideologies discussed in the preceding part, we now may focus on their equally essential social functions.

Racism as example

In order to be able to focus the discussion of the social dimensions of ideologies, I shall again use *racism* as the concrete example of a set of ideologies that have a prominent role in the reproduction of ethnic or 'racial' inequality in 'Western' societies. 'Racism' here will be understood in a broad, political sense, and involves group prejudices and discrimination against ethnic or 'racial' minority groups, anti-semitism, ethnocentrism, xenophobia, and so on. By contrast with many earlier studies of this topic, racism will *not* be equated with a racist ideology, but also comprises the discriminatory practices being enacted on the basis of racist ideologies, as well as the social structures or institutions involved in the reproduction of racism, such as political parties, education and the media. In other words, racism is a complex system of domination, which needs to be analysed at various levels and domains of society, including those of cognition, discourse, group relations, organizations and culture.[3]

Against this background, my examples will focus on the social manifestations and the reproduction of ideologies: Which groups are involved, what are their relationships, and how for instance are racist or ethnocentric ideologies 'invented' and spread in white European(ized) societies? What is the special role of the elites, and of the ideological institutions such as politics, the media and education? That is, I shall analyse racism to see ideology 'at work', and especially its conditions and consequences in the organization of society, and the (dominance) relations between groups, which will allow us to better understand the societal basis and functions of ideologies. The next part of this book will then focus on the microsocial level of the discourses that concretely play a role in the social reproduction of such ideologies.

15

Groups

Who 'has' an ideology?

After such fundamental questions as what ideologies actually are, and what they look like, as discussed in the previous part, perhaps the most crucial question is: *who* in fact has such ideologies? I have provisionally assumed that ideologies are essentially social, and shared by *groups*.[1] However, we have also seen that such an assumption needs qualification: the passengers on a flight, or the pedestrians waiting for a red light, are not likely to share one ideology. Indeed, such more or less arbitrarily composed collectivities might not be called 'groups' in the first place. So, we need to define the notion of group, and determine which groups typically develop and share an ideology.

Traditionally, especially in the Marxist tradition, ideologies are of course associated with the notion of 'class', later described in more abstract terms, such as 'social formations'.[2] More specifically, ideologies were attributed to the ruling class, which disseminated them to conceal or to legitimate its power, inequality or the status quo. Similarly, the Gramscian notion of hegemony implies ideological domination and consent, but also especially in terms of a ruling class or power elite, on the one hand, and a large dominated group of a 'mass public' or simply the citizens whose ideologies are persuasively inculcated by these elites, on the other hand.

At a later stage, however, with the increasing attention being paid to other forms of domination, for instance those of gender and 'race', also other social groups or formations were attributed ideologies, such as men (or male chauvinists) versus feminists, or white people (or racists) versus anti-racists. The same is true for the increasing focus on questions of safety, security, peace, the environment or various (e.g. sexual) lifestyles, in which also different groups, collectivities or social movements of some kind are associated with different positions and ideologies. Peace movements and ecological movements are just two prominent examples of such 'new' ideological groups, in which the basic principles no longer are of a socio-economic kind.

In sum, each social group or formation that exercises a form of power or domination over other groups could be associated with an ideology that would specifically function as a means to legitimate or conceal such power. Earlier it was emphasized that also those groups who resist such domination should have an ideology in order to organize their social practices.

Several of the issues introduced here, such as power, dominance or hegemony, need to be dealt with later. Here we need to examine first what collectivities of social actors may share an ideology, and why.

Groups

Just like various forms of socio-cultural knowledge, and just like natural languages, ideologies are shared. There are no 'private' ideologies, only private opinions. Ideologies are acquired, confirmed and changed by social actors as members of groups, and as a function of the goals and interests of such groups.

The basic question, then, is what counts as a 'group' in the first place. Why are the passengers on a specific plane generally not considered a social group? One reason may be that their membership of the *ad hoc* collectivity is simply too ephemeral, and besides travelling safely to the same destination, passengers will not have joint goals and interests. Indeed, they do not travel as a group, but as individuals who happen to be on the same flight. Hence, one criterion for groupness may be that collectivities of people must have some *continuity* beyond one event.

Of course, the situation is different when some people decide to fly together, that is, engage in *collective action*, or when many airline passengers (and not just those on this flight) *organize* as consumers, that is, as a group with shared goals and interests, such as safety and service. Similarly, when their plane is hijacked, the passengers who before merely travelled as a collection of individuals, may of course become more of a group because of a shared predicament. Such a *shared problem*, or a *common fate*, in which people may become *mutually dependent*, and may want to *act collectively* to overcome their plight, may be other criteria for the formation of a group. More generally, various kind of social *conflicts* between collectivities of people typically create groups.

Shared social representations

Note, though, that besides 'objective' social, political or economic problems shared with others, also cognitive or affective criteria must be involved – members of a group must *know* (or believe) about other members, about a shared problem or conflict, or about possible collective actions. Moreover, they may share *opinions* about their common experiences, conflicts or actions. Finally, they have affective *feelings* of belonging to the group or about their experiences or activities as group members.[3] In other words, sets of people constitute groups if and only if, as a collectivity, they share *social representations*.[4] For the individual group members this means that part of their personal identity (self) is now associated with a *social identity*, namely, the self-representation of being a member of a social group (see also Chapter 12).

Since social representations take time to develop, and presuppose a common history of experiences, interaction and discourse, *ad hoc* collectivities of people do not have such social representations, and hence do not form a group according to this definition.

Finally, we might further require that the individual and collective *actions* of the group members be monitored by these social representations. That is, not only should the collectivity, as a set of people, not be *ad hoc*, but also the decisions, goals and actions of the members of a collectivity should not happen to coincide or be similar, as was the case for the individual passengers travelling aboard the same flight to the same destination. Thus, group members act *as* group members when these actions are (also, though not exclusively) based on shared knowledge, attitudes, ideologies, norms or values (see Chapter 3).

Thus, slightly less ephemeral than the group of passengers on an airliner, we may take the example of a demonstration. Here, membership is not arbitrary, but members share opinions, and at least one goal. They do something together, namely, protest against some social situation, action or policy they disapprove of, and they know it (also about each other). However, although such a protest and the opinions that give rise to it may well be ideological, a protest demonstration – as such – need not be an ideological group either. The goals and opinions shared by the demonstrators as well as the collective action, after all, may be strictly contextual, and not go beyond the occasion at hand.

On the other hand, some demonstrations may be based on shared group attitudes and ideologies, for example a demonstration of environmentalists against dumping nuclear waste, or an anti-racist demonstration against a racist party. In that case, the attitudes and ideology are shared by a broader group than just the participants in the demonstration. Members of the demonstration in that case are a subgroup of a larger group, such as a social movement, and the protest one specific manifestation of ideologically based attitudes.

From this theoretical analysis, as well as from these examples, we may conclude that ideologies and groupness mutually seem to define each other. Only groups may develop ideologies, and the definition of groups in turn presupposes not only shared social conditions, experiences or actions, but especially also shared social representations, including ideologies.

This circularity of the definitions of ideology and groups is both apparent and theoretically welcome in a theory of ideology. First, although all ideologies are group-based, not all groups need to develop an underlying ideology. Shared knowledge and some shared group opinions may be enough for many forms of collective actions and goals, as would be the case for our example of a group of people regularly taking their vacations together. On the other hand, many groups (or maybe social groups stricto sensu) can only reproduce themselves, and continue to exist, if they – or their members – satisfy a number of social criteria, including access to specific resources, as we shall see in more detail below. Some of these resources are not just material, but also symbolic, (knowledge, information, education, status, etc.), as is the case for politicians, professors and journalists, among many others. Since such symbolic resources are defined in terms of socially shared representations that actually define their social value, we again are back at the socio-cognitive level in order to define groups. Moreover, many groups are primarily defined in terms of these social representations (e.g. opinions, ideologies) themselves, as is the case for Christians, socialists, feminists, anti-racists or peace activists and many other social movements.

And finally, even for groups that seem to be constituted also or primarily in terms of material resources (like the poor and the rich, the homeless and the unemployed), we have seen that socio-economic conditions are relevant for the group only if their experience is shared, and hence framed in terms of shared knowledge or beliefs, that is, if group members actually feel and represent themselves as members of such a group; or conversely, if they are represented by members of other groups as such, and are treated accordingly. And finally, for most groups continuity and reproduction presupposes either individual acts of social actors as group members, or collective action, which in both cases presupposes shared social representations of the members.

Note that this does *not* mean that being poor or homeless is 'all in the mind', and that socio-economic conditions are thus reduced to their mental representations. Of course not. But for someone who is poor or homeless to feel and represent him/herself as a member of a *group*, and not just out-of-luck as an individual poor or homeless person, such economic conditions still need to be interpreted and especially also represented as being shared by others.

Nor does this argument imply that groups are *only* constituted by social representations. They are also characterized of course by their (lack of) access to material or symbolic resources, by collective action, discourse and other social practices. However, whatever the 'objective' socio-economic base of a collectivity of people, they can only constitute a group if they share social representations that give collective meaning to these social circumstances. It is also in this sense that groups are not merely a societal construct, but also constituted mentally through shared representation. Groups are also constituted by their members, as well as members of other groups, by feelings of belongingness, shared memories of collective experiences, and more generally by social representations, or precisely by the fact that others do not share these representations or challenge them. And if groups should be defined by the social practices of their members, the same necessary precondition obtains, as we have seen – social actors can only act *as* group members if they develop and share such social representations in the first place.

If groups are constituted by the shared social representations of their members, but not all groups have ideologies, we must later formulate further

conditions on which groups under what conditions actually develop ideologies. Thus, whereas a group of vacationers, as such, may not (need to) do
so, battered women, managers, or peace activists are more likely to develop
some form of ideology. These conditions might be socio-cognitive, for
example when the specific social representations of a group need further
organization and foundation, or when group members need to co-ordinate
their actions or engage in collective action. And they may be socio-cultural
or political, namely, for example for effective group reproduction, organization, sanctions of norms, domination of other groups, conflict resolution, and
more generally the effective realization of its goals. Below I shall return to
these further conditions on the development of ideologies.

Social categories versus social groups

The criteria of group continuity and social identification typically apply to
social categories of people, defined in terms of more or less permanent
properties, such as age, gender, 'race', ethnicity, origin, class, language,
religion, sexual orientation or profession. Hence, women and men, white and
black, young and old, and poor and rich may well develop ideologies that are
related to the position and the interests of the members of this category in
society.

However, general social categories are again too broad to form groups as
defined above. After all, it is not likely that all women, or all rich people,
share the same overall ideology, even when they share similar social
experiences or act similarly in certain social situations. Taking the example
of class struggle, feminism, or the civil rights movement, we see that these
apply to groups of people who belong to a social category, but also share
specific goals, norms, values, and in general some form of awareness about
these. And this awareness or group feeling was defined as social identity and
hence as a form of shared social (self)representation. Social movements may
defend the interests of all workers, women or blacks, but as groups they have
more specific goals and interests that need not be shared by all members of
their respective social categories.[5]

Equally general are those collectivities of people that are precisely defined
by their *ideologies*, such as liberals and conservatives. Again, the question
may be raised whether these are 'groups' in a more narrow sense – do all
conservative people in the world form a group? Should their ideological
stance be taken as a more or less permanent property, as is the case for
gender, age or ethnicity? It may be assumed that members of such 'groups'
identify more or less strongly with them, precisely for ideological reasons. If
shared social identity is a sufficient criterion for the definition of groups,
then this collectivity of people would constitute a group. They may even
have some overall goals. On the other hand, unlike demonstrators or
members of social movements, members of such ideological categories do
not, as such, participate in *joint* activities, but at most in *similar* activities,

such as voting and engaging in liberal or conservative actions and discourse. This is why the analysis in Chapter 28 of a concrete example suggests that 'conservativism' be considered as a 'meta-ideology' that controls dimensions of the ideologies (e.g. those of neo-liberalism, sexism or racism), rather than as a proper group ideology.

Another general type of group is based on *profession*. Doctors, nurses, professors, journalists or carpenters thus may form a professional group, which obviously has similar activities, goals and interests, and with which many or most members may identify. Such groups have professional values and norms, and opinions and attitudes about professional practices, as well as group-specific expert knowledge. Though possibly universal (specialized professions exist in virtually all societies and cultures), this type of group seems like a plausible candidate for the development of group ideologies, especially given the relevance of conflicting interests between different professions. But again, members of the same profession across the globe only rarely engage in joint activities, although some do, for instance at international conferences.

Between these very general (if not universal) categories of social actors on the one hand, and the fleeting group membership of a demonstration or a team, we have the groups of people that constitute *organizations* and *institutions*, such as political parties, parliaments, universities, unions and corporate businesses. Again, identification with such organizations defined as 'groups' is plausible, and there are shared (and even joint) activities, goals and values, as well as similar interests. Note, though, that there is a problem here: As individual institutions or organizations they may no more have their own specific ideologies than their members. We do not speak of 'the' ideology of a specific union, but rather about a union ideology in general. Similarly, in business corporations we may find more general corporate ideologies (or variations of them), and not so much the ideology of one specific business corporation. If such corporations are large, as is the case for multinationals like IBM, however, a common 'culture' may develop, and such a culture of shared norms, values and goals might in a way be identified as the corporate 'ideology'.[6]

Another criterion, maybe a decisive one, for the definition of the social group basis of ideologies, is *social conflict, struggle* or any other kind of interest-based opposition between groups, whether over material or over symbolic resources. This is traditionally the case for classes and class struggle, and in Marxism, obviously, ideologies were primarily related to groups such as workers and 'capitalists'. The same is true for feminists versus male chauvinists, or anti-racists against racists, and so on. In such cases the dominant groups will tend to develop an ideology that serves the reproduction of its domination, and the dominated groups may develop an ideology as a basis for its attitudes, opinions, practices and discourses of resistance or opposition. Membership, activities, goals, social position, values and group resources are all rather easily identifiable here, and given these as basic categories for the definition of ideological schemata, these could be the prototypical ideological groups. Other groups (say, a category like 'women', or a profession like 'doctors', or a party like the Christian-Democrats) would generally be defined by only one or a few of these categories.[7]

If we define ideologies in terms of their social functions (see below), then sharing beliefs, the co-ordination of social action and interaction, providing identification, common goals, organization and in general defending group interests, are major conditions for the constitution of ideological groups. Collectivities of people as defined by one or more properties (such as age, profession, goals, income level, political orientation, etc.) thus will tend to be more like ideological groups if these ideological functions apply to them. We need a detailed sociological theory of social groups in order to be able to make such criteria explicit.

One such criterion may also be the degree of *institutionalization*. This first of all excludes all ephemeral groups, such as plane passengers and participants in a demonstration. It also eliminates general social categories, such as socio-biological ones like men and women, blacks and whites, old and young, or socio-economic ones like rich and poor, or the unemployed. As suggested, these general categories may well be the broader collectivities from which more specific ideological groups are recruited, however, as is the case for feminists as members of the category of women. Many ideological groups, such as feminists, socialists, environmentalists, anti-abortionists and so on, are not merely defined by shared identities, goals, positions or resources, but also by the fact that they tend to organize in institutions, such as parties, non-governmental organizations, Churches, sects, and so on. They often have explicit, self-styled or elected leaders or officers, headquarters, membership fees, publications, meetings and so on. Such institutionalization may play a prominent role in recruiting new members, setting goals, formulating norms and principles (and indeed ideologies), securing resources, and especially the co-ordination and effective execution of actions that realize the goal of the organized group.

We may conclude this discussion by assuming that there cannot be a clear and explicit boundary between social groups in the more specific sense and any other collective of people defined by one or more shared characteristics. Generally, however, I shall assume that a social group must be more or less permanent, more or less organized or institutionalized, and reproduced by recruiting members on the basis of identification on a specific, more or less permanent set of properties (like gender or income), shared activities and/or goals, norms and values, resources, and a specific position (often of competition or conflict) in relation to other social groups. Groups that satisfy most of these conditions will then be assumed to be most likely to develop shared ideologies that will serve as the basis for organization of the actions and cognitions of their members in such a way that the aims of the group are optimally realized.

Groups versus members

There is one thorny theoretical problem we need to address here, and that is the specific, emergent nature of a group as being distinct from the set constituted by its members. Throughout this study many observations are made about the ideologies and other mental or social properties shared by a group. We have assumed, for instance, that journalists as a group develop a professional ideology and that other collectivities of people may do likewise in specific social circumstances.

However, the problem is that we would like this also to be true when one or a few individual journalists do *not* share such an ideology. Indeed, many groups may have ideological 'deviants' or 'dissidents'. If this is the case, the notion of group may at least sometimes be distinct from the set of its individual members. Maybe 'groupness' only requires that *most* or *many* of the members share some property. However, such fuzzy criteria also make groups rather like fuzzy sets rather than strict sets of members. Indeed, as with sets, groups may theoretically exist if they do not (as yet, or any longer) have any members at all!

Apart from the set theoretical and quantitative dimensions of groups, we may also ask whether groups have emergent properties that (sets of) members do not necessarily have. Indeed, are there mental representations (like knowledge and ideology), collective actions or group relations that do apply to the group, but not necessarily to (all of) its members? Obviously, this is the case. As we shall see in the next chapter, social group relations such as power and dominance are defined for the group as a whole, and do not necessarily apply to all members. Indeed, despite male dominance in society, not all men are dominant with respect to all women they interact with, nor do most men act dominantly against women all the time. Groups may similarly have a collective past, history and experiences that not all members personally have, as is typically the case for the Holocaust for the Jews. From this example it is but one step to collective memories and hence to shared social representations: Jews as a group have social representations about the Holocaust and anti-semitism, although there may be individual Jews who don't. These few examples suggest that indeed groups may have attributes that are not necessarily those of (all) their members.

It is likely that the same is true for ideologies. That is, because of their history, collective experiences, social position, and social relations with other groups, groups may develop and reproduce a specific ideology. Like 'having a language', thus, 'sharing an ideology' is such a property that should be defined at the societal level, that is, for the group as a whole. In the same way as a social group is an abstraction, or an ideal type, also ideologies may thus be seen as an abstract property, much like languages such as English or Chinese are abstract systems, at least at one level of analysis. Such a system is not simply the same as the actual language use of all speakers of English or Chinese. Indeed, there are languages that, as linguistic systems, have survived their users. Similarly, socialism as an ideology will still be an ideology even when the last socialist has switched off the light.

The macro–micro problem

These observations, however, require a further analysis of the relations between social abstractions, systems, collective properties, and groups on the one hand, and group members as actual people – as well as their minds and actions – on the other hand. This is an example of the well-known macro–micro problem in the social sciences.[8] In the same way as the system of the Chinese language must at least be partially known in order to be 'used' by concrete speakers, we may assume that a similar condition holds for the role of ideology in the monitoring of social practices in general, and of discourse in particular. That is, if ideologies are defined only for groups, if groupness presupposes shared social representations (or a social identity), if social representations are mental, and if groups as such don't have minds, then we must assume that groups can only 'have' an ideology if at least a qualified number of their members share at least part of such an ideology. Now, what exactly does that mean?

One trivial answer already formulated above is simply quantitative. That is, a group 'has' an ideology if most of its members share most of the propositions that define such an ideology, where the fuzzy quantifier 'most' may be assigned any value between, say, seventy-five per cent and 100 per cent.

Somewhat less trivial would be to replace the quantifier for the number of propositions by the set of 'essential' or 'core' ideological propositions, namely, those that are the specific, defining or prototypical fundamental beliefs of a group. For instance, people would not qualify as neo-liberals if they did not share the core ideological propositions based on the freedom of the market. This is relatively straightforward of course for groups defined primarily by their ideologies.

But what about journalists? Does a journalist who does not believe in the core propositions based on the value of the freedom of the press, exclude him- or herself from the journalistic ideology, and hence from group identification? Would such a journalist not be like a prototypical journalist, and hence be defined (or define himself or herself) as a relative outsider, and actually be marginalized, as we may indeed observe in journalistic (or other professional) practice?

Are the well-known forces of conformity, including socialization, school-ing, the media, sanctions, marginalization and other social practices to enforce ideological alignment of members, a social manifestation of the necessity to defend at least the adherence to a core of ideological proposi-tions by all members? Such seems indeed to be the case. Again, the comparison with language (grammar) may be instructive: use is not merely regulated by mutual intelligibility but also by socially enforced standards of minimal correctness for many social situations, such as schooling and getting or keeping a job. Personal variation is possible, but some normative core grammar needs to be respected in specific social situations.

If at least a minimal ideological core should be respected 'in' the group, then we still need to qualify by how many or which members this needs to be the case. Again, we may use a qualitative criterion, namely, the 'core members', such as leaders, the elites, all people with responsibilities, and in general, thus, the 'ideologues' of any group. This is socially necessary for the group, in the first place, in order to ideologically reproduce itself. At least some members need to teach the ideology to newcomers or new generations. Second, at least some members need to monitor social practices and hence the applications of the ideology by current members. Third, at least some members need to be able to reformulate and adapt the group ideology to new social developments, circumstances or changed relations to other groups. Fourth, at least some members need to be able to formulate and distribute (fragments of the) ideology throughout the group. These and other ideological core activities need to be adequately carried out for any group to reproduce its ideology and the social practices and social position based on it. In other words, we may conclude again, and again rather vaguely, that ideological reproduction presupposes at least a core of elites or ideologues to perform these functions.

Of course, for different groups or institutions such ideological activities may vary considerably: the Catholic Church does this in a different way from the feminist movement or the peace movement. Also, the conditions on either the number of ideological members or the number of ideological propositions to be shared by them, may be very different for different groups. Traditionally, in the Catholic Church one might be excommunicated for adhering to a specific heresy. Something similar might happen for a strictly ideological political party or specific social movements. In some (extreme) cases all members need to ascribe to all ideological propositions, whereas in others only to a core of basic ideological principles, or again, only a core group of people need to know all or most or only the core principles. But if only a small group knows and shares only a fragment of the (original) ideology of a group, so that full ideological reproduction becomes impossible among newcomers, we may expect ideological decline, or ideological change, or indeed the resolution of a group. Since, however, ideologies may often be written down in explicit textbooks, Bibles, catechisms, histories of movements, party programmes, corporate 'mission statements', organizational statutes, and similar ideological writings by ideologues, there is always a possibility that at least some group members are able to keep the ideological fire burning for a long time.

What is sharing?

Finally, there is another aspect that needs to be examined when we study the relations between the ideological group and its members, namely, the precise social and cognitive status of sharing. Above we have seen what kind of social dimensions may be involved, namely, how many, and what kind of members need to share how much of an ideology. Now, the question is what this actual 'sharing' means – identical 'copies' of propositions in the minds of the relevant members, as when computers run copies of the same program, even when different personal uses of the program are made? Again, the comparison with grammars may be instructive. In order to use the language more or less grammatically, we may assume that language users need to acquire more or less the same rules of a grammar. Of course there may be personal variation, for example due to schooling and other forms of learning, in the amount of rules acquired or how the rules are applied. That is, despite such variation, most speakers of the language must have more or less similar copies of the core rules of the same grammar.

The same, we assume, should be true for the basic social representations of a group, that is, its ideology. On many occasions, such ideological principles may actually be formulated, for example in contexts of admission, inclusion, socialization, initiation, teaching, jurisprudence, sanctioning, marginalization and exclusion. Of course, such formulation takes places in variable discourses, and not directly in terms of (abstract) ideological propositions, so that acquisition, even in ideal cases, is often less strict than acquiring the rules of grammar. However, as with other social principles, such as norms and values, there are many social practices and discourses expressing or enacting the underlying ideological principles, so that by continuous repetition and experience, some fairly similar ideology fragments will be acquired. Again, this will be highly variable for different ideological groups. Also, it need not be emphasized that the knowledge that group members have of such ideological propositions need not always be explicit or even conscious (as is also the case for the rules of grammar), if only they are able to apply them more or less adequately.

In sum, for the moment, we have no theoretical alternative but to assume that a group 'has' an ideology if at least some (or most, depending on the group) members share at least some core (or most) ideological propositions. Sharing, in this case, means that these members have fairly similar propositions stored in their social memory. In other words, if an ideology is taken as an abstract system of the group as a whole, it is concretely (mentally) 'distributed' over its members. That such members will make (sometimes vastly) different uses of this ideological system in different social contexts, is obvious, and defines the large variation in ideological discourses and other social practices. We shall come back to such personal and contextual variation later.

Multiple identities and conflicting ideologies

As has been suggested several times above, individual social actors may be members of various social groups, each of which may have its own ideology. This is one of the fundamental reasons why the expression of ideologies by such actors in specific situations may appear incoherent or even inconsistent. The point here is that since different groups may have different interests (membership devices, activities, goals, norms or resources), also their ideologies, which cognitively represent such basic interests, may be in conflict in the decision 'how to speak or act' in a specific situation. Depending on the situation, one identity and hence one ideology may be more relevant or more important, so that strategic choices can be made in the management of conflicting beliefs and interests. We already encountered the prototype of a middle-class female black journalist, who will probably let her journalistic ideologies and practices prevail over those suggested by the other group ideologies, at least if she wants to keep her job.[9]

Only sometimes can such group ideologies and practices be combined. Middle-class ideology will often combine well with the middle-class bias of the media, most sources, most news actors and most of the public. No conflict of interest will be very likely here. As a woman, the black journalist may be partly accepted (or even forced) to 'behave' as a journalist, although she may get story assignments with a women's perspective (but seldom a radical feminist one). This will be even less the case for her as a black person, although in times of ethnic or racial conflict and crises, 'ethnic' stories may be assigned to her. But in general the social rule is: believe and act like most of us in 'our' group. Transgressions of the rule, and outright deviance and dissidence will be sanctioned by marginalization, exclusion or elimination, whether physical, economic, social or cultural.[10]

Group categories and membership

Ideologies have been assumed to be organized by a group schema consisting of a number of fundamental categories that codify the ways people define themselves and others as group members. These categories have mental aspects, but also social ones. Thus, whereas membership may be construed as the mental representation of the relations individuals have with social groups or categories, it also needs to be accounted for in more sociological terms. Thus, it may not be sufficient that group members consider themselves to be members of a group. It is also important how *others* perceive them as such. Indeed, individuals may 'naturally' belong to, and be considered and accepted, as members of groups or categories, as is the case for women, children, or whites and blacks, but in many other groups, the process of admission and recognition follows a more complex social process. This also affects the role of membership in the reproduction of ideology.

Besides the 'natural' categories just mentioned (which obviously are social constructions in their own right), membership should first be examined for those social groups people may be 'born into', and to which they thus have more or less involuntary access. Class and caste are the most prominent example of such groups, and at the same time the classical example for the development of ideologies. Although in later life people may well 'change' class or caste, they are assumed to be class members as long as they are unable or unwilling to change such membership.

Class membership is as complex as the very notion of class and socially constructed in terms of much more than just socio-economic parameters, such as family income, occupation or position. Various types of non-material, symbolic 'capital' may be indicative of one's class, such as status, respect, accent and language use, knowledge of the arts, and so on for the upper and upper middle class, or precisely the relative (real or attributed) lack of such symbolic resources for the lower classes. Changing class, especially upwardly, therefore also requires more than just a change of material resources, as is shown by the negative categorization of *nouveaux riches* as not really belonging to the upper classes. Indeed, specific upper classes (e.g. of nobility) cannot be entered otherwise than by birth. For others, both material and symbolic capital, such as a good education, a good school, and acquired 'culture' may be needed to access the higher class if they did not acquire such resources as 'born' class members.[11]

Both for established members as well as for new members, class membership is also associated with ideologies. Indeed, the very reproduction of the socio-economic interests of the class, including both its material and symbolic resources, is one of the main functions of class ideologies. That is, when matched with the structure of ideologies, class provides a 'membership device' that is essentially resource-based: people define themselves and are categorized, recognized or admitted by other members primarily in terms of a specific set of (socio-economic and cultural) resources. For the successful reproduction of the class, therefore, group members learn either from birth, or as newcomers, the ideology that allows the protection of these resource-based interests. Economically, this may mean opposition against various forms of wealth and income distribution, high taxes for the rich, and so on. Symbolically, this may mean exclusive or preferential access to special schools, clubs, professions and forms of 'high' culture. Ideologically, such privileges will tend to be legitimated by claims of natural or social 'rights' (birth, marriage, heritage) and/or merit (hard work, learning).

For *professional* groups, membership and access are usually well defined in terms of legal or traditional membership criteria, such as education, degrees, diplomas and expertise. Lawyers, doctors and professors can become such only when being officially evaluated and qualified, whereas for journalists less strict qualifications may be needed. Membership of such groups is usually based primarily on type of activity and expertise (advising clients, healing patients or teaching students). The interests of such groups are also tied to specific, symbolic resources such as legal, medical or scientific knowledge and expertise, as well as status and respect accorded the professions in a particular society.

Given their nature, we may expect that professional groups develop ideologies especially as a function of the interests tied to their activities and their special resources. Thus, freedom of the press, independence of the courts, autonomy of the universities, as well as freedom of information and science, are well-known elements of the basic ideological beliefs that reflect such interests. Also for these reasons, membership is rather strictly regulated; the number of people having access to these resources should be kept fairly small, so as to maintain the economic value of professional services and expertise. Most professionals oppose 'lowering standards' or 'mass universities' and insist on a self-regulated threshold of access, such as special exams, in-house training or specialization. Successful reproduction of the group through the protection of these special interests thus also needs to be articulated in various professional ideologies, for instance about the importance, relevance or the functions of these professions (serving justice, health care, knowledge and education, or informing the public). Similarly, in order to protect such interests, the activities of the professional may also internally be judged on the basis of ideological values (justice, truth, reliability, fairness, etc.).[12]

Groups and their membership may be constituted also on the basis of their social goals, usually in relation to their norms and values, as is typically the case for various *social movements*. Feminists thus form a group typically on the basis of their goal to end male domination and gender inequality. The essential values involved in their activities for the realization of that goal are, for example equality, independence and autonomy. The same is true for socialists, environmentalists, human rights activists and similar action or advocacy groups, on the one hand, and for nationalists, racists, and anti-abortionists, on the other hand. Membership criteria in this case will therefore be personal choice, ideological alignment and recognized activities that contribute to the realization of the common goal. As is the case for other groups, ideologies of these goal-defined groups reflect their main interests, such as gender equality or ethnic autonomy. At a higher level of abstraction, the same membership criteria and ideological development apply to ideological groups, such as conservatives and liberals. In this case, the main membership criterion is precisely the ideology itself.[13]

Although most groups and their identity are defined in terms of their relations to other groups (outgroups), some groups are specifically defined in terms of the *social position* of their members within the group. This is the case for leaders, managers, chiefs and in general the elites, in relation to subordinates, underlings, ordinary people, the masses, citizens, the 'people' and so on. That is, apart from hierarchical position, their main resource is power. Membership conditions and criteria may in this case be appointment, election and self-selection. Ideologies of such groups should be primarily articulated in the interest of the reproduction and the legitimation of their crucial resource, namely, power, as is typically the case for leading politicians and managers.[14]

Although not complete, this categorization of various groups and their membership criteria shows that there is a close interplay between ideological categories and the essential dimensions of social access, membership,

activities, goals and resources of groups. Ideological structures have precisely been postulated as the cognitive reconstruction of the main social
conditions for the existence and reproduction of various social groups. In
other words, the essential conditions of existence, organization, reproduction
and the social practices of groups and their members have both social
dimensions and mental ones. Here, ideologies and groups mutually constitute each other. No group can socially exist and act without a group
identity and shared ideological beliefs of its members. Conversely, no group
ideology will develop unless collectivities of people start to act, co-ordinate
and organize as a group. Indeed, a large part of the social practices of many
groups, and especially of teaching, communication and discourse, is precisely geared towards the development of a common ideology.

In sum, in rather general terms, social groups and their members may be
distinguished by

- *who they are*, as defined by more or less permanent characteristics, such
  as gender, 'race', ethnicity, caste, class, age, religion, language or
  origin;
- *what they do*, as is the case for professionals;
- *what they want*, as is typically the case for advocacy groups;
- *what they believe*, as is true for advocacy groups, as well as for religious
  and ideological groups such as conservatives and progressives;
- *where they stand*, as for all groups defined in terms of social position and
  their relations to other groups;
- *what they have or don't have*, as for all groups whose identity is based
  primarily on the special access or lack of access to social (material or
  symbolic) resources, as is the case for the rich and the poor, the
  employed and the unemployed, the homeless and the home-owners
  the famous and the infamous, the educated and the non-educated, the
  intellectuals and the non-intellectuals, and so on.

The categories that define this typology of groups are intentionally the
same as those that form ideological schemata (see Chapter 5). That is, our
approach precisely emphasizes the mutual constitution of the social and the
cognitive dimensions of groups. Most social criteria discussed above for the
constitution of social groups can thus be articulated in terms of categories
that also organize the social cognitions shared by group members.

Ideologies without groups?

The assumption of the mutual constitution of groups and their ideologies
raises an important final question: are groups necessary as the 'social basis'
of ideologies, or would it be more appropriate, at least in some cases, to
allow ideologies to 'exist' more independently? There can be little doubt that
there are collectivities of social actors that can be defined in terms of non-
ideological social conditions, as is the case for socio-economically defined
groups (classes) or professions. That such groups also need to share social

beliefs and ideologies in order to co-ordinate the actions of their members and to reproduce themselves, has been shown above.

But what about groups of which membership is much more fuzzy and primarily ideological, such as the feminist movement or the peace movement? Can we simply say that all 'members' of the feminist movements are feminists, and that those who are not members are not feminists? What about women who share some tenets of feminism, but not others, or those women who do share many feminist propositions, but do not consider themselves feminists? Is the feminist movement a well-defined group in the first place? Or should it be defined in terms of a fuzzy set, in which some women may be 'more or less' members, depending on the amount of their feminist beliefs, or their degree of identification? Or should we use some version of prototype theory and distinguish between more or less prototypical feminists?[15]

In other words, especially for social movements that have a more individualistic orientation, it might not be an already existing group which 'has' an ideology, or an ideology that requires a group, but *individual* social members who adopt, to a greater or lesser degree, ideas of an ideology. Such an ideology would then rather have the status of any other system of ideas, such as a philosophy or a theory, and could have been developed by one or more individuals, whether or not it is being shared or adopted by many people or a collectivity of social actors.

Such a more individualist approach to certain ideologies would at least avoid the theoretical problems associated with the definition of ideological groups as indicated above. It would account, by definition, for the vast individual differences in the adherence to certain ideological propositions, and for a more dynamic process of ideological change and renewal. It would emphasize people's individual decisions in adopting ideology fragments, and explain the personal variation in the enactment of ideologies in everyday social practices. We would not need to worry whether a conservative ideology, for instance, is shared by a group, but may simply say that given such an ideology as a socio-historical phenomenon individual social members may espouse one or more of its tenets, but may reject others.

In this framework, people do not become all-or-none members of, for example, the 'club of conservatives', but simply use (fragments of) a set of beliefs as a resource in the organization of their own knowledge and opinions and the social practices based on these. Ideologies of this kind would be like 'personal organizers' rather than social (group) organizers. Indeed, this approach would also account for the seemingly curious situation, signalled above, that we may have ideologies that have no 'members', or rather adherents, at all, as we also have abolished religions or theories. Ontologically, ideologies like this would only exist as a form of (possibly specialized) historical knowledge, or expressed historical documents or treatises, but no one would still 'believe in' them.

These arguments for a more individualistic approach to (at least some types of) ideology are quite persuasive. They again suggest that an exclusively sociological definition of ideologies is incomplete. The processes as described are fully accounted for in the cognitive theories presented in Part I. Indeed, personal beliefs, experiences and practices have been shown to be associated with specific or general mental models, as well as by other representations in episodic memory. Individual social actors may thus flexibly adopt and personally integrate whatever 'ideas' there are available in the public domain. They may for the same reason more or less identify with one or more ideologies or social movements, or may recombine elements from several ideologies. Women may experience and thus interpret male practices as women, and bring to bear shared social representations of women as a category, but not necessarily identify with feminism as a social movement or interpret their experiences in terms of a feminist ideology. The same is probably true for many religions, political convictions, lifestyle conceptions, and on any other system of attitudes (e.g. about abortion, nuclear energy, or the environment).

Paying due allowance to this individual dimension of ideology, or rather of the 'uses' of ideology, however, does not mean that the social, collective dimension can be simply dispensed with, for the many reasons given throughout this book. Thus, the feminist and the peace movement do not merely consist of sets of like-minded individuals. First of all, at the social side, there is social interaction between such individuals, and some of these interactions are engaged in as a consequence of, or precisely as a condition of, sharing specific beliefs, that is, by social actors *as* 'believers'. Second, social movements are also defined in terms of collective actions, such as demonstrations or strikes. Third, they have many forms of organization and institutionalization; they have leaders, programmes, socio-economic resources, and so on. That is, they may have all the characteristics that define a group.

What a theory of ideology needs to explain, then, is precisely the dynamics that relate social members to ideologies and to the collectivities that are constituted by shared experiences, beliefs and ideologies. We need to know how individual membership, identification, allegiance, solidarity and active participation are being defined in relation to such a collectivity and its organization. It should be examined how groups may grow and decay as a result of the actions and participation of individuals. That ideological 'groups' may be quite loose or fuzzy in their definition, and their membership or adherence flexibly defined in terms of the interplay between personal beliefs and socially shared beliefs, does not mean that we can dispense with the social dimension of ideologies in terms of groups or similar collectivities. It is this interface between the individual and the group that is one of the theoretical problems that need to be examined in a theory of ideology.

Racist groups

This dilemma about ideologies and their relationships to groups and individuals is particular clear in the study of racism. Indeed, which 'group' has a racist ideology? It would be easiest call this group the 'racists'. However, the delimitation of that group would require the definition that racists are all people who share a racist ideology, but, if not circular, this would be rather trivial. Moreover, as we have seen above, many people may share some social opinions (prejudices) based on racist ideologies, but need not share a fully fledged racist ideology.

One could also define 'racists' in terms of their organizations, for example by identifying them as members of racist organizations, but the circularity or triviality would in that case also hold for the definition of such organizations. Moreover, it is obvious that there are more 'racist people' than people who are members of racist parties or organizations.[16]

Another possibility would be to identify the group with all white (European) people. But that is obviously inadequate if we assume that racism is not an inherent or essential property of white Europeans. Indeed, some whites share an explicitly anti-racist ideology, whereas some members of minority groups may support racist ideologies.

Moreover, we have already seen that it is pointless to distinguish sharply between those (whites) who are racists and those who are not. Rather, we must assume that elements of racist ideologies and attitudes are distributed unevenly over the white group: some people will only share some or moderate racist beliefs, whereas others have many and blatant racist beliefs. Indeed, the same is true for anti-racist ideologies.

Instead of distinguishing between racists, non-racists or anti-racists, therefore, it is much more adequate to speak of *racist practices*. Practices may then be called 'racist' if they contribute, more or less directly, to ethnic or racial inequality. Racist practices (and not just any unethical or unacceptable activity) are such also because of underlying opinions, attitudes and ideologies, for instance those that imply any form of non-egalitarian relationships between dominant and dominated ethnic groups.

The example of racism shows that the association of ideologies with social groups is not a straightforward matter. We might say that managers, journalists or other more or less easily definable groups share a professional, occupational or other ideology. But other categories and groups are much less well defined, even if they share an ideology, or especially if all that defines them *is* their ideology and the social practices derived from them. The same is true for feminists, environmentalists, and more generally for ideological groups, such as progressives, liberals or conservatives. They form 'groups' of a very different nature than for instance a specific action group or profession, and are much more distributed over other groups, both socially, regionally and internationally. Sometimes they are organized, as in liberal or conservative political parties, sometimes they form sects or churches, and sometimes also an international movement, as is true for anti-abortionists or environmentalists.

Most people who have racist beliefs and act and speak accordingly, will vehemently deny that they are racists. That label is officially sanctioned as a negative qualification, as is that of being a bigot or intolerant in societies where 'tolerance', 'equality' and 'democracy' are dominant official (ideological) values.[17] Hence racism is a typical example of an ideology applying to a group as it is defined by others.

The provisional conclusion from this brief analysis must be that the notion of group needs to be taken in a broad sense in order to be able to associate ideologies with groups. Crucial, as we have seen, are

1 the development and sharing of social representations;
2 identification of members with the group;
3 the defence of specific resources (such as citizenship or equal rights in all domains);
4 relations to other groups (e.g. resentment against immigrants);
5 specific activities (such as discrimination) and at least a vaguely shared goal (segregation, immigration restriction, etc.).

Social members who identify with these criteria are, by definition, group members, but the boundaries of the group are ill-defined. As is true for cognitive category theories of prototypes, thus, we may have more or less prototypical 'racists' and 'anti-racists'. Skinheads who beat up Turkish women only because they are Turkish are more typical for the commonsense notion of racists than are cabinet ministers advocating immigration restrictions or professors who have less confidence in black female PhD candidates than in white male ones.

These examples again show that ideologies as well as social groups and social relations (and their self- and other-perception) are all social constructs, which both have cognitive and social (societal) conditions and consequences. The distinction between 'cognition' and 'society' in this case becomes purely analytical and theoretical. In the everyday life of group members who participate in a group and its ideology, these cognitive and social conditions and criteria are inextricably interwoven – one may (socially) 'be' a Christian simply by 'defining' oneself as such.

Very often actions and interactions are required if one is to socially display or prove one's membership. However, in that case the socio-cognitive definition or construction also applies to these actions themselves. Doing or saying something also needs to be (mentally) planned or interpreted 'as' feminist, and will not 'inherently' be so. As we have seen already in the chapter on identity (Chapter 12), while acting 'as a group member' it is not merely the action itself that identifies a member, but rather the specific meaning attached to that action. Hitting someone over the head may simply be categorized as an aggressive, norm-violating action. However, it becomes interpreted as a racist act only when the participants in this event are members of specific groups, and if the aggressor is assumed to act on the basis of such group membership, for example as sharing specific racist attitudes.

Against cognitivist or interactionist reduction, these arguments further emphasize the fact that one cannot escape either the cognitive or the social dimensions of ideologies, groups and social reality. Both dimensions or levels are analytically needed to adequately describe and explain the social 'facts' – or rather the socio-cognitive constructs of society, groups and their members.

Inclusion and exclusion

The example of racism shows another important feature of the relations between ideology and group membership, namely, the social and cognitive principles and strategies of *inclusion* and *exclusion*. Racist ideologies and practices basically aim at keeping Others down and especially *out*: out of 'our' country, 'our' city, 'our' neighbourhood, 'our' street, 'our' family, 'our' jobs and 'our' houses. If some limited form of admission is accepted, then only in a lower position: in another (worse) part of town, in worse housing, worse jobs and so on. Superiority may be denied as the leading value involved, for example because of official democratic and egalitarian values. But the implication is always that We, Our Group are self-assigned a better or higher position and that such a position is deserved and can hence be justified ('We were here first', etc.). These ideological principles of superiority and inferiority may of course be combined with others, such as those that regulate competition over scarce resources, so that racism typically gets worse in times of an economic recession or other social and economic pressures on the ingroup.

As we have seen for the discussion of membership, groups thus share beliefs and practices that regulate inclusion and exclusion. Inclusion may be made difficult, as is the case for complex initiation rites, or it may be made easy, as long as the new members identify with the group. Other groups eagerly go out to recruit new members, as is typically the case for religious groups and advocacy groups. Overall, we may assume that if groups have special privileges, that is, preferential access to highly desirable or even necessary resources (freedom, housing, food, income, employment, etc.) also the strategies of exclusion will be more forceful. In this case, the stakes (the interests) being vied for are highest. Typical examples include political oppression, the forceful exclusion of 'illegal' immigrants, or the discrimination of minorities on the labour market. The same is true when the poor are kept from virtually all resources of society, both the material ones (income, jobs) as well as the symbolic ones (education, status, respect, culture).

Inclusion and exclusion may also function in a more positive way, for instance in situations where ingroup solidarity is relevant in the resistance against domination. Blacks may have black-only organizations in order to organize against racism, and women may have women-only bars in order to have a place where they need not confront men. Being among 'one's own' in such situations may have a benevolent effect on self-consciousness, the organization of resistance or simply the reproduction of group beliefs through conversation. But, as is true for dominant groups and their ideologies, also in this case group formation and identity are closely linked to the sharing of common beliefs. Exclusion here may foster the development of an ideology that allows group members to evaluate the beliefs and actions of others, both of the own group, as well as of one or various outgroups.

This informal discussion shows that the notion of group, and the principles and practices of identity and identification, inclusion and exclusion, access and acceptance, and many other social practices and processes are intimately linked to fundamental group ideologies. They involve representations of identity, about who We are and what They are, and especially about what is good for Us and what is not good for Us. Sharing exclusive or preferential access to scarce resources with others will generally not appear to be good for Us, unless people can be convinced that marginalization, discrimination and oppression of Them may eventually also be bad for Us. It may be bad for business (because good candidates or good business are excluded), bad for our moral standing (few people want to be called a sexist or a racist) and eventually bad for our self-esteem if we become convinced that our values, ideologies, morals or practices are inherently wrong. Group membership and its ideological basis, after all, are not only about power and domination, and not only to protect interests, but may also be a source of pride and pleasure. In the pages that follow, I examine some other features of these social dimensions of ideologies.

16

Group Relations

Position

Throughout the earlier chapters of this study, ideologies not only appear to be tied to more or less well-defined groups or movements, but also to various aspects of relationships between groups. One of the fundamental categories of the ideological schema therefore also focused on the *position* of the group in relation to other groups. Racist ideologies, as we have seen, are fundamentally based on distinctions being established by ingroups that simply 'prefer their own' or that feel themselves superior to outgroups, and manifest themselves in all social forms of problematization, marginalization or exclusion of the others.

Journalists, as a group, develop professional ideologies primarily in relation to other elites and other power groups. Thus, they may emphasize the freedom of the press, oppose censorship, while on the other hand they will see themselves as the watchdogs of society in the service of the 'public' at large. Similarly, professors also define themselves as such in relation to their students, and doctors and lawyers with respect to their patients and clients. Sometimes these relationships will be more or less egalitarian, but competitive, in other situations the relationship may be hierarchical and dominant.

In many cases, various interests of our group may have to be defended or legitimated against others. And since conflicts over scarce social resources may be the very core and function of the development of ideologies, group position and relations are the most direct social counterpart of ideological structures, as is most obvious in the well-known *polarization* between *ingroups* and *outgroups*. Indeed, some groups exist by virtue of their hierarchical or more powerful position, as is the case for superiors and subordinates, elites and the 'masses' or majorities and minorities. As discussed in the previous chapter, identification, access and inclusion of (new) members, may be intimately linked to the exclusion of others, thus defining power abuse and domination. Let us therefore examine some of these group relations in somewhat more detail, and see how ideologies are functionally related to (the reproduction of) these relationships.[1]

Power and domination

This is not the place to present a new or better theory of power, which has already filled many studies.[2] In the framework of this chapter I simply take (social) power as a specific type of social relation between groups. Of all the possible dimensions of this complex notion, I focus on that of *control*: a group A has or exercises power over another group B when the members of A are usually able to control the members of B. This may typically involve the control of the actions of the other group and its members, in the sense that the others are not only not (or less) free to do what they want, but may be brought to act in accordance with the wishes or the interests of the more powerful group, and against their own best interests (and usually also against their will). Power relations of age, class, gender, 'race', ethnicity, origin, social position or profession, are typical examples.

Thus, the possession and exercise of (more) power of one group usually implies the loss or limitation of freedom for the other group. Ideological claims for *freedom*, as in freedom of the press, and freedom of the market, are thus usually claims for power. The same is true, though from a different perspective, for the claims for freedom – as empowerment – by dominated groups.

Making others act as one prefers requires resources. Thus, in the most elementary form of power exercise, namely, that of coercion, the resource may be bodily (typically male) or institutional (police, military) force. More sophisticated is the exclusive control over necessary resources (food, housing, jobs or money) by which others may be forced to comply with the wishes or follow the directives of the powerful. Non-compliance will in that case lead to undesired consequences (loss of necessary resources), so that the dominated will have to choose between being dominated but surviving, on the one hand, or resisting and perishing, on the other. Colonialist and capitalist oppression and exploitation, as well as traditional socio-economic oppression, male chauvinism and racism are of this kind.

For my approach to ideology and discourse, a more 'sophisticated' form of power needs to be dealt with, one that is usually called 'persuasive' and which is traditionally associated with ideology and hegemony. In this case, control does not take place (primarily) through physical or socio-economic coercion, but by more subtle and indirect control of the *minds* of the dominated. By controlling the access to public discourse, only specific forms of knowledge and opinions may be expressed and widely circulated, and these may persuasively lead to mental models and social representations that are in the interest of the powerful. Once these mental representations are in place, the dominated group and its members will tend to act in the interest of the dominant group 'out of their own free will'. The dominated group may lack the knowledge or the education to provide alternatives, or it may accept that the dominance of the dominant group is natural or inevitable, and resistance pointless or even unthinkable.[3]

In this study it is this type of discursive and ideological control that will be taken as the main example of power and dominance, one that seems prevalent in contemporary 'information and communication' societies, in which knowledge and the access to the media and public discourse are the crucial resources to control the minds, and hence indirectly the actions, of others. It is here that consent and consensus play a fundamental role in the exercise of power and the reproduction of ideologies that support such power. Obviously, those who have persuasive, ideological or discursive power, also usually have the coercive powers to take care of those who won't comply with the directions of symbolic power. Economic and physical means may then be applied where less blatant power means fail.

Although the notions of power and domination seem to be used as synonyms above, I use them in a different sense. Since domination implies involuntary inequality, I reserve it as a shorthand for *abuse of power*. This also implies that I don't use power only in a negative sense: power may be consensual and beneficial, as is the case in situations where groups elect their leaders and temporarily accord special power to them. Domination, then, presupposes power and deviance from general or universal ethical principles, that defines abuse, for instance the exercise of social power in one's personal interest, hurting other people, and so on. Both power and domination, as relations between groups, need to be based on ideologies in order for such relations to be reproduced in everyday life and the mundane practices of group members.

This may of course involve all kinds of variation, gradual differences between power and counter-power, and the more or less harsh or soft exercise of power, or the more or less tough resistance or compliance by the dominated. It is in this more contextualized way that power is sometimes said to be 'everywhere'.[4] There would be no dominant groups if power were not exercised, sometimes very subtly, through everyday practices. Moreover, there are (members of) dominated groups who comply, and dissident dominant group members who show solidarity with the underdog. Despite these variations and the uneven exercise or distribution of domination and resistance, we may assume that, at a higher level of analysis, relations of domination between whole groups exist, and that ideologies control these relations and their everyday implementation.

Within this framework, then, we first need to examine the role of ideologies in the *reproduction* of power and dominance. Indeed, one of the core notions of classical ideology analysis and critique has always been that ideologies are developed and applied as *legitimation* for the abuse of power (domination) and its resulting social inequality.

In my analysis I have started from the assumption that ideologies are systems of basic principles that are socially shared by groups. Such ideologies have a number of cognitive and social functions, including the maintenance of group cohesion and solidarity, as well as the protection (or acquisition) of scarce social resources. In sum, socially, ideologies are developed in order to make sure that group members think, believe and act in such a way that their actions are in the interests of themselves and the group as a whole. Such a 'co-ordinative' social function is in the interest of the group in its relationships with other groups.

If a group is in a dominant relationship with respect to other groups, for instance on account of its privileged access to social resources, ideologies have the double function of maintaining or confirming the status quo, and at the same time of providing the basic cognitive framework for arguments to persuade its own members as well as others that this situation is 'just', 'natural', God-given, or otherwise legitimate.

Thus, priority in employment and housing for 'our own' people may thus be legitimated by the racist principle of ethnic or racial superiority, by the 'commonsense' nationalist principle that 'our people' should of course have priority over newcomers, or by the opportunistic socio-economic reason that there is a shortage of houses and jobs, and that 'objective' criteria must be applied for 'fair' decisions, and that those who come last have fewer rights than those who were already 'here'.

Thus, we see how power and domination, as a specific form of inter-group relation and societal structure, may be reproduced by various ideologies (at the socio-cognitive level) and by the social practices (at the microsocial level of situations) that 'implement' such ideologies. Whether these social practices already existed before they were legitimated by an ideology, or whether they only can be thus organized because of an ideology, may be a moot point in practice, asking the proverbial chicken and egg question. Rather, we would say that the dynamics of the interplay of cognition and social practice shows that they mutually constitute each other in a 'dialectical' process. Here power abuse is sometimes ideologically justified afterwards, but at the same time (socially or historically acquired) negative attitudes against others may already exist in order for power abuse to be exercised in the first place.

The primacy of ideology over action

Theoretically and historically, the question of the primacy of ideology over action (or vice versa) is less frivolous. It has for instance been asked in relation to the system of slavery, and its abolition: were racist ideologies (e.g. about the attributed inferiority of Africans) invented to legitimate slavery and colonialism, or could Africans be enslaved in the first place only because they were already seen as inferior to Europeans?

Although this is not the place to answer such questions, a socio-cognitive theory of ideology would opt for the latter suggestion – enslavement presupposes knowledge and opinions about peoples that may be legitimately (ethically, etc.) enslaved: for instance non-Christians, people from a different continent or country, people with a different appearance, or simply people that were conquered by 'us', as the history of slavery (also of others than Africans) has shown. These criteria of difference were generally associated with negative opinions about the others, or at least with feelings of superiority of the own group. Hence, engaging in enslavement already presupposes some kind of negative attitude about the outgroup, which allowed slave-traders and slave-owners to legitimately do what they did, for example without being sanctioned by the state or the Church. If not, they could simply – and probably more cheaply – have enslaved people of their own group, namely, the poor, as was the system of capitalistic exploitation that followed the slave system or as happened with indentured whites. However, precisely because of increasing ethical (and at the same time economic) arguments against slavery, it became necessary to further develop the ideological system that legitimated slavery. Various pseudo-scientific reasons, for example, about the differences between the 'races' were adduced as foundations for such ideologies, thus giving rise to more specific and explicit racist ideologies, where earlier, at least until the eighteenth century, the inferiority and hence 'enslavability' of the others was simply taken for granted – and hence ideologically presupposed.[5]

My point here is merely that systems of social practices of groups (and not incidental actions of individuals) tend to be oriented towards the interests of these groups, and such a *co-ordination problem* can only be solved if the group shares specific knowledge, attitudes, norms, values and ideologies in the first place. These may be very simple and elementary in the beginning, but without them social practices would be more or less haphazard and individual. Concerted action in favour of the group and at the same time for its members, thus, primarily presupposes shared social cognitions, and not the other way around.

Legitimation based on such ideologies only becomes relevant when needed, that is, in contexts of opposition, critique and social struggle. They are social (discursive) social practices in their own right, and their absence does not imply absence of ideology, but only that in such a case the ideology may simply have been taken for granted.

Pure power abuse, thus, does not always need social (discursive) practices of legitimation, but it always *does* need belief systems in order to co-ordinate the social practices that keep the system of domination intact. In the case of slavery and exploitation, thus, negative attitudes and ideologies about relevant outgroups are needed to subject outgroup members to the social practices of domination. As is the case with most complex social actions of groups, ideologies are also necessary as fundamental guidelines for the management of domination.

Of course, once systems of power and domination are already existing, the relationships between social practices, social relations of domination and inequality on the one hand, and attitudes, norms, values and ideologies on the other hand, will mutually sustain each other. Thus, slavery was abolished precisely for this double-edged reason: it did not pay (enough) anymore, while at the same time the ideological justification was successfully challenged by abolitionists and their supporters. In such complex social situations, causes and consequences, actions and minds, are difficult to keep separated. Yet, for purely 'psycho-logical' reasons, I assume that people cannot act rationally and purposefully without the appropriate social cognitions. At the level of the maintenance of groups, group interests and group relations, such cognitive conditions require the development of attitudes and ideologies.

These ideologies may themselves be sustained by (successful) social practices, but they are not only 'invented' as a consequence of such actions, for example as forms of *post hoc* justification. They may be acquired simply by discourse, communication or perception, much in the same way as the Europeans of over five hundred years ago 'knew' about Africans through tales, myths, histories, travelogues, and later through 'scientific' discourse. It is that complex, but essentially 'biased' – and later constantly updated – image that was at the basis of the social practices that led to the slave system, even if these were not the only social cognitions that informed such decisions: Of course also socio-economic, geographic, and other belief systems and conditions were involved in these decisions. Many other examples of dominance systems in society and their historical growth, change and demise may thus be explained also as a consequence (and not the cause) of developing or changing ideologies.

As I have shown above, even 'objective' socio-economic circumstances, as such, do not influence social actions directly, but only through their (mental) interpretation and representation. Thus, there are most certainly also powerful social and economic conditions that allowed or favoured the growing feminist movement of the 1960s and 1970s, but it seems historically more correct to maintain that the major 'causes' of that movement were ideological, and brought about by politicians, writers, academics, artists and other women (and some men) who advocated equal rights for women. This happened in a period in which also other forms of ideological change took place, such as the civil rights movement, decolonialization, and challenges to the authoritarian state.

This suggests that the relationships between power, dominance and ideologies need to be analysed carefully, and I already assumed that ideologies may not always (or even seldom) be 'invented' *post hoc* to legitimate patterns of inequality and the social practices that constitute such inequality. Legitimation is usually discursive and often argumentative, and we saw that it may be especially required in specific social contexts, for example of opposition and struggle. However, such opposition itself logically follows the existence of domination, and domination is possible only with at least a minimum of shared social cognition, and hence by ideologies of dominant groups about dominated groups. That ideologies may change as a result of such opposition, and indeed as a consequence of the ideological debate that accompanies such resistance, is obvious, but again suggests that ideologies are more or less autonomous, and may be changing as a consequence of other ideologies and their manifestations in public discourse, and not (always) as a consequence of changing social practices.

Indeed, traditional systems of power were usually coercive, that is, based in physical action control, violence, military power, or the practices of the secret police or strongmen. On the other hand much 'modern' power is persuasive, discursive and (hence) ideological. Dominant groups no longer maintain their position only by force or even threats of force (the latter already being forms of discourse), but by complex systems of discourse and ideologies that make (most members of) dominated groups believe or accept that domination is justified (as in democratic systems), natural (as in gender and racial domination) or inevitable (as is the case for the socio-economic grounds and the 'logic' of the market).

As soon as some and especially many members of dominated groups no longer accept such ideological grounds, and have acquired the symbolic means to propagate counter-ideologies and the material conditions to act upon such counter-ideologies, ideological change will be inevitable, and changes in social practices will (sometimes very slowly) follow. Indeed, many men will today accept at least some basic tenets of feminist ideologies according to which women and men are equal and should be treated equally, but it is well known that their social practices do not yet always meet the precepts of this new gender ideology. That men are aware of such changing ideologies is frequently apparent from their discourses, for example in disclaimers such as 'We do not discriminate against women, but . . .', or 'We have tried to find a woman, but . . .'. That is, disclaimers of this nature, to which we shall be coming back in the next part of this study, are typical expressions of the contradictions, if not the moral dilemmas, between official or dominant ideologies and actual practices, talk and text. At the same time, the disclaimers obviously function as moves in face-keeping strategies of positive self-presentation.

In sum, despite the complexities of the (sometimes mutual) relations between ideologies, power and domination, the theoretical framework assumes that, historically and theoretically, ideas precede actions, and (at least simple) ideologies precede the systems of social practices that define domination. But, once the system of domination is in place, and especially when it is being challenged, then ideologies may well be further developed to provide for the legitimation of the system. This does not imply, however, that ideologies only serve as systems for discursive legitimation, which would suggest a *post hoc* role of ideologies. More relevantly, ideologies monitor and organize group knowledge and attitudes and hence the beliefs that members need in order to construct the models controlling the actions that implement domination.

Practices of power abuse, domination and oppression can be effective only when co-ordinated, when relevant model structures are socially shared – and ideologies precisely serve that 'practical' goal. As soon as ingroup members need to be recruited and persuaded to share in the actions, against outgroup members, which they would not undertake against ingroup members (which by itself presupposes social norms and attitudes about what should or should not be done), these underlying ideologies may need to be discursively expressed and detailed even for 'internal' use and the intragroup reproduction of power and dominance.

Dominance thus requires a fair amount of consensus as well as practical co-ordination, and ideologies are needed both for the maintenance of the relations of power with respect to the others, as well as for the maintenance of ingroup representations that allow such consensus to be reproduced in everyday life – and to marginalize or punish deviants and dissidents that may threaten, as the 'enemy-within', the dominance of the ingroup. The anti-communist scare of Joe McCarthy was precisely designed to protect and maintain the anti-communist consensus and coherence of a country that represented itself as besieged by World Communism.

This suggests that patterns of power and domination and their underlying ideologies also apply within the group itself, namely, between the elites and the rest, between the leaders and the led, between the thinkers and the doers, a point that needs to be discussed separately later. This will also allow us to reflect about who actually 'invents' the ideologies shared by groups, and whether ideologies are spontaneous popular constructions, or rather those of ideologues or intellectuals who conceive of them first.

Another point to be dealt with (again) in this framework is the well-known question whether ideologies are essentially associated with domination and dominant groups, or whether we need a more general notion of ideology for *any* kind of social group in a specific social position, including that of resistance.

Conflict and struggle

Domination usually leads to resistance and struggle to overcome inequality and oppression. It is common practice in the study of ideology to associate ideologies with domination and its legitimation. I proposed that also resistance needs a socio-cognitive basis in terms of group-relevant values, principles, ideologies and its more specific knowledge and attitudes. In the same way as the exercise and co-ordination of power abuse needs an ideological basis, also group-internal solidarity and inter-group resistance needs to be ideologically organized. Whereas it may be in the interests of a dominant group to conceal their power abuse and to hide the forms of equality that are its consequences, dissidents and opponents may be specifically interested in uncovering and exposing domination and inequality, and to manifest and legitimate as 'just' their own, counter, ideologies. Indeed, that was the point of the communist 'manifesto', as it was for many other manifestos and declarations (like that of the various declarations of human rights) in the first place.

From a critical point of view, this may well imply that dominant groups favour falsehood, deceit and manipulation, and that dominated groups advocate truth, openness and rational or emotional persuasion, that is, goals with which also scholars may want to show agreement. Since also most scholars define themselves (ideologically) as people who want to describe 'objectively' the real social relations involved, their interest may in this respect sometimes be consistent with the subjective, self-serving truths of oppositional groups. However, since their ideologies of class and profession may at the same time be inconsistent with the interests and the demands of the poor, the left, the women, or the minorities, most (middle-class, white, male, etc.) scholars at the same time prefer to ignore such demands and to strategically look elsewhere and do their 'objective' research on less-threatening topics.

Hence the insistence on (scientific) truth in much oppositional ideologies and critical studies of ideology. We also know, however, that in many social, economic, political and ideological conflicts, the distinction between truth and falsity is not that clearcut. This and many other theoretical reasons suggest that it is more adequate to adopt a general concept of ideology, and to assume that ideologies by definition represent the interests of a specific social group, whether or not (in our view as observers, critics or participants) the group's beliefs are based on true social analysis, justified claims or legitimate action.

If ideologies represent group interests, and if conflicting interests also imply social conflict of various kinds, it seems logical to assume that ideologies by definition imply conflict. For fundamental group relations such as those of class, gender and ethnicity, this seems hardly controversial: the empirical facts of the international class struggle, the women's movement and the civil rights movements, hardly allow an other conclusion. Conflicts of interests here are so fundamental that open social conflict is a matter of everyday life, and much of this conflict is not only about socio-economic interests, but also about symbolic, ideological ones.

But in the same way as I asked before whether all social groups have ideologies, I should now ask whether all social conflicts between groups are ideological, and whether all ideological differences always lead to social conflict. Theoretically, groups may have different and even conflicting ideologies, but have learned to live with these in relative social peace. Indeed, there may be higher-order goals and interests that prevent social conflict between two groups. This is not merely a question of principle, but also an empirical matter.

Thus, whereas in some societies or cultures, religious differences may be the basis of acrimonious, open conflict (as in Northern Ireland or India), in others mutual religious tolerance may be prevalent. Similar examples may be given about linguistic or other cultural conflicts. Of course, such an empirical question may hinge on the definition of the very notion of conflict. If conflict also includes mere differences of opinion and debate, then virtually all ideological differences will be conflictual. However, if we limit conflicts to any form of dominance, to one-sided or mutual discrimination or other social practices in which ingroup members are favoured over outgroup members in social interaction, then we have a more specific notion of conflict that may be relevant for a more selective use of the combination of ideology and conflict.

It is in this more restricted sense, then, that we might maintain that ideological differences do not necessarily lead to open social conflict. Professors and students, doctors and patients, lawyers and clients, different political groups or parties, non-governmental organizations and action groups may all have different and inconsistent or even conflicting interests and ideologies without therefore exhibiting such conflict in forms of discriminatory or oppressive practices directed against outgroup members. In other words, whereas most social conflicts and struggle presuppose ideological conflicts (especially over scarce resources), the opposite is not true – not all ideological conflicts imply struggle and social conflict. Ideologies may incite to self-serving group actions, but laws, norms, agreements or other, non-ideological self-interests, may prohibit open conflict. Sometimes social peace and co-operation may be the prevailing, also self-serving criterion over sectarian or ideologically based open conflict. In that case, the ideological struggle may be transferred to the level of mutual discursive persuasion, negotiation and consensus policies.

Competition

Indeed, one form of ideological conflict that need not imply social conflict may be based on inter-group competition. Different groups may have the same goal, but want to realize it with different means. Peace, equality, human rights, the equal distribution of wealth, and so on, may be ultimate goals that countless groups and movements, with different ideologies, may want to achieve in different ways. Such groups, trying to realize the same goals, or vying for the same social resources, may just be competitive and not be in open conflict with each other. Indeed, this is the very ideal (idealistic and ideological) principle of liberal market philosophies.

The question may then be raised again: does social competition require ideological foundations, given the differences of goals or interests, and vice versa, do all ideological differences at least imply some form of competition? I think the first question should be answered negatively. First, because competition is not necessarily social and group-based, but may also be inter-personal, and, second, because competition may also exist between groups with the same ideology, as would typically be the case for different companies in the same social domain vying for the same customers. Differences here need not be 'deeply' ideological, but rather practical and strategic, that is, different ways of reaching the same goal and following the same principles.

On the other hand, competition between different political parties during an election, or between two different ecological groups, may well be based on ideological conflicts. This suggests that the second question may well be answered positively: ideological differences between groups usually imply competition, if only when vying for membership and the recruitment of new members, or the persuasion of outsiders. More common is of course the competition for scarce social resources, such as residence, income, housing and welfare on the other hand, and non-material resources such as knowledge, education, esteem and status, on the other. Thus, struggle and open conflict, while based on conflicting interests, usually implies competition, but not vice versa.

Co-operation

We may make a final theoretical step and ask whether also inter-group relations of co-operation may be ideologically based. This certainly seems to be the case. Two groups or organizations may have different ideologies (e.g. Catholics and Muslims), but may well co-operate to realize a common goal, and jointly acquire or defend shared interests (e.g. support for religious activities and freedoms, or the prohibition of abortion). Ideological opponents may thus become allies in pursuing the realization of the same goals. But whereas open conflict and struggle may need ideological foundation as such, especially in categorizing the beliefs about own group position and the relations with other groups, co-operation as such does not need ideological support. One common goal or one important attitude or opinion may be enough to organize the joint accomplishment of social action.

Conclusion

From this discussion it may be concluded that inter-group relations are generally fundamental in the development and support of ideologies, and conversely that ideologies are at the basis of the social practices that implement such group relations. Conflicts of class, 'race' and gender thus pitch dominant groups against (usually) minority groups or groups with less power. These conflicts are usually about access and control over material or symbolic resources. Other conflicts, as well as competition and co-operation between groups, exist but do not seem to be ideological, but rather practical, for example when groups engage in different ways to separately or jointly realize a common or a related goal. Conversely, although ideologies often imply struggle and conflict, this implication does not always hold: ideologies that are in conflict do not necessarily lead to, or emerge from, social struggle and conflict, but may also be needed to manage diversity.

17

Elites

Who 'invents' ideologies?

In order to complete the picture of the social basis and dimensions of ideologies, we should now ask where ideologies 'come from' in the first place. Who, indeed, 'invents' ideologies? Or do they arise and develop spontaneously in a group, as a form of jointly produced social cognition that has no specific authorship, as would be the case for a natural language?

Many ideologies seem to emerge from large groups of people, if not from the 'masses'. Ecologist, feminist, socialist, nationalist or capitalist ideologies are examples of ideologies that are shared and carried by many people, often across national boundaries and continents. That these should be 'invented' by specific individuals, or by a small group of 'ideologues', thus seems to be counter to the basic conception of ideologies as shared, social belief systems.

One question, often formulated in political psychology, is that it remains to be seen whether such large groups of people do indeed have a more or less explicit or articulated ideology in the first place. They may share a few general principles and goals, but not a 'complete' ideology. Such more detailed and explicit ideologies are then typically attributed to the leaders, the intellectuals, the elites or indeed the 'ideologues' of such groups.[1]

As is the case for social and personal differences of knowledge, we may expect variations of attitudes and ideologies within the same group. Experts have access to more and more varied forms of discourse,[2] may communicate more often and more explicitly about the ideologies of their group, and may therefore develop more detailed and more 'articulate' ideological systems. They may be more familiar with ideological arguments against their ideological opinions, and may therefore become more proficient in ideological counter-arguments, which again may contribute to more detailed attitudes and ideologies. In other words, explicit ideological practices as well as ideological discourses are systematically related to ideologies, which mutually may facilitate each other. Leaders, intellectuals and other 'ideologues' of a group typically may be expected to play such roles, especially because of their privileged access to public discourse, and because of their tasks to lead a group, co-ordinate its actions, and make sure that its goals are realized and its interests protected.[3]

At the same time, there is no clear-cut distinction between such 'ideologues' and the other members of a group. Any member who is more or less conscious of her or his group membership and its goals, and who is able to participate, even passively, in public ideological discourse (e.g. by reading editorials in the press), may thus become fairly proficient in the argumentative expression of underlying ideologies, and thus develop detailed ideologies. Thus, in the women's movement, not only the leaders, intellectuals, experts or other 'ideologues' may develop ideologies, but also other relatively active and 'conscious' members. After all, if ideologies are constitutive of 'lived experiences' and common sense, most members will be confronted with ideological practices, and may in principle be able to interpret these accordingly.[4]

There are probably differences between different ideological groups in this respect. Political party members may be less ideologically conscious about their party membership than are members of religious groups or social movements. As a criterion for such differences, we may assume that the nature of socialization in the group, the amount of top-down or mutual indoctrination, the number of meetings and other forms of active participation, as well as the nature of everyday experiences that have an ideological basis, will all contribute to more or less explicit ideologies. Opposition groups, and social movements who have access to public discourse may thus quickly raise broad support for their ideological beliefs, and thus make members more 'conscious' about the reasons for their group membership. The women's movement, the civil rights movement and the ecological movement from the 1960s to the 1990s are typical examples in point.[5]

Moreover, I do not conceive of ideologies only in terms of explicit, detailed systems, for example those of the 'ideologues' of a group. A few basic principles that organize the attitudes of group members may be enough to define a core ideology, which in turn will influence social practices and discourses. Thus, a fundamental value like 'equality' applied to gender relations, will yield the basic ideological proposition, 'Women and men are equal.' Such a proposition may be enough for more specific application in attitudes about equal rights in general, for example in voting, employment, promotion, salaries, family roles and a host of other social practices and situations. In other words, no very sophisticated, theoretical analysis is necessary in the 'invention' as well as the application of ideologies. Sometimes, a single basic value such as equality or freedom may be enough to construct an ideology when it is applied to the evaluation of the position of the own group.

What *is* crucial, though, is access to public discourse. For some social movements, such discourse may literally begin with shouted slogans in the streets. But, in general, groups and social movements historically have their basis in the writings of smaller elite groups of philosophers, writers, academics, politicians, union leaders and other elites who have at least some access to books or the mass media. These writings may be based on critical social analysis, values and other ethical principles, as well as on personal experiences shared with other members of the group. Whereas the latter case is typical for the women's movement and the civil rights movement, group membership of leading elites is not essential, as long as these elites are able to express and articulate the goals, interests and, vicariously, even the daily experiences of the group 'for' which they write and take action. This is typically the case for the class struggle, but also for anti-racists, or people in the North who feel solidarity with those oppressed in the South.

Top-down or bottom-up?

Related to the question whether ideologies are rather the systems known by 'ideologues' or other elites, or also (fully) shared, as such, by the population at large, is the question of development and influence. That is, it is not merely relevant to investigate where ideological beliefs come from, but also how they are shared and communicated.

We have seen that historical evidence suggests that at least many ideologies first seem to be invented and propagated top-down: a small number of more or less conscious and articulate leaders, intellectuals, or 'ideologues' tend to formulate the ideological principles of a group. Then, through various forms of intra-group discourse (debate, meetings, propaganda, publications) and other institutional and organizational practices, such ideologies are slowly propagated among group members and society at large. Indeed, as we have seen, only the leaders or other elites may have access to the means of communication and public discourse that allow propagation and the reproduction of ideologies in the first place.

This assumption probably applies to such broad social movements as liberalism, socialism, feminism, and the environmental movement, among others. Sometimes rather precise historical and even personal antecedents of ideologies may be found, for instance with eighteenth-century French philosophers, or twentieth-century African-American leaders. Specific books of specific authors may spawn a movement and its ideological grounding.

Although all this may be true, it seems at the same time inconsistent with the social, group-based nature of ideologies. If ideologies are inherently social, how can they be 'invented' by individuals? This would historically reduce social movements and their struggles to personalistic initiatives, actions and ideas.

My view of this dilemma is that there is no contradiction here. Specific ideas may well have been 'invented' by one or a few individual thinkers, revolutionaries, writers or other elites. But for such a set of 'ideas' to become an ideology, in my definition, it must essentially be socially shared. One major condition for this process of social sharing and reproduction is, at least in general, that the group members are able to identify with the group and its ideology. Its goals, practices, position, values, and so on must also apply to them, and be relevant for their everyday experiences. Socialist or communist ideologies thus applied to the everyday lives of workers, and so did feminist ideologies for the everyday lives of women. In other words, even when 'ideas' or arguments for such ideas may initially be 'invented' or at least voiced publicly by specific individuals, they may constitute an ideology only when shared and 'carried' by a group of people whose interests are related to these ideas in the first place.

This also suggests that the success and acceptance of some basic opinions as an ideology by a group may indeed presuppose relevant experiences of group members. Gender inequality and oppression already existed before the women's movement, and at least some women were conscious of such relationships and resented them. Feminist ideas about equality and autonomy, partly borrowed from similar ideas in the realm of politics, were thus hardly more than the explicit formulation of more or less implicit ideas about 'what was wrong' and 'what had to be done' among many women. In that respect, the leaders of the women's movement were inspired both by their own experiences as women and by (initially maybe anecdotal) information about and direct observations of the experiences of other women. It is in this respect that elite ideas and the invention of ideologies are not merely conditioned by the acceptance of such ideas by social groups, but at the same time by the very experiences and (possibly informal) discourses of group members in the first place.

That is, initial explicit and public formulations may have taken place especially by a few leaders, elites or intellectuals, but the opinions, attitudes and experiences on which they are based may already have been widely shared by larger groups, and may already have given rise to occasional, isolated forms of protest, resistance or dissidence among such larger groups. In this respect, the development of ideologies is indeed a social, two-way process, in which top-down leadership and influence is closely tied to bottom-up influence, experience and action.

Elite discourse that does not formulate popular opinions is not likely to spawn a popular movement. And once such a movement grows there are numerous ways 'ordinary' members are able to make themselves heard to the elites in mass meetings, demonstrations and other forms of public action. Indeed, those leaders and elites will generally be most influential who are best able to articulate the concerns and the experiences of the group as a whole. And conversely, the historical record also shows that grassroots experiences and opinions alone may not be a sufficient condition for the articulation of explicit ideologies in public discourses that are able to influence wider social debate and to lead to social change, for example among those groups (and their leaders) who initially oppose a popular movement.

This top-down, elite influence is especially noteworthy for those cases where interests and everyday experiences are initially found to be less acute and fundamental for a large group of people. This is for instance the case for the environmental movement, in which the public at large initially was barely aware of the conditions and consequences of pollution. Only when the threat to health and survival, both to that of humanity as well as to that of nature, was clearly demonstrated by research (the Club of Rome) and concrete examples (like Chernobyl), could environmentalism become a popular movement. Awareness and consciousness, thus, often is a social construct, and elites may play a role in the invention of such a construct.

Elite racism

Racism is a well-known example of the complexities of the relations between elite ideas and popular resentment. Research shows that white elites emphatically deny their role in the reproduction of racism, while at the same time blaming poor whites for xenophobic resentment and taking advantage of such resentment to propagate their own ethnocentric or anti-foreigner ideas and policies.[6] Racism thus is also essentially top-down and bottom-up. Bottom-up influences are generated by the everyday socio-economic experiences of poverty, run-down inner cities and unemployment, and the (biased) perception of 'easy' immigration and the alleged favouring of immigrants in employment, housing and welfare. In other words, popular racism and its ideologies are primarily based on the perception of unfair competition for scarce material and symbolic resources.

However, this is only part of the story of racism. Research also shows that xenophobic beliefs are not always or not only limited to poor whites in a social–economic predicament. Indeed, prejudices and discrimination may even be more widespread not so much at the bottom of the social hierarchy, but just one or two rungs higher, for example in the lower middle class, as relative deprivation theories would predict. Here, instead of feelings of competition, the fear of loss of barely acquired resources may be stronger than among those at the bottom who have nothing to lose.

But even this common observation only provides one more element of the complex structure of racism and its ideological basis. Indeed, prejudice and discrimination, though of different types, are widespread throughout white society, also among the elites themselves. Whereas the confrontation with other peoples, languages and cultures as such may be much more familiar among (travelling and reading) elites, this does not mean full acceptance in everyday life of 'racially' or culturally different others, for instance as colleagues or bosses. That is, the general social superiority feeling of class or education among the elites easily transfers to those of race and ethnicity.[7] Instead of the competitive 'threat' to jobs or housing, elite racism is thus much more oriented towards cultural issues, such as habits, religion, language, education and values. The world-wide construction of the threat of Islam, for instance, is not a popular movement, but an elite phenomenon. Widespread discrimination on the job is also managed by elites, namely, the managers. Bias, stereotyping and outright ethnic polarization in the media is the product of journalists, or of the politicians they use as reliable sources, and hence also an elite phenomenon. The same is true for biased textbooks and scholarly research.

In sum, wherever it really counts (immigration, residence, housing, jobs, education, media, health care, welfare, or the arts) the crucial decisions about inclusion and exclusion are made by the elites. It is therefore essentially the elites who pre-formulate many of the everyday ideological beliefs that have become widespread in racist societies. These ideas need not be explicitly racist, unlike those of extremist right-wing scholars who legitimate ethnic inequality through pseudo-research. Although such scholars are often marginal, they may have tremendous influence on racist organizations as providers of scholarly legitimation.

Rather, I am referring to much more mundane beliefs and arguments against immigration and the multicultural society, beliefs that are easily accepted by everyday common sense, even of those among the population at large who have no daily dealing with minorities. To blame immigrants, refugees and minorities for generally felt problems of, for example, unemployment, overpopulation, inner-city decay and the destruction of the welfare state, is relatively easy as long as the mass media and many intellectuals comply, at least in a moderate way. Having generated the popular resentment against foreigners that may follow such subtly racist propaganda, this popular resentment may be used again as a 'democratic' legitimation against immigration, equal rights or affirmative action (see Chapter 28 for a concrete illustration of these and related strategies).

Given the virtually exclusive access to, and control over the mass media by the elites, and the marginal role of ethnic minorities and their economic competition in the everyday lives of most white people, it is difficult to accept that white racism is a spontaneous, popular movement. Indeed, if the elites were consistently and fundamentally opposed to any form of prejudice, stereotyping and discrimination, all the decisions that really count for minorities would not be so consistently against them, as immigration restrictions, job discrimination and bias in reporting and textbooks shows. Indeed, if only and originally popular in origin, racist beliefs would not have access to anti-racist public means of discourse in the first place.

From these arguments (and much research) it follows that whereas racism may at first sight appear as a form of popular resentment, with only small intervention of some marginal, prejudiced elites, or even as a form of inequality that permeates the whole of Western societies, in fact it is largely based on elite ideologies, discourse and social practices. Ideologies pre-formulated by these elites, however, may in the appropriate socio-economic circumstances be incorporated in initially vague and undirected popular resentment. Such resentment and its socio-economic basis may be such that the elites (and especially the politicians) in turn may often be seen as 'soft' on immigration or minorities, on the basis of a more moderate style of public discourse, as propagated through the media.[8]

That is, one might say that in ethnic matters, large segments of the population are able to read between these 'moderate' lines, and expect the more blatant forms of anti-immigrant beliefs as they are voiced in much everyday talk in private situations. Hence, there is no contradiction here between strong popular resentment and moderate elite discourse about immigration and minorities. On the contrary, what is being presupposed or implied by the elites, as well as the actual social practices of discrimination or exclusion by these elites, is enough as a legitimation for popular resentment in the first place. If leading politicians or newspapers focus on the many problems of immigration, and advocate various forms of exclusion, then many people will feel vindicated in their resentment against 'those foreigners' who are blamed for fundamental social and cultural problems and insecurity.

Another proof of such top-down, elite influence in the reproduction of racist ideologies and practices is that in those situations where leaders do take energetic anti-racist positions, also their subordinates or group members tend to follow and accept such beliefs and policies. Although this may not be the case for all social issues, and although ideological influence may sometimes be both top-down and bottom-up, racism seems to be a rather clear case of predominant elite influence. One other reason for this special case is that ethnic prejudices and ideologies have to do with fundamental values of equality and social and cultural acceptance, and less with economic threats and the experiences of everyday life. Minorities are literally of minor consequence in most Western societies, and the consequences of inter-group relations in this case are therefore of a symbolic and ideological rather than of a socio-economic nature. The point is precisely that the elites transform socio-cultural interests into socio-economic interests that may be acceptable to the population at large, for example by blaming social problems (like unemployment or crime) or a lagging economy on immigrants.

Acceptance, tolerance and diversity (and their counterparts) are typical elite issues, and as long as the elites do not wholeheartedly accept the multiculturalization of white Western societies, it is hardly likely that such will be the case among the population at large. The massive presence of ambiguous or negative news, movies, advertising, opinion, social debate or political propaganda about minorities and immigration – all managed by the elites – in this case finds an easy target among those of the population who only too readily accept that prejudice and discrimination of the others are only in their own best interests. Indeed, racist ideologies are so easy to produce and reproduce precisely because of the elite control of the mass media who specialize in the communication of largely symbolic ideologies, and because racism as a system of inequality is in the interest of all (white) group members.

18

Dominant Ideologies?

Introduction

A major debate in the study of ideologies pertains to the question whether ideologies are by definition 'dominant', or should be defined in broader terms, independent of whether or not groups are dominant, or whether ideologies are able to 'dominate' the minds of all people in the first place. In the previous chapters it has already been suggested several times that a general theory of ideology should not limit the notion to dominant ideologies. However, this decision needs to be discussed in somewhat more detail in this chapter.[1]

Following the dictum of Marx and Engels about ruling ideologies being the ideas of the ruling class, it is frequently debated whether such 'dominant' ideologies exist in the first place, whether the dominant 'class' has a unified ideology, and whether or not such ideologies are able to control the (ideologies of the) dominated classes. Similar questions may of course be formulated for other relations of dominance, that is, also for gender, ethnicity, and so on.

Several of the notions earlier discussed with respect to the top-down influence of ideologies and the role of the elites are combined in these questions. This also suggests that, as such, these questions may well be too general and too broad, and may be answered only in a more analytical fashion.

Groups of various kinds (here including classes) develop group ideologies, and do so especially in social structures characterized by conflict, competition and dominance. On a very global level, nothing seems more obvious, then, that if there are 'dominant classes', such classes also will have their own ideologies. The questions which then need to be asked first are what these classes are and whether, how and whom they dominate. Thus, if the 'rich' are such a class, we may assume that they will develop an ideology that is geared towards the maintenance of their special access to social resources, such as capital, income, tax breaks, status, and so on.

However, if (at least leading) politicians, corporate managers, scholars, journalists, professionals and other elites are also part of 'the' dominant class, or form their own dominant classes, then we have a complication. Will they develop an overall ideology shared by these groups or 'classes', or will they each tend to develop their own, more specific ideologies, tailored to their own interests, position, goals and power?

There is no reason why both should not be the case. Obviously (leading) journalists, scholars and politicians have different interests, and will therefore (also) develop specific, group-based ideologies, as discussed above. However, they may well all have a number of interests in common, for example as related to their (usually middle-class) position and power. Such partly shared ideology fragments may for instance pertain to their specific access to scarce resources (income, employment, housing, status, knowledge, power), identity and membership (as elites or leaders), and especially their position relative to non-dominant groups (variously defined by them as the 'masses', the 'public', the 'voters', 'ordinary people', and so on).

That is, despite possible competition and conflicting interests, some ideology fragments may be shared in a common, overarching, 'dominant' ideology. Whether or not such shared fragments exist at any one time and social situation, is an empirical matter, but it seems quite plausible that if dominant groups have at least their 'dominance' in common, they will also have the corresponding ideology fragments in common that sustain and help legitimate such dominance. Indeed, 'popular' revolutions may well target all such dominant groups, not only for socio-economic, but also for ideological reasons. Since the elites of various social groups often share similar forms of education, media, clubs, friends, employment, and so on, and multiply interact, even competitively, it may be assumed that such a dominant or maybe better 'elite' ideology can also be shared by communication and discourse.

Imposition and inculcation

The second question implied by this issue is whether the (shared) ideology – or ideology fragments – of the dominant groups or elites can be somehow 'imposed' on dominated groups. This formulation of the question suggests that dominated groups interiorize the 'dominant' ideology and accept it, wholly or partly, as their own, whether or not that ideology is in their best interests. Given the definition of power, domination and control in Chapter 16, this means that the elites are able (partly) to control the minds of the dominated group. Since ideologies usually and largely are acquired through discourse, and because the contemporary elites obviously control the means of ideological reproduction, and especially the mass media, the question essentially boils down to two interrelated empirical questions, namely, whether the mass media mainly represent the ideologies of the elites, and whether these ideologies have the intended influence on the ideologies of the ('dominated') public at large.

The first of these questions hardly needs to be further investigated: All research shows that the ideologies that are most prominent in the media are largely those of the elites, and not of any dominated or oppositional groups.[2] Where moderate forms of oppositional ideologies (such as feminist or environmentalist ones) have access to mainstream media at all, they are consistent with those of significant 'fractions' of the dominant elites.

Also, this does not mean that the symbolic media elites (defined as senior editors, leading reporters and columnists) always fully agree with for instance political, business or academic attitudes and ideologies, let alone with all specific issues. As suggested, there are different interests and attitudes. However, on fundamental issues, there is a rather broad consensus. Thus, no mainstream Western media, nor other power elites are (today) anti-capitalist, socialist, feminist, pacifist or anti-racist. Moreover, and even more crucially, dominant elite groups have prominent access to the mass media. Whether or not they are occasionally criticized (as corrupt politicians or as polluting industries may), their overall representation is generally favourable or at least respectful. In other words, through the media, other elite groups and their discourses and opinions are at least able to reach the public at large: They have an effective public voice.

The second question, about the ideological influence of the mass media, is as complex as it is crucial in this debate. Much research suggests that the general, ideological influence of the media is pervasive, especially in those domains where media users have no alternative ideological sources or personal experiences that are blatantly inconsistent with the dominant ideologies as conveyed and reproduced by the mass media, as is typically the case for ethnic ideologies or foreign policy ideologies.[3] On the other hand, much contemporary research emphasizes that even where such ideological control takes place, media users are active and flexible and able to reject persuasive ideological statements where necessary, or adapt such ideologies to their own needs, interests or circumstances. Indeed, there are many specific examples where pervasive ideological influence of the elites through the mass media did not take place at all.[4]

In order to explore the implications of such apparently contradictory empirical results, we need to know more about which dominant and dominated groups are involved, what ideologies these respectively may have, and under what conditions which dominant ideologies may be inculcated in which dominated groups. Again, these questions are not merely conceptual but empirical, and their full answers must hence be given in detailed research into the ideologies of various social formations.

What are 'dominated' groups?

One first issue we need to deal with here is whether the very general and hence fuzzy notion of 'dominated' groups, that is, as those dominated by the elites, is a realistic construct. As long as we talk about socio-economically defined 'classes', as is the case in most traditional research and especially in the Marxist tradition, the question may be slightly less complex, but obviously ideologies in contemporary societies are not limited to classes.

The question then is whether these 'dominated groups' collectively have or share (fragments of the same) ideologies. For the same social and economic reasons as it was assumed that the elites must share ideological fragments, the non-elites must share such fragments, if only because of their similar non-dominant position, and hence at least some shared interest, namely, lack of power. Of course women, minorities, the poor, the workers and so on, each have their group ideologies that provide the basic framework that can account for their specific experiences in everyday life, for their (dominated) position in society, and for possible forms of opposition, dissent or resistance, that is, belief systems which Mannheim called 'utopias', because they formulate alternatives to currently dominating ideologies.[5] But although there will be conflicts of interest (e.g. between white workers and black workers, between poor men and poor women), their similar relations to the elites suggest common ideology fragments which may lead to political coalition formation, for example defining movements such as the Rainbow Coalition in the USA.

Theoretically, there is no reason why these various non-dominant groups would adopt dominant ideologies if these are inconsistent with their daily experiences, their opinions about social events and their basic interests. Indeed, if they were to do so, such ideologies would monitor group knowledge and attitudes that would continuously clash with the daily experiences of most group members. Thus, when confronted with (implied) elite ideologies in the media, the public(s) at large would, again theoretically, only adopt those ideology fragments that are also in their own interests and reject or ignore those that do not 'fit'.

For the majority of the white public one prominent example may be the adoption of fragments of racist ideologies, since these are also in their own best interests. On the other hand, liberal market ideology fragments that accept unemployment as a necessary aspect of capitalist production, or promote a further destruction of the welfare state, may well be much less broadly accepted, especially in the working class and the lower middle classes. Following this argumentation, the general dominant ideology thesis would in many instances be invalid, and would only apply for specific ideology fragments and for specific non-dominant target groups, for example whites, or men, or the middle class.

Whenever and wherever it *does* take place, ideological dominance may take many forms and occur in different situations. Preventing solidarity among non-dominant groups is a well-known and powerful device, namely, of conquering the enemies by dividing them. Another strategy is to prevent or mitigate group identification in the first place. We have already seen that group identity and identification is a crucial implication of the acquisition of ideological schemas throughout a group.

For instance, liberal socio-economic ideologies and especially their pervasive and persuasive genre expressions (in news, background stories, advertising) in the mass media, may especially address media users as individuals. In situations of social and economic crisis, thus, ingroup solidarity among non-dominant classes may be prevented by suggesting that each person 'can make it', as was the case in the conservative rhetoric of 'popular' capitalism of Thatcherism and Reagonomics, and the increasing power of the New Right.[6]

At the same time union membership may be discredited as 'communist', 'radical' or simply out of date. Thus, forms of intra-group solidarity of dominated groups may be prevented or obstructed. The same divisions may be created among women by discrediting feminism; they may be discredited among ethnic minorities by emphasizing ethnic crime or by discrediting multiculturalism through allegations of political correctness, on the one hand, and at the same stressing the positive role of the government and the 'offering' of integrated minority 'help' by mainstream institutions, on the other hand. Obviously, such strategies are not always successful, and resistance and opposition may be able to challenge them in many ways, thus leading to specific social changes, including some in the ideologies of dominant groups.[7]

Further complications

Of course, deeper analysis of these ideological processes is in order, because the picture is much more complicated. For one, even within dominant groups, there are ideological *dissidents*. That is, there are elite group members (leading politicians, journalists, scholars, etc.) who reject and resist dominant ideologies and may even 'side with' dominated groups, as has been the case in most ideological revolutions. The converse is also true – members of dominated groups may espouse elite ideologies, if only in order to get, individually, recognition or access to other resources that the elites will provide to them as tokens of their gratitude for their 'defection'. Examples may for instance be found among some minority group members who have espoused ideologies (e.g. about 'political correctness') that are clearly inconsistent with those of their own group (see Chapter 28).

Another well-known complication is the fact that, despite what has been said above, there are cases in which elite ideologies are successful among specific dominated groups even when they are inconsistent with the interests of most group members, as is the case for neo-liberal market ideologies. One, equally well-known, explanation for such success, apart from their pervasiveness in the mass media and public discourse, and the social processes of individualization and competition among the dominated groups, are the various mechanisms of *manipulation*.

That is, what the public discourses of such ideologies typically do is to tone down the obviously inconsistent parts of the ideology and emphasize those parts that may be more attractive. Thus, racist (and some conservative) parties may foment ethnic prejudices, blame immigrants or minorities for social problems, and may thus attract lower (middle) class voters and supporters. They will, however, seldom advertise their conservative policies when it comes to the position of women and the consequences, for the poor, of their market ideologies. At the same time, those who share more subtle versions of racist ideologies may publicly mitigate their racist attitudes, and try to influence those among the population who reject overt racism, but who may be sensitive to, for example, ecological or social ideas. In that case, reference to overpopulation, scarce natural resources, or the cultural 'backwardness' (e.g. in the treatment of women) of some immigrant groups, may be used as 'rational' arguments in favour of an immigration control that may be acceptable even to liberals.

In the same way, the mass media will generally select or focus on those 'facts' that are consistent with elite interests, and vice versa, thereby persuasively influencing the models, and indirectly the knowledge and other social representations of the public at large, as described before. Most prominent are examples of nationalist war propaganda, and the public praise of the blessings of the 'freedom' or the 'flexibility' of the market, in which the multiple negative consequences for large groups of the population will be selectively obscured or simply ignored.

Strategies of ideological control

Thus, elite ideologies may well be adopted more broadly among the population at large or among specific dominated groups under the following conditions.

1 They are able to divide the non-dominant groups, by being at least attractive to, or in the interest of, some non-dominant groups, thus preventing intra-group solidarity and the organization of counter-power, for example sexism and especially racism, thus preventing non-elite solidarity and sharing of dissident ideologies, for instance among women and minorities.
2 Preventing ingroup solidarity of (important) non-dominant groups by creating divisions within the group and by addressing group members as individuals, for example dividing women between 'feminists' and the 'others', or enticing lower-class members with liberal rhetoric of personal responsibility and upward mobility.
3 There are no (strong) popular alternatives to elite ideologies, or these alternatives are unknown or marginalized, for example racism, because anti-racism is virtually excluded from the mass media; or neo-liberalism after the demise of socialism and communism.
4 The elites (and especially media editors) prevent or limit the access to public discourse of leaders of non-dominant groups (no feminist, anti-racist or political 'radicals' in mainstream media), or will marginalize or discredit them among the population at large or even among their own groups.
5 Popular ideologies are seemingly adopted by the elites, but in a very moderate way, thereby avoiding major conflicts with the interests of the elites, for example environmentalism and – partly – feminism.

6 If elite ideologies are largely inconsistent with relatively strong and known ideologies of dominated groups, the elites have the special means of media access and control, and discursive strategies of manipulation of knowledge and opinions, for example by emphasizing the ideological implications that are less inconsistent with the interests of dominated groups, or de-emphasizing those that are inconsistent with these interests, for example nationalism, militarism, and especially neo-liberalism and neo-conservatism.

Of course, there are other means of ideological control, but these cover a wide variety of forms of ideological dominance. The more specific but crucial discursive strategies involved in these forms of ideological domination will be discussed in more detail later.

Concluding remark

This discussion suggests that the arguments for the dominant ideology hypothesis are not very persuasive, but that in many situations and under specific conditions it does seem to hold true. It is the task of a more detailed theory of ideology to specify how and where it does apply, and where it does not apply. It is, however, a very general and abstract thesis, and it is clearly necessary that it be translated into the detailed structures of social cognition, discourse, communication and social structures, before it can be evaluated more rigorously. Despite the large ideological variety and confusion of contemporary society, the evidence strongly suggests that, given the increasing control of the elites of the mass media, and the increasing role of the mass media as the major means of ideological control of society, elite ideologies will generally tend to be dominant, as defined above. Popular ideologies may become dominant only (a) if they have broad support within or across several dominated groups, (b) if leaders of such groups have access to public discourse, and especially the mass media (which implies that at least some mass media need to collude with them), and more generally (c) if these ideologies are not fundamentally inconsistent with the interests of the majority of the elites.

19

Institutions

Organizing the reproduction of ideologies

In the analytical sequence that carries us from the psychology of individual cognition and action, and the microsociology of everyday situated interaction (including discourse), to the macrosociology of group relations, power and shared belief systems, we finally need to examine the role of institutions that organize, manage or propagate such cognitions, actions, interactions and group relations. In the discussion about the role of discourse in the reproduction of ideologies, we shall further investigate how ideologies are reproduced in and by the text and talk of families, peer groups, schools, media, churches, unions, clubs, social movements, agencies, corporate businesses, and so on. In the previous chapters, we have found that the media play a central role in the reproduction of dominant elite ideologies. Therefore, before I discuss the discursive details of such reproduction processes, a sociological analysis needs to focus more generally on the ideological role of organizations and institutions.

In many ways, institutions or organizations are the 'practical' or social counterpart of ideologies. That is, in the same way as ideologies organize group cognition, institutions and organizations organize social practices and social actors. Merely being a 'group' of women, journalists, teachers, or anti-racists, may not be enough to organize members' actions effectively, and to achieve desired group goals, either individually or jointly. Institutions and organizations may co-ordinate common goals and actions, provide or distribute resources and other conditions and constraints, elect or impose leaders, and so on.

Similarly, in order to organize ideological practices, we may assume that *ideological institutions* are needed.[1] In other words, ideological institutions are created that (also) have as their task the 'realization' of a shared ideology. Probably there are few institutions that are exclusively ideological, that is, geared towards the propagation of belief systems only. *Churches* may still be the most obvious example, although in practice, and in order to realize their ideological goals, they also have several (other) social aims and activities, such as welfare and community services. At a more basic level, also *families* and their socialization practices are partly ideological, because of their role in the socialization of norms, values and fragments of ideology.[2]

Schools, *universities* and the whole education system are among the most complex, elaborate and pervasive ideological institutions, if only because they involve virtually all members of society, intensively and daily, sometimes for more than twenty years. Geared mainly towards the reproduction of knowledge and the acquisition of skills, they obviously also operate as major means for the reproduction of the dominant ideologies of society, although in some cases they also facilitate the propagation of counterideologies. Indeed, schools and especially universities are among the few institutions where enough freedom (from state intervention, from the market, etc.) exists for 'dissidents' to voice their opposed ideologies.[3]

Despite this pervasive role of education, in contemporary information societies much of the ideological work of the family, the Church and the school is taken over by the *mass media* as an institution. While mainly geared towards the production of information and entertainment, they at the same time constitute the most complex institution for the public expression and challenge of ideologies. Without the media, and given the reduced role of the church, and the limitation of schooling to children and adolescents, public debate about issues, and shared knowledge about what happens in society and the world, would at present be unthinkable. It may therefore be assumed that in the reproduction of ideologies, the media play a central role. Social representations are easily and widely shared because of these forms of accessible public discourse, and the same is true for the ideologies that underlie these representations.

The structures, strategies and practices of these social institutions need not only be oriented by practical reasons of organization, efficiency, the distribution of roles or resources or the attainment of goals. They may also reflect and facilitate ideological concerns. Lessons, textbooks, exams, assignments, corrections and sanctions in educational institutions, thus, may be organized partly by ideologically based aims to teach and inculcate 'the right things', including the 'right' ideologies in the first place. In a less organized way, the same is true for the various socialization discourses in the family.

The media

Though less explicit, but therefore probably more pervasive and influential, the same is true for the media. The production of news, advertising, documentaries, movies, games, talk shows and other shows, among many other media genres, may thus be examined in detail for the ways they organize actions, discourses, sounds and images in such a way that ideological production and reproduction, including processes among the audience, are most effective. In news gathering, such ideological concerns monitor assignments, beats, interviews, press conferences, press releases, selection and decision procedures, among other practices. That is, these practices are governed by professional expertise and attitudes and ideologies about what is true or false (fact or opinion), interesting or uninteresting, newsworthy or not, relevant or irrelevant, and so on. News values are among the many ideological systems that guide such practices – these specify, for instance, the preference for news about elites, negative events (especially those caused by others), our own cultural group and world region, and so on.[4]

But, less directly, the same is true for seemingly less ideological decisions about who has access to the media, who is interviewed, covered, and who will be quoted. It is well known that elite persons, organizations and states are predominant in these patterns of access, and hence also the opinions and ideologies of such elites. And since most journalists in the West are white, male, middle class and heterosexual (among other identities), it is most likely that they will favour the access and the opinions of 'similar' news actors. Most research confirms this assumption.

In sum, the routines, actors, events and institutional arrangements in newsmaking are biased towards the reproduction of a limited set of dominant, elite ideologies, as we have seen in a previous chapter. This is not only true for news production, but also for current affairs programmes, documentaries, shows, and other categories of media discourse.

What has been said about institutional production routines and constraints is reflected in their products. Thus, preferential access is reflected in preferential quoting, favourable opinions and hence style, access to the opinion page, preferred topics, and in general in all aspects of media discourse. For such complex ideological reasons, thus, we get more news and opinions about alleged or socio-economically less destructive 'minority' crimes than about real crimes of discrimination by employers or other elites, more news by and about men and about topics that interest men more than women, and so on. These are familiar research findings, and my point is merely to recall them in order to illustrate the ideological conditions, practices and products of institutions.

Crucially, the same is true for the consequences of such ideological institutions for the reproduction of ideologies among the population at large, as I have already discussed when examining the dominant ideology thesis. Despite the personal differences and freedom of media users in their processing and use of media discourse, the overall ideological effects of the media are undeniable – the range of acceptable social ideologies is more or less identical with those that have preferential access to the mass media. Fundamental norms and values, the selection of issues and topics of interest and attention (agenda setting), selective if not biased knowledge about the world, and many other elements or conditions of ideological control, are presently largely due to the mass media, or indirectly to the groups and institutions, such as those of politics, that have preferential access to the media. Of course there will be debate, opposition, differences of opinion, as well as differences among newspapers. However, these are well within the boundaries of tolerable ideological variation. No serious newspaper advocates, for instance, the abolition of the market, the abolition of all arms and armies, a total reversal of all gender roles, so that women will be put in charge of the world and all major institutions, let alone the control of the mass media by independent monitoring organizations that will evaluate their truthfulness, quality, and the total absence of gender, class, ethnic or other biases. In sum, within a theory of ideology, the pervasive role of ideological institutions such as those of politics, education and especially the mass media explains the very social conditions of ideologies, namely, the means and the ways of their being shared by large numbers of people and groups in the first place.

Institutional racism

Taking up again the example of racism, we should ask how racist ideologies are sustained and reproduced by institutions and organizations. The most obvious example in most countries in Europe and other white-dominated countries is the presence and activities of racist *political parties*.[5] Although politically nowhere dominant beyond the local level of some neighbour-hoods and cities, and although often marginalized by the mainstream media, their indirect ideological influence is considerable. Even when covered in a context of conflict, for instance by quoting provocative statements of their leaders, or by highlighting counter-demonstrations and protests, they are as widely known as their ideologies are. The radical versions of these ideologies may be generally rejected by the elites, but it has been often observed that more moderate versions of their xenophobic or anti-immigrant slogans have found wide currency and even support among mainstream parties, as has been the case for instance for the conservative parties in the USA, the UK, France, the Netherlands, Germany, Austria and Italy, among other countries.

Increasingly harsh immigration restrictions, earlier advocated only by racist parties, are now standard government policy everywhere. The same is true for various policies that turn back (or never introduce) the gains and claims of the civil rights movement or similar movements in other countries. Popular support for such policies among large sections of the white population is guaranteed, after the ideological onslaught of racist and conservative propaganda, which tends to blame many social ills on the presence or the activities of immigrants and minorities. Immigration can thus easily be targeted as one of the major causes of unemployment, diminishing welfare or the real or alleged increase of crime. The mass media, and especially the conservative popular press, play a crucial role in the persuasive support and propagation of these ideologies.

And although I focus here on the production and reproduction of ideologies, it hardly needs to be added that such ideologies also sustain concomitant social and political action. Ideologies are translated into actual policies, which are executed in concrete practices, for example of the immigration services, the police or the courts, or the media. The negative examples of the elites and state agencies are followed, often more blatantly or even violently, by organizations or youth groups who openly discriminate or attack immigrants and minorities. In a few domains in society, the institutional and elite propagation of ethnocentrist, xenophobic and racist ideologies clearly and directly influences everyday practices of exclusion, marginalization, problematization and violence directed against others, as is the case in the area of ethnic relations. Colonialism, slavery, segregation, Jim Crow, the Holocaust, and at present Rwanda, Bosnia and South Asia, are the well-known illustrations of that observation.

In sum, racist ideologies, and especially their popular and populist versions, are sustained by a large number of important institutions and organizations. Extremist right-wing parties, conservative parties and think-tanks, the popular press, phone-in radio, racist pamphlets, marginal but influential racist scholars and their publications, are among the many institutional factors that are involved in this reproduction process.[6]

Again, although the radical versions of these ideologies may not be predominant, moderate versions may well have become dominant in Western societies where conservative forces are in the majority. Even leftist and social democratic parties and organizations don't escape the pressures of the broad popular (white) support for such ideologies, and adapt their ideologies and policies accordingly. This does not only show in the support of anti-immigration or anti-minority attitudes, but especially also in the marginalization of anti-racist groups and ideologies.

Indeed, one of the main problems in Western societies may not be that moderate racist ideologies are influential, but rather that the official non-racist norm, as established by law and constitution, is not institutionalized in such a way that such ideologies are energetically combated. There are anti-racist groups and institutions, but these are minor and often have a bad press or little support among the population at large, as well as among the elites. They may be officially marginalized as much as the extremist-right, while allegedly being too 'radical'. In such a political evaluation, thus, both racism and anti-racism are rejected, thus leaving a vast consensus intact in which anti-immigrant ideologies may flourish because they are simply deemed not to be racist, but commonsense. We shall later see how political and media discourse constructs and sustains such a broadly organized consensus of white domination.

Part III

DISCOURSE

20

The Relevance of Discourse

The special relevance of discourse

In the third part of this study I finally focus on another crucial dimension of ideology, namely, its expression and (re)production in social interaction in general and in discourse in particular. Having assumed that ideologies are shared social representations that have specific social functions for groups, we need to find out how such ideologies are acquired, constructed, used and changed by social group members. This means that, after the excursion into the social macro domain of groups, group relations and institutions, we now need to get down to the micro level again, that is, to the level where ideological production and reproduction is actually being achieved by social actors in social situations.

Against the background of the classical approach to ideology, such a micro-level study of interaction and discourse is especially relevant. Not only does the traditional account of ideologies tell us little about the precise nature of ideologies (namely, as mental representations), but it is also unspecific about how exactly ideologies come about, and what role social actors play in their construction and reproduction. This also means that such approaches largely ignore how a typical macro notion such as ideology should be related to typical micro notions such as actors, actions, social practices, discourses and social situations.[1]

By focusing especially on the role of discourse in the reproduction processes of ideologies, I do not imply, as some current approaches do, that I *reduce* ideologies, or their study, to discourse and discourse analysis.[2] Discourse, language use and communication do play a special role in such processes of reproduction, but ideologies are *also* being expressed and reproduced by social and semiotic practices other than those of text and talk. From the study of racist and sexist ideologies, for instance, we know that many forms of non-verbal discrimination also exhibit ideological beliefs. Besides these well-known practices of discrimination, also other semiotic messages (e.g. photographs and movies) may of course express underlying ideologies.[3] When social members observe and comprehend such (non-verbal) practices, they may also infer underlying opinions of actors; and across contexts these may also be generalized to more abstract underlying social attitudes and ideologies. They may do so through an inferential step that tells group members: 'This apparently is how we do it' or, 'This is apparently the way to deal with members of such and such a group.' In sum, although discourse is often crucial in the expression and reproduction of ideologies, it neither is a necessary nor a sufficient 'medium' of reproduction.

Although this part of the study focuses on discourse, we should bear in mind that it is paradigmatic for a broader study of ideological practices in all domains of society, from non-verbal communication to the myriad of other social actions and interactions that define everyday life. Also, we should not forget that discourse is often embedded in or otherwise related to such non-verbal interactions, as is the case for talk and text at home, in parliament, in school, in the newsroom, the workfloor, the office, the shop, the agency, the hospital, the police station or in prison. Ideologically based dominance and inequality, conflict and competition, resistance and opposition, as discussed before, thus, are implemented and reproduced in many ways, both discursively and in other interactions.

Discourse, however, has a special status in the reproduction of ideologies. Unlike most other social practices, and in a more explicit way than most other semiotic codes (such as photos, pictures, images, signs, paintings, movies, gestures, dance and so on), various properties of text and talk allow social members to actually *express* or *formulate* abstract ideological beliefs, or any other opinion related to such ideologies. Specific actions only allow more or less indeterminate inferences about the underlying opinions of actors, but as such cannot express general, abstract or socially shared opinions.

With *visual* messages this is somewhat easier, and in some cases more effective than through discourse. But in general, there is no semiotic code as explicit and as articulate in the *direct* expression of meanings, knowledge, opinions and various social beliefs as natural language (and of course in various sign languages). If an image is worth a thousand words, this is mostly because of the visual details that are hard to describe verbally. This means that images may be particularly apt at expressing the visual dimension of mental models. If images express opinions or general beliefs and ideologies, they do so rather indirectly, and hence are in need of (indeterminate) interpretations. This does not imply that, in communication, such indirect expressions of opinions and ideologies need to be less persuasive. On the contrary, a dramatic photograph of a specific scene, event or person may be a much more 'powerful' means of expressing opinion than words. However, this persuasiveness is precisely based on the concreteness of the 'example', and needs reader-based inferences about what the picture actually 'means', as is also the case for model-based storytelling or other examples used as a means to convey abstract opinions and ideologies.

Discourse enables social actors to formulate general conclusions based on several experiences and observations. It is able to describe past and future events, it is able to describe and prescribe, and may describe actions and beliefs at any level of specificity and generality. And for us, most interestingly, discourse not only exhibits ideologies indirectly, as other social practices may do too, but also explicitly formulates ideological beliefs directly.

Thus, in many situations of intra- and inter-group text and talk, social members are able to tell or remind others or novices about the ideological beliefs shared by the group. Ideological socialization, therefore, largely takes place through discourse. In interactional confrontations with members of other groups, people are similarly able to discursively explain, defend or legitimate their ideologies. In other words, discourse allows direct and explicit expression of ideologies, but the crucial function of such (usually generic, general) expressions is in their social consequences, namely, the acquisition, change or confirmation of social beliefs.[4]

In this and the next chapters, I shall describe some of the dimensions of the relations between discourse and ideology. This investigation is merely illustrative – many volumes can be written about the many ways ideologies are expressed in text and talk. My approach here is primarily conceptual and theoretical. I want to know, more generally, *how* discourse expresses or reproduces underlying ideologies, and not study specific ideologies or specific language or discourse structures (such as topics, pronouns or metaphors). In a later study I hope to focus in more detail on the role of discourse structures in the reproduction of ideologies.

The concept of discourse

In order to understand how ideology relates to discourse, let me first summarize my discourse theoretical framework, especially since this is somewhat different from others that study both discourse and ideology, such as the more philosophical approach by Foucault.[5] As indicated before, my approach is essentially multidisciplinary, and combines an analysis of linguistic, cognitive, social and cultural aspects of text and talk in context, and does so from a critical, socio-political perspective.[6]

The concept of discourse used here is just as general, and hence as fuzzy, as that of language, communication, society or, indeed, that of ideology. Although its 'definition' is the task of the whole discipline of discourse studies, a few remarks are in order about my use of the term 'discourse' in this study. This is also necessary because in many current studies of ideology and its relations to discourse, other (sometimes confusing) discourse concepts are used.[7]

Communicative events versus verbal products

The primary meaning of the term 'discourse' as it is used here, and as it is now generally used in more socially oriented discourse analysis, is that of a specific *communicative event.* Such a communicative event is itself rather complex, and at least involves a number of social actors, typically in speaker/writer and hearer/reader roles (but also in other roles, such as observer or overhearer), taking part in a communicative act, in a specific setting (time, place, circumstances) and based on other context features. This communicative act may be written or spoken, and, especially in spoken interaction, usually combines verbal and non-verbal dimensions (gestures, face-work, etc.). Typical examples are an everyday conversation with friends during dinner, a dialogue between doctor and patient, or writing/ reading a news report in the newspaper. We may call this the *extended* primary meaning of the term 'discourse'.

In the everyday practice of discourse studies, however, we often also use a more *restricted* primary meaning of 'discourse.' In that case, we abstract the verbal dimension of the spoken or written communicative act of a communicative event, and usually refer to this abstraction as *talk* or *text*. That is, in this sense 'discourse' is rather being used to refer to the accomplished or ongoing 'product' of the communicative act, namely, its written or auditory result as it is made socially available for recipients to interpret. 'Discourse' in that case is the general term that refers to a spoken or a written *verbal product* of the communicative act.

In earlier text linguistics, and still among some discourse linguists, a related distinction is made, between 'discourse' and 'text'. Here 'discourse' is used to refer to the actual, socially displayed text or talk, and 'text' to its abstract (e.g. grammatical) structures. This distinction implements for discourse analysis the well-known distinctions between *langue* and *parole* or between *competence* and *performance* in structural and generative linguistics. 'Discourse' is then a unit of language use or performance (parole), and 'text' an abstract theoretical unit (like a noun phrase, clause or sentence) that belongs to the realm of abstract linguistic knowledge or competence or to the system of the language (langue). Although relevant, I no longer use this distinction. In contemporary, multidisciplinary discourse analysis it has become either too confusing or obsolete – discourse studies now generally analyses discourses as forms of language *use*. Such a focus on concrete, ongoing language use does *not* mean that the theoretical account itself is less abstract. In the same way as linguists abstract grammatical properties from actual verbal utterances, discourse analysts do so when they describe, for example, gestures, intonation, pauses, repairs, graphical design, narrative structures, metaphors, turns, closing sequences, and so on.

Tokens versus types

Whether in its extended or restricted meaning, namely, as talk/text or as complex communicative event, 'discourse' in this primary meaning is used to refer to *particular* objects or *tokens*, that is, to unique occurrences involving particular social actors in a particular setting and context. This uniqueness is for instance defined in terms of the unique combination of *these* words, intonation, gestures, meanings or acts being accomplished *now* by *these* participants. To mark this specific use of the notion of 'discourse', we use indefinite or definite articles or demonstratives: we speak about 'a discourse', 'the discourse' or 'that discourse'. That is, 'discourse' is a count noun here.

In the age of printing, xeroxing and computer files, *copies* may be made of the spoken or written expression of such a unique discourse, for instance on tape or in a book or newspaper. But even then we say that these are copies of (the expression of) the 'same' discourse.

As elsewhere, there are the usual delimitation problems: Where does one discourse end and the next one begin, for instance in a sequence of conversations, or in a collection of printed texts, for instance in a newspaper, book or encyclopedia? Are the different instalments of an article, a TV film, or a daily story, one or more discourses, even when they are physically non-contiguous in time or place? There are many examples where there is an ambiguity between such discontinuous instalments of the 'same' text or talk, on the one hand, and sets of 'intertextually' related discourses, on the other hand. Indeed, whereas a continuous spoken dialogue is usually considered as representing one discourse, a written dialogue or debate is rather seen as an intertextually related sequence of texts, even when it may be called 'one' debate in both cases.

This is not the place, however, to solve such well-known problems of delimitation and definition. To simplify matters, I simply follow commonsense practices here, and speak about one dialogue when it is continuous in time (not in space, because participants may talk to each other over the phone), has the same participants, and has a marked beginning and end. And for written texts we assume that they have the same writer(s), have marked beginning and end, and usually, though not always, that they are physically continuous (exceptions are, indeed, several instalments of the 'same text' appearing at different times, or separate parts of the same time appearing in different locations of the same medium (e.g. a front page story in the press, continuing on an inside page). Both for spoken and for written discourse, we usually further require that they are globally coherent, that is, that they form a meaning unit, and not only a physical unit of continuous expression. But this requirement is itself problematical for everyday conversations that are characterized by several unrelated topics, or for instance literary texts, like poems, that do not seem to have an obviously unitary, global meaning.

These problems and examples also show that 'discourse' is a highly complex and ambiguous notion, and that as soon as we really want to give a 'definition' we already need to start making all kinds of analytical distinctions, use other concepts, and indeed start to theorize about discourse. Hence it is usually a rather pointless exercise to give exact definitions. As suggested above, thus, discourse is as general and therefore as vague a notion as 'language', 'society' or 'culture'.

Besides the specific (extended or restricted) notion of 'discourse', there is also a more abstract concept. Instead of specific, unique tokens, we may also use 'discourse' to refer to abstract *types*. Thus, instead of referring to this *particular* conversation, story or news report, we may also use the notion of discourse in order to designate conversations, stories or news reports in general. When we make theoretical, that is, general, assertions about discourse, they are of course about types, not about tokens. We may say that 'a' or 'the' news report or story consists of a number of conventional categories, such as an initial summary (e.g. a headline and a lead) or a concluding coda. That is, in this case we characterize a potentially infinite set of real or possible tokens that satisfy such properties. This abstract notion of discourse may similarly be restricted as well as extended. We may refer to a dialogue as the verbal result of a communicative event, or to the whole communicative event. In this chapter, we only talk about discourse and its properties in general, not about particular instances or tokens of text or talk as we would do when analysing concrete examples.

Text and talk of social domains

To make things even more complicated, there are at least two other main meanings of the concept of discourse. First, closely related to the notion of discourse referring to an abstract type, the concept may be used to refer to specific *genres*, mostly in combination with an adjective denoting a genre or social domain, as in *political discourse*, *medical discourse* and *academic discourse*. In this case, the notion of discourse is also general and abstract, but selects a specific set of (abstract) discourses or genres. Thus, political discourse may be the overall designation for all discourse genres that are used in the realm of politics, or the discourses used by politicians, and so on. In this sense, 'discourse' is not simply a specific genre (like a parliamentary debate or a propaganda leaflet), but rather a socially constituted set of such genres, associated with a social domain or field.

Finally, we may distinguish an even more abstract and higher-level notion of discourse. Instead of referring to all the text and talk, or the discourses of a specific period, community or a whole culture, we may also use the very abstract and generic notion of the 'discourse' of that period, community or culture – including all possible discourse genres and all domains of communication. Other notions sometimes used here are *discourse formation* or *discursive formation*, and *order of discourse*, following sociological uses of the terms 'social formation' and 'social order', respectively. Depending on one's theory of discourse and society, also this highly abstract notion of discourse may be restricted (all text and talk) or extended (all communicative events, including language users, contexts, etc.). It is this last, very abstract and general notion of discourse that is often related to the equally general, abstract, social and shared notion of ideology. Indeed, this notion of discourse is sometimes even collapsed with that of ideology, a practice of reduction that I rejected as theoretically, empirically and analytically misguided.

Confusion here is even worse when this broad, philosophical concept of discourse also includes the ideas and ideologies of a specific period or social domain. As is of course often the case, the most general and ill-defined concepts may sometimes become most popular. After all, in cultural fads and fashions, ambiguity, myth and vagueness are often more attractive than conceptual precision. This is currently also the case for many postmodern uses of 'discourse' in the humanities and the social sciences.[8]

Whatever the ambiguities and fuzziness of the various notions of discourse introduced above, most share verbal (and related other semiotic) properties. That is, I do not use the word 'discourse' (or 'text' for that matter) for social structures, interactions or communicative events that do not have (also) a verbal character. Thus, societies, (sub)cultures or social practices will *not* be described as discourses or texts here, even when they may need understanding or interpretation, or when they are routinely 'accomplished' much like discourses.

Other semiotic 'discourses'

Finally, another well-known case comprises 'messages' in other semiotic codes, such as (sequences of) images, movies, a dance and so on, especially when these *also* have a verbal dimension.[9] I shall, however, limit myself to commonsense notions here, and again only use the *restricted* notion of 'discourse' (text or talk) when referring to the *verbal* dimension of communicative interaction. Obviously, the *extended* notion of discourse, when referring to a whole communicative event, may well also feature other (visual, gestural) dimensions of communication and interaction, sometimes closely intertwined with the verbal aspect, as is the case in spoken movies and advertising. The only problem is that there is no everyday word to refer in general terms to either integrated (verbal/non-verbal) 'discourses', or to exclusively non-verbal semiotic 'messages', except by their specific words, such as 'picture', 'photo', 'movie' or 'advertisement'.

I do not use the semiotic terms 'signs' (or indeed 'signifier' or 'signified') here. For discourse analysis these have generally become obsolete after more than thirty years of increasingly sophisticated linguistics and discourse studies. These notions were useful in early semiotics in order to describe, in the terms of early structural linguistics, some properties of non-linguistic semiotic codes or objects, such as stories, movies, non-verbal sign systems, or other cultural artefacts. Moreover, the notion of 'sign', following early structuralism, is mostly used to denote minimal meaning units (like words), and not maximal meaning units like whole discourses or movies.

Where necessary, I shall simply speak of non-verbal discourses, or use specific genre designations. As is the case for other, more sophisticated disciplines (such as linguistic, logic or communication studies), it is hardly relevant to keep using traditional semiotic terminology to describe discourse structures. However, as long as the study of other semiotic practices does not have its own theoretical terminology, the integrated description of verbal and non-verbal 'messages' may still make use of such semiotic terminology. This is especially so if such semiotic descriptions go beyond the mere identification of isolated signs, signifiers or signifieds, and focus on more complex structures of expression (signifiers), meaning (signifieds) and use.[10]

The study of discourse

Discourse studies, as it is understood in this book, is a cross-disciplinary field of research that has emerged, especially since the mid-1960s, in virtually all disciplines of the humanities and the social sciences. Initially developed in linguistics, literary studies and anthropology, it soon also spread to sociology, psychology, communication research and other disciplines. In principle, discourse studies as a separate cross-discipline besides linguistics (or semiotics for that matter), would not have been necessary if linguistic theories had paid attention to the study of actually occurring text and talk in the first place. However, most hard-core linguistics focused on grammar and on isolated sentences, even if there are directions of research that may focus on the textual or interactional 'functions' of grammatical structures of sentences. Hence, together with such other cross-disciplines as socio-linguistics, pragmatics and the ethnography of speaking, discourse analysis focuses on the systematic account of the complex structures and strategies of text and talk as they are actually accomplished (produced, interpreted, used) in their social contexts.

As suggested above, such a brief characterization of what I understand by 'discourse studies' (or the less adequate, but better-known term 'discourse analysis') is relevant in order to distinguish this field from (some) more impressionistic studies of discourse, especially in philosophy and literary studies. Discourse studies of course focuses on the broad social and cultural functions, conditions and consequences of text and talk, including, in our case here, the role of discourse in the study of ideology. However, more specifically, discourse and conversation analysis will typically always also focus on systematic, detailed and theory-based analyses of actually occurring structures of text and talk. Thus, a mere paraphrase or summarization of the 'content' of discourse, as also language users often do on the basis of their knowledge of discourse, is usually found not to be a form of discourse analysis in the sense intended here.

In its thirty years of existence, discourse studies has developed into a quite sophisticated discipline, and it would be no serious contribution to our insight into discourse (or ideology) if we were to simply ignore the many advances in the many areas of this new discipline.

However, given the ambiguity of the term 'discourse', we may expect the same for 'discourse analysis', and there are therefore many directions and approaches of research, and many fields of inquiry. Besides linguistic (grammatical) studies of discourse, thus, we may find pragmatic studies of (speech) acts, conversation analysis, stylistics, rhetoric, or the socio-linguistic study of discourse variation in its social context. Most of these studies focus on the various structures or strategies of text and talk, to be discussed in the next chapter. However, also the psychology of discourse production and understanding should be included in a broad, multidiscipli-nary discipline of discourse. The same is true for the study of microsocial dimensions of interaction and contexts, in which relations between discourse structures and, for example, properties of participants are being theorized.

In other words, the field of discourse studies as a discipline obviously follows the study of text and talk in the various disciplines in the humanities and the social sciences, and now also includes social psychology, communication research, political science and history. Ideally, an integrated study integrates the analysis of discourse structures *per se* with the account of their cognitive, social, political, historical and cultural functions and contexts. It is in this broad, integrated and multidisciplinary approach that I locate the study of the discursive expression and reproduction of ideologies.

21

Discourse Structures

On levels, structures and strategies

Typical for a discourse analytical approach to ideologies and their reproduction is that ideologies are not simply related to undifferentiated forms of text or talk, but mapped on to different levels and dimensions of discourse, each with its own structures or strategies. These various properties of discourse are the result of theoretical analyses and therefore may vary widely in different approaches.

Thus, conversation analysts exclusively focus on spontaneous, everyday dialogues, linguists on the grammatical structures of discourse, whereas pragmatics focuses on more specific properties of action and interaction, such as speech acts, illocutionary force or politeness strategies. Whereas earlier 'text linguistics' in practice tended to study mostly written texts, most other contemporary approaches, especially in the social sciences, have a preference for the analysis of spoken discourse, sometimes with the implicit assumption that 'natural' language use is essentially oral and interactive. Psychology on the other hand favours the study of (written) text comprehension, probably also because this is easier for experimentation in the laboratory.

It needs little argument, however, that both spoken and written/printed forms of discourse are the object of discourse studies, and that there is no more or less 'natural' priority here, at least not for all cultures that have writing systems. Any approach that uniquely associates ideologies or social representations with the interactive, face-to-face social construction of 'meanings' is therefore by definition incomplete: ideologies are also expressed and reproduced by written text. Indeed, when it comes to the mass-mediated reproduction of ideologies in contemporary society, face-to-face interaction may even play a less prominent role than textual or one-sided spoken/visual communication by newspapers and television.

From the sprawling cross-discipline of discourse studies that has emerged from anthropology, sociology, linguistics, psychology and other disciplines in the humanities and social sciences, we may hardly expect anything else but a large variety of approaches, theories, methods and their underlying philosophies. In order to give some background to the chapters that follow, let us briefly summarize some of the main structures usually studied in discourse analysis. At the same time, I give a brief indication of the ways ideologies may impinge on such structures during their communicative manifestations. Note, though, that these indications are merely illustrations. A proper discourse analysis of ideological expressions of course would involve a much more detailed and systematic account of relevant structures and strategies.

Graphics

Neglected in virtually all approaches of discourse studies, and obviously irrelevant for the study of spoken dialogue, graphical structures of written or printed text are literally a prominent, while actually visible, property of discourse. Apart from some semiotic work on images or textual graphics, theory-formation in this field is still scarce, and analyses hardly go beyond impressionism. Yet, little theory is necessary to understand that variations of graphical prominence may constitute a crucial element in the expression of ideologies. Whether a news report appears on the front page or on an inside page of the newspaper, high on the page or at the bottom, left or right, or whether it has a small or a banner headline, is long, short or broad, that is, printed over several columns, with or without a photograph, tables, drawings, colour and so on, are all properties of the graphical representation of just one genre that may have a serious impact on the readers' interpretation of the relevance or newsworthiness of news events. Many advertisements are inherently associated with images, colours and other graphical elements, and sometimes lack verbal text altogether. The visual element of TV programmes is crucial, and also includes special discourse graphics. Modern textbooks have a graphical layout that is assumed to raise and keep the interest of children and adolescents. And so on for a large variety of other written or printed genres.[1]

Graphical structures may have several cognitive, social and ideological functions. Cognitively, they control attention and interest during comprehension, and indicate what information is important or interesting, or should be focused on for other reasons, and may therefore be better understood and memorized. They may signal communication forms and genres, such as the difference between a news report and an editorial in the press, or between theory and assignments in a textbook. Socially, graphical structures, including photographs, have a large domain of associations, for instance with groups, organizations and subcultural styles, as the difference between a popular tabloid and a serious mainstream broadsheet shows, or the type of advertising in fancy magazines, street billboards, the subway or a supermarket leaflet.

At all these levels the possible expression of ideologies is obvious, for instance through the graphical emphasis of positive values with ingroups, and negative values with outgroups. Through images, photos, text placement, page layout, letter type, colour and other graphical properties, thus, meanings and mental models may be manipulated, and indirectly the ideological opinions implied by them. A serious theory spells out *what* graphical structures exactly may have which of these various functions.[2]

Sound

The phonetic and phonological expression structures of discourse (the 'sounds'), though systematically studied since the beginning of modern linguistics and phonetics, have also been neglected in discourse analysis.[3] Articulation or auditory reception or phonemes may be marginal to a typical discourse analyst who prefers to look at discourse structures beyond those of words, phrases or sentences. Yet, pitch, volume and intonation are a rich source of variation by which, as in graphical expressions, emphasis, prominence or distinctiveness may be controlled as a function of semantic and ideological importance and relevance, as well as of opinion, emotion and social position (as in authoritarian commands versus polite requests). Since most conversation analysts work with transcripts, precisely these 'sound structures' tend to be partly ignored in analyses, or reduced to rather crude forms of representation or description, with the exception of the study of applause in public address.

Especially interesting for ideological analysis is the fact that subtle sound variation may directly code for underlying opinions in event and context models, that is, without explicit semantic articulation: Admiration, praise, derogation, blame and many other functions of discourse may thus be signalled implicitly – and hence deniably – as a function of ideological beliefs. The sound structures of talk to or among women and men, whites and blacks, superiors and subordinates, and generally ingroup and outgroup members, may thus display, emphasize, conceal or persuasively convey ideologically based opinions about events or the participants in the context.[4]

Morphology

The study of word-formation is not exactly a main focus of concern in most types of discourse studies, and usually associated with traditional sentence grammatical research. Since stylistic variation, compared with other levels of utterances, is limited here, the ideological impact on the way words are formed in text and talk seems to be marginal, especially in languages that do not allow compounds. Where relevant, for instance in the study of neologisms, such ideological effects usually will be studied in lexical stylistics.

Syntax

On the other hand, the study of sentence forms, syntax, has drawn attention from (critical) linguists interested in ideological analysis from the start.[5] Variation in the order or hierarchical relations of the structures of clauses and sentences is a well-known expression of dimensions of meaning as well as of other underlying semantic and pragmatic functions. Thus, order and hierarchical position may signal importance and relevance of meanings, and may thus play a role in emphasizing or concealing preferred or dispreferred meanings, respectively.

Agency and responsibility for actions may similarly be emphasized or de-emphasized, for example by active or passive sentences, explicit or implicit subjects, as well as word order. It needs little analysis to show that such an important function of syntactic variation may have an impact on the description of ingroup and outgroup actions, and hence on ideological implications of text and talk. Position and role of clauses may signal implications and presuppositions, which are closely related to what language users should or should not know, and hence to the ideological discursive functions of exposing or concealing information.[6]

Among many other features of syntax, pronouns are perhaps the best known grammatical category of the expression and manipulation of social relations, status and power, and hence of underlying ideologies. Ingroup membership, outgroup distancing and derogation, intergroup polarization, politeness, formality and intimacy, and many other social functions may thus be signalled by pronominal variation. Ideologically based respect to others may be given or withheld by using familiar or polite pronouns of address, as in French *tu* and *vous* and Spanish *tu* (or *vos* in some Latin American countries) and *Usted*. Given the group-based nature of ideologies, group polarization and social struggle is thus prototypically expressed in the well-known pronominal pair of Us and Them. Indeed, there are few words in the language that may be as socially and ideologically 'loaded' as a simple *we*. The close relationship between group identity, identification and ideology, as discussed before, explains this particular function of this pronoun.[7]

The specific set of choices that are made among the possible structures of syntactic form in one specific discourse, is usually called the (syntactic) *style* of that discourse. Combined with lexical variations in the choice of words (lexical style, see below) such syntactic style is often studied in a separate domain of discourse analysis, namely, *stylistics*. Style may generally be described as the overall result of the consistent use of variable grammatical structures as a function of properties of the context (or rather of the interpretation of the context as represented in context models). This means that style is by definition a function of the ideological control of such context models, as we have seen for the example of polite or impolite uses of forms of address.

Semantics

Graphics, sound and sentence forms are usually categorized as 'observable' expressions of discourse, traditionally called 'surface structures' in gen-erative grammar. In some critical and ideological studies (often but not only in a Marxist tradition), such structures may even be called 'material', although, as suggested before, there is very little 'material' in abstract structures (one reason I used 'observable' between quotes). Yet, in a somewhat sloppy but practical sense, we may say that surface structures are the kinds of things that are actually and 'observably' expressed, shown and displayed for interpretation by recipients. But we should remember that also these 'observable' structures of expression are in fact abstract or mental structures being assigned, by theorists as well as language users, to the various physiological, auditory or physical (phonetic, printed) properties of communication.

The meaning of 'meaning'

Undoubtedly crucial in all ideological analyses of discourse are the *meanings* expressed by or assigned to surface structures by discourse participants. Unfortunately, there are few notions in the study of language and discourse that are so complex and vague as that of meaning. Especially also in critical or ideological studies, the notion is sometimes used so broadly that it has lost virtually all 'meaning'. That discourse expresses, conveys, has, constructs and does many other things with meaning is both commonsense and scholarly knowledge. Yet, we need a sophisticated semantics, or even various types of semantics, to be able to spell out *how* exactly, what *kinds* of meanings, are involved here. Simply talking about the 'production of meaning', as is usual in much contemporary critical studies, does not tell us much about the role of discourse or ideology in communication, interaction and society.

Thus, it can't hurt to recall old linguistic, philosophical and logical distinctions between (conceptual) *meaning* or *intension*, on the one hand, and *reference*, that is, as a relation between expressions and things being referred to, denoted or talked about (i.e. the referents, denotata or extension), on the other hand. Similarly, in an abstract analysis, it also makes sense to distinguish between word or sentence meanings, utterance meanings, speaker's meanings, hearer's meanings and socio-cultural meanings (including ideological meanings).

As is the case for all structures of discourse, all these different 'meanings' result from different theoretical approaches. In traditional linguistics as well as in common sense, words are associated with (word) meanings, as is still the case in dictionaries. In structural and generative grammars, meanings of sentences are formally constructed as a function of the meanings of words and syntactic structures. In philosophical logic, meanings are abstract functions that make sentences true or false, or that pick out referents or extensions (objects, properties, facts) in some situation or possible world.

Meaning and interpretation

In the philosophy of language as well as in psychology and most of the social sciences, meanings are not so much abstract properties of words or expressions, but rather the kinds of things language users *assign* to such expressions in processes of *interpretation* or *understanding*. This also allows for contextual variation: a speaker and a hearer may assign (intend, interpret, infer) different meanings to the same expression, and indeed, the same expression may therefore also mean different things in different contexts. Hence, meanings of discourse or language in use are contextual or situated, and depend on the (interpretation of the) participants.

Psychologists will then further spell out how such meaning assignments or interpretations take place mentally, and what *memory representations* (such as models or knowledge) are involved in meaning production and understanding. Socially oriented discourse analysis will usually ignore such cognitive 'processing' of meaning, and focus exclusively on the interactive or social construction of meanings in or by discourse. In this case meanings are usually inferred intuitively by the analyst, and are not further analysed. It is on this (rather shaky) basis that much ideological meaning analysis often takes place.

As we shall see later, discourse meanings are the result of selecting relevant portions of mental models about events. That is, knowledge about events is thus mapped on verbally expressed meanings of text and talk, and hence partly constrained by the possible word and sentence meanings in a given language or culture. Since models embody opinions, which may in turn have an ideological basis, also the meanings that derive from such 'ideological' (biased, etc.) models may embody ideological aspects.

Many of these opinions may be conventionalized and codified in the *lexicon*, as the respective negative and positive meanings of the well-known pair 'terrorist' versus 'freedom fighter' suggest. Lexical analysis is therefore the most obvious (and still fruitful) component in ideological discourse analysis. Simply spelling out all implications of the words being used in a specific discourse and context often provides a vast array of ideological meanings. As a practical method, substitution of one word by others immediately shows the different semantic and often the ideological 'effects' of such a substitution.

Theoretically, this means that *variation* of lexical items (that is, lexical *style*) is a major means of ideological expression in discourse. Depending on any contextual factor (age, gender, 'race', class, position, status, power, social relation, and so on) language users may choose different words to talk about things, people, actions or events. Personal and group opinions, that is, attitudes and ideologies, of participants are a prominent contextual constraint, and hence a major source of lexical variation. Given the obvious ideological implications of lexical choice, we may also expect that language users are often (made) aware of their style, and may hence also partly control it, and thereby either emphasize or precisely conceal their 'real' ideological opinions. The current debate on 'politically correct' language, precisely focuses on this aspect of ideologically based lexical style, and especially shows people's positions in the relationships between dominant and dominated groups.

Propositions

Beyond lexical semantics, the study of discourse meaning of course has many other aspects that are relevant for the mapping of ideology on text and talk. Thus, first of all, the *propositions* that represent the meaning of clauses and sentences have an internal structure, of which for instance the various semantic roles (agent, patient, object, etc.) may exhibit the ways participants are associated with an event, actively or passively, responsibly or as experiencers of events and actions. In other words, semantic structures result from model structures. Such semantic representations are obviously a function of how events are interpreted and evaluated (in a model), and may therefore be ideologically controlled, depending on the group membership, the position or the perspective of the speech participants. Who is seen as the hero or the villain, the perpetrator or the victim of an act, which roles need to be emphasized or concealed, are questions that organize many ideological attitudes, and such perceptions may directly be mapped into propositional structures and their variable syntactic formulations (actives, passives, nominalizations and so on).[8]

Local and global coherence

Whereas most of the structures mentioned above are within the traditional realm of linguistic grammars, discourse analysis was precisely developed in order to account for structures and strategies beyond the sentence boundary. Semantics (as well as pragmatics and interaction analysis) is especially well suited to account for such more complex 'textual' meanings. Thus, sequences of sentences (or rather, of propositions) constitute discourses if they satisfy a number of *coherence* conditions, such as (a) *conditional* relations between the 'facts' denoted by these sentences, or (b) *functional* relations (such as generalization, specification, contrast) among propositions.

Such coherence is based on the interpretation of events as represented in the mental models of the language users, and may therefore also be ideologically influenced. Whether language users see a social event as a cause or not of another social event may thus have an effect on the coherence of their discourse. In other words, coherence is both contextually and socially relative, and depends on our ideologically controlled interpretation of the world.

The same is true for the kind of overall coherence represented by *topics* or *semantic macrostructures*, which also signal what speakers or recipients think is the most important information of a discourse. Such a judgement may obviously be ideologically based. What for some is defined, topically, as a 'race riot by a violent black mob', for others may be semantically summarized as an 'act of urban resistance against racist police officers'. In other words, semantic macrostructures (derived by special semantic 'reduction' rules or strategies from propositions in models about an event) not only define such important discourse structures as topics, overall coherence, or importance of information, but essentially also explain the well-known ideological practice of 'defining the situation'.

The implicit and the explicit

Another ideologically relevant property of meaning is propositional relations, such as *implication, entailment* and *presupposition*. Thus, information that is explicitly asserted may emphasize negative properties of outgroups or positive ones about ingroups, whereas the reverse is true for implied or presupposed meanings. The well-known ideological function of concealing 'real' social or political facts or conditions may be semantically managed by various ways of leaving information implicit. This also shows the importance of distinguishing between mental models (beliefs) and discourse meanings, although we often may infer what people 'really mean' (their models) when they say something.

Similarly, we may describe acts or events in great detail, or do so only with few details, or at higher levels of abstraction. Such variation may also encode ideological positions – who, indeed, has interests in knowing or concealing such details about social events? In sum, semantics is a rich field of ideological 'work' in discourse, and virtually all meaning structures are able to 'signify' social positions, group perspective and interests in the description of events, people and actions.

Schematic structures

Whereas topics represent the global meaning of discourse, overall schematic structures or superstructures represent the *global form* of text and talk. Such global discourse forms or schemata are organized by a number of conventional categories, such as introduction and conclusion, opening and closing, problem and solution, premises and conclusion, and so on. Stories, news reports, conversations, meetings and scholarly articles, among many other genres, are thus organized by conventional schemas that define the order and hierarchical position of such categories (as well as the semantic macrostructures or topics that define the 'content' of these categories).

As is the case for the syntax of sentences, also this 'discourse syntax', may vary and hence 'code for' ideological positions. As is true for all formal discourse structures, these schemata may signal importance, relevance or prominence. What information appears in a headline, what is emphasized in a conclusion, or what event descriptions count as complication or a resolution of a story, depends on the ways events are interpreted, and hence on ideologically variable positions. Obviously, some of these categories are obligatory (as is the case for headlines of news reports), but others are not (for instance background information in news reports), and also categories may appear in different positions. Thus, greetings and leave-taking are usually obligatory categories of conversation. Besides interactional functions, for example of address and politeness, they may also have ideological functions, such as when their absence is intended as an ideologically based insult. Similarly, if verbal reactions in a news report appear up front, we know that the source of such reactions is found important, as are his or her opinions, a structural feature that obviously has ideological implications.[9]

Rhetorical structures

Discourse features a number of special structures or strategies that have been amply described already in classical rhetoric, and that are usually called 'figures of style', but which will here be called *rhetorical structures*. These structures appear at all levels of discourse described above, and assign special organization (repetition, deletion, substitution, etc.) to these levels, for instance by the figures of rhyme and alliteration at the level of sounds, parallelism at the level of syntax, and comparison, metaphor, irony, etc. at the level of meaning. Unlike other discourse structures, these are optional, and serve especially in persuasive contexts, and more generally to attract or manage the attention of recipients.

In an ideological analysis this will usually mean that rhetorical structures are studied as means to emphasize or de-emphasize meanings as a function of ideological opinions. Metaphors may be chosen that highlight the negative character of our enemies, comparisons in order to mitigate the blame of our own people, and irony to challenge the negative models of our opponents. Rhetoric, defined in this sense, is essentially geared towards the persuasive communication of preferred models of social events, and thus manages how recipients will understand and especially how they will evaluate such events, for instance as a function of the interests of the participants. It is therefore not surprising that rhetorical structures play such an important role in ideological manipulation.[10]

Speech acts

Whereas utterances were traditionally analysed along two main dimensions, namely, expressions (*significants*) and meanings (*signifiés*), the philosophy of language and the social sciences have added an important third dimension: action. Uttering words and sentences in text and talk, in a specific situation, is also and at the same time the accomplishment of a large number of social actions, as well as participating in social interaction. Thus, assertions, promises or threats are made, and such *speech acts* are typically defined in terms of social conditions of participants, namely, their mutual beliefs, wants, intentions, evaluations and goals that have social implications. Speech acts like threats presuppose power, and tell recipients that the speaker will do something negative if they do not comply with his or her wishes. Commands also presuppose power but require that the recipient must do something. That is, relations between speech participants are crucial in the ways speech acts are accomplished.

This also means that if these social relations are ideologically grounded, for instance in relations of dominance and inequality, such relations may well also be displayed in the kind of speech acts speakers are (or feel themselves) entitled to accomplish. At this point, the ideological control of social practices directly impinges on speech acts, for example when whites of equal social position feel entitled to give orders to a black person, or when men threaten women. In sum, whenever relations between participants as well as other dimensions of the context (time, location, etc.) are ideologically based, this may show up in the kind of speech acts being accomplished by the participants.

Interaction

Finally, within the vast field of the social actions being accomplished in or by discourse, we find a number of interaction strategies that express, indicate, reflect or construct specific social relations between participants, and which therefore are ideologically relevant. It is especially at this level of analysis that social position, power and control of social members may be exercised, opposed, mitigated or emphasized.

Interactional control may affect virtually all levels and dimensions of text and talk. Powerful speakers may control context structures by requiring or prohibiting the presence of specific participants, setting a time or place, allowing specific genres and not others, prescribing or proscribing the language or professional jargon spoken, by initiating or changing preferred or dispreferred topics or an agenda for a meeting, by sanctioning formal or informal lexical style, by being polite or impolite, by (requiring) the accomplishment of specific speech acts or the management of turns at speaking, or by opening or closing the interaction, among many other ways text and talk may be controlled. In all these forms of control, it is the social position of the participants, and more generally the ideologically based interpretation of the context that is thus being enacted, expressed or constructed in talk.

More specifically, the interaction dimension of discourse is relevant in everyday conversation and other forms of spoken, face-to-face dialogues such as meetings and parliamentary debates. Such conversations are organized by a number of specific structures and strategies, for example those of turn-taking, interruption or beginning and ending. Many of these are obligatory and hence not directly controllable by ideologically variable contextual factors. However, as is the case for interaction in general, ideologically based group membership, power, positive self-presentation or outgroup derogation are among the underlying social relationships that may impinge on conversational structures and moves. That is, who may (or must) begin or end the conversation or meeting, who may initiate or change topics or who may interrupt whom, are among the many forms of power display in discourse that may also have an ideological dimension, for example those based on gender, 'race' or class.[11]

Ideology and discourse control

In these and many other ways, thus, we see most concretely how relations of dominance, conflict or competition between speech participants may implement and enact relations between groups. People not only engage in such verbal social practices as individuals and as cultural members, but also as members of specific groups, and such identities and membership may also be locally negotiated. That is, group dominance is not simply mapped on contextual relations between participants, but may be flexibly managed and exercised in situationally variable ways.

The same is true for the ideologies that sustain such practices. From the abstract level of group representations, they may provide particular opinions about other group members which together with specific contextual constraints provide the unique interactional configurations we observe in ongoing discourse. More generally, also for the levels we introduced above, ideological mapping on discourse structures is seldom direct. It takes place through more specific group knowledge and attitudes, the formation of 'biased' models of events and contexts, the construction of meaning representations, and the expression in variable forms and surface structures, in ways that are a function of many social and contextual constraints, of which ideological beliefs are only one element.

For the practice of ideological analysis this also means that ideologies cannot simply be 'read off' text and talk. What is an ideologically relevant expression in one discourse or context may not be one in another, or may have an opposed ideological function at another moment. This means that ideological discourse analysis is very complex, and needs to take into account all levels of text and context, as well as the broader social background of discourse and interaction. In the following chapters, I shall discuss some of the topics of such an ideological discourse analysis.

22

Context

What is context?

A broad characterization of discourse as a communicative event not only features the various levels, structures or strategies of text and talk discussed in the previous chapter, but also those of the context. Despite many informal discussions in socio-linguistics, pragmatics and discourse studies of this notion of context, there is strictly speaking no *theory* of what exactly a 'context' is.[1] The term itself suggests that it is all that comes 'with the text', that is, the properties of the 'environment' of discourse.

I shall stay as close as possible with this linguistic version of the commonsense notion of context, and define it as *the structured set of all properties of a social situation that are possibly relevant for the production, structures, interpretation and functions of text and talk.*

Thus, it is well known that, for example, the setting and the various group memberships and positions of participants (e.g. age, gender, power) play a prominent role in the way discourses are shaped and understood, and how they function in the social situation. Other features of the social situation may well be socially relevant but neither usually nor systematically influence specific structures of discourse, for instance the beauty, height or clothing of the participants, although there may be some societies, cultures, or situations where also such properties of a social situation become contextually relevant for discourse.

Why is such a theory of context relevant for the theory of ideology? As we shall see, contexts – defined as structures of discourse-relevant properties of social situations – instantiate many properties of social events and social groups that are monitored by ideologies. Thus, group domination, conflict and competition will be multiply exhibited in everyday practices of social actors, including their communicative practices. That is, ideologically relevant interests such as group identity, activities and goals, norms and intergroup relations of dominance and resistance, as well as social resources, are also locally exhibited and reproduced in social situations, and hence in communicative contexts. More specifically, we will find that ideologically based dominance also involves the control of context. Specifying contexts thus provides insight into the details of the exercise of social dominance and its underlying ideologies.

Context models

In most studies of context, typically so in conversation analysis, socio-linguistics, pragmatics or the ethnography of speaking, contextual properties are assumed to directly affect (or be affected by) discourse properties. Within the socio-cognitive framework presented here, no such direct relation exists. Rather, the notion of relevance implies that models are relevant only *for* language users, and hence only may influence discourse through the ways they are being subjectively *constructed* by language users.

Such constructions again imply mental modelling. That is, it is not the context itself (whether or not it 'exists' objectively) that influences text and talk, but rather the *context models* of language users.[2] Such context models are stored in episodic memory, just like the event models that are used to represent what a discourse is about. Context models, thus, represent how participants in a communicative event see, interpret and mentally represent the properties of the social situation that are now relevant for them. This is important, because it is precisely this subjective nature of context models that also allows for personal variation and contextual uniqueness – it is not the objective fact that speakers are women or men, white or black, young or old, powerful or not, but how they see and construct themselves, in general or in the current social situation. In other words, the essential pragmatic notion of relevance may now simply be defined in terms of context models.

Context models are organized by the usual schema for interaction in general, and thus feature a hierarchical structure of categories of the social situation that language users find relevant for their production or reception of text and talk. Below, I shall briefly discuss some of these categories. In a later chapter, I shall explain how context models provide the 'personal' interface between socially shared representations such as knowledge, attitudes and beliefs, on the one hand, and discourse structures on the other. For now, it should suffice to say that context models monitor virtually all 'pragmatic' aspects of discourse, that is, all properties that may vary as a function of the (interpretation of the) social situation, such as conversational and speech acts being accomplished, as well as style, rhetoric and the ways in which meaning incorporates information of event models (what people know about an event being talked about).

As is the case for all mental models, also context models feature an important evaluative component. That is, they not only represent the knowledge or beliefs of language users about the social situation, but also their *opinions* about it. Thus we may know our interlocutor, or the author of an article in the newspaper, but also have an opinion about her or him, and this opinion will of course also influence our interpretation of the discourse itself, for example as more or less truthful or reliable. Similarly, our model of the recipient (part of the context model) will also influence what we say to him or her, and especially also *how* we do so, for example more or less formally, intimately, politely or authoritatively.

Obviously, as is the case for event models, such opinions may be instantiations of socially shared attitudes, for example when men speak to women or whites to blacks. Similarly, our beliefs about the current social situation will also be instantiations of more general knowledge we share with others about such situations, for example when we visit a doctor or participate in a lesson at school. In sum, context models are also part of the interface between socially shared representations and personal talk and text. In part they simply represent what social members share, as well as their own personal knowledge and opinions as based on their personal experiences, such as the beliefs about their friends, the settings of their everyday conversations, their relevant goals, and so on. It is this combined personal and social nature that makes models the necessary interface between social cognition (and social structure) and discourse, between social macrostructure and microstructure, and hence between ideology and discourse. Without the notion of context model it would be impossible to explain how ideologies may impinge not only on what we say (via event models), but also on *how* we do so.

It should be emphasized that context models are not static but *dynamic*. They represent the *ongoing* interpretation of language users of the social situation. That is, context models may be partly planned, but ongoing interaction and discourse, as well as other changing aspects of the social situation, need continual updating of the context model. Indeed, during a conversation or during the reading of a text, we may completely change our initial interpretation of the genre ('This is an interrogation and not an informal chat') the goals of the speaker or writer ('Is this a threat or a promise?'), and so on. This dynamic nature of context models also implies that current fragments of discourse will become part of the 'previous context' as soon as they have been accomplished.

This cognitive account of indirect, mentally mediated, context–discourse relations does *not* mean that we *reduce* social contexts to cognition. Obviously, contexts need their own social analysis, and so do discourses, as forms of social interaction that are part of or constitute such contexts. It is only the relationship between social context and action, on the one hand, and the subjective understanding of context and discourse, on the other hand, that needs such a cognitive interface. Indeed, without variable context models, all language users of the same group would speak in the same way in the same social situation.

As we have seen in Chapter 7, context models are a special case of *models of experience*, which we construe from the moment we wake up in the morning until we go to sleep at night: breakfast, going to work, and so on. That is, the way we represent the social situation in which we engage in a communicative event is only one of such daily experiences. People's episodic or autobiographical memories are constituted by such models of their personal experiences. Events of talk and text are merely special cases of such mental models, namely, those that involve discourse as the relevant event or action category. We still have few ideas about what such general experience models look like, but we may assume that self occupies a very central participant role in them. The subjectivity, perspective, point of view or social position of self thus becomes the core of the model, which indeed represents what I am doing when communicating.[3]

Note, finally, that general experience models as well as context models only represent specific, particular, concrete personal experiences of social events. Episodic memory, however, also features more general information, beliefs and opinions about oneself and others. Such general but personal knowledge does not have the same episodic structure as models of events, but is represented in a more abstract form. Yet, besides the influence of socio-cultural knowledge and beliefs, also these personal beliefs are crucial in the formation and updating of context models. In other words, in their ongoing construction, context models are constructed from information from the following sources: (1) a general schema, or goals or expectations about the current social situation; (2) activated previous models (being reminded of a previous conversation with X, reading the same newspaper in the same situation, etc.); (3) general personal beliefs about such a situation ('My neighbour always talks about his work, and I don't like that'); (4) socio-cultural knowledge and beliefs about communicative events (how to write news stories, etc.); (5) previous parts of the ongoing discourse; and (6) previous parts of the text. It is important to remember this variety of underlying sources for context models, especially when we want to explain how context models may be a function of social ideologies.

Dimensions of context

Let us now examine some of the situational properties that usually are assumed to constitute the context, keeping in mind that it is *not* the properties themselves that influence discourse (or that are influenced by discourse) but their mental construction, as categories, in model schemata of such social situations. In other words, despite the general, social and cultural dimension of situational relevance, it is the personal construction of such relevance criteria that for each discourse exercises the actual constraint on current text and talk. Obviously, this also means that context models of speakers or writers may be at variance with those of recipients, and lead to communication conflicts about the 'definition of the current situation', as well as with that of the group or culture as a whole.

Provisionally, then, we assume that the following situational parameters may constitute categories of context models.

Domain

Communicative events are usually tied to a specific social or institutional domain. In some cases, they may be constitutive of such a domain. Thus, the many types of legal discourse constitute the domain of the 'law', whereas types of political discourse largely constitute what we understand by 'politics' or the 'polity', and educational discourse the domain of education. That is, a domain is the typical contextual property that defines overall classes of genres, such as political discourse, medical discourse and scholarly discourse. For the definition of context they signal what social field the context is a constituent part of.

For participants, contextual knowledge about domains serves as a global orientation for the management of functions and circumstances of communicative events, for example in the use of professional jargon. Since domains may be related to for instance professional group activities (e.g. those of journalists in the domain of the media), and ideologies may be associated with such groups, domains at the same time may function as 'ideological domains', that is, as those sectors of society in which they define their identity, exercise their activities, realize their goals, interact with relevant groups and enact their power and where they protect or control their resources.

In sum, ideological domains are sites of domination, struggle, conflict and interests. Domains may be ideologically protected by groups as 'their' domain, in which other groups should not 'interfere'. Thus, it is a main tenet of market ideologies that the state should not interfere in the markets, of journalistic ideologies that the state should not abridge the freedom of the press, and of professors that nobody should interfere with the freedom of teaching and research. Many of the properties of discourse signal such ideological embedding in social domains. Indeed, legitimation is a domain-sensitive function of communicative events.

Overall interaction and type of speech event

For the planning, ongoing interactional management, understanding and recall of speech events, participants need to be able to categorize them at an overall level. They often use a name or *genre* description to do so. Thus, participants may describe what they participated in as a conversation, a chat, a meeting, a lesson, a parliamentary debate, seeing the doctor, reading the newspaper, or writing an application letter, among a very large number of other genres. These genres may then be characterized by several of the discourse structures discussed in the previous chapter and by the context features listed below. That is, genres are types of discourse that require definition in terms of both text/talk *and* context. Thus, genre knowledge of participants will monitor many formal properties of discourse (such as schematic organization and style) and well as the choice of topics.[4] If ideologies are typically being reproduced in, for example, lessons, propaganda and news reports, then this reproduction process needs to be studied for all relevant properties of the context as well as of text or talk itself of these genres.

Functions

The genres defined by the various context properties discussed here usually have specific *functions* in an action sequence or domain, for example as condition, consequence, purpose or goal of other social acts or events. Exams for instance function as a test of the successfulness of educational instruction and the qualification of students as participants; interrogations are carried out with the goal of obtaining knowledge, typically about criminal acts; parliamentary debates are constitutive of political decision making; news reports are written and read in order to provide or to obtain information and opinions about new events, and so on. In the accomplishment of their discourses, language users orient to these overall social or institutional functions of the communicative event, and thus will adapt many properties of their text or talk (or their understandings of such text and talk) to these functions, either because such is the norm or rule, or because such is strategically more efficient or successful.

Social actors as group members may of course have ideological representations of the functions of their discursive practices. Thus, journalists may see their newswriting as serving as a 'watchdog of society', professors their research as 'establishing the truth', and judges their judgements as 'doing justice'. Similarly, genres may have illegitimate or immoral ideological functions in the exercise of power, as may be the case for torture sessions in order to obtain confessions, some police interrogations or racist propaganda in order to incite racial hatred. Well-known ideological functions of discourse, to be discussed in more detail later, are, for example, those of legitimation, defence and control.

Intention

Communicative acts, like all forms of action, are intentional. Theoretically this means that participants construe mental models of what they want to do (say, write) in the present context. The discourse itself is thus accomplished in order to realize the intention and its represented outcomes. Obviously, and especially in spontaneous conversation, such intentions may be negotiated and interactionally modified or abandoned in the ongoing context. Despite such possible modifications, speakers usually manage and execute their talk and text according to their intentions, and often display such intentions in various strategic positions of the discourse, for example by such expressions as 'What I am calling for is . . .', 'What I wanted to talk to you about was . . .', and 'This article will be about . . .'. Ideologically relevant is precisely the concealment of the 'real intentions' of speakers, for example when a talk is announced as a friendly chat, but in fact is intended as an interrogation, as political manipulation or as racist propaganda. That is, overall genre or communicative action type are essentially related, from the point of view of the speaker or writer, with specific intentions, but recipients may or may not be able to detect such intentions, and may thus be manipulated. I shall later discuss some of the mechanisms of such forms of ideological manipulation.

Several directions of research, and especially also conversation analysis, reject analyses in terms of 'intentions', for example with the argument that such would ignore the fact that intentions (if any) are personal and private, and only become socially relevant when displayed in text and talk. I disagree with this position. First, intentions do play a fundamental role in social contexts, namely, as necessary antecedents of social action, and there is no reason to privilege the interpretations of recipients over those of speakers or writers in that respect. Second, recipients continually construct the possible intentions of speakers *even when these are not fully displayed in text or talk*. From their own experiences (and their own intentions) they know that speakers often do not say (exactly) what they intend to say, and recipients may worry about that, ask about it, and otherwise topicalize intentions. Indeed, they also think about them without saying so, and such thoughts may again monitor what they will (not) say next. Third, for the same reason, intentions not only monitor what is said or socially displayed, but also what is *not* said. That is, the non-said may be interpreted by recipients also as part of what speakers or writers intend with their utterance. Fourth, it is inconsistent to reject intentions with the argument that they are personal or private and relevant only when displayed in talk, and not do the same with the (social?) *understandings* of the recipient. That is, hearer perspective is not more social than speaker perspective, and *both* intentions and interpretations are both mental and social in interaction. Fifth, rejecting intentions as irrelevant is inconsistent with the broad acceptance of other mental representations as underlying discourse and discourse production, namely, knowledge and rules. In sum, a fully fledged theory of discourse and context is impossible without assuming the relevance of intentions of speakers or writers as part of the 'cognitive' dimension of the context. No doubt they are crucially important for language users themselves, given their frequent references to, and inferences from their mutual representations of each others' intentions.

There is no way to account for actions, and hence for discursive acts, without their cognitive counterpart, namely, intentions as represented in action models. These are integrated in the more complex model of the whole communicative context. Theoretically, actions are combinations of such intentions and the 'doings' that actually realize them, much in the same way as discourse is a combination of (mental) meanings and the 'observable' utterances that realize such meanings. Conversely, understanding an action means the tentative reconstruction of an 'intended' model, as inferred from observable 'doings' in some context of interaction – co-participants or observers try to figure out what actors 'mean' or 'intend' by their displayed 'doings'. We see again how closely discourse and (inter)action are related to cognitive representations.

Intentions may appear purely individual and tied to the personal circumstances and biography of speakers. So, how could such a context category possibly have ideological functions? If ideology is defined as a group self-schema consisting of a number of categories, it soon becomes apparent how intentions (as plans for action) may of course also be ideologically based. They may represent (plans for) typical group activities (e.g. writing news reports by journalists), include norms and values about *how* to do so appropriately, identify the social position of self (as speaker) with that of the group (e.g. as being dominant or not), and the implementation of specific social resources (such as knowledge or access to public discourse). More specifically, they may instantiate social attitudes, for example when whites intend to derogate blacks with a slur, or when anti-abortionists intend to argue against abortion. Indeed, as we see, speech acts as well as many other discourse properties, as suggested in the previous chapter, may be a function of ideologies, and this will often be the case intentionally for the speaker, or as intentions attributed to the speaker by recipients in their model of the context. In other words, ideologies often can 'reach' discourse structures precisely through the intentions of the speakers: discourse is action, and hence intentional, and such intentions may also extend to specific properties of discourses. This does *not* imply that all ideological discourse structures are intentional, or that ideological functions of discourse are always intended. Speech acts by definition do, and so may topics and some elements of style. More detailed surface structures (e.g. intonation or stress, syntactic clause structure) or semantic dimensions may be sometimes intended, and sometimes be more or less 'automatic' expressions of the representation of the context. In other words, not all characteristics of context need to 'pass' through the intention category.

Purpose

Often confused or collapsed with the notion of 'intention', also purposes need to be introduced as a separate category in context structures. Thus, whereas intentions are mental models of (discursive) acts, purposes or *goals* are mental models of the broader consequences of such acts, for instance of the *functions* of discursive acts as discussed above. Thus, contributions to a parliamentary debate may have as their purpose to enact or defeat a bill, and a lesson to teach students some knowledge or skill, as discussed for discourse functions above. The difference between purposes (as well as intentions) and functions, as defined here, is that functions are social, and intentions and purposes are mental representations of speech participants. This theoretical distinction is crucial. It allows us to assign different social functions to discourses accomplished with the same 'purpose in mind', to account for 'unintended' social consequences of intentions and purposes, to describe and explain the role of individual speech events in the social structure, to explain conflicts between purposes and functions, and so on. Obviously, there are many forms of ideologically based implications of such a distinction. Manipulation, for instance, is precisely to successfully accomplish a speech event of which the recipients do not know or understand the ultimate purposes.

Date, time

Discursive events by definition have beginnings and ends. That is, they take place in time, on specific days and dates, and for a specific more or less strict or variable duration. Most official and institutional discourses (meetings, appointments, sessions, etc.) have pre-set times of beginning and often also of closing. Lessons and formal exams may last for instance one or two hours. Sermons, depending on the religion, are usually pronounced on holy days, and so on. Even informal talk has negotiated beginnings and closings, namely, when people will meet, call or stop talking. Newspaper stories have deadlines and datelines, and people may read the newspaper only in the morning or evening. Most informal and virtually all formal talk involves ongoing time management. Speaking turns may be restricted or cut off by chairs 'when speaker time is up', for instance in meetings, court sessions or parliamentary debates. In relationships of dominance and inequality, for instance, people may not be allocated speaking time at all, or their rightful time to speak may be cut off. Such unequal treatment may be based on age, gender, race, class, education, or status, and hence be ideologically based as well as thus reproduced.

Location

Many communicative events typically take place in specific locations. Where everyday informal conversations may occur virtually everywhere (although in some situations they may be prohibited, e.g. during many institutional communicative events: lessons, court sessions, meetings, etc.), a lesson will typically take place in a classroom; an interrogation in a police station or in court; a verdict always in court; a parliamentary debate in the 'House'; and so on. Those in power not only set time and period, but often also location for talk, as is the case for appointments of patients with doctors or students with professors. Depending on power relations, similarly, journalists will go and interview important people where these want it and not where the journalists propose. Hence, place of talk may be an element of power, and hence ideologically relevant in the accomplishment of discursive practices when location decisions break norms or rules of acceptable communication as a form of power abuse.

Circumstances

Many speech events can only take place when specific social or other *circumstances* or *conditions* are in effect. A verdict can be pronounced only 'when the court is in session'; some meetings only when a specified number of participants (a quorum) is present. These circumstances may themselves be discursive, thus defining *intertextual complexes* like court sessions or conferences. Sentences may be pronounced only after a verdict, and a verdict after indictments, defences and pleas, among other legal discourse genres. Discourse may take place in 'inappropriate' circumstances, or conversely, it may be inappropriate in the given circumstances. Such communicative and social conflicts may play a role in the reproduction of dominance: defendants may be interrogated without the presence of their lawyers, women be made sexual advances at work, and so on.

Props and relevant objects

It may seem strange to include various props as part of a broader discourse analysis, but if the analysis of context is part of such an extended account of text and talk, then it makes sense to take them into account. Thus, the context of a lesson may feature educational props such as a blackboard, chalk, or an overhead projector, among other props, and usually relevant furniture, of which the table of the teacher, usually placed in front, will be different from that of the students. Similarly, a doctor's consultation may have its own typical props, beginning with a white coat (at least in hospital), a stethoscope, and many more, all objects that are both indexical of ongoing medical routines of investigation, as well as symbols of the doctor's status and role. Attorneys for the state or the defence may be asked to 'approach the bench' by the judge, and such will also influence their manner of speaking (confidential, non-public, whispered talk). Judges and chairs of meetings will probably have and handle a gavel to open and close meetings or to mark decisions being made, and so on for many other institutional communicative events.

As suggested, these props may also be indicative of ideologically relevant properties of the interaction or the social domain, such as hierarchical relations and dominance. Those who control meetings and sessions will often sit in front, and possibly somewhat higher than the rest (as the judge behind the 'bench', or the speaker of the house in a special position and seat), if only to mark their current (powerful) role. Participants (police officers, military, doctors, nurses, lawyers and judges, etc.) may wear uniforms that index their position, profession, role or status, and these and other props may be legally obligatory, such that the communicative event may not even 'count' as a socially or legally binding act without them, or they may be optional (as the flag in the president's or governor's office) and merely symbolic of the participants 'office'. From these few examples, we see that props such as furniture, uniforms, objects, and so on, have many social and symbolic, and hence ideological implications, and as such they may also be represented in the context models of the participants.

Participant role

Social actors participate in communicative events in several types of role. First of all they usually take part *as* speakers, writers, listeners (hearers) or readers, and some of these roles, as is the case in interaction, will alternate, such as that of speaker and recipient. But there are complications. The reader of the news on TV may well have a speaker role, but is not always the person who actually wrote the news reports, say a writer, editor, or reporter, who may have the role of the 'originator' of the relevant news text. Indeed, we know that many other people may be involved in the *joint* production of that news broadcast, such as producers, directors, camera people, reporters 'on location', and so on. That is, the production of institutional discourse may have several layers or stages of actual text making, of which the person who broadcasts, publishes or distributes may only be the last one.

The same is true for the various recipient roles. In a conversation with one other person, this is easy and straightforward: the addressee is the same as the hearer. But as soon as more people are present, they may not be there as addressee even if they listen and hear what is being said; they may be there in the role of 'overhearers' or as an audience in a talk show. And a talk show will have participants who speak to each other, but the TV viewers are the 'real' addressees and listeners of this mass mediated dialogue. A doctor may speak to trainees or nurses at the bed of a patient in hospital, but obliquely also addressing the patient, or when speaking in medical jargon trying to conceal from the patient what is being said. A secretary who takes the minutes of a meeting is certainly supposed to hear what is being said, but at the same time is seldom an addressee of the various turns at talk. A defendant in court or during an interrogation at the police station may have to talk when asked to do so (and when a lawyer is present), but may also decide to remain silent under special conditions. Students in class are expected if not required to listen and to speak when being asked to do so.[5]

In sum, in most institutional situations there is a complex structure of participant roles, usually defined in terms of the social roles of the social interaction but in this case only defined in relation to the kind of contribution they make to the whole event, what rights and obligations they have, and hence who must speak or may speak, who must listen or may listen in a given situation. Ideological dimensions of these various communicative roles are as obvious as they are in social situations and practices in general. Again, power and dominance may be enacted, and these may express ideologically based inequality, for example when those in power abuse their communicative roles, and prevent others from assuming their rights as speakers or listeners, or force them to speak when they have the right to remain silent.

Professional role

Similar remarks hold for the various professional roles participants exercise when participating in communicative events.[6] The earlier examples also put many of these on stage: professors, judges, police officers and so on. That is, in this case the participants derive their communicative roles (e.g. as speakers, producers, or chairs) from their socially or legally established professional roles. Each of these professional roles may be associated with a set of participant roles, as well as with types of communicative events or discourse genres. Thus, whereas public prosecutors have access to the genre of indictments, and may interrogate defendants and witnesses, they are obviously barred from verdicts or sentences, genres to which only juries and judges have access, respectively. Similarly, professors have active access to explaining things in a class and to asking questions during exams, and students will have the obligation to act as respondents.

As is the case for the other relevant categories discussed above, also this category is a proper element of the context if it systematically relates to the structures of text and talk. Thus, in their participant role as speakers and their legal professional role as 'chairs' of trials, judges may control the kinds of speech act (defendants must make assertions), topics (defendants must speak about the facts being discussed), style (defendants must speak politely or else may be held in 'contempt of court'), genre (defendants may or may not be allowed to tell a personal story of their experiences), and especially the many interactional features of the dialogue: defendants are not allowed to interrupt the judge, they must begin and end their contribution when required to do so, and follow many other rules of judge–defendant discourse in the courtroom. Indeed, the whole point of a contextual analysis is precisely to single out those properties of the communicative event that may have such systematic relations with such properties of talk and text.

The ideological implications of these relations between professional roles on the one hand, and participant roles and genres or speech acts on the other hand, are fairly straightforward, as discussed above. As soon as professionals break the rules of communicative interaction and limit the rights of co-participants they may enact forms of domination that may be based on ideological beliefs. This may be the case for male doctors in relation to patients, for male professors in relation to female students, and so on. Note that here, as well as in the other examples given above, domination as well as the ideology on which it rests, are enacted and thus reproduced by talk itself.

Social role

In the complex network of various types of role of speech participants, we may distinguish yet another type, which we may simply call *social role*. Unlike communicative roles, these are not limited to contributions to text and talk, and unlike professional roles, they need not be related to organizations and institutions. Indeed, these social roles obtain in virtually all action and interaction. For instance, whatever our position or professional role, we may act and speak as a friend, an enemy, an ally, a proponent or an opponent of other participants. Speakers in parliament, in their professional role of parliamentarians (or cabinet ministers) affiliated with the legislature of a country or state, may also speak as opponents of a bill, or as allies of those who introduced the bill. The same may be true in everyday conversations as well as in formal talk. Such social roles will usually be enacted by specific discourse features, such as forms of address, politeness moves, strategies of positive self-presentation (face-keeping) or negative other-presentation, arguments (against opponents, or in support of allies, etc.) and favourable or unfavourable rhetoric.

Note that even within this category there are levels or layers of roles. In everyday conversations or parliamentary debates opponents may be 'direct' and confront each other face to face. In a debate on the op-ed page, opponents may also be confronting each other personally, but not face-to-face and not at the same time.[7] But, as is the case for various communicative roles, there may be indirect, long-term addressees or relations. Opposing a speaker may stand for opposing her or his boss or organization, and speaking as a member of an action group may be interpreted as advocating the stance of the action group itself. Thus, in parliament, speakers may oppose what the previous speaker has said, they may, more broadly, oppose the bill being proposed by someone, and by so doing they may oppose the party to which that person belongs, and at the same time they of course advocate their own position, and/or that of their own party (which need not be identical), and as political representatives they may at the same time represent or oppose the 'special interests' outside of parliament. In other words, deeper and more sophisticated analyses of contexts in principle uncover complex sets or levels of various roles.

We have seen that besides membership of groups and organizations, ideologies typically involve polarization, struggle, conflict or competition, and these relationships precisely map onto the social roles being introduced into the context here. Ingroups and outgroups and their associated ideologies thus manifest and reproduce themselves precisely by the 'position' their members take in situations of debate and conflict, also in communication. Arguing in favour of a bill that restricts immigration, may by its very stance be part of the reproduction of nationalism or ethnocentrism. An anti-communist speech in parliament is thus taking a stance in an ideological conflict. In other words, social roles are contextually variable enactments of positions, including ideological positions.

Affiliation

Participants in professional roles often don't speak 'for themselves', but as representatives of an organization or institution, and as representatives who in principle can be replaced by any other institutional member. That is, their affiliation plays a prominent role in the context: confessing to a police officer or in court, doing an exam, making a declaration for a tax auditor, and so on, are the kind of speech events that are often appropriately accomplished in the presence of any representative (in the same professional role) of the organization. People speak in parliament or congress, but usually do so as representatives of their parties, as they do when listening to such speeches. More generally, these events and their participants are also integrated in a web of institutional affiliations. Some of these may be very strict, and legally well described (also with respect to kinds of communicative events), while others may be looser and open to variation and negotiation. Thus, teachers will usually have more leeway in the accomplishment of their communicative and professional roles than speakers of parliament or judges.

One of the many implications of the institutional or organizational affiliation of communicative events is precisely the fact that such participants take part *as* representatives of the institution, and hence often carry the institutional ideologies, if any, into the ongoing context. Indeed, the representatives of an organization are by habit, norm or law entitled or obliged to represent the 'interests' of the organization, and hence their talk and text will multiply index or signal such ideological commitments. Thus, a teacher may thus implement the educational ideology of the school or university, the journalist an ideology of the press, and so on. Such ideologies may pertain to the content of text or talk (such as newsworthiness of events for news interviews or news reports), but also to the very nature of the interaction itself. Educational or medical ideologies may or may not allow a more or less independent and autonomous initiative to students or patients, depending on whether the ideology is more authoritarian or permissive.

Membership

More generally, participants may speak, write, listen or read (also) *as* members of *groups* or *social categories*, in addition to the organizational affiliation and the various roles described above. People may be male or female, white or black, old or young, and so on, and either they themselves or their co-participants will categorize them as such, and act (speak, write) accordingly. Since such social groups and categories are the basis of ideologies, these ideologies will in principle also exhibit in the relevant communicative social practices in which group members engage. That group membership affects the structures of text and talk themselves has been shown in much socio-linguistic research, for example on intonation, lexical items, topics, rhetoric or interactional moves, as discussed in the previous chapter. In terms of the context, people of different social groups or categories are defined and treated as such, also in the communicative event – they may be given preference in turn taking, freedom in topic selection or style, but they may also directly be discriminated against along the same lines, only because they are a member of a specific group. Probably more than any other category of the context, thus, social group membership is what projects ideologies into communicative events. Later we will see how this is being accomplished in text and talk.[8]

It should at this point be emphasized again that roles, affiliation and group membership are not always 'given' in social situations, and this is a fortiori the case in subjectively construed models of such social situations. That is, such social 'positions' may be negotiated, changed, oriented to, deviated from, ignored, forgotten or otherwise become less (or more) relevant in a specific situation. That is, a dynamic theory of discourse emphasizes such situational and personal flexibility. The same will be true for the ideological conditions and consequences of the ways such categories are constructed in the current context by the participants. Men may temporarily disassociate from their group and speak on behalf of women; speakers may defend the position of their opponents when they act as devil's advocate; and dissidents are by definition speaking in defiance of dominant group ideologies.

The social others

So far, the relevant participant roles discussed above pertain to people involved in various capacities in the communicative context itself. However, text and talk are often also *about* other people, usually people who are not present in the ongoing context at all. Strictly speaking this is a property of the *meaning* of discourse, and hence part of a semantic and not of a (pragmatic) context analysis. That is, discourse referents are not part of the context model, but part of the event model (partly) expressed by the discourse. Thus, men routinely speak about women, whites about blacks, and doctors about patients, and these *social others* are thus the referents of their talk. It is also in this way that the ideologies relating communicative participants to the social others, as members of outgroups, are projected into the meanings of a discourse. Yet, one might also argue that these social others are some kind of 'absent participants' in the context.

Racist talk addressed to other whites may obliquely be addressed, in a broader social context, to the social others, and thus not only be semantically relevant, but also pragmatically, that is, as an inherent element of the act of discriminatory talk, as a form of reproduction of racist ideologies. That is, the social others, as part of the targeted outgroup, may be talked *about* but at the same time indirectly, socially and ideologically *addressed*. That is, acts of discrimination also may be categorized and interpreted as such when the discriminated party is not present – yet, they are somehow 'party' to such communicative interaction.

Social representations

Most context categories discussed above have a proper social nature, and are typically made explicit in sociological terms. Obviously, however, participants not only have positions, rights, duties and relations in social situations, institutions and overall social structures, but also share social representations, such as knowledge, attitudes and ideologies. Some of these mental dimensions of participants have been discussed in terms of intentions and goals, which are more individual and contextual.

However, especially as members of various social groups and institutions, communicative participants also share social representations that have an impact on ongoing interaction, text and talk. Thus, crucial for all communicative events is the respective knowledge of the participants, both personal as well as social and cultural. Thus, speakers have *knowledge* about each other (that is, they have a model about Self as well as about others), and such knowledge may instantiate more general knowledge and beliefs about the group to which the others belong.[9]

Similarly, *ideologies* of participants in many ways affect the ongoing definition of the communicative situation, the various actions, participant roles, as well as the discourse itself. The same is true for the socially shared attitudes monitored by these ideologies. Indeed, these attitudes may even be specific and tailored to the communicative event at hand. Thus, trivially, in an informal discussion about abortion, or a parliamentary debate about nuclear energy, speakers bring to bear their specific attitudes about these issues, and such attitudes multiply influence the event and context models that monitor ongoing talk: who is defined as proponent or opponent, whether a speaker is seen as a representative of a social group (man or woman in the abortion debate), who will be treated more or less politely, and so on.

In sum, all social aspects of the complex communicative event are variously monitored by the social representations of the participants as members of groups, categories or institutions. Knowledge will be mutually presupposed accordingly, for example when doctors or lawyers speak with members of the same professional group, or when women presuppose both knowledge, attitudes and ideologies of other women of the same feminist movement. Indeed, most of the communicative context and the discourse need not be made explicit because of such presupposed sharing of social representations within the same group, society or culture.

Together with mental models of individuals, social representations are part of the cognitive interface between social structure, group membership and discourse. If people speak or write as members of groups, their group membership will largely be brought to bear in the current context in terms of the social representations shared with the group, that is, as instantiations of group knowledge, attitudes and ideologies.

This does *not* mean, incidentally, that social representations, including ideologies, cause or determine text and context. It has been explained in some detail in Part I, that there is still a vast 'mental distance' between social representations, and hence the influence of social groups, on the one hand, and discourse structures (including context) on the other hand. Most crucially, although variably so in different situations, speakers are also individuals with their own biography, goals, preferences, plans and emotions – that is, with their own personal models. Intentionally or unwittingly, such models may instantiate shared elements of social representations, but even then the context and the individual and hence their text or talk will be unique. If not, and as suggested before, all members of a group would say or write the same thing in the same situation. This is also one of the reasons why I include relevant aspects of personal models (e.g. intentions and purposes) in the current context.

Social representations may not only apply to the semantic dimension of discourse (e.g. abortion as a topic of talk), but also to the discursive interaction itself: who may/must speak/write about what/whom, to whom, in which way? Journalists know how to interview news sources or news actors, how to write news reports and follow rules and strategies they have learned as group members, and the same is true in all other professional roles discussed above. Thus, both in conversation and in parliament, people instantiate the very ideological forms of membership that we routinely assign to speakers: he is a conservative, she is a liberal, and so on.

At this point we have come full circle. Ideologies may indirectly control the properties of all categories of context models for discourse. But it now appears that one of these categories itself pertains to the social beliefs, and hence the ideologies, of the participants. In other words, ideological control is, so to speak, not external nor deterministic, but internal, that is, through the beliefs of the participants themselves. Thus, I may participate in a conversation as an anti-racist, and this stance influences the way I construct the current context as well as what I say and how I say it. At the same time, both the recipient and I myself represent (part of) my anti-racist beliefs as part of our respective context models, of ourselves as well as about each other (indeed, I may know that my interlocutor knows that I am an anti-racist, and may shape my talk accordingly).

There may even be a discrepancy between my role and my role as represented in my model of myself in the present context. People may speak as anti-racists without much self-control or self-monitoring and thus more or less directly express and enact their group membership. However, they may also do so by monitoring their current identity and by carefully managing their 'image' as an anti-racist, for instance for recipients that are hostile to anti-racists. Also this subtle interplay between 'real' social identities of discourse participants, on the one hand, and those that are locally and intersubjectively represented in their current context models and displayed in their discourse, on the other hand, shows how complex the relations between ideology and discourse may be.

Concluding remark

The context analysis presented above shows that the discursive reproduction of ideologies also applies to the contextual aspects of communicative events. Contexts, or rather context models, explain personal, situational and social variations in the ways underlying ideologies may or may not affect text and talk. They thus serve as another layer of constraints, another interface, between ideology and discourse, and explain that ideologies are not 'deterministic' in the sense of necessarily affecting discourse structures – this will always, literally, depend on the context. Therefore, no discursive theory of ideological expression and reproduction can be adequate without a detailed analysis of context. We shall later spell out in somewhat more detail how exactly mental models of such contexts intervene between social representations, including ideologies, and structures of discourse.

23

Reproduction

What is reproduction?

It has often been argued, above, that ideologies are typically *reproduced* by social practices, and especially by discourse. What exactly does this mean? As with most general notions, the concept of reproduction is not very precise. In general, it implies that ideologies are 'continued', 'made to remain, last, persist . . .', and so on. Like its second part, however, it implies an active, human dimension: It is what people do, make happen, while also making something new, creating something. The repetitive 're' part implies that the act of production is being repeated. For social practices and discourse this usually implies that such acts of production take place every day, are routine, and are part of the definition of everyday life.

More specifically, however, when we refer to the reproduction of ideologies, we are dealing with an equally vague sociological notion, also used to denote the reproduction of groups, social structures, or even whole cultures. Again, reproduction here implies continuity of a system or structure as well as human agency. More theoretically, the notion is used to bridge the well-known gap between the macro-level and the micro-level of social structure. Systems or abstract structures, such as ideologies, natural languages, and societal arrangements are thus said to be both manifested in, as well as made to persist as such through, social practices of social actors at the micro-level. A language like English is reproduced, daily and by millions of people, by its everyday use. And so are capitalist, sexist or racist ideologies.[1]

The active concept of 'production' is relevant here because such systems are not only being 'applied', 'implemented' or passively 'used', but at the same time constituted and reconstituted, as well as gradually changed, by such contextual uses by many social actors. Indeed, also the gradual development of ideologies of a group is based on such social practices. That is, ideologies are (re)produced as well as (re)constructed by social practices.

There is another macro–micro dimension involved here. This time not just that of an abstract system on the one hand and actual practices on the other hand, but the distinction between the group and its members, and especially its new members. Just as groups are reproduced (also) by getting or recruiting new members, also ideologies are reproduced by getting new 'users,' as is also the case for natural languages. Whether by socialization or other processes of sharing social representations (initiation, teaching, training, preaching, propaganda), ideologies are continually reproduced because new social members 'acquire' or 'learn to use' them.

As we shall see in more detail later, this may happen directly through explicit ideological discourse, or indirectly by making inferences from discourse and other social practices about what opinions other group members share. White people 'learn racism' by accepting general racist statements such as 'Black women are welfare queens' as expressed in conversations with friends or colleagues, or they infer such a belief from repeated stories in the media in which black women are portrayed as being on welfare, or because they overgeneralize from one or a few black women they know who are on welfare. This last case, as a personal experience, however, is usually told in stories to other group members, and the relevant inference may then be jointly produced in talk, as a conclusion suggested or accepted by co-participants. That is, sharing is usually not simply a one-sided, passive event, but a complex, co-operative procedure, involving people who (already) 'know', as well as people who 'still don't know'. In other words, reproduction also implies socialization, learning, inculcation or adoption by young or new members, of the socially shared representations of a group.

And finally, besides its macro–micro (system–actions, group–members) dimensions, we also have the local and contextual versus the global and decontextualized dimension of reproduction. Members having learned how to make an inference from one case or example, or to express an ideological opinion in one context, are typically able to do so for similar cases and in similar contexts. That is, reproduction is not only top-down and bottom-up, but also allows for transition from token to type and from type to token, from today to tomorrow, and from here to elsewhere. Reproduction thus also implies generalization. Combined with the vertical relations between system and actions, this also explains the bottom-up nature of reproduction – social representations are not merely acquired directly, in an abstract (and usually discursive) manner, but also as generalizations from daily experiences. In specific social situations of ethnic inequality, such generalizations may be morally unacceptable overgeneralizations (prejudice), but they may also be forms of (correct, justified) social learning, for example when minorities learn to detect and interpret racist events as such, and thus acquire an anti-racist ideology.[2]

Summarizing these various aspects of the social reproduction of ideologies, we thus have the following dimensions.

1   System–Action: top-down application, use and implementation of general, abstract ideological beliefs in concrete social practices.
2   Action–System: bottom-up sustaining, continuing and changing the socially shared system by its daily uses in social practices. Along this dimension, ideologies are effectively being constructed, constituted and changed by social practices, including discourse.

3   Group–Members: ideological communication, inculcation, teaching, socialization and initiation of new members by (knowledgeable) group members.

4   Members–Group: acceptance and compliance or non-acceptance, resistance or dissidence of one or some groups members, against the ideology of the group or its elites.

5   Local–Global: generalization, extension, decontextualization of specific experiences and opinions to similar or abstract contexts, experiences, cases or circumstances; social learning, overgeneralization, stereotyping, prejudice formation and ideology construction.

In 4 we see that the group–member relation may also be conversed, that is, when individual members reject, refuse or do not accept a group's ideology. This may not seem to be a dimension of reproduction, but it is necessary to account for personal variations and change of ideologies, which are also part of their reproduction. Obviously, as soon as most members reject ideologies or some ideological beliefs, then change may eventually lead to the abolition of ideologies.[3]

Discourse and reproduction

Many of the types and modalities of reproduction discussed above appear to be discursive. Ideologies may be expressed in many genres and contexts of discourse and their respective structures as discussed in the previous chapters. Such ideological discourses have several functions, such as a display of group knowledge, membership and allegiance; comparison and normalization of values and evaluation criteria; evaluating social practices; socialization; or persuasion and manipulation. Some of these functions will be dealt with more specifically in the next chapters. Here I focus on some of the more general aspects of the discursive reproduction of ideologies.

Context

In the previous chapter we saw how ideologies may intervene in the social construction or interpretations of the contextual categories which in turn constrain (or are influenced or constituted by) text and talk. Thus, participants may act as speakers, as proponents, as journalists, as representatives of an institution like a newspaper, and as members of various groups (age, gender, ethnicity, nationality, etc.). In all these roles, participants may enact (and sometimes disregard) the social representations, including the ideologies, related to their social identity. That is, social situations in general, and contexts of discourse in particular, are literally the site where ideologies are being enacted in society. As long as speech participants identify with or willingly or unwillingly (have to) represent the groups and institutions of which they are members, they thus by definition contribute to the use and the reproduction of the ideologies associated with these social formations.

The examples mentioned in the previous chapter suggest, however, that such ideological alignment is not straightforward. First, language users may have their own personal models, and these may be more or less at variance with the social representations they share as group members, given the constraints of the present context. Indeed, their interests as group members may be less salient or less relevant than their current personal interests, and their intentions and goals may be formed accordingly. Second, language users are members of several social groups, and thus share in several social representations at the same time. Again, some of these may be more relevant or more powerful than others. The result is that the event and context models that monitor the communicative event may have contents and structures that in many ways are inconsistent with those expected of loyal group members. If such is the case for models, this will also be the case for the discourse properties that are a function of these models, such as the meaning derived from event models (including specific opinions), as well as the surface structure, style, speech acts or interactional strategies that are controlled by context models.

The consequences of these complex and subtle acts of interactional and communicative management in specific social situations are that ideologies are not simply reproduced in talk and text by the members of the groups that share such ideologies. There is more or less substantial variation, there is explicit and intentional deviance, there are dilemmas, and there are personal and interpersonal conflicts that need to be negotiated and resolved.[4] Hence, not all news reports in a newspaper will show the ideology or political allegiances of that newspaper. Not all journalists always give priority to journalistic ideologies in their reports, and not all racists will treat minorities always and everywhere with derogatory remarks.

The empirical picture emerging from this variation may be that ideologies do not seem to 'exist' in the first place – the local and personal constraints of context may distort or prohibit their unfettered expression. The question is then in what respect we are able to speak of the 'reproduction' of ideologies, when social situations so often prevent their direct implementation. Theoretically, then, we are able to account for ideological reproduction only when we assume that across language users and contexts, there are 'enough' instances of ideological expression.

How much is 'enough'? Obviously, this may vary. For instance, it may be assumed that journalists most of the time will have to follow the ideological principles of their profession. If not, they will not be hired or they will be fired. Exceptions will be allowed, especially for highly qualified or popular journalists, but there will be a margin of variation within which each journalist will have to remain when working for one of the mass media. In some cases, for example in public office, even one deviation from the ideological 'party line' may be enough for a politician to be marginalized, discredited or voted out of office.

Interestingly, quantity as such may not be the right measure. One public racist statement may be enough to conclude that someone is expressing a racist ideology, even when in most other situations these expressions were better controlled. The rationale behind such a conclusion is that people who do not have a racist ideology will simply never make such a blatantly racist remark in the first place. In actual practice, there will be a broad range between regular and unique expressions of ideology, on which basis other participants and observers will be able to draw conclusions about the underlying ideologies of group members. Some of these expressions may be very indirect or subtle, and participants and observers may not even notice them if the ideology that inspires them is taken for granted. Thus, the quality press, including the liberal quality press, may not daily make blatant remarks about ethnic minorities or immigrants. Yet, more subtly and indirectly, for example by the choice of its topics (e.g. about crime, violence or cultural deviation), it may well slowly create a negative image of the cultural others, and thus contribute to the reproduction of an ethnocentric ideology.

Given the processes of memory, attention and recall, readers may selectively focus on and memorize even the occasional story in which minorities are represented negatively, and forget about the larger number of negative stories in which members of their own majority group are represented negatively. This is a familiar finding in differential attribution for ingroups and outgroups.[5]

In sum, the conditions of reproduction are as complex as the structures of context and discourse, and the strategies of information processing and social representation, combined. Under what conditions specific text and talk is being attended to, read or listened to, understood, and represented in models, and under what conditions these models are accepted as true and generalized to more abstract social knowledge and beliefs, are all questions that need to be answered in a theory of reproduction.

All this also applies to the projection of ideologies in context models and hence in the enactment or interpretation of the context itself. Negative beliefs about minorities when uttered by prominent members of minority groups themselves or by a white cabinet minister of a respectable party, may be much more credible than those of a member of a racist party. That is, credibility is one element of the process of acceptability, and itself a function of the group membership of the speaker, that is, a category of the context.

Generally, thus, acceptability of beliefs, which is the core criterion in the reproduction of ideologies, depends also on the interpretation and the evaluation of context structures, and especially on the various roles and positions of the participants. Even the context categories of communicative domain, action type, and circumstances may be especially conducive to ideological reproduction, as is the case for classrooms and education, parliament and politics, newsrooms and the media. This is so first because of the credibility or the prestige of the social actors involved, as well as the mass-mediated consequences of text and talk. One 'unhappy' but widely publicized remark of a prominent politician about immigrants may contribute more to the reproduction of ethnic prejudices and ideologies than thousands of blatantly racist conversations taking place in the homes of citizens.

Discourse structures

Although context categories themselves may strongly influence the acceptance of social representations, the really influential factors should generally be searched in the discourse structures themselves. That is, are there discourse structures that prohibit, impair or favour ideological reproduction? The analysis of the structures and strategies of discourse in Chapter 21, suggests that ideologies may in principle map onto all levels and dimensions of discourse: graphics, intonation, syntax, local meanings and coherence, topics, style, rhetoric, speech acts and interactional features. Still, expression structures *as such* usually do not code for ideology – this mostly happens in relation to underlying meanings and functions. To persuasively convey ideological 'content', thus, the semantics of text and talk plays an especially important role.

To prove such an assumption, we need to find out how semantic variations have different consequences for the construction of models, and how these models may in turn be used to confirm or construct social representations. For instance, topics or semantic macrostructures of discourse represent salient and important information, and will therefore generally be attended to, and be used to construct key (top) propositions in models. If such topics are repeated (e.g. 'Black West Indians rioted' in the popular press in the UK), then model construction may become routine and generalized to a negative attitude about black youth, or about blacks in general, if no alternative, counter-ideologies are present that may cause rejection of such models.

At the same time, readers with ambiguous attitudes about minorities, may find such prominent expressions of bias too crude to be credible, and may not construct the biased models as intended. They may, however, be unable to detect more subtle forms of semantic ethnic bias in news reporting, and following their interpretation construct models whose generalization also leads to a negative attitude about minorities. That is, besides contextual conditions of credibility, also the nature of the semantic (and other) structures may (for different participants) have different influences on model construction and acceptance, and on the subsequent generalization to social representations that are part of ideological reproduction.

Reproduction, however, is not limited to interpretation and the influences of discourse on mental representations. Also the production side of the communicative event needs to be taken into account. Part of this has been done in the analysis of context. This means, among other things, that access to specific social roles, and especially elite roles, provides group members with vastly more influential means to reproduce ideologies than ordinary citizens without much access to public discourse. These, then, are the now familiar social conditions that control the context of production.

But besides these contextual categories of position, roles and group membership, we also need to establish which discourse structures can be more or less explicitly controlled in the first place. Some of this control, as is the case in TV programmes, may be the result of complex production processes. Ideological control in that case presupposes that most participants, and at least the more influential ones, are ideologically on the same line. Another questions is whether speakers or writers who have control over discourse are always able to 'translate' their ideologies into the more or less subtle properties of text and talk.

Thus, again, the explicit choice of negative topics in order to derogate outgroups, is fairly easy and straightforward, and simply involves the projection of ideologically biased models of events onto topics of talk and text, as is the case for crime stories about minorities. However, many other discourse structures, such as the syntax of headlines, local semantic disclaimers, or the choice of metaphors, is only moderately or not at all consciously controlled. Ideological influence of discourse in this case is barely intentional, but a more or less automatic expression of biased models.

Of course, this does not prevent ideological reproduction. On the contrary, since it is not consciously controlled, it cannot usually be 'self-censored' either because of prevailing norms or values (e.g. those of non-discrimination), so that ideological reproduction takes place without the speakers' being aware of it. Indeed, when confronted with critical analyses of such subtle racist practices, they will generally deny that they are racists. Thus, besides explicit manipulation of models and social representations, ideological reproduction may more indirectly and unintentionally take place through the routine and taken-for-granted processes of discourse production. In the chapters that follow, I shall study a number of more specific instances of these various aspects of the discursive reproduction of ideologies.

24

From Cognition to Discourse

Introduction

After the more general outline of the role of discourse in the reproduction of ideologies in the previous chapter, I am now in a position to detail some of the components of a relevant theory of discursive ideological reproduction. I shall begin where I left off in Part I, at the cognitive level of analysis, and then I shall move to the various structures and strategies of text and talk that are relevant for the expression of ideologies.

It should be recalled here that the cognitive basis of a theory of ideological reproduction is neither a luxury nor a reduction of the social to the personal. First, I have stressed that the mind is social – socially acquired, shared, used and changed. Many aspects of social structure presuppose such shared knowledge and beliefs of members. A large part of our mind consists of socially and culturally shared representations. These are also needed in the understanding of personal experiences and the accomplishment of individual actions, and hence also for discourse production and understanding.

Thus, second, if we want to describe and explain how group ideologies affect discourse, and vice versa, we need to spell out how to get from social representations to the individual ones that represent personal experiences or personal text and talk. The only way to do this is in terms of a cognitive theory of discourse processing.

There is at present no serious alternative theory that explains how social structures, including those of communicative contexts, are able to constrain the structures of text and talk. We simply need the theoretical construct of people's 'minds' as an interface between the social and the personal. As is the case for all theories, however, these may change, so that the mental 'architecture' as it was adopted from current cognitive science is of course merely a hypothesis about the ways people produce and understand discourse and accomplish many other tasks.

The same is true for the 'information processing' metaphor prevailing in cognitive science. This is at present the only viable theoretical framework to account for language use, communication and the ways knowledge and other (e.g. ideological) beliefs interact with discourse. However, it was also emphasized that such a framework is incomplete when it is not embedded in a broader theory of (verbal and other) social interaction and social structure. That is, beliefs and discourse have both cognitive and social dimensions, and the crucial point of this book is precisely to connect these two major dimensions.

Discourse production

Discourse production involves a set of representations and complex operations that together may be thought of, theoretically, as a discourse production unit in the mind. This unit has three main modules – a pragmatic, a semantic and a formulation module – which operate in close collaboration.[1]

The pragmatic module

As soon as people want to speak or write, they first construct a relevant context model. This model selects the relevant information from the speaker's beliefs about the social situation, as described in Chapter 22, for example the current communicative event (e.g. informal conversation with friend, writing a news report, giving a lesson, or visiting one's doctor), current goals or intentions, a setting, and the speech participants. As suggested before, such a context model may simply be a relevant specification of the current experience model speakers have of the ongoing episode.[2]

The context model thus specifies what relevant speech acts must be accomplished, and generally provides the information needed in the other (semantic, formulation) modules for the production of a discourse that is appropriate in the present context. In other words, a context model contains a 'plan' that features all information needed to accomplish an appropriate speech act. For instance, beliefs about the nature of the social relation between speaker and hearer provide the relevant information for the accomplishment of deference or politeness, such as specific pronouns or the use or avoidance of specific lexical items. All possible variations of discourse structures that are not a function of the semantic module are controlled by the pragmatic module and its current context model. That is, speech acts, interaction, as well as the stylistic and much of the rhetorical dimensions of text and talk, are controlled by this pragmatic module.

In other words, whereas the semantic module specifies *what* people want to say or write, the pragmatic module controls *how* they must do so in an interactionally and socially appropriate and effective way, how discourse 'fits' the current context, and what social acts are accomplished by the discourse.

Whereas in writing or monological communication, the context model may be relatively fixed during production, in conversational interaction such a model is of course continually updated, according to the feedback received from other participants. Models of each participant in a communicative event will partly be identical or similar, but also partly different – each participant interprets and represents the 'current context' in an at least slightly different way. These different constructions may be the basis of communicative misunderstandings and conflicts, although language users have effective strategies to solve such problems of misunderstanding.

The semantic module

The semantic module provides the information needed for the meaning construction of discourse. It may draw on virtually all representations in personal and social memory. This is not surprising, since we may speak about virtually everything we know or believe, including what other people know or believe. In order to talk about past and current personal experiences, as well as about intentions for future actions, or what language users know from others or the media about any situation or event, they draw upon relevant experience and event models in personal memory. But they know and believe much more than the specific facts represented in their models about personal experiences. For instance they may also want to express social representations, namely, what *we* know and believe in our group or culture.

Obviously, people do not usually express all they know or believe, simply because all this would not be relevant in the present situation, because the recipients already may know or believe many of these things, or because for whatever reason they do not want the recipients to know what they know or believe. These constraints are contextual and therefore provided by the pragmatic module and the information in the context model (the representation of what the speaker believes about the beliefs of the recipient). Generally, then, only a small fragment of contextually relevant information of event models will be selected for the construction of discourse meaning. Other information may be left implicit, and may at most be signalled by appropriate discourse structures, so that the recipients will be able to infer it when they need or want to do that. Obviously, the more beliefs already shared by the participants, the more discourse may leave meaning (representing such beliefs) implicit.

The output of the combined (ongoing) operation of the pragmatic and semantic modules is a semantic representation. Whereas our knowledge, as represented in personal event models, may well be accessible and available, we usually do not know in advance what model information will be included in this semantic representation. That is, language users have recourse to effective strategies that allow them to continuously adapt the selection of what they know and believe to the constraints of the ongoingly constructed and updated context model (e.g. what they think is interesting for the recipients, what they need to say in order to remain coherent, and so on).

What language users normally do know in advance, however, is the overall *topics* or themes of the discourse (or discourse fragment) they are about to produce. In the semantic module, therefore, these overall topics or semantic macrostructures play a fundamental strategic role – they allow not only global planning (and global understanding) of discourse, but also the management of a large amount of information over a longer period of speaking or writing (or reading).[3] Topics thus also allow language users to make their discourses coherent and to announce to recipients what they are going to speak about (which may be essential to get the floor or attention in the first place). It is also for this reason why many discourse types typically express their 'upcoming' topics up front, for instance in various forms of announcements, summaries or headlines. In comprehension this will allow the recipients to activate or build up the top structure of relevant mental models. They will know what the discourse will be 'about', and this knowledge facilitates further understanding.

Under the overall control of topics, the semantic production module finally produces the actual 'meanings' of discourse, in the form of a locally coherent sequence of propositions. This happens by selecting the more detailed, lower level propositions of the model a speaker has about an event. As suggested, the context model specifies which lower-level information will be relevant for actual expression, and which information may be left implicit. Besides the construction of minimal local coherence, the speaker may also shape its semantic representations following a number of strategies that allow the differentiation of importance, focus, foregrounding and other forms of information distribution and emphasis. Obviously, this linear production of the meaning(s) of a discourse is also a strategic, ongoing process, in which constraints from other modules may influence current meaning production: ongoing thought and inferences, current perceptions and experiences, interpretations of reactions of recipients (in oral discourse), as well as any change in the ongoing context model.

The formulation module

The formulation module takes the output of the pragmatic and semantic modules and produces actual utterances in a given natural language, using the various discourse rules, grammar and lexicon of that language. This production process is exceedingly complex. It takes place in working memory and also has a strategic nature, with continuous feedback from the pragmatic and semantic modules. Production is linear, and proceeds word by word, phrase by phrase, clause by clause, gradually translating units of semantic representations, such as concepts or propositions, into lexical expressions, in their appropriate grammatical order. Although mistakes can be corrected, the strategic nature of discourse production allows for a lot of 'imperfection', as long as the language user is being understood and speaks or writes appropriately in the present context.

Specific semantic structures of the meanings to be expressed may thus be mapped onto specific syntactic structures (word order, clause structure); agency may for instance be embodied in the expression of a lexical item in first ('topical') position and as the subject of the sentence; relations between propositions may be marked by conditional or functional connectives, and main topics may be placed up front in headlines.

From these examples we also see that the formulation module not only calls upon the grammar and the lexicon, but also on other discourse structure rules and strategies, such as the structures of stories or news reports. To write a news report, a journalist knows that the report should have a headline (or will expect someone else to write one for the report) and a lead as initial discourse categories, and that these should express the most relevant information in the present context, namely, the topics being constructed for the present discourse.

Finally, when combined with lexical expressions, semantic 'content' derived from the semantic module (and its event model) and controlled by the pragmatic module (and its context model) will be actually expressed in talk or writing, following the usual phonological rules, for example of intonation, or the graphical rules for the current genre.

Producing ideology

The details of these respective modules are not relevant here.[4] My brief summary is merely intended to give an idea of how mental representations 'get into' actual text and talk. Conversely, they also explain how the understanding of text and talk may contribute to the construction of mental representations. The question now is how ideologies may interfere in these processes. Again, there are several ways in which this may happen.

Direct expression

Since under special conditions all accessible mental representations are available for direct expression, ideological propositions may sometimes be expressed directly. That is, if the contextual constraints of the pragmatic module allow this, the semantic module may directly select the relevant ideological propositions as input for the semantic representations (meanings) of discourse. This is for instance the case in explicitly ideological discourses, such as propaganda, theoretical analysis, and for discourses in which ideological explanation, justification or legitimation is at stake. People in that case primarily speak as group members, and express what 'we' believe in. In a dispute with the unions or the government, for instance, managers may directly state that 'the market does not want any government interference'. Obviously such direct expressions may be combined with more particular ones, such as personal experiences. Moral conclusions of stories about minorities, for instance, may express the negative group evaluation that 'we are not used to that here'. Given the abstract and general nature of ideological beliefs, also the meanings (and their formulations) need to be general and abstract, and feature generic concepts and expressions.

Instantiated direct expression

Ideological beliefs may also be expressed through instantiation (or specification) in mental models in episodic (personal) memory of the general propositions in social memory. For instance, instead of talking about markets and governments in general, thus, specific managers may express that *they* do not like the interference of *this* government. Disclaimers often feature such instantiated direct expressions. As a strategy of positive self-presentation, people may begin negative statements about minorities, by saying 'I have nothing against minorities, but . . .'. The first clause of this type of utterances, realizing an apparent denial, instantiates for the current speaker the general opinion, derived from a non-racist ideology, that one should not say negative things about minorities. That is, as soon as general moral rules, attitudes and ideologies are applied to the present context and its participants, we have an example of an instantiated direct expression of ideologies. In formal terms, this means that variables are replaced by the constants (for participants, time, place, etc.) of the present context.

Direct expressions of ideological attitudes

What has been said for the direct expression of ideologies also applies to the direct expression of the domain-specific *attitudes* controlled by ideologies. For instance, under the control of a racist ideology, group members may say that they are in favour of a restriction of immigration of non-European people. As with the expression of ideologies they may do so in general, abstract terms, and use the group-reflexive 'we', or they may do this in the instantiated form and use personal pronouns ('I', 'we') referring to specific participants or subgroups.

In all the cases mentioned above, the information of social representations is directly combined with the constraints of the pragmatic module and entered into the semantic module of the discourse production unit. Conversely, in interpretation and (critical) analysis, discourse produced in this way may be understood as explicitly expressing or indirectly signalling such ideological beliefs. We should not forget, however, the possible constraints of the context model. Both recipients and analysts should know that such expressions may be made for a number of special social reasons, such as social compliance, or the realization of specific goals (e.g. get a job). That is, the pragmatic module may require people to be polite, tactical, or otherwise forced to hide their 'real opinions'.

Event model expression

Most discourse is about concrete experiences and events, and therefore derives its information from event models, as described above. Ideological and attitudinal group beliefs in this case may be instantiated and applied to concrete personal situations. Instead of general opinions about non-interference of the government in the market, we may for instance have a concrete news story in which specific managers resent a government policy to have them register the number of members of ethnic minorities groups in firms in order to get information about minority employment and discrimination. Similarly, beliefs about the criminal activities of a Turkish neighbour, which may or not be based on personal experiences of the storyteller, may similarly be an instantiation and application of the general ideological opinion that minorities are criminal. Once part of the event model (the personal construction or interpretation of the event), this personal opinion may be used as input to the semantic module. Under the constraints of the context model, people may or may not include such opinions in the semantic representation of a story or an argument.

Context model expression

Since all models may thus be ideologically influenced, this is also the case for the context model. People may represent co-participants in a negative way only because they are members of specific social groups. Their intentions, goals and actions may enact beliefs derived from ideologies and attitudes, for instance when they directly intend to derogate co-participants. Thus, intentionally or unintentionally issuing a command instead of a polite request in a context where this would not be appropriate, may count as an act of discrimination. The same is true for the contextual constraints on deference and politeness, and other interactional conditions of appropriateness.

Negative representations of other participants in many ways influence the semantic and formulation modules. Beliefs of events models that normally would not be expressed because of contextual constraints of politeness or non-discrimination may now be admitted to the semantic representation of the discourse. Similarly, also various expression structures may directly be affected by such 'biased' context models, for instance in the use of impolite pronouns or intonation, and lexical items may be selected that signal negative opinions about people spoken to or spoken about.

The fundamental role of context models in shaping (and interpreting) discourse by the participants of communicative events, should again warn us that a 'direct' ideological analysis of discourse is theoretically and practically impossible. We should always know the details of the context in order to know whether and what type of ideological control is at work. Indeed, the 'same' statement in one context may have an ideological source, which it may not have in another context – depending on the speaker, group membership, intentions and goals, circumstances and so on. People may for many reasons want to conceal their personal or group beliefs, or they may express beliefs they do not have. They may feign, lie, dissimulate, be ironic or metaphorical, and in many other ways say what they do not mean literally. Thus, contexts in many ways 'key' the meanings and expressions of discourse, and, without knowledge of that key, we are unable to understand, infer or criticize their discourse or communicative act. In the studies of specific ideological and discursive strategies in the following chapters, this important warning should be heeded.

Concluding remark

The discourse production processes briefly discussed in this chapter appear to overlap with the ways underlying ideologies control other social representations, such as attitudes, which in turn may influence the opinions of context and event models, which finally define the contents for the modules of discourse production. Discursive and ideological production and reproduction thus run parallel, but at the same time it has been shown that the expression of ideologies usually requires several stages. Few discourses are wholly ideological in the sense that they express 'pure' group ideology. However, general ideological opinions may of course be 'applied' in specific models and thus provide the ideological basis for actual discourse production.

25

Persuasion

Influencing the mind

Although the theoretical framework proposed in the previous chapters explains both the expression and the reception side of the relations between discourse and ideology, the theory has focused mostly on the ways ideologies are expressed in text and talk. In this and the next chapter, I shall take the other perspective and examine some of the discursive and cognitive strategies of the ways ideological discourse may be persuasively used in the formation or change of ideologies. Thus, assuming that members of a group effectively express their ideologies in their discourses, we now need to know the 'effects' of such discourses on the minds of both ingroup and outgroup members.

As is the case for the other fundamental notions studied in the previous chapters, the notions of 'effects' and 'persuasion' have generated an enormous literature in social psychology and mass communication research.[1] The empirical results of all this work, especially in the traditional effects-research in mass communication studies, have at best been rather inconclusive. The mass media, which undoubtedly also are the main means of ideological reproduction in contemporary societies, have variously been described as powerful or as rather powerless in influencing the minds of the audience. Some research emphasizes that at most they are able to set the agenda of public discourse and opinion. That is, they may not tell people what to think, but they are quite effective in influencing what people will think about.[2]

This is not the place to review this vast research tradition. One major problem of much earlier research is its theoretical inadequacy in the account of the two main domains involved in the notions of 'effect' and 'persuasion', namely, discourse and the mind. That is, in order to be able to say something analytically acceptable about the influence of discourse, one needs an explicit theory of the various structures of text and talk and their contexts, as well as a cognitive theory of discourse comprehension and other mental representations involved in understanding and cognitive effects. It is only recently that the latter problem has begun to be dealt with, whereas discourse analytical approaches still remain scarce in effects and persuasion research, mainly as a consequence of the unfortunate insularity of empirical (read experimental) research in much social psychology, especially in the USA.

Another problem that is relevant for my discussion is the confusion about the kind of mental representations involved in the processes of change involved in the persuasive effects of discourse. No distinction has usually been made between opinions and attitudes, nor between personal or contextual changes and long-term socially shared ones, as is the case for ideological influence. Although there is work on attitude change in more natural settings, most experimental work focuses on short-term, experimentally controlled changes observed in the laboratory. Moreover, much of the work is also marred by the strange division of labour between cognitive and social psychologists, of which the first deal with knowledge and learning, and the second with opinions and attitudes, although in both cases the processes and representations involved are closely related.

Different types of influence and persuasion

Against this background, then, the analysis of persuasion must be based on the theory of cognition and text processing summarized in the previous chapters. The implications of this approach for the study of the ideological influence of discourse are the following.

1   Discourse understanding and influence is a complex process that is a function of both the structures of discourse as well as of the mental processing and representation of recipients. That is, whether or not, and how, people are influenced by talk and text also depends on what they already know and believe.

2   Discourse understanding not only involves the processing of structures of text and talk, but also, and very crucially, those of the context as it is subjectively construed by the recipients in their context models. In my terms this means that the construction or change of any mental representations of events is a function of the contents and structures of ongoing context models. One well-known notion to be explained in such terms is for instance that of 'credibility'.

3   Although the relations between factual beliefs (knowledge) and evaluative beliefs (opinions, attitudes) are quite complex, it may be generally assumed that discourses have an influence on evaluative beliefs only when they are at least marginally understood. In other words, persuasion presupposes comprehension. Only in very specific circumstances may people be persuaded by discourses they do not understand, and, even then, at least partial understanding is a minimal condition of opinion formation and change.

4   If persuasion is defined as a process in which people change their opinions as a consequence of discourse, it is crucial to make a distinction between different kinds of evaluative belief and hence between different kinds of persuasion. Thus, a distinction has been made between personal opinions and socially shared opinions. The first are represented in both event models and context models, stored in episodic (personal) memory;

the latter in social representations, such as attitudes and ideologies, stored in social memory. Moreover, one should distinguish between particular and general or abstract opinions. Most socially shared attitudes are by definition context-free, and hence abstract and general. Personal opinions may be both particular and general: I may dislike my boss today, I may dislike my boss in general, and I may dislike all bosses. Socially shared opinions may also change, but because they are acquired fairly slowly, also such changes take time. In sum, unlike much traditional work on attitudes and attitude change, I do not simply collapse all evaluative beliefs into one undifferentiated category of 'attitudes'. The concept of attitude is used here in its original sense of a (set of) socially shared opinions.

5   From these distinctions it follows that discourses may variously affect these different types of evaluative beliefs. My talk now may temporarily lead to the formation or change of a particular opinion of my recipient today, or may have more general effects: opinion change may be more permanent, or it may affect more general and abstract opinions of the recipient. And finally, a large number of discourses may have persuasive effects on a large number of group members and thus gradually construct or change their social representations, as is typically the case for the more 'structural' learning from educational discourse or media discourse. Obviously, the acquisition or change of ideologies belongs to the latter type of discursively based changes of the 'social mind' shared by the members of a group, society or culture.

6   In principle all discourse may have ideological effects, whether or not it expresses ideologies explicitly or implicitly. In practice, however, we often limit research into ideological influence to those discourses that express ideologies. That is, if we are interested in the production and reproduction of ideologies, we usually will focus on the presence or lack of ideological effects of ideological discourse.

7   It also follows from the theoretical distinctions made above that the analysis of all processes of effect, influence or persuasion needs to relate detailed structures of text and context, with those of short-term discourse processing, as well as the details of mental representations both in episodic (personal) and in social memory.

Ideological influence

After this brief summary of some of the main principles presupposed in the analysis of the ideological influence of discourse, let us now turn more specifically to the discursive and cognitive structures and strategies involved in the formation and change of ideologies as a result of verbal communication.

Besides verbal discourse also other semiotic messages (images, photos, movies, etc.) as well as other social practices may have ideological 'effects' on social members. Indeed, many sexist practices as well as ideologies of men may be inspired by observation, interaction and watching movies, and not just by male ingroup talk and text about women. Yet, in the rest of this book, I shall take such other semiotic and 'practical' influences for granted and focus on discourse, with the understanding that the basic processes of ideological influence involved are very similar.

Cognitive conditions

Discursive influence on ideologies presupposes a number of cognitive conditions. Before ideologies are being acquired and changed, people already have vast amounts of factual and evaluative beliefs, represented in the ways explained before. During socialization, education and peer group interaction, thus, personal knowledge of members of groups and cultures about concrete people, events and facts is thus gradually extended with socially shared beliefs. That is, people learn that other people in similar circumstances have the same or similar beliefs, or, vice versa, they learn to accept (or reject) what they are told by others. In other words, the acquisition of new ideologies by competent language users and social members does not take place 'on a clean slate'.

   Thus, we may generally assume that ideological persuasion is facilitated by lacking social and political knowledge, if recipients have no alternative opinions, and if ideological propositions do not obviously clash with their personal experiences.[3]

   More specifically, social members have gradually learned to distinguish between (true or false) factual beliefs and evaluative beliefs, that is, between beliefs that in principle should follow or be made plausible by truth criteria, and those beliefs that represent people's personal evaluation of situations, events, objects, people or their properties in terms of cultural shared values. As suggested, they also have acquired the cognitive competence that allows them to distinguish between their personal opinions and those of others, and that groups of people sometimes have the same or similar opinions.

   And finally, people have learned that their own knowledge as well as their beliefs, and those of others, may change as a consequence of what others tell them. For the change of knowledge this usually means that facts must be supported by commonsense (or scientific) truth criteria, such as those of reliable observation, correct inference or communication from credible sources. For opinions on the other hand, change is usually related to 'good arguments', based both on facts as well as on basic values about what is good or bad, right or wrong.[4]

   In sum, the acquisition of ideologies takes place in a rich and well-developed social and cognitive environment: people know that others may have the same or different opinions about the world and that such opinions may be influenced by discourse. In a later stage they learn to discern that the distribution of opinions of 'others' is not random, but that various 'kinds' of people also tend to have various 'kinds' of opinions, and that many opinions hang together. As is the case for all social learning, they may acquire insights either indirectly on the basis of their own observation and action, as well as more directly through discourse: they may hear from their parents, friends, children stories or TV that people not only have opinions that may change or remain more or less the same, but also that group membership may be related to what people typically do or ought to think. Indeed, the early acquisition of gender knowledge and roles is an example where boys and girls learn that they may have different opinions precisely because they are boys and girls.

At the same time, they learn to understand that many of the earlier general opinions (e.g. about boys and girls, children and grown-ups, or in general 'us' and 'them') seem to be relevant for the evaluation of many different situations and events. It is at this point that the more complex attitudes they have acquired during adolescence begin to crystallize into fragmentary ideological systems with which they can personally identify.

Social conditions

The acquisition of social representations not only has a number of cognitive conditions as informally summarized above, but also social conditions. People have learned that social interaction in general and discourse in particular is relevant in the way they and others acquire or change their opinions. They know they have to defend theirs against others, and they understand that others give arguments for their own opinions. And they have understood that opinions are not only personal but may also be related to group or category membership (being a boy, being a girl, or being a child). In sum, they know that opinions are often about social events or issues, often shared or disputed by others, acquired or challenged in social interaction, and tied to social groups and different for 'us' and 'them'.

Obviously, such knowledge about opinion acquisition and change has its 'empirical' social base in the many forms of social interaction, communication, and group relations of which social members are part. That is, ideologies just like other social representations are both a cognitive as well as a social construction – they are not only mentally shared with others as forms of social cognition, but also socially produced with others as group members.

All this also applies to the cognitive and social dimensions of discourse and its ideological influences. Members have acquired the social competence not only to understand opinions of others, but also that these are typically expressed in text or talk, and often in the forms of arguments. They know that people may persuasively express both their own opinions as well as those of the group or organization they belong to. Everyday discursive interaction in which such opinions are being expressed are themselves often part of broader social arrangements, organizations or institutions.

Children read or hear stories and watch TV and know that opinions may be expressed by politicians speaking or quoted on TV or in the newspaper;

and the same is true for the expressions of opinions by priests in sermons in church, by teachers in lessons at school, or by fathers or mothers at home. Many of these opinions seem to recur in the same social situations, expressed by members of the same group (other politicians, other teachers, other parents, other girls) and it is in such social contexts, then, that groups and systems of social beliefs tend to be associated to social structure, to social groups, to social interests, and to self-serving talk and text of members of such groups. In sum, through quite complicated processes of social perception, interaction, communication and discourse, group members gradually acquire the very notion of group attitudes.

The social and cognitive complexity involved here suggests that the very notion of ideology, which is hardly a commonsense notion for younger children, as well as the ideologies themselves, are only gradually acquired during adolescence. Indeed, the definition of ideology in terms of a complex schema of categories defining the evaluations of the own group and its properties (identity, activity, goals, norms, group relations and resources) suggests that people will only acquire ideologies when they have learned what it is to be a group member. That is, from thinking in terms of 'I', they have to learn to think in terms of 'we' and 'them', distinguish a number of group differences, identify with the group, participate in its activities, share some of its goals, be subjected to its norms, values and rules, have participated in inter-group interaction and conflict, and have been given (or denied) access to social resources.

As such, these ideological schemata and the social conditions of their (social) acquisition need not be acquired only in later adolescence: many of the social experiences, social groups and social relations involved, children already have acquired for age and gender – they know that grown ups often have different opinions than children, and that boys/men and girls/women also may have such differences, and children will thus have learned to identify themselves as children, have acted as children, defended their interests or special resources, and so on. In other words, even when socio-political ideologies are acquired much later, the social conditions of primary and secondary socialization are such that children already learn at an early stage the relevant cognitive and social conditions of group membership and the ways in which such membership is related to opinions.[5]

Opinion discourse understanding

Under the social and cognitive conditions summarized above, social members are routinely and daily confronted with many types of discourses that express socially relevant opinions. For such discourses to have implications for the formation of ideologies, they need to be understood in general, and need to be understood as expressing opinions in particular. This does not mean that discourse expressing factual beliefs does not play a role in ideology formation. It does. We may daily learn about the hard facts of killings in Bosnia, and may ourselves associate with these facts the evaluations that may sustain or challenge for instance attitudes about Serbs, Croats and Muslims, or about armies, or ideologies about ethnic conflicts or about pacifism in general. Although obviously the media accounts of the events in Bosnia are replete with critical opinions, which also will influence our own attitudes, this example also shows that the formation of specific ideologies need not take place through explicit opinion discourse. It may be sufficient that people get what they see as the 'facts', and give their own personal or socially shared evaluation of them on the basis of specific values, in this case those of non-violence, or those of defending the weak against the strong.

With this important caveat in mind, however, the opinions that are being inferred from discourse are often pre-formulated in those discourses themselves. Understanding such opinion discourse has two different cognitive consequences. People represent the events (such as those of the war in Bosnia) in their event models, and at the same time represent the opinions about these events, also in the event model. On the other hand, they may represent the events in the event model, but the opinions expressed by the text as those of the speaker or writer, and then store those opinions in the speaker/writer model that is part of the context model.

In the second case, the recipient may or may not agree with such opinions, but merely represent them as the opinions of a particular writer or speaker. That recipients construe such models of speakers/writers may be concluded from the fact that recipients are usually able to reproduce later the opinions of the speaker/writer. When generalized, these models may later even allow recipients to conclude that the speaker/writer is a pacifist or a militarist, pro or contra the Serbs, and so on, even without remembering the concrete facts of the event model.

If opinions are stored with the mental representation of the events themselves, that is, as part of the event model, we might assume that the opinion is provisionally accepted or adopted by the recipient. In the same way as the discourse being understood may be evaluated as more or less factual and as probably true or false on the basis of truth criteria, arguments and what recipients already know or believe to be the case, also the opinions expressed in discourse may thus be evaluated. If they match the general personal or social opinions of the recipient, then the opinion may be provisionally adopted and associated with the event in the event model. If the result of this evaluation process is negative, then the opinion may simply be attributed to the speaker/writer and stored in the context model, as explained above. Probably the same is true for the factual beliefs expressed in the discourse as well. That is, if the recipient does not believe that what is said is true, then it seems pointless to construct a 'model of the events', because the events don't exist in the first place. Instead, the speaker/writer will also be attributed with what he or she 'claimed' to be the case, and no event model is then constructed.

Although this solution for the well-known problem of 'acceptance' of opinions seems elegant, it also has its drawbacks. Mental models were introduced in cognitive psychology in order to account for a variety of problems in (discourse) understanding. That is, beyond semantic representations, understanding a discourse involves the construction of a model. When people are able to construct at least a fragmentary model of what the discourse is about, we say that they have (at least partly) understood a text. The question of truth or falsehood is not a condition of such understanding. Indeed, since we were children we have learned to understand and construe models for myths, fairy tales, lies and fiction. That is, a model represents any kind of event, fictional or real. In fact, one of the reasons to introduce the notion of model in the first place was that such models are constructed by people whether or not they believe or know that the events being talked about are true or false.

If this is the case, we should conclude that at least for the representation of 'factual' (true, false, fictional or not) beliefs, language users construe models. That is, even 'false' discourse needs to be understood, and the way to do that is to build a model for it. It will not do to simply construe 'what was said', that is, a semantic representation, and associate that with the 'discourse model' that is part of the context or speaker models of the current situation.

Now, if this is true, we still need to account for an independent assessment of the truth or falsity of the events represented by the model. Again, the easiest way would be to simply 'tag' the model as being truthful or false (or assign it a probability value), as a result of the evaluation procedure that compares the 'facts' of the model with other (true) models or with instantiations of general, shared 'certified' knowledge. This would also mean that if such a tag were no longer accessible later, people might erroneously 'believe' what they once represented in the model, a condition that is quite familiar in media reception studies. Another option would be to store 'true' (believed) models in a separate memory location, and mark that location as (personal) 'knowledge'. The advantage of such a solution would be that such a separate knowledge reservoir would be more easily related to socially shared, 'accepted' knowledge.

Theoretically, however, these two ways of representing subjective truth and falsity would be practically 'notational variants', as linguists would say, although empirically one or the other proposal might have different processing consequences. The main point is, though, that all models get stored in episodic memory, and most of them will get evaluated during processing (or sometimes later), and then marked as being (more or less) truthful.

The same argument, however, does not apply to the representation of opinions. Indeed, opinions are not properties of facts but of people, so opinions are not stored 'with' the event, unless they are (like truths) the result of the evaluation procedure of the recipients themselves. That is, if the recipient represents a fact like the rapes of women in Bosnia, then it will be her or his opinion being associated in his or her own model of these facts that gets represented. Opinions of speakers or hearers on the other hand do not thus attach to the events and the event models, but to the speakers/

writers and their models as part of the context model. This seems to be confirmed by the fact that for instance readers of news are able to construct a model (their model) about an event independently of the possibly biased opinions of the speaker/writer. Indeed, they may even disregard the biased style of the discourse, and reconstruct the model contrary to the persuasive intentions of the writer/speaker. I shall return to this notion of 'preferred' interpretations later.

Unfortunately, there is as yet no theoretically satisfactory and sophisticated way to represent what we are dealing with in the first place: opinions. It was decided to simplify matters for the moment and represent these as 'evaluative' propositions, that is as propositions with an evaluative predicate, where such a predicate is any concept that is derived from some social or cultural value. But we have seen in Chapter 11 that the difference between 'factual' and 'evaluative' propositions and predicates is more complicated. Although many predicates are generally treated in a specific society and culture as being evaluative ('beautiful', 'kind', 'right', 'wrong', etc.) or as factual (e.g. 'chair', 'stone', 'paper' or 'car'), there are many others where it depends on the perspective, values and indeed the ideologies of the group members whether these are factual or evaluative notions (e.g. 'thief', 'terrorist', 'heavy' or 'pollution').

Given this theoretical uncertainty about formats of representation, we have at the moment no other alternative than to represent opinions in models as evaluative belief propositions. But it should be added that this implies precisely what ideologies are supposed to do, namely, that some people will represent as models of 'facts' what others represent as context models of opinions of other people. This nicely ties in with the proposal that the kind of 'bias' of mental representations as a function of different ideologies is exactly what it is, namely, a differently organized system of models. We may assume that various processing tasks, including the use of models in discourse comprehension and production will be affected by such different representations. That is, in the various structures of discourse, as well as in processing such discourse, it should become clear whether an event is being represented as truthful, or whether it is represented as false, and especially it should show whether my opinions about such an event are part of *my* model of the event, or whether they are attributed to the speaker or writer. In the latter case the opinion is represented in the model I have about the models of the speaker or writer, and that representation is part of my context model and not of my event model.

What was just proposed also shows how opinions about contexts are being processed. That is, people do not only construct models of speakers or writers (with their opinions about them) on the basis of what these say, but also on other grounds, which have been discussed before, such as group membership, appearance, non-verbal activities, and so on. The same is true for the rest of the context, such as the ongoing communicative event as a whole, the setting, props or circumstances, and so on. Obviously, these may play a crucial role in the construction of event models and opinions. The familiar insights of credibility research obtain here. Thus, when a statement about an event is made by someone who is known to be a specialist in the study of such events, then such statements will be more credible than those made by a non-specialist, unless other information (like special personal interests of the specialist) overrides this truth criterion.

In other words, contexts, or rather subjective interpretations of context, that is, context models, provide the resources being used in the application of epistemic evaluation of discourses in the construction of event models. People draw on their personal and social knowledge as well as on what they know about the context (identity of the speaker, etc.) to decide whether what is being said is more or less truthful. We have also seen that this also explains the ideologically biased evaluation of the context (and hence of the discourse) – if for racist reasons blacks are deemed to be less competent or truthful, whites may assign a lower truth value to what blacks say. That is, perceived group membership influences the construction of both context models and event models, including the opinions and overall (truth) evaluations being assigned to them.

Generalization and abstraction

Having construed the event and context models featuring the opinions derived from opinion discourse or construed by recipients as their own opinion about the events or the context, other strategies will be applied to make such opinions more useful for social members. That is, opinions should also be relevant in other situations, and in the judgement of other events and contexts. This requires decontextualization, abstraction and generalization, as described before – models of particular events and contexts will be abstracted from in such a way that they may be used in the understanding and evaluation of other events. This may yield general personal models, representing the personal experiences and opinions of each person, but also social representations that are shared by others. For my purpose, especially this latter strategy is relevant.

Again, little is known about the details of these strategies and under what conditions they take place. For social group members to know that specific factual or evaluative beliefs are shared by most or many other members, a process of 'normalization' should take place – own beliefs, based on personal experiences, need to be compared with those of others. This will again usually require discourse – speakers belonging to a group who are talking to other members (or reading texts from other members, e.g. in the press) construct models of their interlocutors and their beliefs, and may generalize such models to social representations featuring the shared beliefs of the own group. A variety of contexts, speakers, and circumstances as properties of contexts, as well as specific features of discourse, such as presuppositions, may thus suggest to group members that it is apparently 'generally accepted' that such or such is true or false. We see that the abstraction and generalization of context models, that is, decontextualization, precisely provides the crucial criterion for the transformation of personal knowledge into social knowledge.

The same is obviously true for opinions. If social members repeatedly represent many other group members as expressing a specific opinion, they may generalize and assume that this is a typical opinion of the group as a whole. This holds true both for the generalization of ingroup opinions as well as for outgroup opinions, although ingroup opinions may be encountered more often, be found more credible, and so on, and therefore more easily acceptable than those of outgroup members. Inter-group perception and differentiation thus also takes places at the level of opinion differentiation. Our facts or opinions may be sufficient reason to reject, a priori, those of others, disregarding an 'independent' evaluation of their validity. In fact, group differentiation may be based only on the perception of different social opinions and not on other social membership criteria.

Finally, social opinion clusters (attitudes) may be further generalized and abstracted from as ideologies, as described earlier. In this case, further 'decontextualization' regards specific social domains or circumstances. For instance, women may acquire a number of relevant attitudes, for example about equal pay, glass ceilings, child care or abortion, and then abstract from the various roles (and inequality or lack of autonomy) in situations at work, the family or in politics, and derive the general ideological propositions that represent what these different social situations have in common. Theoretical and empirical details of these processes are as yet unknown.

It was suggested earlier that the acquisition of ideologies need not be indirect and based on models, but may also be direct, that is, based on general statements about social representations and ideologies in discourse. Instead of personal experiences and opinions, thus, social members may be confronted with explicit attitudinal or ideological discourse and derive relevant opinion propositions directly from this discourse, without the intervention of models. Since no 'facts' sustain such social representations, contextual conditions are crucial – speakers/writers need to be very credible before people accept their general statements as valid. Again, decontextualization may operate here – the same statements are being made by many other ingroup members, so that such consensus information alone will enhance credibility. Yet, social members may still want to evaluate such general statements with respect to their other social representations, and may then accept them as valid when they are consistent with these other representations, suspend judgement when there is no consistency, and reject them as biased when they are inconsistent with (many) other representations, or eventually re-evaluate their current social representations. It is only this latter process that one should call 'attitude change'.

We now have an approximate idea about the ways (opinion) discourse influences the mind, which representations are involved, and how social beliefs, including ideologies, may be confirmed or changed by discourse. We have found that context models play a crucial role in the construction of personal and social opinions, and the same is true for the event models and social representations of social members. Both sources are used as the basis for the evaluation of discourse as valid or invalid. Ideologies may be acquired 'empirically' but indirectly through the decontextualization of particular and personal models to more general and more abstract representations, or they may more directly be formed by explicit expressions of social beliefs. Evaluation of social beliefs usually requires decontextualization, however, so that even for explicit ideological discourse, repetition may be needed by various and credible sources before an ideology is being accepted. Most crucially, however, for all social representations, and especially their ideological underpinnings, is that they should 'work'. That is, they should be applicable in people's everyday lives, in the adequate accomplishment of social practices, in understanding such practices and other people, and in the successful participation in discourse.

26

Legitimation

What is legitimation?

Legitimation is one of the main social functions of ideologies. In classical approaches, thus, dominant ideologies were usually described in terms of their role in the legitimation of the ruling class, in particular, and the dominant order, in general. In this chapter, I examine some properties of legitimation and its relationships to ideology and discourse.[1] In philosophy, law, and the social and political sciences, legitimation is a notion that has been extensively studied.[2] However, in discourse analysis, it is much less studied than, say, politeness or persuasion, although legitimation is a prominent function of language use and discourse.

As may be expected in the framework of this book, legitimation will primarily be defined in a discourse analytical framework.[3] It is obviously a social (and political) act, and it is typically accomplished by text or talk. Often, it also has an interactive dimension, as a discursive response to a challenge of one's legitimacy. Pragmatically, legitimation is related to the speech act of defending oneself, in that one of its appropriateness conditions is often that the speaker is providing good reasons, grounds or acceptable motivations for past or present action that has been or could be criticized by others.

However, the communicative act of legitimation has several further constraints, and does not, like defences, presuppose actual attacks or challenges, but at most possible ones. Theoretically, legitimation is not an illocutionary act at all, but (like argumentation and storytelling) a more broadly defined communicative act that usually requires more than the utterance of one single proposition. Legitimation may be a complex, ongoing discursive practice involving a set of interrelated discourses.[4]

Legitimating discourse is usually accomplished in institutional contexts. Although people may perhaps be said to 'legitimate' their everyday actions in informal conversations, such usage would probably count as being derived from a more formal lexical register. In everyday informal talk, we would rather speak of justifications, explanations or accounts. In all these cases, the crucial point is that speakers explain why they did or do something, and why such an action is reasonable or, in general, socially acceptable. In such acts, we may expect arguments, that is, references to reasons and to courses of action that had or have to be taken because of contextual constraints, causes or opinions. Moreover, this family of communicative acts is interactively engaged in especially, as we already saw, when these reasons or these actions referred to are not obviously acceptable. People justify or account for their actions mostly if they know or expect that others might be puzzled or, more strongly, if others disagree, condemn, challenge or attack them because of these actions.[5]

Legitimation, then, is the institutional counterpart of such justifications. That is, speakers are usually described as engaging in legitimation as members of an institution, and especially as occupying a special role or position. Legitimation in that case is a discourse that justifies 'official' action in terms of the rights and duties, politically, socially or legally associated with that role or position. Indeed, the act of legitimation entails that an institutional actor believes or claims to respect official norms, and hence to remain within the prevalent moral order.

Legitimation presupposes institutional restrictions of social power, as defined by law, regulations, rights or duties that set the boundaries of institutional decision-making and action. All those who have no absolute power may routinely need to legitimate their action, although, for many (e.g. face-keeping) reasons, even dictators will regularly engage in various forms of legitimation.[6]

Because of this institutional nature, legitimation may not be restricted to a justification of official action, but even of the position, role or institution itself. Accusations of illegitimacy often make normative inferences from actions to the actor, or about his or her very incumbency in the position. Indeed, in a democracy, a president of a country, when found to have engaged, *ex officio*, in serious illegal action, may expect to be impeached. And the security services of a dictatorship accused of breaches of human rights may be abolished by democratic governments because of their illegitimacy.

These examples also suggest that legitimation is not only engaged in by persons in some official position, but also by institutional actors, such as organizations, official bodies, parliaments, and so on. That is, legitimation may be a form of collective action, and hence aims to justify the actions of the institution itself.

Legitimating discourses presuppose norms and values. They implicitly or explicitly state that some course of action, decision or policy is 'just' within the given legal or political system, or more broadly within the prevalent moral order of society.

Given the relation between legitimation and institutional power, legitimation discourse is prototypically political. Those expected to legitimate themselves are those who occupy or are appointed to public office and who exercise power because of such office. In a state of law, this implies, obviously, that they not only respect widely shared social conventions, agreements and norms, but especially the law.[7]

In the real world of politics, legitimation discourse may, however, be expected especially when officials are accused of breaking the law, or when they expect principled opposition against their decisions, policies or political action. Indeed, legitimation may not be necessary in normal courses of events, in routines, and when no challenges to institutional power or authority are imminent. They become imperative, however, in moments of crisis, when the legitimacy of the state, an institution or an office is at stake. Legitimation, then, becomes part of the strategies of crisis management, in which ingroups and their institutions need self-legitimation, and outgroups must be delegitimated.

Note that the concept of legitimation used here has a *top-down* direction: elites or institutions legitimate themselves especially 'downwards', that is, with respect to clients, the citizens, or the population at large. There is also a complementary form of legitimation, which is *bottom-up*, and involves the legitimation of, for example, the state, elites or leaders by the 'masses'. For instance, it has often intrigued social scientists why many forms of oppression and inequality are so often accepted or condoned, or even normatively approved by people in subordinate positions.[8] One explanation for such approval is 'equity': people often think that their subordinate position or the dominance of the elites are deserved because of their respective actions or performance. The criteria for this kind of self-evaluation, however, are often established by the elites themselves, so that in fact this form of popular legitimation is rigged from the start.

Legitimation and ideology

Within these succinctly summarized general principles of legitimation, we now need to examine what the role is of ideology in such acts of legitimation. Indeed, how can ideologies be an 'instrument' of legitimation?

We have seen that legitimation presupposes moral or legal grounds for the judgement of official action, such as norms, values or formal laws. In our analysis of ideology, we have seen that ideologies, as the basis of the social representations of groups and their members, also presuppose norms and values. For specific groups, thus, ideologies provide the foundation of judgement and action, and hence also the basis for group-related legitimation. Thus, democratic ideologies provide the basis for judgements about the legitimacy of 'democratic action'.[9]

Similarly, xenophobic groups or parties may engage in racist actions, but usually deny that such actions are racist, and hence outside of the moral order.[10] Instead, they will claim that it is 'natural' to make a distinction or even to establish a hierarchy between Us and Them, to accord priority to Us, or to give preferential access to symbolic or material resources because of Our blood, soil or innate characteristics. Racist ideology, self-servingly appropriating general social norms and values about precedence and rights of the ingroup, thus embodies the basic principles of the shared opinions that control racist actions as well as their legitimation.[11] As is the case for justifications and accounts in general, socially shared representations, and especially the evaluative ones, provide the grounds for judgements about what is right and what is wrong, good or bad.

In sum, ideologies form the basic principles of group-internal legitimation. They do so by specifying the ideological categories of membership criteria, the activities, the goals, the social position, the resources (or power base) as well as the norms and values for each group. These norms and values not only regulate and organize the actions of group members, but also may be used to justify (or indeed to challenge) the social position of the group in relation to other groups.

It is at this point where ideology and legitimation interact most specifically, in the control of inter-group relations, such as those of power, dominance and resistance. Indeed, as we have seen, the classical approach to ideology was to define them in terms of their role in the legitimation of dominance.

Since, however, ideologies are by definition group based, and hence feature propositions that are in the interests of the own group, their consequences for group action may conflict with those of others. Indeed, membership criteria, actions, goals, values or access to resources of one group may be inconsistent with those of other groups. This means that to legitimate group action not only for group-internal purposes, but also for inter-group purposes, a group needs to show that its basic principles are just, and possibly that those of the other group are wrong. Or rather, it may claim that its basic principles are general, if not universal, and hence apply to everyone.

To legitimate actions in a social conflict and in a situation of inequality in which one group is or may be challenged by another, usually involves the claim that these actions are within the general moral order, and hence not justified only by partisan, self-serving grounds. Group ideologies may thus be declared to be 'common sense', or principles that should be followed by all social members, also those of other groups. As we have seen, persuasion and manipulation may thus be combined with legitimation as soon as one group tries to impose its ideology on another group or is able to have it adopted by more subtle means.[12]

Delegitimation

At the same time, this obviously implies that opposing groups, as well as their basic principles (ideologies), will be delegitimated. Ideological and social conflict thus take the form of a struggle not only over ideas, or over scarce social resources, but also over legitimacy. Domination in this case will crucially involve those strategies that are geared towards the delegitimation of internal dissidence as well as outside competition or 'threat'. These strategies may themselves follow the categories of the ideological schema, and thus challenge the very existence or identity of the other group, for example as follows for the case of delegitimating minority groups, refugees or other immigrants.[13]

1 Delegitimating membership: they do not belong here, in our group, in our country in our city, in our neighbourhood, in our organization.
2 Delegitimating actions, including discourse: they have no right to engage in what they do or say, for example work here, or accuse us of racism; criminalization of actions (e.g. 'illegal entry').
3 Delegitimating goals: they only come here to take advantage of our welfare system.
4 Delegitimating norms and values: their values are not ours; They should adapt to our culture; We are not used to that here.
5 Delegitimating social position: for example, they are not real refugees, but merely economic ('fake') ones.
6 Delegitimating access to social resources: they have no priority to get jobs, housing, work, welfare, education, knowledge, etc.

For each social group that is seen to challenge the dominant group(s) or the status quo, the main identifying categories defining the group may be delegitimated. Thus, for goal-defined groups such as social movements, the strategy will focus on the delegitimation of their goals, as is the case for the women's movement or the peace movement. If for instance the goal is to end patriarchy or sexism, this goal may be delegitimated by denying that gender inequality is a major problem in society.[14] For ideological opponents, the basic ideologies will be attacked as being inconsistent with the dominant values. And in the neo-liberal moves to abolish welfare, such access to a crucial resource will be delegitimated by reference to the need to push back the role of the state, and to emphasize the need for people to take their own initiative to find a job.

These examples also show that strategies of delegitimation generally presuppose norms, values and ideologies that are claimed to be universal or widely accepted in society. Dominant groups will in such a case not openly refer to their own interests, but on the contrary engage in arguments that claim that their actions or policies are for the common good or are good for the dominated groups themselves. This is for instance typically the case in the political delegitimation of immigration and hence of all immigrants. It is not surprising that the most pervasive adjective in official discourse about immigrants is that they are 'illegal'. By thus portraying immigrants as people who break the law, the strategy at the same time implies that they are criminals, and place themselves outside of the civil society, so that immigration restriction, expulsion and withholding social services to immigrants become legitimate.

Thus, in Europe, the elites will not refer to their own privileges when opposing immigration, but will focus on the consequences for poor (white) people in the inner cities, or may emphasize that it would be better for immigrants if they would help to build up their own country.

In the same way, the peace movement may be delegitimated by emphasizing its violence, and hence violating the value of non-violence.[15] Unions, or strikers may be delegitimated by focusing on the dire consequences for the economy (the common good) when their demands are realized, if not on their illegal actions, their violence, their 'communist' ideology, or the threat to freedom (of the market).[16]

Legitimation, delegitimation and discourse

It has become clear above that legitimation is a complex social act that is typically exercised by talk and text. Strategies of legitimation and delegitimation are similarly discursive, and involve the usual moves of positive self-presentation and negative other-presentation we shall further examine in the next chapter.

But as is the case for all social action, discourse itself may also be (de)legitimated. This is a crucial strategy, because discourse was found to have a primary role in the formation and change of underlying attitudes and ideologies, that is, in persuasion. If the public discourse of any social group can be controlled or delegitimated, a dominant or competing group can establish hegemony over the symbolic domain, namely, the control of the meanings and minds of the recipients of such discourse. In war, civil war, revolution or social conflict, one of the main targets of attack will be radio or television stations, or the exercise of censorship. And where coercive force, prohibition or other legal measures are impossible or ineffective, strategies of delegitimating or otherwise marginalizing opponent discourse will be resorted to.

Strategies geared towards the delegitimation of discourse take several forms. First, they may focus on the context of production, on access and use of discourse, for example by challenging the legitimacy of communication participants (who has the right to speak, or to speak for others?), speaker roles, setting, goals, knowledge, expertise and so on. Newspapers may thus deny representatives of 'illegitimate' groups access to the newspaper, boycott press conferences, ignore press releases, or represent leaders or speakers of movements as unreliable sources in newsgathering.[17]

One very effective form of ideological speaker control is when dominant groups are able to influence the minds of the speakers themselves, through the interiorization of dominant beliefs, attitudes or ideologies. There are many examples, for instance in the domains of class, gender or 'race', where dominated groups have been confronted so consistently with legitimate, official discourse, that they may accept that they are indeed inferior, deviant or otherwise illegitimate. We have seen in the previous chapter how subtle processes of persuasion and manipulation are able to create preferred mental models of events. These models may then be generalized to more fundamental, shared social self-representations of a group. These will in turn control the everyday judgements and social practices of the members of the dominated group, in such a way that they are consistent with the interests of the dominant group. Of course, this is the standard example of how dominant ideologies work in the formation of 'false consciousness', and we have seen that in the real world, such ideological hegemony is seldom complete, given the many forms of mental and social resistance by dominated groups. Obviously, these forms of counter-power and resistance are themselves again in need of legitimation, which itself is based on a counter-ideology.[18]

Yet, given the close relation between ideology and social identity, such ideological brainwashing may also affect the very self-confidence of whole groups. This has often been observed for women and blacks confronted with pervasive derogating discourse by men and whites, respectively. It is only through raising group self-consciousness and ideological de-programming that the effects of this form of ideological hegemony may be countered.

Second, once access to public discourse cannot be prohibited or denied, opponent discourse may itself be delegitimated by many moves. These may include, for example, citing out of context, focusing on negative or threatening elements in discourse, emphasizing the violation of common values, or by framing such discourse in a specific way, for example through negative speaker description ('militant', 'Marxist', 'radical', 'fundamentalist', etc.). Thus, of the speeches of 'radical' Nation of Islam leader Farrakhan, the media will typically focus on his anti-semitic remarks, as they also did when African American leader Jessie Jackson spoke of New York as 'Hymietown'. In this case, it may be left to the readers to draw conclusions about the reliability and the legitimacy of the speakers of the others. Another framing strategy is to use authoritative, and hence 'legitimate' speakers, for example police officers or the mayor, in order to correct possible accusations by minority groups after a 'riot'. Indeed, as I have found in my work on racism and the press, minority representatives seldom are allowed to speak alone, and hence function as the only source about ethnic events. This is especially the case in crucial accusations, for example of racism. Not only will these be presented as fundamentally doubtful, and hence between quotes, but also they will never go unchallenged by the (white) authorities.

Finally, the delegitimation of opponent or dissident discourse by dominant (political, media, etc.) groups and organizations may focus on the possible effects of such discourse, and hence on the recipients. Of course, this may be done, indirectly, by presenting speakers and discourse themselves as illegitimate, for example while being unreliable, violent, radical or deviant. Event models and context models of recipients are thus persuasively oriented towards negative representations of the 'illegitimate' speakers or to a rejection of what they say as being true. But, even reception itself may be obstructed, for example by programming broadcasts at times when the audience is small, publishing items on inside pages or inconspicuous places, by jamming the airwaves, imposing duties on distribution of radical media, preventing the public from listening to speeches, and so on.

Also in democratic systems that celebrate free speech, there are many ways to delegitimate dissident or opponent discourse in many overt or subtle ways. This essentially happens by preventing or impairing access – to the media of public discourse, to fair representation, and especially to the minds of the audience at large. At the same time, of course, own group discourses will be favoured in the opposite direction, and will have optimal access to context, text and reception.

For the discussion in this book, this analysis of the (de)legitimation of discourse is important in understanding ideological conflict and reproduction. If dissident or opponent discourse is delegitimated, and hence the 'normal' processes of communication and persuasion are impaired, also the construction of alternative ideologies is made more difficult. In social, political and ideological conflict and crisis, it is vital that members of the ingroup, or members of allied or neutral groups do not become 'infected' by the ideological virus of the opponents. Once such an ideology is allowed to spread, it will increasingly control the social representations, models and hence discourse and other actions of the population at large. In that case, not only may the ideological struggle be lost, but the social and political struggle as well, if the persuaded others act in accordance with their new ideology. The strategies of the virulent anti-communist witch-hunt by Joe McCarthy in the USA are a prominent example of the forms of ideological delegitimation described here.

As we have seen, strategies of delegitimation presuppose power and imply dominance, that is, power abuse. In the domain of discourse and communication, such power need not merely be political or socio-economic. It may also be symbolic. That is, dominant discourse may be presented as legitimate because it has authority and prestige, and hence is associated with truth.[19] Thus, politics and especially the media and science exercise ideological control because their discourses are legitimated by the control over truth criteria, such as information, evidence and expertise. If no counter-evidence, counter-expertise or alternative information is (made) available by their opponents, thus, such elite discourse is self-legitimating because of its exclusive access to such symbolic resources as authoritative knowledge and opinion.

Moreover, powerful elites also control the institutions that organize such special access to knowledge, truth and opinion, such as universities, laboratories, think tanks, intelligence agencies, secret services, bureaucracies and so on. That is, their authority defined in terms of truth claims may be effective not merely by preferential access to public discourse or media control, but also by the 'incontrovertible' (reliable, scientific, etc.) evidence that will back up such claims. Thus, the strategies of legitimation are most effective when they are able to establish the very norms, values and ideologies by which both dominant and dominated groups and their actions are judged. In the next chapter, we will examine some of the discursive properties that may be brought to bear in such ideological legitimation and control.

27

Ideological Discourse Structures

Introduction

The expression of ideology in discourse is usually more than just an explicit or concealed display of a person's beliefs, but mostly also has a persuasive function: speakers want to change the mind of the recipients in a way that is consistent with their beliefs, intentions and goals. This means that a more detailed study of 'ideological discourse structures' has implications for our insight into the ways in which discourse is used to express ideologies and at the same time into processes of reception and persuasion. That is, I here focus on the double-edged core of the ideological reproduction process, namely, the ways in which ideologies are expressed and spread within groups as well as across group boundaries in society as a whole.

The notion of 'ideological discourse structures' may, however, be misleading in the sense that it suggests that specific structures are used in the expression and persuasive communication of ideologies. Nothing is less true. On the one hand, we should assume that in a given text and context virtually *any* structure or strategy may be used in this way. On the other hand, specific structures that in one context function ideologically, may not have that function in another context.

With this important reminder, we may nevertheless examine some of the structures that often or typically exhibit or imply ideological beliefs and/or those structures that typically may have ideological 'effects' upon recipients. That is, I here focus more specifically on a selection of the discourse structures introduced in Chapter 21. At the same time, I will briefly explain what role such discourse structures may have in the cognitive and social (re)production of ideologies.[1]

The relevant relations between cognition and discourse have been discussed before and form the backdrop to the more discursively oriented analysis in this chapter. It was found that there are essentially two ways in which ideologies may be expressed or conveyed, namely, directly through general (generic) expressions of abstract, ideologically based social beliefs, or indirectly through the formation of specific personal beliefs in event and context models. Since I focused on the persuasive acquisition of ideologies in Chapter 25, without examining the discourse structures that typically appear in such persuasion, I shall here pay special attention to such discourse structures and particularly to the 'social' side of the language users confronted with ideological discourse as recipients. It is, however, understood that these same structures should also be seen as intentional or unintentional expressions of underlying ideologies of speaker/writers.

Since explicit expressions of ideological beliefs hardly produce any problems for the (critical) analyst, specifically those structures should be studied that persuasively express ideologies in a more indirect, implicit or subtle way. We have seen that the understanding of discourse involves the construction of mental models. Communication in general, and hence also ideological communication, is geared towards the management of such models, which from the point of view of the speaker/writer may be called 'preferred models', since these represent what the speaker/writer wants the recipient to know or believe. The question then is which discourse structures are particularly relevant in the persuasive management of such models.

Context constraints

It has been repeatedly stressed that the discursive reproduction of ideologies in many ways depends on the perceived communicative contexts of text and talk, that is on the context models of the participants. It was already suggested for instance that the same discourse structure may function ideologically in one context and not in another, depending for instance on the intentions, goals, roles or group membership of the participants. To wit, blacks may speak of 'niggers' without racist implications, whereas whites may do so only in very specific circumstances without expressing a racist ideology. A debate on immigration policies in a critical scholarly study usually has different ideological implications than a debate on the same topic in right-wing, extremist propaganda.

Each of the context categories discussed in Chapter 22 may thus become relevant for the expression, interpretation and social functions of ideological discourse, and, for each type of structure discussed below, it should therefore be spelled out what the precise contextual conditions of their ideological effects are. In order to be able to focus on the discourse structures themselves, I will do so here in a more global way for all structures mentioned below.

Of the ideologically relevant context structures, I shall only mention two: (1) the type of the communicative event as a whole, that is, the communicative genre (e.g. an informal conversation among friends, a parliamentary debate, an op-ed article in the newspaper), and (2) types of participant and participant roles.

The first contextual constraint, namely, the type of communicative event, as well as the overall discursive intentions and goals that are associated with it, has many implications for the production and comprehension of discourse structures, and therefore also on the ideological functions of text and talk. Thus, we may expect that in an op-ed article, a parliamentary debate, a propaganda leaflet or sermon, several ideologically based opinions may be persuasively expressed. Although in principle all discourse types may express ideologies, we may nevertheless assume that other communicative events have a lower level of ideological expressions, implications and functions, as may be the case for a TV instruction guide, an article on phonology, or a daily conversation on horticulture. That is, some genres more typically function as persuasive expressions of opinions than others, if only through the kind of topics that are associated with it. Most genres that have persuasive functions or implications and that are on social topics have ideological implications.

The second set of contextual constraint is the type of participant. Again, people expect ideologically relevant social opinions from specific group members rather than others. Thus, a politician, corporate manager, priest or journalist writing or speaking about social issues is more likely to be (heard as) expressing ideologically based opinions than a child or a carpenter talking about how to make a table. Indeed, representatives of specific social groups speaking about issues relevant to the group, for example women, blacks, pacifists or environmentalists, will more typically be heard to express ideologies than people who are not primarily speaking as group members. This not only puts constraints on discourse structures, but also and importantly on the definition of the communicative situation by the recipient, that is, on the recipient's context model, which will in turn monitor comprehension and event model formation.

That is, in many situations recipients already know that ideologically based discourse may be expected from the speakers or writers. This implies that ideological communication may be most effective when recipients do *not* or hardly expect ideological implications, for instance in children's stories, textbooks or TV news, whose main functions are usually assumed to be free of persuasive opinions. For news in most of the Western media it is one of the major (ideological) criteria that 'facts' should be separated from 'opinion'. It needs no comment that when such assertions are made, that is, when ideology is denied, it is especially relevant to do ideological analysis.

Besides types of communicative event and participants, there is another context feature that is crucial in the reproduction of ideologies, namely, properties of the intended recipients. That is, mass mediated or any other kind of public discourse will have more serious ideological consequences, if only because of the size of its audience, than mundane interpersonal dialogues. Both genres may in specific contexts be equally ideological, but ideologies expressed in public discourse convey opinions to many more ingroup and outgroup members. Moreover, public discourse, such as that of politics or the media, usually features institutional speakers or representatives who have more authority and hence more credibility. Much of the ideological consensus construed among groups or in society today would be difficult to obtain without coverage of relevant issues in the mass media. This size of the audience of a discourse will be called its 'scope'. Trivially, and all other things being equal, the larger the scope of a discourse, the greater its ideological effects. And since those who have active access to, and control over the mass media are generally members of the elites, larger scope will often be combined with higher credibility of the speakers/writers and hence a higher chance that models will be construed as preferred.

Topics

Let us now turn to the question of what discourse structures are typically involved in the expression or formation of ideology.[2]

There are probably no structures of text and talk that have a more prominent effect on the construction and further processing of models than semantic macrostructures or topics. Derived (formally or by production and comprehension strategies) from the propositions of a discourse or an event model, they embody what is most relevant or important for the participants. Unless recipients have alternative 'readings' of a discourse, topics will head the model, and will generally be most accessible for further processing. If people remember anything of a discourse at all after some delay, it is the topic and maybe some details that are personally relevant for the recipient.

Since topics are represented by (macro) propositions, they may also express opinions, and hence ideologies. These propositions may be expressed in specific schematic categories of a text, for instance in the initial summary of a story (of the type 'What I particularly dislike of foreigners is that they don't want to learn our language') or the headline of a news report ('Black youth involved in crime wave'). Ideologically based stereotypes and prejudices may thus be highlighted twice: by their important semantic function of a topic that organizes the semantic microstructures of a discourse, as well as by their schematic emphasis in the beginning or on top of a story (often marked by special graphics, such as a banner headline, or by special intonation in conversational dialogue). Obviously, the scope of the newspaper report in this case, and hence the contribution to the reproduction of racist ideologies in society, is vastly greater than that of an everyday story among neighbours.

Since topics as expressed in discourse suggest preferred macrostructures of event models and since such macrostructures remain more accessible, they also provide the 'facts' that are used in the rhetorical arguments of everyday conversation in support of ideological opinions ('Yesterday it was in the newspaper that . . .'). Similarly, these model structures will also be used for further abstraction and generalization and hence as the basis for the confirmation or construction of ideological attitudes and ideologies themselves, unless counter-information discredits the discourse or its writer/speaker as being biased. In sum, discourse topics are crucial in the formation and accessibility of preferred ideological models and, thus, indirectly in the formation or confirmation of ideologies.

Local meaning

In discourse comprehension, prominently expressed topics play an important role in the local comprehension of text and talk. They define the overall coherence of the discourse. At the same time, they activate relevant knowledge and help construct the top level of the models being used for the possibly biased interpretation of the rest of the discourse. Local meanings may thus be ignored or literally 'down-graded' to the level of insignificant detail.

Examining these local meanings as such, we deal with the actual 'content' of discourse, and it is here that most ideological beliefs will be incorporated in text and talk. As we have seen before for the process of expression, this means that beliefs in event models are selectively constructed to form the semantic representation of text and talk. For obvious contextual reasons, not all we know about an event needs to be included in the meaning of a discourse, so that speakers/writers make a selection, and it is this selection that is liable to multiple forms of ideological control. The general constraint is contextual relevance: Those propositions are expressed which the speaker/ writer thinks the recipient should know. That such relevance decisions may be in the interest of the speaker/writer is obvious; for instance, information about an event that may give a bad impression of the speaker/writer, or which in any other way may later be used 'against' the speaker/writer, may be left out in order to influence the models of a recipient in the preferred direction.

Here we encounter two important principles of ideological reproduction in discourse, namely, the presence or absence of information in semantic representation derived from event models, and the function of expression or suppression of information in the interests of the speaker/writer. This last principle is part of an overall strategy of ideological communication that consists of the following main moves:

1　Express/emphasize information that is positive about Us.
2　Express/emphasize information that is negative about Them.
3　Suppress/de-emphasize information that is positive about Them.
4　Suppress/de-emphasize information that is negative about Us.

These four moves, which constitute what may be called the 'ideological square', obviously play a role in the broader contextual strategy of positive self-presentation or face-keeping and its outgroup corollary, 'negative other-presentation'. Unlike the self-presentation moves usually discussed in the literature, however, these are not primarily focused on participants as individuals, but on participants acting as group members. This suggests a third important principle of ideological discourse analysis, namely, the fact that since ideologies are social and group-based, also the ideological opinions expressed in discourse must have implications for groups or social issues.

Detail and level of description

When applied to semantic analysis these principles and strategies allow a wide variety of options. One was already suggested above – in descriptions of situations (as represented in models of the speaker) some information may be expressed and other information may be left out. That is, in relation to the original model, discourses may be relatively incomplete. If a news report of a 'riot' only mentions the violence of 'a black mob' and not of the police, or not the causes of the riot, then we typically have a description which is incomplete relative to what is known and what would be relevant information about the 'riot'. The consequence of such *relative incompleteness* may be incomplete models of recipients (e.g. the readers of the newspaper), which may again have implications for the biased construction of attitudes, as described earlier.

This semantic feature may also work in the opposite direction: discourses may be relatively *overcomplete* when they express propositions that are in fact contextually irrelevant for the comprehension of an event (that is, for the construction of a model), but which are nevertheless included in the semantic representation of a description. Following the moves of the ideological square, we may assume that this will typically happen when such overcomplete information negatively reflects back on outgroups (or positively on ourselves). The standard example in reporting on ethnic affairs is to mention irrelevant ethnic group membership in crime reporting.

The same principles not only apply to the selection, inclusion or exclusion of model propositions in the meaning of a discourse, but also to the *level* of the propositions included. These may be quite general and abstract (as in topics), but also very low-level and detailed. The ideological conditions and consequences are the same. Biased discourses will tend to be very detailed about Their bad acts and Our good acts, and quite abstract and general about Their good acts and Our bad ones. Although the precise mental consequences of levels of description are not known, it seems plausible that their results are more or less detailed models of events. Mentioning many 'preferred' details requires organization, that is, mapping on topics, so that more or less detailed text fragments nevertheless get topical status. This will in turn allow them to be recalled better than a description of the same sequence of events with just one global proposition. This is especially also the case when details are 'vivid', for example when much 'visual' detail is presented of actions. Precisely such details may imply (unstated) negative evaluations which in turn may be taken up in the topical proposition summarizing this event in the model of the recipient. Although these and many other assumptions of this theoretical analysis of ideological discourse structures need to be empirically tested, they are consistent with what we now know about discourse processing.[3]

Implicitness versus explicitness

The well-known semantic properties of implicitness and explicitness of discourse can easily be explained in terms of mental models – implicit information is the information of a mental model that could or should have been included in the semantic representation of a discourse. As is the case for the level of specificity and the relative in- or overcompleteness of descriptions, we may more generally say that propositions may selectively be made explicit or left implicit as a function of the interests of speakers as group members. Besides relevant components of actions, this may typically be the case in the expression of conditions (causes) and consequences of events, as was suggested for the frequent omission of causes of ethnic conflict that negatively reflect on our ingroup (e.g. police brutality, inner city neglect, poverty, unemployment or discrimination by employers). On the other hand, ideologically blaming the victim in this case means that the negative properties attributed to the outgroup (e.g. drug abuse, cultural deviance) will be made explicit. Research on the representation of ethnic affairs in the media has often found such ideological dimensions of semantic implicitness or explicitness.[4] (For detailed examples, see Chapter 28.)

One step between presence and absence of information is when propositions are not as such expressed in discourse but implied by other propositions that are expressed. *Implication* and *presupposition* are the familiar semantic relations involved here, and both involve inferences based on models and social knowledge. The ideological function of the use of such semantic relations is not always straightforward. Following the ideological square, we may assume, as above, that implied information is not explicitly asserted, and hence not emphasized, and will therefore typically be information that needs to be concealed in the interest of the speaker and the ingroup. This is especially so when the implied information cannot be readily inferred from socially shared knowledge. When such implied information needs to be known in order for propositions in the text to be true or false, we speak of presuppositions, and these may have the same ideological functions – information is assumed to be 'given' or 'true' and is therefore presupposed by the discourse, but it may well be that the presupposed information is questionable or not true at all. That is, in this case it is obliquely asserted to be true, but without emphasizing such an 'assertion'. Following the strategies of the ideological square, it is easy to spell out what information about ingroups and outgroups will typically be expressed and which information will be left implicit.

Local coherence

Sequences of propositions are linearly connected by relations of 'local' coherence. Such conditions of coherence are first of all defined relative to the event models. Two propositions are coherently related if they express 'facts' in a mental model that are (e.g. causally, conditionally) related. But if mental models are ideologically biased, this also means that discourse coherence may be biased and have biased models of recipients as a result. Taking the same example of a 'race riot' discussed above, a police report whose version of the facts, that is whose underlying model, is adopted by the press, may describe the events such that criminal behaviour of black youths is taken as the cause of the riot, and not 'tough' policing. Similarly, coherent explanations of social events are in general based on assumptions about causes and consequences, such that the ideological bias of coherence may presuppose or imply biased models of the social situation.[5]

Propositions may also be related in a sequence by means of 'functional' semantic relations, such as generalization, specification, example or contrast. In ideological discourse these play an important role because they manage the way statements are understood in relation to other ones. For instance, a prejudiced story about minorities may feature descriptions of negative events about minorities, followed by the generalization, 'They always do that.' Such a generalization is of course crucial in the transition from models to generalized models and social representations. It persuasively suggests that this was not merely an incident or a personal experience, but a general, structural phenomenon. In this way, concrete events (and their models) are related to, and at the same time explained and legitimated by general attitudes.

Also the converse takes place: a speaker may make a general, prejudiced statement about immigrants, and knowing that such a generalization might be understood as prejudiced, may then add 'evidence' in the form of an example, specification or a whole story. Similarly, group polarization may be discursively emphasized by typical semantic and rhetorical contrasts, as in, '*We* always have to work hard, and *they* only have to ask for welfare.' We find another well-known type of contrast in disclaimers such as 'I have nothing against Turks, but . . .', in which something positive about Me (Us) is being combined with a negative statement about Them. That is, such disclaimers also play a role in the complex strategies of positive self-presentation and negative other-presentation which is so typical for ideological discourse.[6]

Lexicalization

The most obvious and therefore most widely studied form of ideological expression in discourse may be found in the words being chosen to express a concept. The pair 'freedom fighter' versus 'terrorist' is the paradigmatic example of this kind of ideologically based lexicalization. That is, a negative concept of a group is represented in a model, and depending on context, the most 'appropriate' word is selected, in such a way that an outgroup is referred to and at the same time an opinion about them.

Following the ideological square, this means that in general we may expect that, depending on context, outgroups will be described in neutral or negative words, and ingroups in neutral or positive terms. And conversely, we may also expect that in order to describe groups and their practices, various forms of *mitigation* and *euphemisms* may be selected, thus adding a rhetorical dimension to lexicalization.

Finally, lexicalization may also extend to the *nominalization* of propositions, such that agents or patients are left implicit. Inner city 'policing' thus focuses on a verb, without actually making explicit *who* is being policed, whereas the role of the police is also de-emphasized. It need not be repeated what influence such nominalizations may have on the structuring of action roles in the models of recipients.

Discourse schemata

Discourses not only have a global meaning but also a global form or conventional schema, which consists of a number of characteristic categories appearing in a specific order. Thus, arguments may feature various kinds of premises and a conclusion; stories are organized by narrative schemata with such categories as orientation, complication and resolution; and news reports begin with the well-known category of a Summary consisting of a headline and lead. As is the case for global meanings or topics, also such schemata function as organizers for complex information, and at the same time as properties that help define discourse genres. Stories organized by a conventional schema are thus easier to tell, understand and memorize, while a headline in a news report has the conventional function of expressing the main topic, so that readers know what the report is about and may decide to read it or not.

Since these categories are conventional, and vary between genres and cultures, they also have important *social* functions. Making headlines for a news report is part of the routines of newsmaking, and so is finding quotes for a verbal reaction category in a news report. As is the case for the organization of everyday conversations (beginning with greetings and ending with leavetaking) or the schematic organization of meetings, sessions and other institutional communicative events, these schemata organize discourse as much as they do interaction.

Given the important cognitive and social functions of schemata, it stands to reason to assume that they may also have ideological functions. It is vital whether information is being expressed in a headline or not, and this may of course influence the form of resulting models; negative information or opinions about minorities may thus appear in the headline, and information that is important but positive about them may be excluded, as much research on 'ethnic' news shows. The same is true for the appearance of opinions in conclusions of arguments, which social groups have 'access' to the verbal reactions category of a news item, and so on. Information and opinions about Us and Them may be further organized, and be made more or less prominent through such schemata.

Style

Lexicalization may vary as a function of opinions, and if such takes place throughout a discourse, we would then speak of a specific lexical style. Generally, then, given specific meanings or model information, different expressions may be used to express such 'content', and this variation may signal in many ways the social context of the communicative event.

Depending on the nature of the communicative event, the genre, setting or participants, thus, 'surface' structures (lexical items, syntactic structures, pronunciation and graphics) may vary in order to intentionally or unintentionally signal their contextual boundedness: the situation may be more or less formal, the relations between the participants may be friendly, familiar or distant, and participants may have various opinions about each other. The result may be a more or less formal, familiar or polite style, and at the same time an indication of underlying ideological 'stances' of speakers. Everyday racist events, for instance, frequently involve 'breaches' of appropriate interactional style, for instance when white speakers use derogatory words or impolite pronouns to or about minorities.[7]

In sum, lexical and grammatical style is one of the most obvious means speakers have to explicitly express or subtly signal their ideological opinions about events, people and participants. The same is also true for syntactic structures and their possible variation. Sentences may be expressed in an active or passive voice, and agents and patients of actions being described by such sentences may in this way be made more or less prominent or completely left implicit, as is the case in nominalizations, as suggested above.[8] More generally, word order, clause structure or clause relations may put information in more or less prominent positions, and as is the case for all structures and strategies discussed here, this will subtly effect processing and the construction of models. According to the ideological square, we will thus find that positive action roles of outgroup members will be put in less prominent order or position, and vice versa for their negative action roles (and conversely for the positive and negative roles for ingroup members).

Style thus may signal in many ways the structures of the social context, including relationships of power. A powerful social position of a speaker will thus not only be 'expressed' by the words or syntax being chosen, but is at the same time enacted and reproduced by it. This may become apparent in stylistic differences between male and female talk and text, as well as that between majorities and minorities, doctors and patients, civil servants and clients, professors and students, judges and defendants, or police officers and suspects. Style thus defines positions of participants, and wherever these are controlled by ideologies, as is the case with the examples just mentioned, style will be a direct 'trace' of ideologies in discourse. Social discrimination is thus implemented directly by those who control the style of text and talk.

Rhetoric

Several examples have already been given above of the rhetorical dimensions of discourse, defined here (rather narrowly) as the system of special 'rhetorical figures' that have specific persuasive functions at various structural levels of discourse, such as metaphors, euphemisms, irony or contrasts at the semantic level, or alliteration and rhyme at the phonological level.

Similar observations may be made for graphical structures, which are mainly organized to control attention and steer interpretation through emphasis.

The main function of such rhetorical structures and strategies is to manage the comprehension processes of the recipient, and hence, indirectly the structures of mental models. A specific negative opinion may be emphasized by a catchy metaphor from a negative conceptual domain (for instance, describing outgroup members in terms of animals such as rats, dogs, bloodhounds, snakes or cockroaches), by comparisons of the same type, or by hyperboles describing their negative characteristics. Repetition moves such as syntactic parallelism, rhyme or alliterations may further increase the attention paid to such semantic properties of the discourse, and thereby enhance the possibility that they will be stored, as intended, in the preferred model of an event. The converse is true for negative properties of ingroup members, in which case we will expect various forms of rhetorical mitigation, such as euphemisms, understatements and other ways to deflect attention from specific meanings.

Interaction strategies

Finally, and specifically for spoken dialogues, many of the structures discussed above will be further accompanied by moves and strategies of an interactional nature. If the basic aim of ideological communication is to influence the models and social representations of recipients in such a way that preferred opinions are prominently represented, recalled and eventually accepted, also several forms of interaction management will play a role in this form of social 'mind control'.

First of all, however, it should be stressed that interactional strategies themselves are liable to ideological control, as is also the case for the context and its models. Ideologically based dominance and inequality is not only expressed in the structures of text and talk discussed above, but also in group relations as embodied in participant roles and actions. In the same way as speakers may control topic or style, they may control turn taking, 'schematic' sequences (who begins or closes a dialogue, meeting or session), pauses, laughing and so on. Power abuse by speakers of dominant groups may thus also be blatantly or subtly enacted by limiting the conversational freedom of others. If women, minorities, students, clients, patients or 'ordinary people' have less to 'say' in society, this will also show and be reproduced in many conversational situations. Detailed conversation analysis has shown how such forms of social inequality may be enacted in the subtle details of mundane and institutional talk and interaction.[9]

At the same time, these interactional strategies may have an effect also during the construction of (semantic) event models. This is obvious for the interactional control of meaning, for instance in topic management, as described above. However, control of interaction itself, such as in turn taking and sequencing, may also influence the ways recipients construe models of events. For instance, participant roles are important in ideological communication, for instance in the management of credibility. Power and status of speakers is a well-known condition in the way assertions are accepted by recipients. However, conversation analytical research would correctly observe that such social properties are not simply something people 'have', but that they are (also) interactional accomplishments. Status and power are contextually enacted and thus reproduced in many subtle ways, such as bodily position, distance between speakers, clothing and props, and the ways speakers control talk.

Crucially then, models and their representations depend on who says what, and interactional management may control such effects. For instance, speakers may be prevented from saying dispreferred things by interruptions, or alternatively be encouraged to speak by selective turn allocation if they are expected to say preferred things. Similarly, interactional strategies of displaying agreement and disagreement play an important role in the management of event models and their opinions. Specific speech acts (commands, orders) may be enacted to implement social power, but also to emphasize the negative characteristics of outgroup members (accusations, blaming the victim). These are merely some of the many examples of the ways interactional moves and strategies express, implement, enact or accomplish ideologically based opinions, perspectives and stances of speakers, and the ways the models of recipients are shaped according to the preferences or interests of speakers or the groups or organizations they represent.

Manipulation

Ideological communication is often associated with various forms of manipulation, with strategies that manage or control the mind of the public at large, and with attempts to thus manufacture the consent or fabricate a consensus in the interests of those in power.[10] Indeed, modern power and ideological hegemony are precisely defined in terms of effective strategies in the accomplishment of compliance and consent, so that people will act as desired out of their own free will. In that case, power and dominance will seem natural, legitimate and commonsensical, and will be taken for granted without significant opposition.

Formulated in this way, we get a simplified picture of the complex processes at work in the enactment of dominance and the accomplishment of hegemony. Without a much more detailed study of the social, cognitive and discursive elements of the structures, strategies, processes or representations involved in this form of the 'modern' reproduction of dominance and ideologies, such analyses barely go beyond easy slogans or superficial social analysis and critique.

In the previous chapters and above, I have outlined some ideas about the mental structures, social conditions and discursive reproduction involved in the reproduction of dominance and hegemony. A study of manipulation, mind control or the manufacture of consent needs to take place in such a complex framework.[11] Above, I have given some examples of how ideologies are expressed and especially persuasively conveyed by text and talk, and how models and social representations may be effected by the structures of discourse and context.

Thus, manipulation basically involves forms of mental control of which recipients are not or barely aware, or of which they cannot easily control the consequences. Models are constructed of events in a way that has implications for the construction of shared social representations people have about the world, which in turn influence the development or change of ideologies. Given the fundamental role of ideologies in the management of social cognitions and models for discourse and other social practices, ideological control and compliance are the ultimate goal of hegemony. We have seen how specific discourse structures and strategies, such as the control of topics, style or interaction strategies, may have such influences on models and other representations of the mind. Because of such discursive properties, knowledge about events will be incomplete or biased in favour of speakers or their ingroup, and this may affect more general knowledge about the world. Even more crucially, this is the case for the management of opinions, in such a way that a negative opinion about specific outgroups seems the most 'natural' or 'logical' conclusion from the models as persuasively controlled by discourse.

Conclusion

Of the vast richness of discourse structures and strategies I have mentioned only a few. A detailed study will be necessary to chart all possible ways in which contextualized text and talk exhibits and reproduces ideologies. However brief, the discussion shows the basic principles at work. Ideological communication is a double-sided process, in which ideologically based beliefs are expressed (or concealed), and persuasively control the minds of recipients. Mind control is obviously an exceedingly complex process. But also here, some basic formats of ideological influence seem to emerge from the analysis – in order to contribute to the construction of preferred models in a given context, discourse structures must be shaped in such a way that specific model structures are the most likely consequence.

In the ideological situation of dominance, power abuse, group conflict or competition, this in general means that (members of) outgroups need to be treated and portrayed negatively, and (members of) ingroups positively. This principle applies both to the pragmatic or interactional context, as well as to the forms and meanings of text and talk. At each level of analysis, thus, we find emphasis (prominence, importance, focus, etc.) on our good things and their bad things, and vice versa for our bad things and their good things. Besides this control of group-related opinions about Us and Them and their properties and actions, discourse structures more generally control the management of the structures of models and social representations, for example through explicitness versus implicitness, manifestation versus concealment, levels or details of description, the distribution of agency, responsibility or blame, the relationships between facts, and so on.

In sum, whatever the ideological shape of underlying attitudes, they will appear in models of speakers, and these will try to appropriately and effectively express such social representations in text and talk and their contexts, in a way that most likely results in the construction of preferred models. Often, and especially in what we call manipulation, this happens without the awareness of recipients. It is more or less in this way that ideologies are reproduced in everyday life. Later studies of discourse and ideology will have to spell out the details of the general framework presented here.

The Ideology and Discourse of Modern Racism

A concrete example

After the theoretical chapters of this book, let me finally analyse a concrete example. In line with my choice of racism and racist ideologies as illustration of general principles, this chapter examines in some detail the ideology and discourse as expressed in a recent book: *The End of Racism: Principles for a Multiracial Society*, by Dinesh D'Souza (New York: Free Press, 1995). Also in some of his other books, for example on multiculturalism, D'Souza has made himself a vociferous spokesman of the New Right in the USA, and a staunch defender of conservative ideas. Indeed, we might call D'Souza one of the main 'ideologues' of contemporary conservative ideologies in the USA.

In the *End of Racism* D'Souza deals with what he sees as a 'civilizational crisis' in the USA, and focuses on what he consistently calls the 'pathologies' which, according to him, characterize the African American community in general, and the black 'underclass' in particular (in my analysis, words in my running text actually used by D'Souza will be indicated by double quotation marks). Given the size of this book (724 pages), this is no mere ideological tract. On the contrary, D'Souza has set himself the task of writing a broadly documented study of the ethnic and racial situation in the USA. An endorsement by George M. Frederickson in *The New York Review of Books*, printed on the cover, says: 'The most thorough, intelligent, and well-informed presentation of the case against liberal race policies that has yet appeared.'

Thus, D'Souza deals with what he sees as the breakdown of the 'liberal hope' of race relations in the USA, the origins of racism, slavery, the rise of liberal anti-racism, the civil rights movement, Eurocentrism and Afrocentrism, the IQ debate, finally culminating in an apocalyptic vision of the 'pathologies' of black culture. In many respects, this book may be seen as the ideological foundation of a conservative programme of race relations in the USA. Since D'Souza is a scholar attached to the conservative think tank of the American Enterprise Institute, we may conclude that his book does not merely express a personal opinion, but also has a powerful institutional backing. We already saw in Chapter 19 that contemporary ideologies are often produced and reproduced by such ideological institutions.

Given his right-wing radicalism in ethnic–racial matters, D'Souza has been severely criticized, and accused of racism (in the introduction to the second edition of the book he discusses and rejects such critique). After having examined his theses and evidence in detail, and analysed the discursive formulation of his underlying ideologies, I have come to the conclusion, with others, that this book indeed articulates a special form of 'cultural racism', celebrating white, Western cultural and civilizational hegemony, and especially problematizing and attacking African-American culture. As is also clear from much of the literature on 'modern racism', most forms of racism are no longer biologically based, but take a more 'acceptable' form as cultural racism: others are not vilified for what they are, but for what they do and think. More generally, D'Souza defends ideas that are sometimes called 'symbolic racism': a forceful rejection of any form of affirmative action, a strong repudiation of egalitarian values, problematization of blacks, blaming the victim, and so on.[1] Indeed, he even proposes the repeal of the Civil Rights Act of 1964 (p. 544), and he favours 'rational discrimination' in the private sphere.

Our ideological and social enemies and Us

Given their multiple group memberships, individuals may acquire and personally adapt several ideologies or ideology fragments. This means that D'Souza's book is not merely an expression of conservatism and modern racism, but a personal combination of these and other ideologies, attitudes, beliefs, values, models and other social and personal representations.

Yet, where he expresses positions and opinions that seem to be widely shared, at least among conservatives, in the USA (and also in Europe), we may assume that he is not merely writing as an individual, but also as a member of several ideological communities. At the end of his book, thus, he explicitly aligns himself with other 'cultural conservatives' (p. 521). His opinions about multiculturalism, affirmative action, the inner city ghettos and related topics are widely shared by other conservatives in the USA. Hence, abstracting from more personal views, we may read and analyse his book as a formulation of group ideologies.[2]

The ideological enemy

Ideologies are often formulated, explicitly or implicitly, as attacks against ideological opponents or enemies. Anti-Communism has been the most prominent example, especially in the USA, of this kind of anti-ideology. In D'Souza's book, this ideological enemy is what he calls 'cultural relativism', whose major tenet is that all cultures are equal, and that we should not assume any value hierarchy between different cultures. D'Souza traces this tendency to early twentieth century anthropology, and especially to Franz Boas and his students.

Throughout his book, cultural relativism is frequently blamed for virtually all ills of US society, and especially as the ideological source of contemporary 'anti-racist' policies and practices in the USA:

[1] [The main problem is] Liberal anti-racism. By asserting the equality of all cultures, cultural relativism prevents liberals from dealing with the nation's contemporary crisis – a civilizational breakdown that affects all groups, but is especially concentrated among the black underclass. (p. 24)

[2] Fundamental liberal principles are being sacrificed at the altar of cultural relativism. In its fanatical commitment to the relativist ideology of group equality, liberalism is inexorably destroying itself. (p. 530).

[3] Relativism has become a kind of virus, attacking the immune systems of institutional legitimacy and public decency. (p. 532)

As these examples also show, the reference to liberalism as an ideological orientation is at least ambiguous. On the one hand, the specific US sense of politically or culturally 'progressive' may be meant by it (as in example 1, whereas D'Souza himself does not deny his allegiance to the original, philosophical-political meaning of the term, as in example 2. We may therefore expect, as was argued in the previous chapters, that the ideological conflict presented in his book will be articulated in starkly polarized terms, where all They think is inherently bad, and all We think is inherently good. The rhetoric and lexical style of these examples expresses this ideological polarization, as is shown in the use of metaphors from the domain of health ('virus', 'immune system') in 3 and from traditional religion ('sacrificed on the altar of'), as well as by the use of hyperboles ('civilizational breakdown') in example 1. The rhetorical contrast in 3 suggests that there is a struggle between Us and Them. *They* are enemies who 'attack' us, and We defend – as an 'immune system' – legitimacy and decency in the USA. Framed in those terms, the ideological debate turns into a fierce struggle between Good and Evil, as was also the case in classical anti-communism until the Reagan era.

The social enemy

D'Souza and his fellow cultural conservatives not only have an intellectual, ideological enemy, but also a social one, namely, African-Americans. Although, as we shall see in more detail below, he emphasizes that his animosity is not directed against blacks as a 'race', but rather against African-American culture, his special focus on blacks can hardly hide the fact that he is not merely fighting a cultural war. It is this reason why in his book, and its underlying ideology, 'culture' and 'ethnicity' represent the respectable mask behind which (acknowledged) ethnocentrism mingles with various brands of modern racism. Although much of his fury targets the black 'underclass' and its social 'pathologies', he often forgets this specification and problematizes the whole black 'culture', which he sees as coherent and associated with all African-Americans in the USA.

This is a very anti-black book. If D'Souza had more generally been worried by the 'breakdown of civilization', as he so hyperbolically calls the present 'crisis' in the USA, he could have targeted many other social or cultural groups. With many of the same arguments and examples, he could also have focused on Latinos, on Native Americans, on the 'dependent' white underclass, on all unmarried mothers, all criminals, or all minorities who profit of affirmative action. He does not. He specifically singles out blacks, and his extremely biased, if not racist, judgements barely leave another conclusion than that these are his real social enemies:

> [4] The last few decades have witnessed nothing less than a breakdown of civilization within the African-American community. The breakdown is characterized by extremely high rates of criminal activity, by the normalization of illegitimacy, by the predominance of single-parent families, by high levels of addiction to alcohol and drugs, by a parasitic reliance on government provision, by a hostility to academic achievement, and by a scarcity of independent enterprises. (p. 477)

This quote sums up D'Souza's major points of resentment against the African-American community. Indeed, he does not speak here of a (relatively small) section of this community, but of the community as a whole. Where many others would talk of 'social problems' of some inner-city areas, D'Souza's view is more apocalyptic. He sees 'nothing less than a breakdown of civilization'. In many places of his book, he explicitly speaks of African-Americans as a 'threat' not only to themselves but to the whole society:

> [5] The conspicuous pathologies of blacks are the product of catastrophic cultural change that poses a threat both to the African-American community and to society as a whole. (p. 478)

Whereas conservatives before had communists as the major internal as well as external enemy, this kind of socio-political paranoia now targets blacks. In order to emphasize the 'pathologies' of blacks, the Asian community in the USA is held up as the good example, an example that at the same time serves as a strategic argument against those who might see racism in D'Souza's attacks against blacks:

> [6] By proving that upward mobility and social acceptance do not depend on the absence of racially distinguishing features, Asians have unwittingly yet powerfully challenged the attribution of minority failure to discrimination by the majority. Many liberals are having trouble providing a full answer to the awkward question: 'Why can't an African-American be more like an Asian?'

One might easily explain this racial divide-and-rule principle by the fact that D'Souza himself is an example of the Asian success story (he is from India), but there are few other traces of his Asian (or Indian) allegiances in the book. He does not speak for immigrants or minorities at all. On the contrary, as is true of many conservative immigrants, he completely identifies with Western civilization, and the dominant white majority which, obviously, could not have a more persuasive spokesman when it comes to attacking multiculturalism and affirmative action: who is more credible in attacking the others than one of them? As may be expected, conservative blacks and other people of colour in the USA are extensively celebrated and promoted, and have full access to the media and other ideological institutions, especially when they serve as 'useful idiots' and sustain the dominant consensus of the white elites.

Obviously, such groups and group relations need to be located in the more complex, socio-political and intellectual framework of US society. Thus, among the ideological enemies (the 'relativists' or the 'Boasians' – from Franz Boas, famous US anthropologist) he further identifies most liberal (progressive) scholars, politicians and journalists, proponents of civil rights and affirmative action, anti-racists, and all those whom he portrays as condoning or having vested interests in the continuation of 'black pathologies'. One stylistic ploy in the derogation of his ideological enemies is to call them 'activists', including professors whose opinions he dislikes. In passing he also includes some other target groups and ideologies of conservative scorn:

[7] . . . activists draw heavily on leftist movements such as Marxism, deconstructionism, and anticolonial or Third World scholarship. (p. 345)

[8] . . . solutions [of African-American scholar Cornell West] are a quixotic combination of watered-down Marxism, radical feminism, and homosexual rights advocacy, none of which offers any realistic hope for ameliorating black pathologies. (p. 520)

In sum, although not the main target of his ire, his ideological enemies stretch far along the social horizon, and include all progressive, alternative or otherwise non-mainstream groups and the institutions associated with them.

Us

Whereas there is little ambiguity about who his enemies are, who are *We* in this polarized representation of the civilizational conflict? As usual in this kind of discourse, *We* are largely implicit and presupposed, and in need of much less identification. In a large part of this book on the 'breakdown of civilization', *We* are simply all civilized people. More specifically, also in the historical sections of the book, *We* are those (mostly Europeans) who invented 'Western' civilization. Within the context of the USA, *We* may variously be all non-blacks, or whites, or all those opposed to multiculturalism, affirmative action and state interference.

Whereas his positive descriptions of all these different We-groups with which D'Souza identifies leave no doubt about his allegiances, his closest ideological reference group comprises what he calls the 'cultural conservatives':

[9] The only people who are seriously confronting black cultural deficiencies and offering constructive proposals for dealing with them are members of a group we can call the reformers. Many of them are conservatives. . . . (p. 521)

They are the ones who, at the end of the book, have 'understood' the seriousness of the 'civilizational breakdown' in the African-American community, and have made proposals to amend it. Quite predictably, D'Souza includes a group of conservative blacks among their ranks, and does not seem fazed by the inconsistencies such a selection engenders when he at the same time lambasts the entire African-American community. Apparently, and as always, there are exceptions, and those are Our friends.

Since ideologies articulate within and between groups, we now have the first elements of the social framework that sustains D'Souza's ideologies. We know his enemies and we know his friends, and we know that he serves as the ideologue for these friends, and as the ideal opponent of his enemies.

The conflict and the 'crisis'

Ideological struggles are rooted in real political, social or economic conflicts. They do not merely involve arbitrary groups, but involve group relations of power, dominance or competition. At stake is access to scarce social resources, both material as well as symbolic ones. The conflict that serves as the background for the ideological struggle in which D'Souza takes part involves both 'race' and class, and especially focuses on the relations between the white majority and the African-American minority in the USA.

As is also obvious from the historical chapters of his book, this conflict has a long history: European world exploration and colonization, the enslavement of Africans by Europeans (and Arabs), the plantation economy in the rural South, abolition, the emergence of scientific racism, the Jim Crow laws, racial segregation, the civil rights movement, the end of formal segregation and official racism, affirmative action, large scale immigration from Asia and Latin America, multiculturalism in education, and finally the conservative backlash of which D'Souza's book is a salient example.

Despite their 'real' socio-economic backgrounds, conflicts are sociopolitical constructs, which are defined differently by the various groups involved in them, depending on their ideological orientation, group goals and interests, as well as the everyday experiences of their members. Ongoing sociopolitical conflicts such as that of race relations in the USA are characterized not only by the many structural properties of social inequality and occasional reform. They also know a series of 'crises', which are also defined by shared mental representations of (and hence differently interpreted by) groups in conflict. A crisis may occur when one of the participant groups enhances its political, economic or ideological dominance and oppression or when the dominated group engages in explicit forms of resistance. Thus the conservative backlash that coincided with conservative Reagonomics and the victory of neo-liberalism in the 1980s and 1990s, is one of such crises. This crisis in turn found its ideological motivation in the reaction against the (modest) political and economic gains of African-Americans that resulted from another crisis, namely, the civil rights movement and the social government policies of the 1960s and 1970s.

The social and political function of D'Souza's book should be defined against this general background of race relations, politics and policies in the USA, but draws its rhetorical relevance and persuasiveness especially from a self-defined 'civilizational crisis'. That is, structural properties of US society (such as poverty, especially in the black ghettos or overall socio-cultural changes) are interpreted and presented as a major threat. Once defined as 'catastrophic', such a perceived threat demands urgent action and policy, and D'Souza's book provides the ideological principles for such a 'multiracial society', as its subtitle specifies. We have seen that just talking of (well-known) 'problems' will not do in such a rhetorical book. Hence such social problems need to be magnified to a disaster of major proportions, as also the frequently hyperbolic style of D'Souza shows:

[10] . . . the nation's contemporary crisis – a civilizational breakdown that affects all groups . . . (p. 24)

[11] . . . a deterioration of basic civilizational norms in the ghetto. (p. 241)

[12] The conspicuous pathologies of blacks are the product of catastrophic cultural change that poses a threat both to the African-American community and to society as a whole. (p. 478)

[13] For many whites the criminal and irresponsible black underclass represents a revival of barbarism in the midst of Western civilization. (p. 527)

In other words, we do not merely have a conflict between two groups, whites and blacks, in the USA, but a momentous struggle, namely, that between (white) 'civilization' and (black) 'barbarism'. And, as may be expected, D'Souza is the hero who has taken on the Herculean task of fighting the forces of barbarism, as also the Greek heroes defended their civilizations against the barbarian foreigners. D'Souza explicitly refers to the Greek history of 'Western civilization' and democracy, as an example which, until today, deserves emulation, including 'rational', ethnocentric discrimination of the barbarian others. Thus, his struggle is not just one that tries to safeguard the interests and privileges of the dominant, white middle class, but more grandly presents itself as a valiant defence of Western civilization against the onslaught of a 'rainbow' coalition of blacks, immigrants, leftists, gays, lesbians, multiculturalists, Boasian relativists and others who threaten the status quo. In that respect, D'Souza and his book, and the ideologies he defines, are quite coherently conservative and ethnocentric. Let us now try to reconstruct these ideologies and other social representations from his book and then examine in some more detail their persuasive discursive manifestations.

Reconstructing ideologies

Recall that ideologies, defined as basic social representations of groups, should not be identified with their discursive expression. Indeed, the relation between ideologies and discourse may be very indirect – usually, more specific beliefs from social attitudes and from personal models of events show up in text and talk, further modified by the constraints of context models of speakers and writers. That is, more often than not, ideological beliefs need to be inferred, hypothetically reconstructed, from actual discourse, for instance by comparison with repeated (contextually different) discourses of other group members. Since we only have one (large) text here, such comparisons can only be made within the book itself, as well as with those texts or examples the author refers to and agrees with. Moreover, in typical ideological treatises of this kind, the very formulation of the 'principles' involved may be close to the underlying ideologies because D'Souza does not tell many concrete stories, but argues at a general, abstract level. Moreover the overall, contextual purpose of the book is to attack what he sees as a threatening ideology (cultural relativism) and to promote another, which he does not name explicitly, although he aligns himself with what he calls 'cultural conservatism'.

As may be expected from a book that deals with various political, social, economic and cultural issues, also D'Souza's book manifests several, related ideologies, depending on his respective identifications with different groups or communities, as explained above: Western, white, middle-class, male, heterosexual, professional, conservative elites. However, D'Souza focuses on his main ideological and social enemies, namely, the cultural relativists and African-Americans. Also class is a salient dimension, as is obvious from his special wrath against the black 'underclass'. His frequent generalizations show, however, that he takes the whole black community as a metonymic (*totum pro parte*) representation of the black poor.

In sum, we may expect four types of ideology here, those of race–ethnicity, class, culture and politics, and an overall 'meta-ideology' organizing these, namely, that of conservatism. It is this over-arching conservative ideology that establishes coherence and numerous links between the beliefs in the respective ideologies. For instance, where D'Souza defends socio-political, neo-liberal beliefs about limited state intervention, we may expect racialized beliefs about African-American dependency on the state in general, and about black welfare mothers in particular. And where his cultural ideologies defend the uniqueness and hegemony of Western civilization, we may expect both the class and race ideologies to feature beliefs about the 'barbarism' of the underclass. The same cultural ideologies may be connected to ideological beliefs about the 'bankruptcy' of relativist multiculturalism, whereas conservative–liberal individualism emphasizes the importance of personal merit against group-based, collective affirmative action. Similarly, the conservative ideology of law and order will be 'racialized' in this case in the evaluation of 'black crime'. Many other such cross-linkages between main ideologies and specific attitudes may be reconstructed from this book.

As we shall see in more detail below, such an ideological complex will be brought to bear in the central attitude that provides the basis and the title of this book, namely, that contrary to what is maintained by blacks and their liberal white supporters, the USA is not (or at least no longer) a racist country. As suggested in the previous chapters, it is this denial of racism which constitutes one of the core attitudes of modern elite racism. Disguised by what is defined as a 'culture war' between liberal relativists and conservative cultural supremacists, we thus discover the continuation of the ongoing 'race war' that has characterized the 'American dilemma' for centuries. Indeed, the book's subtitle advocates a 'multiracial' society, but the contents of the book show that the supremacy of the dominant white 'race' should not be challenged. 'Rational discrimination' is a 'natural' right of this dominant ethnic group:

> [14] The Greeks were ethnocentric, they showed a preference for their own. Such tribalism they would have regarded as natural, and indeed we now know that it is universal. In some situations an instinctive ethnocentrism is inevitable, as when one's society is under external attacks and one must rally to its defence. (p. 533)

We see here at work one of the most prominent devices of the ideological legitimation of inequality, namely, that such a situation is 'natural' and hence 'universal'. At the same time, such a passage shows another device in the representation of the others, namely, how outgroups are constructed as enemies against whose 'external attacks' we must 'naturally' defend ourselves. Thus, racism is not only made respectable, while natural, but also a patriotic duty of whites in the 'culture war' and the 'civilizational crisis' (p. 535).

After this brief overall characterization of the various ideologies involved, let us now examine some of their contents and structures.

Conservatism

It was argued, above, that 'conservatism' it not so much a (group) ideology, but rather an overarching, meta-ideology that organizes other ideologies. For instance, applied to neo-liberal ideologies in the realm of the political economy, conservative ideologies typically advocate a limited role of the state (or government) in the market. Similarly, when applied to cultural ideologies, conservative meta-principles may take two complimentary variants: limited state intervention in some cultural domains (education, media, religion), or active state intervention, for example through tough legislation, in the domains that are seen to threaten the moral order (family values, sexuality, multiculturalism). And finally, when applied to racial or ethnic ideologies, conservatism will similarly allow (condone or not strictly police) various forms of discrimination, as the right of each person or ethnic group to 'prefer one's own'.

Values   As all ideologies, also conservative meta-ideologies are based on a selection and combination of values drawn from a cultural commonground. D'Souza for instance positively refers to the following values (of which the ideological, attitudinal and discursive constructions will be examined below):

- freedom
- personal merit
- discipline
- prudence
- moderation
- responsibility
- self-restraint
- hard work
- authority
- order
- decency
- elitism
- non-permissiveness.

Such an ideological selection of rather general cultural values usually also involves a set of counter-values when the ideology is brought to bear in an ideological struggle with ideological opponents. Thus, these values are selected and emphasized especially against (certain variants of) those of egalitarian, progressive liberalism: equality, social responsibility, social support, moral freedom, cultural relativism, freedom from oppression, representativeness, anti-authoritarianism, permissiveness, creativity, self-critique, progress, democracy, and so on.

Given these values and their counterparts, some of the conservative ideological beliefs defended by D'Souza in his book are the following.

1   The social and civilizational status quo is being threatened.
2   The state should not interfere where it does not belong.
3   Social programmes to help the poor are counterproductive.
4   People should be judged individually by their own achievements.
5   Inequality has individual not social causes.
6   People have duties, and not only rights.
7   A coherent society does not allow multiple cultures or worldviews.
8   There are natural inequalities between (groups of) people.
9   Society must be characterized by law and order.
10   All individuals should take initiative and pursue excellence.
11   Children shall be born in wedlock.
12   All people must work.

These ideological principles are not always directly formulated in the *End of Racism*, but especially appear in the negative evaluation of the ideologies and attitudes of D'Souza's enemies, for example in favour of state intervention in the ghetto, welfare, affirmative action, social responsibility of business companies, social disadvantage, the legitimacy of single mothers or other family structures, decent jobs, equal group representation, equal outcomes, and so on.

As suggested before, these conservative values and ideological beliefs will appear to be manifested in more specific group ideologies and attitudes. Indeed, some of the ideological beliefs mentioned above might even be omitted because they are domain- or group-specific general beliefs. Thus, the freedom from state intervention in fact implies that the state should also not be (very) active in the social domains, for example with social programmes for the poor or the elderly. Similarly, the opposition to 'illegitimacy' of children or to unmarried mothers, is of course a further specification of overall conservative beliefs about family values.

Ethnocentrism/modern racism

Although conservatism is the overarching ideological framework that organizes the social and cultural beliefs in *The End of Racism*, ethnocentric modern racism is its specific ideological core. This conclusion may be rather ironical given the title of D'Souza's book, but within the framework of our elite theory of racism, such denials are paramount in all forms of modern racism. Hence D'Souza's rage against anti-racists, his systematic mitigations of the continued relevance of 'race' in the USA, and his alleged 'ignorance' of widespread discrimination against of African-Americans in virtually all social domains. For the same ideological reasons he attacks civil rights 'activists', those who plead for (or see no alternative for) affirmative action, and those he sees as using racism as an excuse for own failure and 'civilizational breakdown'.

As group ideologies, ethnocentrism and modern racism feature the following basic beliefs about the own group, namely (white) Westerners, and its relations to other groups. Most of these ideological principles are based on the core value of (cultural if not natural) inequality between groups.

1   Our Western culture is superior.
2   Ethnocentrism is natural and sometimes inevitable.
3   Discrimination may be rational.
4   The USA is not and should not be a multicultural society.
5   Cultural assimilation of culturally deviant groups is necessary.
6   We are tolerant.
7   The USA is not a racist society. / We are not racists.

Related to these ideological self-representations is the, polarized, negative representation of the others: first the liberal cultural relativists, for example in terms of the following beliefs.

1   They think that all cultures are equally valuable.
2   They advocate multiculturalism.
3   They criticize Western civilization.
4   They accuse us of colonialism and racism.

5   They want proportional representation of ethnic minorities.

The second main enemy, the social opponents, are blacks, African-Americans, and more generally all non-Westerners in the book. They are variously described on the basis of the following ideological beliefs.

1   They are primitive, uncivilized, barbarians.
2   African-American pathologies are cultural.
3   They are culturally deviant.
4   They break the law.
5   They tend to be criminal.
6   Their culture(s) are stagnant.
7   They depend on the state.
8   They take no initiative.
9   They are promiscuous.
10   They are not striving for excellence.
11   They use racism as an excuse for own failure.

In other words, and as we have seen in Chapter 6, negative other-presentations deriving from ethnocentric and racist ideologies are often articulated around the attribution of violations of our basic values and ideological principles. Thus, where we are tolerant, anti-racism is intolerant; where we value personal merit and discipline, they lack such values; where we are decent they are promiscuous, where we work hard, they are too lazy to work, and so on.

Ideological structures

One of the theoretical issues dealt with earlier in this book is that of the structure of ideologies (Chapter 5). On the basis of repeated general propositions in D'Souza's book, a number of beliefs were selected that are general enough to be included in the conservative meta-ideology and the ideologies of cultural racism or ethnocentrism. It was, however, argued that ideologies probably have some kind of internal organization, for instance a schematic structure of fixed categories. Such a schema would be relevant each time people need to acquire or change an ideology, for instance when they become new members of a social group. Searching for a format for such a schema, I assumed that given the close link between group ideology and the self-representation of the group, a group schema modelled on the fundamental societal co-ordinates of the group would be a good candidate. The question now is whether the ideological propositions inferred from de D'Souza's book can be validly assigned to such a schema.

Thus, if we have to design a framework for the ideologies of racism and ethnocentrism, we may propose the following (simplified) structure:

- *Membership Criteria* – only members of our own culture, ethnic group, 'race' or nation;
- *Activities* – discriminate others;
- *Goals* – exclusion, segregation or assimilation of others;

- *Values* – natural inequality, cultural homogeneity;
- *Societal Position: relation to other groups* – we (our culture) are (is) superior to the others;
- *Resources* – Western civilization, (political and economic) power, whiteness.

Obviously, since group self-schemata are usually (though not always) positive, and 'racism' is culturally and socially sanctioned, at least officially, most people who share this schema will not describe themselves as 'racists', but for instance as nationalists. Recall that the group schema and its categories will feature those fundamental group beliefs that define the identity as well as the basic interests of the group. When these interests are under threat, they will most energetically be defended, or when lost they will be reclaimed.

This is also the case for D'Souza's book. Thus the membership criteria category defines who does or may belong to Us, and hence the others are defined by racists or ethnocentrists as foreigners, aliens, immigrants, outsiders, and so on. The activities of the members should be geared towards the realization of the essential group goal, which is basically to keep others out or down, or if that is impossible to fully assimilate them (in this case culturally). These aims are the basis of the negative evaluations in the attitude of multiculturalism, as we shall see below.

The basic value of ethnocentrism and racism is to emphasize 'natural' inequality between groups, against the egalitarians and the relativists. It is not surprising that such a value only serves the interests of those who are dominant, and therefore, in the societal position category, we find the fundamental definition of Our position, namely, that We are superior to Them (i.e. Our civilization, culture, knowledge, etc., is better than Theirs).

Since dominant group position and reproduction need resources, the crucial resource in a racist ideology is the symbolic power of being part of (Western) civilization and of being white, that is, the very criteria of their membership of their own group. Given the fundamental nature of resources for group power and reproduction, these are the ideological interests that will be defended most forcefully. This is indeed the case in D'Souza's book, wherein the repeatedly expressed concern is that (Western) civilization is breaking down, that other cultures may get the upper hand, and that Our (Western, white, male, middle-class, etc.) group and its interests may lose power.

The societal position category in the ideological schema typically features a relation to other groups, in this case obviously the group(s) that are the very target of racist or ethnocentric groups, namely, foreigners, immigrants, aliens, minorities, and so on, especially those of another culture and/or appearance ('race'). Given the relationship of superiority involved here, the other-group schema associated to this self-schema typically will feature those categories and beliefs that are opposed to those for our own group.

Their membership category (as defined by Us) is, say, 'being black', or as D'Souza's insists, 'having a coherent black culture'. It is also here that the 'essential' evaluation of the others is being represented, namely, as being primitive, uncivilized, barbarians, lacking initiative, being promiscuous, and so forth.

Their (negative) activities may be ideologically summarized as 'They violate all our norms' (are criminals, push drugs, get illegitimate children, don't want to work, accuse us of racism, etc.). Their goal is represented, for example, as equal rights, multiculturalism and an equal economic share. Their values are all those opposed to Ours: egalitarianism, relativism, permissiveness, dependency on state, disrespectfulness of order and authority, indecency, and so on. Their position is represented on the one hand as (culturally) inferior, and on the other hand as a threat to our culture, civilization and other resources; moreover, they accuse us of racism and intolerance. Since the other group is hardly powerful, few resources will be attributed to them, and the point is precisely to make sure that they will not get access to our resources, or their resources (such as their own culture) will be negatively valued, as is the case, as we shall see, for the attitude about Afrocentrism.

These basic ideological group schemas for Us and Them will then be further detailed for specific social domains in a number of more detailed attitudes about specific groups, for example about African-Americans, or about Us (whites, etc.) in the USA, and for specific issues, such as racism, multiculturalism or affirmative action, as I shall spell out below.

Note, finally, that I did not attempt to schematize the list of conservative basic beliefs, since conservatism is not a specific group ideology, but rather a meta-ideology that organizes some basic principles of other group ideologies. The typical conservative beliefs (about state intervention, individualism, law and order, family structure, etc.) are in fact all specifications of fundamental conservative values. Thus freedom is defined as freedom from state intervention, and personal merit is inconsistent with social welfare, decency prohibits illegitimate children, and so on. If we would have to define conservatives as a 'group' we might say that it is constituted precisely by the category of its values (against progressives). That is, the identity, actions, goals, position and resources of conservatives all focus on the realization of those values. It is in this way that the meta-ideology of conservatism constrains other (group) ideologies, such as those of racists, or professors, or business people, for whom the conservative value system will have different applications depending on the interests and specific group goals of these groups.

Attitudes

Theoretically, ideologies control and organize more specific attitudes. Thus, whereas basic ethnocentric and racist ideologies represent the overall properties of Us (Westerners, whites) and Them (non-Westerners, blacks), attitudes feature more specific social beliefs, such as prejudices, about specific outgroups. Thus, African-Americans are further represented as follows.

1 They are the cause of the breakdown of civilization.
2 They have one coherent (black) culture.
3 (Poor) blacks have scandalous pathologies:
   - excessive reliance on government;
   - conspirational paranoia about racism;
   - resistance to academic achievement;
   - celebration of the criminal;
   - normalization of illegitimacy;
   - single-parent families.
4 Their pathologies are due to African-American culture.
5 Their culture is functionally inadequate.
6 They are themselves racist:
   - they have ideology of black supremacy.
7 They are violent and criminal.
8 They abuse drugs.
9 They have an expensive lifestyle (they are 'flashy').
10 They may have lower intelligence.
11 They have fewer skills.
12 They have no mores.
13 They celebrate or condone broken families.
14 They do not adapt to the dominant (Our) culture.
15 They do not take responsibility.
16 They have paranoia about racism.
17 Their middle class has an unfounded black rage.
18 They are weak in developing businesses.
19 They repudiate standard English.
20 They celebrate the 'Bad Nigger'.
21 They dress in conspicuous clothes.
22 They use obscene language.
23 They do not want to work.
24 They are not punctual.
25 They do not respect matrimony.
26 They cause the bastardization of America.
27 Their intellectuals refuse to criticize underclass pathologies.

These beliefs may be further organized in a more structured schema of which, however, the overall principle is again clear: the others (here the blacks) are represented as our negative mirror image – literally as our dark side. Whatever values and principles We share, They don't have them.

The core concepts organizing these beliefs are *difference*, *deviation* and *threat*, applied in all social domains, for example those of culture in general, habits, language, dress, work ethic, family values, character, tolerance, modesty, industriousness, individual merit and achievement, and so on. That is, their cultural mores are not only different from ours, but they also deviate from our norms and laws, and ultimately, their cultural deviance as well as their aggression, crime and other behaviour are a threat to Us and the whole nation, including themselves. Note that within the attitudinal representation of African-Americans, we also encounter some specific beliefs about black subgroups, such as black intellectuals, women or the 'underclass'.

Often, however, the text is not that specific, so that many negative attributes ascribed to a relatively small group of young men in the ghettos are in fact generalized towards the whole group. It is this (over)generalization that is one of the hallmarks of racism: they are all alike. Although D'Souza recalls (without much conviction) that 'it is not in their genes', and that he therefore cannot be called a racist, the distinction between African-American 'culture' and 'race' is very subtle in his argument, and often non-existent. Indeed, most blacks would see his very negative and aggressive stereotyping as little more than a form of racist derogation hiding behind a thin veil of cultural critique.

In his rejection of racism as the cause of the deplorable social condition of the African-American community, D'Souza has no other option than to blame the victims themselves (a strategy he energetically denies and even attacks as one of the criticized forms of anti-racism). That is, he focuses on 'black pathologies' and sees these as a 'civilizational breakdown', as discussed above. Hence the blacks, and no other group or organization, are the cause of the 'catastrophe' that is threatening 'Us' in the USA.

More sober analysts of the socio-political situation in the USA (and elsewhere in the world) would probably wonder why D'Souza's rhetoric focuses on just those 'pathologies' and why these should constitute something as dramatic as a 'civilizational breakdown' and a 'threat' to the whole nation. Since when is welfare, when no jobs are available, a pathological form of 'parasitic reliance'? If so, most of the Western European welfare systems would not be an object of envy. And what about single-parent families? These are increasingly normal in many parts of the world, especially in highly developed nations, such as those in Scandinavia, where up to around 40 per cent of mothers are not married. What we have here, obviously, is a socio-cultural difference, and hardly a pathology, and even less something as apocalyptic as the 'bastardization of America' as D'Souza so delicately describes black families. And how would D'Souza's black conservative friends who are prominent professors (as well as all other blacks with an academic degree) interpret his conclusion that African-Americans are 'hostile' to achievement? Surely, there are other, more fundamental, social and economic problems in the USA, such as the poverty of many millions of families and children.

What is important for my analysis, however, is not so much a critical challenge of D'Souza's work (many others have done that already) but a demonstration of how values, ideologies and attitudes influence the definition and evaluation of the social situation. Where many see poverty, racism, marginalization and many other social ills in the USA, D'Souza's ideology has blinded him to such realities. On the contrary, in a grand movement of reversal he blames the victims of this situation. Even a well-founded analysis of US society, not only by blacks, is thus claimed to be patho- logical. Hence, we see how different ideologies may lead to opposed assessments of the 'facts'.

Attitudes about racism

D'Souza's ideologies also control attitudes other than those about African- Americans: for instance, as we have seen, about racism. Again, both his knowledge and opinions about racism appear to be heavily biased by his underlying ideology of ethnocentrism and modern racism. First, however, it is crucial that his opinions about race and racism be safely protected against any accusation of racism. He does this, as is usual in much other elite discourse, also among several social scientists, by limiting the definition of racism to a 'belief in intrinsic, biologically based superiority'. Since only small groups of white supremacists share this belief, his beliefs and those of most other modern racists are safeguarded against any accusation of racism. Racism defined as he does, is indeed a marginal problem in the USA or anywhere else. The problem is that the system of ethnic/racial inequality in the USA (and other countries dominated by Europeans) is much more complex than that, and not limited at all to beliefs about biologically based superiority. Rather, especially when associated with appearance, all feelings of group-based superiority, also those of culture, and the many everyday forms of discrimination based on them, are forms of contemporary racism.

The same is true for most other beliefs about racism D'Souza expresses in his book. That is, they are geared towards protecting himself and dominant white culture and civilization from the uncivilized taint of racism. Thus, a whole chapter is dedicated to a historical treatise about racism (and slavery) as existing in many other countries and civilizations, and concludes that white Europeans were not the only 'guilty' ones. Such a chapter should also be interpreted as a tactical move to at least share the blame of racism. And when the title and much of the content of his book emphasizes (correctly) that racism is not universal, but has a specific beginning and end, he (falsely) concludes that (therefore?) racism in the USA has ended (on a par with ideology and history which other influential conservative authors before him declared to have 'ended'). Once established (without proof, and disregarding libraries full of evidence to the contrary) that racism has ended, the real aim of the argument becomes clear: if there is no significant racism in the USA anymore, the blacks can safely be blamed themselves for their 'pathologies', and We (whites) are again in the clear. And even more forcefully, those may be accused of bias or lies (or worse, reaping profits) who claim that racism is alive and kicking today in the USA as long as we do not limit its definition to marginal phenomena such as beliefs in 'biological superiority of the white race'. Thus, where D'Souza claims that 'accusations of racism are a rationalization of black failure', others may reverse the claim and state that D'Souza's denial of racism is a rationalization of continued white failure to come to terms with blacks in US society. No wonder that in D'Souza's hierarchy of ideological values, the real problem is not racism, but anti-racism – defined as 'intellectual and moral coercion'.

In D'Souza's attitude to racism, even when defined in his way, racism is a legitimate opinion (p. 538), which may be criticized, but which is no crime, despite many international laws, United Nations charters against racism, and the Universal Declaration of Human Rights. We see that at this point the conservative values of law and order clash with the principles of his racist ideology – enforcing the many laws against discrimination does not exactly have priority in this attitude. On the contrary, discrimination, as D'Souza argues, may well be rational and legitimate in some situations. Ethnocentric supremacy, and neo-liberal freedom to discriminate (e.g. in business) are ideologically superior to the liberal principle of not violating the rights of others.

Wherever discrimination and racism cannot be bluntly denied it is mitigated, their current relevance and seriousness played down, or even legitimated in specific situations. Systematic everyday discrimination in the USA is thus euphemistically reduced to such improprieties as 'slights of taxidrivers who pass by African Americans' (p. 525), a form of discrimination that is fully legitimate for D'Souza, because it is 'rational'.

Similarly, although structurally very similar and socially equally destructive, US segregation is deemed to be totally incomparable with apartheid, a familiar move of mitigating denial. And when D'Souza claims that 'we do not know how much racism exists in the USA', such a well-known move of apparent ignorance ('nobody knows how to measure it') is curiously inconsistent with his own repeated claim that racism has declined in the USA. But should some racism still exist, it is especially due to the behaviour of the black underclass, which violates all social and cultural codes of US society – another reversal by blaming the victim.

There are several points where D'Souza's beliefs about racism coincide with those of critical scholars who have studied racism. Thus, as we have seen, racism is certainly not universal, but a scientific invention of eighteenth- and nineteenth-century Europeans, for example, used to explain observations of the 'primitivism' of other cultures. D'Souza does not mention here that it was also invented to legitimate slavery, genocide, land grab, colonization and many other highlights of Western 'civilization'. Indeed, racism is not an irrational antipathy of stupid, uneducated people, but had a scientific basis (and such science should never be called 'pseudo-science' warns D'Souza). True, as is exemplary for his own book, racism, ethnocentrism and many other forms of inequality have always been preformulated and legitimated, in more or less respectable academic terms, by the elites. For D'Souza, however, the argument has other implications: if discrimination is not irrational, but rational, this means that (white) people may have good, even respectable, reasons to discriminate against blacks.

Thus, D'Souza defends the attitude that prejudice, discrimination and ethnocentrism may be natural, rational, expedient (good for business) and hence justified.

Given his attitude to racism, we should not be surprised by D'Souza's attitude to colonialism, another invention of Western 'civilization'. Denial, mitigation, legitimation and simply ignoring the historical facts are only some of the strategies employed to protect the ideology of Western civilizational supremacy against overly critical examination. Thus, explorations were not 'carried out with hostile intentions', D'Souza claims, and should not be seen as rapacious land grabs, theft of resources, or (sometimes) genocide, but as Europe's contribution to 'world transformation', as a sign of progress, and as intellectual enterprises. What is clear from such attitudinal beliefs is that ideologies have a very powerful control over the very selection, focus, representation and construction of historical 'facts'. And where ideologies, such as that of Western civilizational supremacy, might be inconsistent with these facts, they may be insulated against these facts by an entirely different version of reality.

Affirmative action

Little speculation is necessary to predict D'Souza's attitudes about affirmative action (AA), given his denial of racism and his conservative values and ideologies of personal merit, discipline, hard work and rejection of any government intervention. Whereas, on many other accounts, D'Souza rejects egalitarian values, social policy should, according to him be 'colour blind'. He insists that this principle of Martin Luther King should be respected, but he especially does so to demonstrate that contemporary black intellectuals violate King's legacy: a well-known tactic of dividing the enemy.

Whereas elsewhere in his book he makes a case for the legitimacy of 'rational' discrimination, affirmative action is strictly rejected because it is defined as discrimination – of whites that is. Following his own criteria that allow discrimination, one might ask whether affirmative action is an 'irrational antipathy', rather than a rational policy to end inequality and many remaining disparities in hiring, promotion and work conditions of minorities in general, and blacks in particular.

That AA would corrupt US firms, as another of D'Souza's attitudinal beliefs suggests, is another definition of the situation biased by the fundamental ideological belief that social and ethnic inequality should not be taken very seriously. It certainly does not explain why many big companies, when free to decide whether to apply AA, choose to do so.

The most familiar attitudinal belief about AA is that it would 'lower standards', which presupposes that minorities (and especially blacks) are generally less qualified. D'Souza extensively cites all statistics to prove just that. Since he has rejected a 'racial' (biological) explanation of such lower qualification, he is free to play the 'culture card', and hence accuse blacks of lacking a culture of achievement. Of course, other social explanations (bad schools) are hardly highlighted, nor may we expect the conclusion that if blacks (as a group) perform less well, not they, the victims, but the schools should be blamed.

Finally, in this sequence of accusations, reproaches and blaming the victim, D'Souza's attitude on AA, as well as on civil rights more generally, is that this system means Big Bucks for the 'civil rights industry', and especially also for black intellectuals and (other) 'activists'; how much, he does not tell us, one of the many claims about which suddenly his footnotes are scarce, nor how much white civil servants profit of the system. That attitudes are not always consistent among each other, shows here, because where the 'Civil Rights Industry' (and their black employees) are accused of gobbling up mega-dollars, blacks are elsewhere accused of not taking enough corporate or financial initiatives, This 'pathology' D'Souza traces back to black attitudes during slavery: 'a series of measures to avoid, postpone and minimize work' (p. 97). In more traditional parlance such an attitude was routinely expressed as 'They are lazy.' The point, thus, is not to try to establish a balanced picture of the social situation of African Americans and race relations in the USA, but to find *any* argument to derogate blacks.

Multiculturalism

The ideology of cultural conservatism is not very friendly towards multiculturalism. As D'Souza also has shown in his earlier work,[3] in which he ridicules educational, curricular and scientific diversity, his ideology of Western cultural supremacy is inconsistent with the cultural relativism of the 'Boasians', and with that of most social scientists in the world, for that matter.

The specific attitudinal cluster organizing his beliefs about multiculturalism is organized by a number of familiar dimensions, such as the conceptual triple, encountered before for the representation of African-Americans: difference, deviance, threat. Multiculturalists are different from us, deviate from our cultural and educational norms and are even a threat to our Western civilization.

To make the case for the 'threat', various devices of hyperbole are of course necessary, as has been the case more generally in the debate about multiculturalism.[4] In such an attitudinal framework it is not consistent, for instance, to consider alternative versions of reality, for instance the fact that multicultural education in US schools, colleges and universities is, as yet, marginal with respect to that of the teaching and research about dominant Western culture from Aristotle, to Shakespeare and Einstein.

Another ploy to emphasize the deviance of multiculturalism is to associate it with other evil cultural developments, as seen by the cultural conservatives: Marxism, deconstructionism, and Third World scholarship, none of which is exactly a dominant force in US academia. However, appeals to anti-communist (i.e. un-American), ideologies, ethnocentric doubts about the excellence of Third World scholars, and anti-intellectual ridicule of (also foreign, while French) deconstructionism, are of course consistent with both conservative and ethnocentric ideologies.

That multiculturalism would 'result in imbalance and distortion', as another belief of this attitude states, is a final strategy in the negative representation of curricula that emphasize the need for educational diversity for an increasingly ethnically varied population. Of course, the imbalance of restricting education largely to Western authors and scientists, is not further considered, nor has D'Souza nor other representatives of cultural conservatism written alarming books about this form of scholarly distortion, which has dominated US (and other Western) education until today.

Afrocentrism

The combined ideologies of cultural conservatism, ethnocentrism and modern racism are brought to bear in the construction of an extremely negative attitude about Afrocentrism. Ridicule, over-generalization and hyperbole are also the major strategic moves here. Afrocentrism is thus represented as a dangerous philosophy. As usual in the representation of blacks, the views of a radical minority are first generalized and exaggerated by selective quotes, and then derogated. Alternative representations of Afrocentrism, as a correction to dominant Eurocentric ideologies, and as a means to enhance group identification and pride among blacks, would imply a relativist position that is of course inconceivable for D'Souza.

Where arguments about scholarship, the arts or other elements of culture do not suffice, there is always the option to ridicule and derogate the appearance or behaviour of blacks who indulge in Afrocentric beliefs, following the familiar constraints of modern racism:

> [15] . . . the hardened gleam in many Afrocentric eyes . . . virtually cultic pattern of lockstep behavior: everyone dresses alike, and when the leader laughs, everyone laughs. . . . (p. 381)

Depending on one's ideology and social attitudes, such a description would of course fit many outgroups, ranging from the military to the denizens of Wall Street. That is, there is no aim to correctly describe the others, but to construct a negative stereotype, according to which others are typically 'all alike' and lack humanity, individuality and autonomy.

The IQ debate

Finally, D'Souza engages in a lengthy discussion of the IQ debate, spawned by the controversial book by Hernnstein and Murray, *The Bell Curve*. His position is very ambiguous here. He feels ideologically related to these authors because they also question 'the foundation of twentieth century liberalism: the denial of natural differences and the premise of the inherent equality of groups' (p. 434). Indeed, he asks:

[16] Why should groups with different skin color, head shape, and other visible characteristics prove identical in reasoning ability or to construct an advanced civilization? (p. 440)

He thus goes a long way towards agreeing with many of the racist presuppositions of Hernnstein and Murray. He extensively cites all scientific evidence that claims to show genetic black inferiority, as he also does when discussing the presumed lack of academic achievements of blacks. He thereby ignores the vast literature that shows that intelligence is largely contextual and socio-economical, and may even change dramatically within the same group within one generation. This shows that, typically for ideologically based persuasion, evidence is selectively focused on and presented in accordance with one's group attitudes: only those data that confirm the negative characteristics of the others will be given due attention.

The whole argument of biologically based racial differences of intelligence (and culture), of course presupposes the viability of the very notion of 'race', which he claims most scientists accept:

[17] Most anthropologists and biologists agree on the existence of three broad racial groups: the Caucasoid, the Negroid and the Mongoloid. (p. 449)

Again, he is virtually silent about (or simply rejects) all the scholarly literature that concludes that, despite obvious and undeniable differences of appearances between people in the world, a classification of people into 'races' on the basis of such (superficial) differences of appearance only makes sense in common sense. It is the same common sense, rather than scholarly evidence that makes D'Souza smugly use the following *argumentum ad absurdum*:

[18] If the concept of race is entirely fictional, shouldn't all civil rights laws which rely on racial classification be struck down by the Supreme Court as meaningless and unconstitutionally vague? (p. 447)

One of the many problems with this argument is that he disregards the difference between a biological classification and a socio-political or legal one. 'Race' is a social, commonsense construct, and racism is based on such a commonsense classification. Legal measures to counter racism of course recognize the existence of a social category of 'race' on which racism is based, but do not presuppose the existence of biological classifications of people into races.

Again, the strategic aim of D'Souza's argument is not so much to prove or disprove the existence of biological races, but rather to provoke supporters of civil rights, and hence his ideological enemies, into accepting biological races through the back door of the social and legal classifications of 'races'. Moreover, the argument is inconsistent with his critique of the 'one drop of blood rule' that (socially) defines people in the USA as 'black' if they have one drop of 'black' blood. If, indeed, most blacks in the USA do have 'mixed' ancestry, then the very point of their biological classification as black (and hence their racial inferiority on IQ tests) makes little sense. Thus, what African-Americans do have in common, though, is their social position, namely, as being self- and other-defined as being black.

Ultimately, however, D'Souza rejects (without much argument) the biological account of 'racial' differences and the IQ gap between blacks and whites, because that would be inconsistent with his ideologies of cultural conservatism and ethnocentrism. After all, if the 'pathologies' of the black community were largely caused by their genetic predisposition, they could hardly be blamed for them. A cultural explanation, by which deviant black culture is seen as the source of all problems, is much more persuasive in an argument that sets out to emphasize Western, white civilizational supremacy. Such an argument also rules out, as we have seen, any socio-economic explanation of African-American 'failure':

[19] My conclusion is that it is an illusion to believe that racial differences between blacks and whites are largely a phenomenon of socioeconomic class and that such differences will disappear with the current menu of preschool and public-school government interventions. (p. 457)

[20] Contrary to the assumption of cultural relativism, the problem, it seems, is not test bias but the functional inadequacy of African-American culture. (p. 461)

These discursive manifestations of underlying attitudes show again how beliefs are strategically shaped in accordance with prevalent ideologies. According to ethnocentric and modern racist ideologies, blacks need to be represented as inferior to whites. The cultural ideology then provides the explanation of such inferiority in terms of the 'functional inadequacy of African-American culture', which again is the belief that sustains the vehement attack against African-Americans. Biological explanations of black inferiority would invalidate such an argument, although D'Souza seems quite impressed by the biological evidence that might explain the IQ gap as well as the cultural inferiority of blacks. However, if D'Souza were to accept that blacks are genetically unable to compete with whites (or Asians), one solution would again be affirmative action and remedial schooling, and hence (more) government intervention, which is of course off limits for the conservative ideologue.

Models

We already briefly indicated, above, that ideologies and the social attitudes they control not only appear directly in discourse, as general statements, but also affect mental models, that is, personal interpretations and opinions about concrete events. D'Souza's book has few stories of such personal experiences: the 'definition of the situation' he presents is generally quite abstract. However, when he does tell about such an experience, we do see how underlying ideologies also control his mental models. Here are small fragments of one of the stories that express such a personal model, namely, his experience of the celebration, on 28 August 1993, of the thirtieth anniversary of Martin Luther King's march and 'I have a dream' speech:

[21] . . . One by one the leading civil rights spokespersons took the podium, gravely invoked the memory of Martin Luther King, Jr. and demanded that Americans do more to vanquish the forces of white racism so that blacks could achieve what one speaker termed 'meaningful equality'. . . .

But I did not hear anyone invoke King's principle of a race neutral society in which laws and policies are indifferent to colour. The reason for this reluctance was implicitly expressed by black activist Benjamin Chavis's rallying cry. 'We don't just want equal rights,' he said. 'We want our fair share of the economy.' Other speakers decried what they termed 'institutional racism', although they were not specific about this term. The rhetoric suggested the existence of a new civil rights agenda, in important respects different from the one which Martin Luther King, Jr. championed. . . .

Certainly the style and tone of the 1993 assembly differed in two important respects from that of King's march three decades earlier. First, many of the audience seemed middle-class, and there were conspicuous signs of prosperity. A number of speakers arrived in chauffeured cars. I overheard talk of appointments and schedules. 'I have to be at the coalition meeting at six.' I hope that they hold my dinner reservation.' . . . Some activists engaged in minor turf warfare, sparring over whether they had been booked at the Willard or the Madison hotel, over who spoke first at the podium, over who sat where on the dais, and so on. One black professor who felt neglected erupted, 'This event replicates the structures of oppression in American society.' Despite this distress, it was gratifying to see indications that the lives of many blacks in the United States have improved dramatically. People whose condition is economically and socially desperate do not fret over speaker schedules and hotel bookings. (pp. 201–2)

As this passage shows, his personal model of the event closely follows his general attitudes about the condition of black America: a successful black middle class which do not care about the black underclass, black people being 'conspicuous' with their wealth, and attributing all problems to racism, whereas the 'real' problem is the violence of the ghetto. Strategically aligning himself with Martin Luther King (a move of positive self-presentation), he sees the manifestation as a contradiction to what King and D'Souza favour: a 'race neutral society'. The description and the ironic and derogatory style of this story obviously define the event in terms that are consistent with this attitude about the black community. Prominent in that attitude is the rejection of racism as the main problem of black America, and an emphasis on violence and other 'pathologies' of the inner cities and of 'a second black America'. That is, not *our* failure (racism) but *their* failure (pathologies), are then explained in terms of an overall 'black culture' (p. 204). Such an overall classification ignores class division so that the whole black community can be blamed, as he also does in the passage just quoted. In other words, the ideologies of modern racism and cultural conservatism combined produce a mind-set that has such biased models as a result: D'Souza can only 'see' the events the way he describes them.

Discourse

Social representations and personal models control the style and content of text and talk. Let us therefore finally examine how D'Souza's ideologies and attitudes, as well as his personal views, impinge on the discourse of his book. Space limitations do not allow me to provide a detailed discourse analysis of a book of 724 pages, however, so I must limit myself to brief comments on some significant passages. Since ideologies about groups and cultures are involved, I shall focus on the well-known ideological square of *positive self-presentation and negative other-presentation*. Also, the analysis will be relatively informal so as to enhance its readability. Within the broader framework of a critical discourse analysis, I shall also occasionally formulate critical comments on D'Souza's book, but my aim is to illustrate the relations between ideologies, attitudes, models and actual discourse, rather than to denounce D'Souza's book or the ideologies that he represents.

Above, I have already given some text examples from D'Souza's book, and also briefly made some analytical remarks about them. Typical for a rhetorical book like this, which intends to contribute to an ongoing ideological debate, and which aims to sharply criticize the black community, are the various strategies that represent Us and Them. Thus, Our group as well as those with whom D'Souza identifies himself, namely, the West, Western civilization, Europe, white people, conservatives, and so on, are consistently described in positive terms, whereas any negative characteristics will be ignored or mitigated, whereas the others and especially African-Americans are consistently described in negative terms.

Derogating African-Americans

Thus black 'pathologies' are described in stark contrast to Us, and with the usual forms of hyperbole. Lexical choice, comparisons, metaphors and any other device that may be used to paint a negative picture of blacks will be used. Here are some examples, which I cite at length in order to get a good impression of D'Souza's discursive style (some repeating earlier quotes):

[22] . . . the hardened gleam in many Afrocentric eyes . . . virtually cultic pattern of lockstep behavior: everyone dresses alike, and when the leader laughs, everyone laughs. . . . (p. 381)

[23] . . . black racism is more explicitly menacing. (p. 421)

[24] Louis Farrakhan reportedly uses the profits to subsidize a lavish lifestyle which includes expensive silk suits and stretch limousine. (p. 426)

[25] The last few decades have witnessed nothing less than a breakdown of civilization within the African-American community. The breakdown is characterized by extremely high rates of criminal activity, by the normalization of illegitimacy, by the predominance of single-parent families, by high levels of addiction to alcohol and drugs, by a parasitic reliance on government provision, by a hostility to academic achievement, and by a scarcity of independent enterprises. (p. 477)

[26] The conspicuous pathologies of blacks are the product of catastrophic cultural change that poses a threat both to the African-American community and to society as a whole. (p. 478)

[27] Of course no one is to blame for being a victim. But if as a reaction to being victimized, a group develops dysfunctional or destructive patterns of behavior which perpetuate a vicious cycle of poverty, dependency, and violence, then continuing to inveigh against the oppressor cannot offer the victim much relief. (p. 482)

[28] Yet black culture also has a vicious, self-defeating, and repellent underside that it is no longer possible to ignore or euphemize. As more and more blacks seem to realize, no good is achieved by dressing these pathologies in sociological cant, complete with the familiar vocabulary of disadvantage and holding society to account. Society must do its part, and blacks must do theirs. But first, the magnitude of the civilizational crisis facing the black community must be recognized. This crisis points to deficiencies not of biology but of culture; yet they are deficiencies and they should be corrected. (p. 486)

[29] For them [middle class blacks], apparently, antiracist militancy is carried to the point of virtual mental instability. It is hard to imagine whites feeling secure working with such persons: surely such inflamed ethnic insensitivities are now what companies have in mind when they extol the diversity of work environments. Yet if these individuals are cranks, they are in respectable company. (p. 492)

[30] [Jobs?] Yet it seems unrealistic, bordering on the surreal, to imagine underclass blacks with their gold chains, limping walk, obscene language, and arsenal of weapons doing nine-to-five jobs at Procter and Gamble or the State Department. Many of these young men seem lacking in the most basic skills required for steady employment: punctuality, dependability, willingness to perform routine tasks, acceptance of authority. Moreover studies show that even when jobs are available, many young blacks refuse them, apparently on the grounds that the jobs don't pay enough or that crime is more profitable. (pp. 504–5)

[31] With some discomfort, we see that there is some truth to the historical stereotype of the black male stud, or, at least in the case of the black underclass, what used to be a stereotype now contains an ingredient of truth. (p. 517)

These passages give a representative impression of the various strategies of negative other-presentation employed by D'Souza. *Person descriptions* of black activists and Afrocentrists draw on familiar racist stereotypes about conspicuous dress and lavish lifestyles. Blacks are poor and so also their leaders should dress soberly, and at least not more conspicuously than 'we' do. Cultural difference is here interpreted as cultural deviance, if not as a lack of solidarity with the black underclass. And whereas the middle class is described as living conspicuously, underclass youths similarly are characterized in terms of the street counterpart of deviant conspicuousness (gold chains, limping walk, obscene language, etc.) (example 30), described in such a way as to legitimize that they are not being hired.

Thus, black young men from the 'underclass' are seen to violate all basic values of the conservative ideology: 'punctuality, dependability, willingness to perform routine tasks, acceptance of authority' (example 29). No wonder they get no jobs, and they are themselves to blame for it. Black individuality is denied when they are described as a mindless group following their leaders (as in example 22), behaviour that is inconsistent with the dominant white norm of individualism. If not seen as different and deviant, blacks and their rage are characterized as a threat (example 23). D'Souza's conclusion is to admit that these may be stereotypes (e.g. about the 'black male stud'), but then accepts the grain of truth hypothesis to prove he must be right about his generalizations (example 31). His analysis thus is reduced to creating the familiar racist stereotype of the 'bad nigger' (p. 524), who is portrayed as the 'menace of society'. For young black women, as we shall see in more detail below, the stereotype is similarly predictable: they have too many babies, at a too early age, are unmarried, and thus contribute to the 'bastardization' of America.

Social problems of the black ghetto are hyperbolically characterized in terms of a 'civilizational breakdown' (example 25) or as 'catastrophic cultural change' (example 26). Having to be on welfare is negatively represented and blamed on the victims by expressions such as 'parasitic reliance on government provision' (example 25). In other words, blacks are lazy parasites who live out of 'our' pockets. Being ill-prepared for university study because of bad schooling, is similarly blamed on blacks themselves, also in terms of aggression. Based on a few examples of some blacks who see such achievement as 'acting white', D'Souza concludes that (all?) blacks share a 'hostility to academic achievement'. Black behaviour is interpreted with formal style expressions such as 'dysfunctional' or less formally as 'destructive' (example 27), whereas black culture is said to have 'a vicious, self-defeating, and repellent underside'. Black people who have lost patience over everyday racism, and developed a standing rage against white-dominated institutions, are deemed to be 'mentally unstable' (example 29), so that whites seem to have a good reason not to want to hire 'such people'.

Black women

Black women constitute a special target for D'Souza's diagnosis of black 'pathology'. Their double jeopardy when it comes to discrimination and prejudices is clearly illustrated by D'Souza's derogatory discourse itself:

[32] Perhaps the most serious of African-American pathologies – no less serious than violence – is the routinization of illegitimacy as a way of life. The bastardization of black America is confirmed by the fact that nearly 70 percent of young black children born in the United States today are illegitimate, compared to 22 percent of white children. More than 50 percent of black households are headed by women. Almost 95 percent of black teen mothers are unmarried, compared to 55 percent of their white peers. (p. 515)

Note the usual hyperboles, here further emphasized by the phrase 'perhaps the most serious'. For outsiders of the conservative ideology, it may seem preposterous to assume that the phenomenon of mothers who decide not to marry has become a threat bigger than violence, and at the top of the list of the 'pathologies' D'Souza attributes to the African-American community. They might conclude that if *that* is the main problem facing the USA and

Western civilization, apparently D'Souza is incapable of sensible judgements about what the real social problems are that affect US and Western societies.

They might look at the figures and recall that many, also wealthy and prosperous societies (like the Scandinavian countries) have similar percentages of unmarried mothers, and that most of these mothers are doing very well, thank you. They might wonder about the functions in a book of the 1990s of old-fashioned terms such as 'illegitimate' and especially 'bastardization', other than to bluntly derogate, criminalize and marginalize black women and children.

Staying within the familiar 'number game' rhetoric, suggesting scientific credibility, more realistic observers might again look at the figures (assuming they are correct and not themselves very selectively framed, as is usual with statistics), and wonder about the fairly high percentages among *white* women. Do these also contribute to the 'bastardization' of the USA? And how come (as D'Souza does not say) that all these percentages, in most Western countries, are rising? Might there be a cultural change in family values that attaches less importance to being married, and are African-American (like Caribbean) families simply more advanced in this cultural change, for example, by attributing more value to the leading role of women?

Or they might ask about one of the other causes of one-parent families, not in the stereotypical terms of irresponsible black fathers who act like 'studs' (as D'Souza so delicately uses old racist stereotypes), but in terms of the broad social marginalization of poor black men in white America. D'Souza is even cynical when he openly legitimizes 'rational' discrimination of such young men.

Indeed, as is also clear in example 32, within the conservative framework of D'Souza's attitudes, racism and sexism are closely related. That such rhetoric is not altogether without effect may be concluded from recent decisions by local, state and national governments in the USA to dramatically reduce social welfare for poor families, a policy of which young black women will take the brunt. In this respect, D'Souza's book and its discourse is not merely an innocent conservative and racist-sexist diatribe against black women and men, or against liberals who prefer to deal with social problems as such and not as incriminating pathologies.

In the area of race relations, ideologies and their discourses, and even the details of their rhetoric, may be very dangerous. They may further marginalize millions of poor black women, children and men, driving them further into the 'pathologies' selectively and hyperbolically attributed to them especially in order to highlight white cultural supremacy.

It is not surprising that most African-Americans and many white liberals agree that this kind of 'respectable' racism of cultural conservatives is more insidious than the blatant irrational kind of the old days. They will agree with D'Souza on one point, namely, that racism is not an 'irrational antipathy'. His elite racism is, indeed, a deliberate, explicit and very rational attempt to inferiorize blacks and thus to exacerbate racial inequality in the USA.

In sum, middle- and lower-class blacks, women and men, are negatively portrayed lexically and rhetorically in terms of cultural deviance and threat, as violating norms and values of white America, in such a way that the 'civilizational breakdown' of their community is fully blamed on them. Where sober situation descriptions of social problems do not suffice, apocalyptic hyperboles about the 'breakdown of civilization' or 'catastrophic cultural change' are used. Metaphors are borrowed, as usually in such a case, from the domain of threatening animals or plants: blacks on welfare are parasites. D'Souza is aware of his negative style when admitting 'frankness' and when boldly stating that we can no longer 'euphemize' (example 28) our language, a familiar disclaimer when whites engage in derogatives against blacks.[5] We have earlier seen that although African-Americans are the main target of D'Souza's book, also other non-Europeans (except Asians) may share in accusations of barbarism, primitivism, threat, deviance or lacking civilization. Of course, in the contemporary world, Muslims are a preferred target:

[33] Muslims in the United States should be allowed to practice their religion but not to the point where it threatens the religious freedom of others, as through the practice of *jihad* against non-Muslims. (p. 548)

Thus, historically, the others were described as 'savages', and one would expect D'Souza to take some distance, but his own style is simply a contemporary continuation of the old style of racist ethnocentrism.

Of course if there are bad others, there must be good others that serve as the Good Example, and at the same time serve as evidence that 'we' are not racist. That role, in the USA, is now played by the Asians, who have become the model-minorities whose commercial and academic success is often used to shame African-Americans or Latinos. So much so, that since they often out-perform whites in universities, measures have been considered to *limit* their numbers, so as to give the poor whites a chance. Of course, D'Souza does not discuss such developments of reverse affirmative action. For him, Asians serve especially to marginalize blacks and to discredit the argument that discrimination is still a major factor in the situation of African-Americans:

[34] By proving that upward mobility and social acceptance do not depend on the absence of racially distinguishing features, Asians have unwittingly yet powerfully challenged the attribution of minority failure to discrimination by the majority. Many liberals are having trouble providing a full answer to the awkward question: 'Why can't an African-American be more like an Asian?'

This passage has several interesting presuppositions, such as that Asians actually *are* upwardly mobile, and that they *are* socially discriminated against like the blacks. Implicit is the argument that Asians and African-

Americans live in the same socio-economic circumstances, and have the same start position.

Interestingly, if whites are doing worse than Asians, the question might of course be raised about *white* pathologies that cause such a lag, and why also an Euro-American cannot be more like an Asian. Many other comparisons come to mind, such as why Americans cannot be more like Europeans when it comes to rights of workers and social provisions, and why despite such European 'pathologies', and despite Euro-racism, there are no ghettos in Europe comparable to those in the USA. In other words, liberals may have many more awkward questions than D'Souza will ever be able to answer. Probably the only sensible answer is the one he himself provides at the end of the book:

[35] No race has a monopoly on achievement. (p. 472)

If 'mixed' groups have significantly contributed to the economy and the culture of the world, as D'Souza claims, then one might wonder why he denies such a contribution to the typically 'mixed' African-Americans. In the full 724 pages of the book he does not once even try to assess such contributions. That is, he can only see African-Americans in light of his racist ideology.

Ideological enemies

Although his social enemies bear the brunt of his discursive attack, also his ideological enemies, the 'Boasian relativists' are not exactly described in positive terms, as may of course be expected from an enemy. First of all, their theories are derogated in terms of a 'deep rooted ideology' (p. 527), a description D'Souza hardly uses of his own ideas and those of fellow conservatives. And because the Boasians criticized 'American customs and mores' but refrained from criticizing other cultures, they are accused of using a 'double standard' (p. 155). Relativists have allegedly caused the 'contemporary crisis' and do not 'allow social progress', because they treat all cultures as equal. Relativists do not carry out research, and do not attach conclusions to their findings, but they 'dictate' their opinions:

[36] Cultural relativism dictates that non-Western cultures be considered victims of Western oppression: of colonialism, imperialism, racism, and so on. (p. 358)

In the same way, the relativists are seen as the source of the legal 'doctrine' of proportional representation, which implies that such representation for D'Souza is not a democratic 'right'. In a more hyperbolic way, the ideas of the others are not merely derogated as an 'ideology', but its adherents have a 'fanatical commitment' to such an ideology (p. 530). This lexical association with religious fundamentalism is further metaphorically emphasized by representing liberal ideas as the innocent lamb being butchered by the relativists: 'Fundamental liberal principles are being sacrificed at the altar of cultural relativism' (p. 530). And as we have seen, also the metaphor of threatening forms of life will typically be employed here:

[37] Relativism has become a kind of virus, attacking the immune systems of institutional legitimacy and public decency. (p. 532)

Apart from calling relativists 'dogmatic' as is normally the case for ideological opponents, another useful form of negative other-presentation is to represent the ideological enemy metaphorically as tricksters:

[38] Multicultural activists rely on the sleight-of-hand in which 'I cannot know' becomes 'I cannot judge' which becomes 'I know that we are all equal'. A skeptical confession of ignorance mysteriously becomes a dogmatic assertion of cultural egalitarianism. (p. 383)

In other words, such scholars are not scholars at all, but 'activists', who hide their ignorance behind ideological dogmatism in order to avoid judging others. Thus, relativists are routinely accused of being 'blind' to the facts, for example about alleged 'black racism' (p. 88). Obviously, since D'Souza does claim to know, he also has the right to judge about the black community, as his book amply shows. Such a rejection of liberal scholars may in fact extend to scholarship and academia in general, a well-known feature of US conservatives, as also has become obvious in the debate about multiculturalism and political correctness:

[39] . . . no good is achieved by dressing these pathologies in sociological cant, complete with the familiar vocabulary of disadvantage and holding society to account. (p. 486)

The derogatory label 'sociological cant', familiar also from tabloid reactions against anti-racist academics in the UK,[6] apart from expressing the conservative and anti-relativist attitudes of D'Souza, also may be interpreted as a move in a broader 'commonsense' strategy, in which ethnic relations and racism should rather be examined in populist terms (of course those of the conservatives). Sociologists might persuasively argue and prove that the conservative solutions offered by D'Souza will only exacerbate the social misery of many inner-city blacks, as neo-liberal policies elsewhere tend to exacerbate poverty, and make the rich richer. Or they might show (as they *have* done, but all those studies about modern racism are either ignored or rejected) that racism is still prevalent in the USA, and that it is still a major factor in explaining the many social and economic gaps between black and white.[7]

No wonder that such sociologists are simply dismissed by D'Souza. Their insights might be dangerous for his conservative analysis of the situation, as is the case for a book by Joe Feagin and Melvin Sikes, *Living with Racism*: the authors, who are not called 'distinguished scholars' or simply 'sociologists', but 'activist scholars' (p. 491). Thus, any serious evidence of everyday racism is simply marginalized or ignored and negatively presented by derogating their authors as 'activists', and hence as not being 'objective'.

The same is true for those black professionals whose experiences with everyday racism are presented in Feagin and Sikes's book. The powerless rage and discourse of these black women and men are clinically diagnosed by D'Souza as a form of 'mental instability' (p. 492), another well-known strategy to problematize and marginalize the others. Thus, D'Souza brings to bear all discursive devices to ward off any inconsistencies with his claim that racism in the USA is no longer a problem. Thus, prominent black scholars who are not members of his league of conservative blacks, may simply be ridiculed, as we have seen before, as is the case for Cornell West, whose

> [40] solutions are a quixotic combination of watered-down Marxism, radical feminism, and homosexual rights advocacy, none of which offers any realistic hope for ameliorating black pathologies. (p. 520)

One needs few explicit discourse theories to analyse the derogatory labels of such a passage, and inferring who the various bad others are in D'Souza's universe. Ironically, when blacks *do* make it in white America, and become prominent professors, they still do not seem to escape the 'pathologies' diagnosed by D'Souza, unless of course they espouse, as some do, D'Souza's ideology. His condemnation of the African-American community, thus, is one of principle, and not one of fact or generally shared criteria.

This, then, is the hallmark of the conservative and racist ideologies promoted by D'Souza, by whose standards blacks (with some window-dressing exceptions) are inferior, whether they are poor mothers in the ghetto, or prominent scholars at Princeton, especially when they write books, as West did, aptly called *Race Matters*. Indeed, many passages of D'Souza's book about the 'inferiority' of blacks show how valid are conclusions like those of West, as is the case in the following combination of the metaphors of 'incantation' and 'demons' intended to ridicule scholars and to deny racism:

> [41] The charge of racism becomes a kind of incantation intended to ward off the demons of black inferiority. (p. 529)

The most fatal accusation levelled against scholars is that their relativism 'ends up denying the possibility of truth' (p. 384), a truth which of course D'Souza claims to uncover in his book. Since relativists have been shown to be 'blind' about black racism, D'Souza sees it as his task to enlighten his readers about what he does see. The others, relativists and black intellectuals, are thus accused of 'moral paralysis' (p. 520). This example also shows the close relation between group ideologies and the self-attribution of truth in social representations, as well as the relation between ideology, truth and the moral order.

Thus, D'Souza sums up the derogation of his ideological enemies by accusing them of condoning if not promoting 'barbarism', and hence of being enemies of the nation, if not beyond the pale of Western civilization in general:

> [42] By refusing to acknowledge that one culture is better than another – by erasing the distinction between barbarism and civilization – cultural relativism cruelly inhibits the nation from identifying and working to ameliorate pathologies that are destroying the life chances of millions of African-Americans. (p. 528)

Of course, the apparent empathy expressed by the phrase 'the life chances of millions of African-Americans' is merely a device of impression management of the harsh racist ideology underlying such passages, namely, that of white cultural supremacy.

Positive self-presentation

Contrary to this apocalyptic picture of blacks and their culture, as well as all other others, the description of Us, whites, Western civilization, European explorers, and even racist scientists, is squarely positive or mitigated, when they are obviously engaged in loathsome action. Early racism itself is described as 'a scientific ideology to explain large differences in civilizational development that could not be explained by environment' (p. 22) and thus given at least some scientific legitimacy, as also the descriptors 'leading scientists' and 'progressive thinkers' (p. 120) suggest. Ethnocentrism is merely an 'intense preference for one's own group' (p. 35). Of Western technology spreading over the world, only the positive 'comforts' and a 'cosmopolitan awareness' are mentioned, and not a single of the negative consequences.

That such a positive evaluation is not limited to historical racism but still applies today may also be seen in the many ways present forms of racism or ethnocentrism are euphemized, mitigated, excused or explained away, if not plainly denied:

> [43] . . . it is entirely possible that prejudices might be prudent, stereotypes may contain elements of truth, and racial discrimination may be warranted under some circumstances. (p. 120)

That is, except when used in connection with 'black racism', such 'white racism' (a term seldom used by D'Souza, of course), is consistently being put between quotes, or in accusatory contexts, except in its extremist, irrational forms (largely deemed to be occurring only in the past). Racism, thus, becomes something the others 'invent' (p. 238) or that is 'imaginary'. If recognized at all, it is mitigated, relegated to the past or rationalized as 'natural' ethnocentric 'preference for one's own group'. Or in more scholarly terms it can be denied by claiming that 'It is impossible to answer the question of how much racism exists in the United States because nobody knows how to measure racism and no unit exists for calibrating such measurements' (p. 276). Such scientific style merely functions to impress or persuade those who have no knowledge of scholarly studies of racism.

The denial or mitigation of racism, thus, not only serves within the strategy of positive self-presentation, but at the same time may be used, by turning the accusation around, to blame the blacks, as in the following passage, which deserves to be quoted in full, and analysed in some more detail, because it expresses many of the beliefs of D'Souza about racism:

> [44] Sometimes racism is all too real, but it is bad enough to endure real racism without having to suffer imaginary racism as well. Racism has become the opiate of many middle-class blacks. For society, promiscuous charges of racism are

dangerous because they undermine the credibility of the charge and make it more difficult to identify real racists. For blacks, the risk of exaggerated and false charges of racism is that they divert attention from the possibilities of the present and the future. Excessive charges of racism set up a battle with an adversary who sometimes does not exist. . . . Once again, racism becomes the culprit, now accused of having taken an even subtler and more insidious shape. (p. 487)

This passage begins with a familiar strategic move of positive self-presentation, namely, a so-called apparent concession. This concession is apparent because in the rest of the passage, and the rest of the book, hardly any white racism is being detailed. Secondly, 'it is bad enough . . .', is another move, this time of apparent empathy, which I call 'apparent' because D'Souza's book is not at all empathetic with the victims of racism. Both moves here serve as introductions to the reversal, which is introduced with the claim that blacks not only imagine racism but that it even serves the interests of the black middle class. Thus, the victims of racism are not just blamed for it, they are even accused of enjoying it, as the use of the metaphor of addiction ('opiate') shows, a charge that is of course consistent with the dominant prejudice about blacks as selling or being 'on drugs'.

In the next sentence, another dimension of black 'pathologies' is expressed, namely, the well-known element of 'threat' to society. The same sentence further emphasizes ('promiscuous') the well-known counter-accusation that racism is only in the mind of the accusers. Note that 'promiscuous' here ties in with the other 'pathology' of the black commu-nity, and of black women in particular, namely, sexual promiscuity. Having conceded 'some' racism, it needs to be identified, and so it is attributed to the 'real racists', who were earlier defined as those who believe in biological racial superiority and 'irrationally' discriminate blacks. Such usage implies, of course, that most of white society is *not* racist, as the underlying attitude has shown.

Similarly, where racism is denied, mitigated or safely attributed to 'real racists' (a move that may be called blame transfer, which is typical for elite racism), the opposite is true for the accusations of racism, which are called 'excessive', thus enhancing the contrast between Us and Them. The 'imagi-nary' nature of racism is further emphasized by accusing blacks of paranoia, of imagining non-existent adversaries, thus bringing failing mental health into the picture, as we have seen earlier, for those whose 'rage' cannot be understood. Finally, this passage ridicules the accusation that modern racism is more subtle and insidious than the old one, and thus also rejects that charge. In sum, D'Souza uses several discursive devices to persuasively formulate his attitude about racism, and these devices all background white racism and foreground black pathologies (imagining things, the use of an opiate, excessiveness, paranoia).

Whereas throughout the book, thus, the rosy picture of Western Civiliza-tion, including the abolition of slavery ('Abolition constitutes one of the greatest moral achievements of Western civilization', p. 112), is highlighted, not a single word is used to describe the negative dimension of Our culture.

Slavery? No, that was not our invention. Moreover, D'Souza claims, 'the American slave *was* treated like property, which is to say, pretty well' (p. 91). And in any case, slavery can't be blamed anymore for black 'pathologies' today. Colonialism? No, because colonialism only brought progress and put an end to barbarism and primitiveness, it was a 'bold intellectual enterprise to dispel ignorance' (p. 121).

Only sometimes do we find a very tentative disclaimer about Our failure, for example as in the following (duly euphemized) apparent concession about 'mixed motives':

[45] Whatever their shortcomings and mixed motives, the Europeans who voyaged abroad were the historical instruments of a major world transformation. (p. 49)

In other passages, we find plain denials, sometimes accompanied by a complete reversal of the charge, as in example 38:

[46] These Europeans did not approach Asia, Africa and the Americas with hostile intentions. (p. 48)

[47] What distinguished Western colonialism was neither occupation nor brutality but a countervailing philosophy of rights that is unique in human history. (p. 354)

Thus, our Western civilization is described in terms of 'powerful ideas' and 'progress' (p. 50), as 'moving ahead' while 'other groups' are portrayed as 'stagnant', thus rhetorically enhancing the contrast between Us and Them. Of course, describing Our culture in such terms generates a bit of uneasiness, but there is a strategy to deal with that, namely, to blame the others for not doing the same:

[48] Since contemporary scholars do not like to think of cultures as superior or inferior, advanced or backward, the very subjects of primitivism and progress, development and underdevelopment, frequently generate discomfort and even indignation. (p. 55)

No words, of course, about other highlights of Our culture, such as the Holocaust, or pollution, or world wars, or the atom bomb, to name only a few. Thus, the underlying ideology of Western supremacy also shows in the one-dimensional attitudes and finally in the lexical and rhetorical forms of selectively positive or euphemistic self-descriptions. The contrast with the black 'barbarians' could not be greater, as the polarized structure of inter-group ideologies predicts.

Conclusions

The aim of our partial analysis of some passages of D'Souza's book *The End of Racism* is to see ideologies at work. I examined some of their propositional contents, their structures, and how they control specific attitudes about a number of issues. Finally, I showed how such underlying social representations also control many properties of discourse.

The analysis has shown how a specific ideological text of an individual author combines influences from several ideologies, within a broader framework of cultural conservatism. Thus, we find a combination of ethnocentric, racist, sexist, anti-relativist and neo-liberal ideologies in the construction of complex attitudes about African-Americans, racism and anti-racism, multiculturalism and Afrocentrism and other attitudes. The conservative framework and its propositions and underlying values assign coherence to these attitudes and show how they are mutually related. Ideological polarization has been shown for the representation of blacks and whites, barbarians and the civilized, realists and relativists, Us and Them. Ideological schemata organize such propositions in terms of what They are, what they typically (if not stereotypically) do, what their aims and values are, how Us and Them are related (namely, as superior and inferior) or what their resources are.

A succinct and informal discourse analysis has further detailed this overall ideological analysis, and highlighted the social and political functions of this text, and how its discursive devices are tuned to the persuasive communication of the ideology of modern racism. Group polarization is thus expressed and enhanced by a series of well-known devices that emphasize how bad They are and how good We are, or that mitigate their success and our failures. Overall, derogatory lexical style, rhetorical devices (such as metaphor and hyperbole), local semantic moves of denial and apparent concession, the rhetoric of factuality by the use of (selective) statistics, and many other features of this text can be described and explained on the basis of the underlying ideologies and prejudiced attitudes.

It was concluded that such racist ideologies and the discourses that convey or reinforce them are not merely academic exercises nor food for media debates. They explicitly formulate and propose harsh social policies. They are read by influential conservative politicians and other elites, eagerly accepted as a scientific legitimation of racial bigotry, prejudice and the marginalization of blacks, and actually used as the basis for racist policies that contribute to ethnic and racial inequality in the USA.

29

Conclusions

Instead of a lengthy discussion of the findings of this theoretical study, I shall merely list its major conclusions in the form of brief statements.

General

1 Within the vast field of the study of ideology, a *multidisciplinary theory* is needed to account for the nature, the structures and the functions of ideology.

2 In this study, this multidisciplinary approach is represented by an analysis of ideology in terms of the 'triangle' of (social) *cognition, society* and *discourse*. This complex disciplinary basis is necessary to avoid reduction. Especially lacking in earlier work is insight into the socio-cognitive nature and functions of ideologies, and how these are related to their expression and reproduction in discourse.

3 Many of the traditional approaches to ideology are rather of a *philosophical* than of a systematic, analytical and theoretical nature. The confused and often vague nature of traditional ideology studies is also due to the repetition and uncritical acceptance of a number of standard concepts of studies of ideology in the past. A typical example is the notion of 'false consciousness'. Perhaps the most promising work on ideology is currently especially done in the study of political cognition and social representations.

4 In a general and abstract sense, ideologies are conceived of as the *interface* between fundamental properties (e.g. interests, goals) of social groups and the shared, social cognitions of their members.

5 Compared with commonsense and traditional Marxist or other socio-political definitions, ideologies are here defined in a *general, non-pejorative* sense (and not necessarily as false, or distorted ideas).

Socio-cognitive analysis of ideologies

6 The cognitive analysis of ideologies does *not* imply that ideologies are individual or only mental. They are *both* mental and social, and also their mental properties are socially acquired, shared and changed.

7 Ideologies are most generally defined as *systems of beliefs*, especially in political psychology. However, it was argued that there are many types of

belief, many of which are not 'ideological'. So, a theory of ideology needs to focus on specific, ideological beliefs.

8   The traditional distinction between episodic and semantic memory is used to distinguish between *personal beliefs*, on the one hand, and *social beliefs* or *social representations*, on the other hand. Ideologies are of the latter kind, and hence first (and as yet incompletely) defined as *shared, social beliefs of (specific) social groups*.

9   Since on the other hand there are also several types of socially shared beliefs (knowledge, attitudes, norms, values, etc.) some of which are not ideological, it is further proposed that ideologies are the *general, abstract beliefs* that underlie (other) social representations. In that respect, they are like the basic *axioms* of the system of social representations shared by a group.

10   Ideologies are not arbitrary lists of propositions, but organized by specific social *categories* that constitute an *ideology-schema*, such as Membership, Activities, Goals, Values, Position or Resources. These categories are the cognitive (re)construction of the basic social criteria for groups. Cognitively, this schema functions also as the *self-schema* of the group, defining its *social identity* and *interests*.

11   Ideologies also may have other structural characteristics, such as those of group *polarization* (Us versus Them).

12   Ideologies are the basic social beliefs of specific groups, but themselves rooted in the general beliefs (knowledge, opinions, values, truth criteria, etc.) of whole societies or *cultures*. This allows the very understanding, communication and interaction between (members of) different groups.

13   Ideologies, as *social* representations, are generally assumed to be at least coherent. Such coherence explains the frequently observed coherence and continuity of ideological opinions, practices and discourses among different social members and in different situations.

14   Ideological coherence does *not* imply that ideologies are always *used* coherently by group members. That is, the equally frequently observed *variability* of discourse or social practices monitored by ideologies, is not due to lacking ideologies or incoherent ideologies, but by several other factors, such as the interaction of several ideologies (and group memberships) for social members, personal experiences, and the constraints of the situation.

15   Ideologies are coherent and complex only at the group level for which they are defined. Depending on their social position and socialization, different (sub)groups of social members (e.g. the ideologues) may have different *ideological expertise*.

16   The main *cognitive function* of ideologies is to organize the social representations of a group. Indirectly, that is, through more specific, domain-relevant, attitudes and knowledge they thus monitor social and personal beliefs and ultimately the social practices and discourse based on the latter.

17   Attitudes are here defined as socially shared complexes of the shared opinions of social groups, and are carefully distinguished from *personal opinions*.

18   A distinction is also made between *factual beliefs* (true or false knowledge) and *evaluative beliefs* (opinions, attitudes, ideologies) which are based on the application of socio-cultural values.

19   The well-known problem of the relation between social *knowledge* and *ideology* was resolved by making a distinction between (historically variable) cultural knowledge that serves as a 'common ground' for all (competent) members, on the one hand, and the specific knowledge of a group (which may be called 'opinions' by members of other groups). It is the latter kind of group knowledge that may be ideologically controlled. Group knowledge may sometimes become general cultural knowledge and vice versa.

20   Although ideologies may thus also control group knowledge, they especially monitor the shared *evaluative beliefs* (opinions) of a group. They are the basis of the *social judgements* of groups and their members.

21   Ideologies are *not* defined as wrong, misguided, false, or distorted beliefs of a group. Epistemically, whatever their truth status for the group itself, they may be true or false. It is not their truth value, but their cognitive and social role (e.g. effectiveness, usefulness) in the management of thinking and interaction that is the criterion for their evaluation.

22   The socio-cognitive notions introduced above explain more analytically such notions as ideas, beliefs, (false) consciousness, common sense, in traditional studies of ideology.

23   In order to explain how socially shared representations in general, and ideologies in particular, can be related to personal cognitions (and then to discourse), the notion of mental *model* is used, for example to account for the *subjectivity* of personal experiences, interpretations and representations of discourse and action and the representation of contexts.

24   Models are the *interface* between the social and the personal, between the general and the specific, between the macro and the micro. They apply or instantiate socially shared information (knowledge, attitudes, ideologies) in relation to self, to current situations, tasks, problems, actions and discourse. Conversely, they are the experiential basis for the generalization of personal beliefs to social knowledge, attitudes and ideologies.

25   Models embody personal and applied social beliefs, and thus, indirectly, ideologies. It is through *ideologically controlled models* that ideological social practices and discourse can be produced by social members.

Social analysis of ideologies

26   Ideologies are by definition *social*; they are socially shared by groups. They are only individual in their *personal*, contextual *uses*, applications or implementations by individual social members. In that respect they are like language systems (or grammars, or discourse rules).

27   Ideologies are not generally social or cultural, but defined for specific social *groups*. Not all collectivities of people form such groups, but only those collectivities that satisfy a number of group-criteria, such as (more or less continuous, permanent and organized) membership conditions, joint activities, interaction, goals, norms and values, a specific position in society and social resources, and especially shared social representations. These precisely map onto the cognitive structures of shared ideologies. Thus, groups constitute ideologies (and hence social identity) just as much as ideologies constitute groups.

28   The *social functions* of ideologies are tied to these properties of groups. They represent group identity and interests, define group cohesion and solidarity, and organize joint actions and interactions that optimally realize group goals. That is, ideologies resolve the fundamental problem of social and interactional *co-ordination*, namely, that, despite personal and contextual variation, individual social actors are generally able to act *as* group members, and often in the interest of the group as a whole.

29   Ideologies are especially relevant for the management of *social group relations*, such as those of domination and conflict, but also those of competition and co-operation. It is in this respect that ideologies may function as legitimation of power abuse and inequality, on the one hand, and as a basis for resistance, challenge, dissidence and change on the other hand.

30   Given the definition of ideology in terms of social groups, they are *not* limited to dominant groups. Such would unduly restrict the notion and make it theoretically much less interesting. For one thing, it would prevent an ideological analysis of dominated groups and practices of resistance.

31   Because of their preferential access to, and control over, public discourse, and especially of the media and education, various *elites* have a special role in the formulation and reproduction of ideologies. Although ideological reproduction is both top-down and bottom-up, this suggests that a relatively small number of 'symbolic' elites (writers, thinkers, politicians, scholars, journalists, etc.) may exercise the special role of ideological leaders, who preformulate and stimulate ideological debate.

32   The effective reproduction and implementation of group ideologies often requires *organization* and *institutionalization*, typically so by ideological institutions such as those of politics, the media and education.

Ideologies and discourse

33   As described above, social group ideologies *indirectly* (and hence non-deterministically) monitor *social practices* in general, and *discourse* in particular, via social beliefs (knowledge, attitudes) and personal beliefs (models).

34   Discourse has a *special function* in the expression, implementation and especially the reproduction of ideologies, since it is only through

language use, discourse or communication (or other semiotic practices) that they can be explicitly formulated. This is essential in contexts of acquisition, argumentation, ideological conflict, persuasion and other processes in the formation and change of ideologies.

35 Despite the fundamental role of discourse in the expression and reproduction of ideologies, *ideologies cannot be reduced to discourse*. That is, they should not be defined as statements, and their nature and structure should not be identified with the structures of text or talk. An analytical distinction should be made between ideologies as general, abstract, socio-cognitive (mental) representations shared by a group, on the one hand, and the specific, personal, interactional, contextualized uses of the ideology in specific social situations by individual social members, on the other hand. Indeed, if ideologies were to be reduced to (or identified with) discourse, it would be impossible to explain how they can influence other social practices.

36 An analysis of the discursive expression and reproduction of ideologies requires a *detailed, systematic account* of the various levels, structures, units and strategies of text and talk, defined as communicative events. Such an analysis should not, as was traditionally often the case, be limited to a vague study of the 'production of meaning'. Besides complex semantic analysis of various types of meaning, also explicit other theories are needed to account for these discourse structures and how they may express underlying ideological contents and structures, for example, phonological, graphical, syntactic, lexical, stylistic, rhetorical, schematic (e.g. argumentative, narrative), pragmatic and conversational structures.

37 Besides an account of the levels and structures of text and talk, discourse analysis also provides a detailed analysis of the many properties of the *context*, defined as the discourse-relevant structures of the social situation. Context influences discourse 'uses' (production and comprehension) through subjective mental models of language users, that is, through *context models*.

38 *Ideological discourse production* is a complex social and cognitive process in which underlying mental models are mapped on discourse structures – for example, mental models of events map on to semantic structures, and mental models of context on to the large number of variable discourse structures (forms, expressions, schemata, etc.). Context models exercise the overall control of such discourse production and ensure that discourses are socially (or indeed, ideologically) *appropriate* in the social situation.

39 Ideologically based mental models as well as more general social representations may thus be expressed or signalled at all levels of discourse structure, that is, forms, meanings and actions. The overall strategy hereby is in line with ideological polarization and other structures, such as self-serving *positive self-presentation* and *negative other-presentation*.

40 This overall strategy may be implemented by a *large variety of forms and meanings* that emphasize (or mitigate) positive (or negative) properties

of the ingroup and the outgroup, respectively, for example through intonation, stress, volume, clause structure (transactivity: e.g. actives and passives), lexical selection, implicitness, presuppositions, local coherence, overall topics, rhetorical devices (e.g. metaphors), schematic organization (argumentation, fallacies), the selection of speech acts, and conversational and interactional management (e.g. of politeness).

41   Conversely, in *discourse comprehension* and *persuasion*, these various discourse structures may in turn be used to influence the formation, the contents and structures of mental models and, often indirectly, of social representations and hence of ideologies. These strategies are generally tuned to the formation or change of preferred models or their structures, again under the general constraints of positive self-presentation and negative other-presentation strategies.

42   However, *ideological influence* and reproduction are not merely a function of discourse structures but also of the social context (or rather of context models), and of the (other) mental representations of the recipients, such as existing ideologies, attitudes, knowledge, models of experience, current goals and personal interests, and so on. This means that ideological influence may not always have the intended effects. Despite their group membership, and the powerful influence of social representations, social actors are in principle autonomous individuals, and hence largely in control of their opinion formation and change, for example as a function of personal interests, goals and wishes. Ideological influence, and hence reproduction, will hence be most successful if ideologies are consistent with personal experiences (models), if social actors have no (better) alternatives than the proposed ideologically based models for their opinions and actions, or if they can be manipulated to believe and prefer (misguided) information ('facts', opinions) even if it is not in their best interests.

43   A sample analysis of a book about race relations in the USA shows (a) that social attitudes, personal opinions, event models and discourse may exhibit an interaction between various ideologies, (b) that conservatism is rather a 'meta-ideology' than an ideology, (c) how social groups (Us and Them) are represented in attitudes and discourse, (d) how at many levels of text and by many devices ingroups are presented positively and outgroups presented negatively, and (e) how ideological discourse is (made) sociopolitically relevant in times of (real of imaginary) social crisis, as a means to confirm group dominance and to legitimate inequality.

Limitations and prospects

The outline of the theory of ideology presented in this book and summarized above is just that: an outline. Yet, it tries to offer a comprehensive framework for detailed theoretical and empirical studies of ideology.

As suggested, such studies need to be multidisciplinary. One of the main limitations of traditional studies was that they ignored systematic and analytical insights from other theories and disciplines. Indeed, I have shown that the cognitive and especially the discursive dimensions of the theories were hardly developed.

This meant that the classical, socio-economic approach could only be formulated in very general, abstract and often vague terms. Ideologies empirically only 'show' in social interaction and discourse, as well as in their organizational and institutional structures, and hence they need to be empirically studied at those levels.

Moreover, a social explanation of ideological interaction and discourse is unable to relate social structure to interaction and discourse structure, and needs a cognitive interface. This cognitive interface, however, cannot simply and vaguely be identified with 'belief systems'. We need a much more detailed analysis of mental representations and mental strategies in order to understand how ideologies relate to social practices, and to discourse, and how they are thus reproduced.

I have tried to elaborate a theory that establishes these various relations. Obviously, many elements of the theory are not yet fully worked out. For instance, given the predominant social nature of traditional studies, I have only paid attention to some aspects of the role of social interaction and social structure in the formation, functions and reproduction of ideologies. I have assumed that ideologies are by definition group-based. However, we need to spell out in more detail under what conditions groups develop ideologies, and indeed how ideological groups are formed. We need to pay much more attention to the organizational and institutional dimensions of ideologies and the ways they function and are reproduced in society. Ideological conflicts need to be analysed in detail in order to understand the role of ideologies in such conflicts.

Similarly, despite the relative detail provided for some of the cognitive aspects of ideologies, there are many blank spots on the mental map of the structures, contents, organization and functions of ideologies. We have provisionally assumed an ideological schema based on social group self-schemata, but such a schema may be too specific, and not adequate for more general and 'universalist' ideologies (such as religions and complex political ideologies). We need to know much more about the ideological control of the (structures) of other social representations, such as attitudes and knowledge. We only have tentative ideas about the relations between (personal, subjective) models of experience, and the socially shared representations of the group. Indeed, how and under what conditions are mental representations personal, and when are they socially 'shared' or 'known' in the first place? We know as yet very little about the internal organization of mental models and how they embody (ideologically based or other) knowledge and opinions. And finally, we have only vague ideas about the precise relations between models and social representations on the one hand, and discourse structures or social practices on the other hand.

Finally, only a beginning has been made to an explicit analysis of those structures of text and talk that systematically express, convey, signal, communicate or influence underlying ideologies. Although in principle all or most discourse structures may be so used, it may very well be that some do so more typically or more effectively. Much empirical work will be needed to show how some groups use (and abuse) discourse in very specific ways. Indeed, what kind of ideological discourse is typical for what groups, what are its properties, and how is it in turn socially and institutionally embedded? How are ideologies discursively expressed and reproduced in such important social domains as politics, the media and education?

In sum, there are many more questions left open than answered in this book. It should therefore rather be seen as a sketch for a research programme than as a complete theory of ideology. As strongly suggested, such a research programme can only be carried out successfully if scholars from different disciplines (and knowledge about each other's theories and concepts) combine to elaborate the theoretical and empirical details. The development of a fully fledged theory of ideology cannot be left only to psychologists, or only to social scientists, or only to discourse analysts, or, indeed, only to philosophers.

Notes

Chapter 1

1 Indeed, few scholars today would claim to practise a 'science of ideas', although there are some who come close, such as French sociologist (philosopher, etc.) Edgar Morin, whose four-volume sequence *La méthode*, ends with a book on *Les idées: leur habitat, leur vie, leur moeurs, leur organisation*, in which also the 'organization of ideas' (the object of the discipline of 'noology') is studied (Morin, 1991). Of course, there are historical antecedents here, for example, in phenomenology, such as Husserl's book *Ideas* (Husserl, 1962).

2 Indeed, most studies of ideology in philosophy and the social sciences have a prominent historical dimension. This is less the case for work on ideology in psychology, anthropology and linguistics, which in general are less historically oriented. Since many of these studies will be referred to more specifically in the next chapters, we here only mention the most prominent books that provide such a historical background: Abercrombie et al. (1980, 1990); Billig (1982); CCCS (1978); Eagleton (1991); Freeden (1996); Kinloch (1981); Larrain (1979); Manning (1980); Meszaros (1989); Rosenberg (1988); Rossi-Landi (1978); Seliger (1976, 1979); Skidmore (1993); Thompson (1984, 1990); Zeitlin (1994).

3 For a review of this 'restrictive' concept of ideology, see especially Seliger (1979), who critically discusses the work of Bell (1960), Lipset (1960, 1972), Sartori (1966, 1969) and Shils (1958), among others. See also the critical comments of Geertz (1973) on the pejorative use of the concept of ideology.

4 See Marx and Engels (1974).

5 For a discussion of these contemporary changes in the theory of the relations between superstructure and infrastructure, see, for example Wuthnow (1992).

6 A particularly interesting collection of studies documenting this evolution of European neo-Marxism within British cultural studies, and especially within the work of Stuart Hall, may be found in Morley and Chen (1996).

7 One major study that advocates such a more inclusive concept of ideology, and one of the few systematically theoretical approaches to ideology, is that of Seliger (1979), who defines ideology as a 'group of beliefs and disbeliefs expressed in value sentences, appeal sentences and explanatory statements'. These sentences may refer to moral and technical norms, and express views that relate to human relationships and socio-political organization. Such an ideology may legitimate 'concerted action for the preservation, reform, destruction or reconstruction of a given order' (Seliger, 1979: 119–20). Many of these contemporary debates have their roots in the detailed theoretical analysis of Karl Mannheim's *Ideology and Utopia* (1936), which also discusses the distinction between evaluative and non-evaluative ideologies. Also Mannheim thus emphasizes the role of ideologies in the context of the 'collective action' of diversely organized groups.

8 For discussion on such political belief systems, see Chapter 2, and Chapter 2, Note 8, for references.

9 See, for example, Rosenberg (1988) for such a psychological (Piagetian) approach to ideology. See also the references in the next chapters.

10 Of course, as also Geertz (1973) points out, ideologies are not always rooted in, or devised in order to legitimate, interests and power. They may also be a response to social problems and contradictions ('strains') as lived and experienced by social members. At the same time, the analysis in this book responds to a critical conclusion of Geertz that both

approaches are indequate while failing to formulate in detail how 'the trick is really done', that is, how exactly interests are related to ideology, and how social contradictions are 'symbolically expressed': 'Both interest theory and strain theory go directly from source analysis to consequence analysis without ever seriously examining ideologies as systems of interacting symbols, as patterns of interworking meanings' (Geertz, 1973: 207).

11 One example of a recent text in which ideologies (of contemporary movements) are simply defined as 'discourses' is Garner (1996: 15).

12 Note that 'social cognition' in this book is *not* used (only) in the restrictive sense of the information-processing approach, prevalent especially in the USA to the study of the social mind (for survey, see, e.g., Fiske and Taylor, 1991), in opposition to the various European approaches in social psychology, for instance on social identity, social categorization or social representations (see, e.g., Farr and Moscovici, 1984; Tajfel, 1981; Spears et al., 1997). Rather, I advocate an integration of these two approaches. For discussion and further references see the chapters in Part I.

13 Such ideologies of opposition or resistance may of course be given a different name. Thus, for instance Mannheim (1936) distinguished ideologies and utopias, the latter being belief systems 'for a better world' which we also will call ideologies.

14 This position, currently formulated especially within the framework of Critical Discourse Analysis (CDA), has been explained in more detail in van Dijk (1993b). See also Fairclough (1995), Wodak (1989, 1996).

15 For a discussion of the current relevance of Critical Theory and its relations to ideology, see, for example, Agger (1991, 1992); Bailey (1994); Rasmussen (1996). For a discussion of this critical study of ideologies and social inequality in the 'postmodern' world, see Simons and Billig (1994). See also Larrain (1994) and Morley and Chen (1996) for a discussion of the postmodern critique of ideology. See Ibáñez and Íñiguez (1997) for a collection of work in critical social psychology. Note though that the term 'critical' in these various studies has rather divergent meanings and applications.

16 This does not mean, of course, that there is no earlier work on racist ideologies, but only that there is as yet no work on racist ideologies that uses the framework proposed here. See, for example, Note 6 of Chapter 19, for scientific ideologies of race. For the relations between discourse and racist ideologies, see, for example, van Dijk (1984, 1987); Wodak et al. (1990), and references in various later chapters.

Chapter 2

1 One of the (vast) areas of research that will be largely ignored in this book is that of the 'history of ideas', and related fields of historical inquiry, such as the study of 'mentalities'. See, for example, Lerner (1991).

2 The mind-body debate keeps haunting cognitive science, if only as a pseudo-problem. For recent discussion, see, for example, Warner and Szubka (1994). Interestingly, most psychologists simply ignore the question about the 'existence' of the mind, and go about their everyday business of describing and explaining psychological phenomena with the tacit assumption that minds do exist. The ongoing debate, especially among philosophers and neuroscientists mainly involves the relations between mind and brain. See, among many other contemporary studies: Clancey et al. (1994); Kosslyn and Koenig (1992); Pinker (1994); Searle (1992, 1995).

3 For an explicit social-developmental (Piagetian) approach to ideology, see Rosenberg (1988).

4 Such 'interactionism' may be found in certain directions of research in ethnomethodology and discursive psychology, in which the (socially) 'real' things we need to deal with are interaction and discourse. That is, whatever 'mental' things may exist, they are relevant only through their expression or formulation in social practices, text and talk (Coulter, 1979, 1983, 1989; Edwards, 1997; Edwards and Potter, 1992; Harré, 1995; Harré and Stearns, 1995; Potter and Wetherell, 1987). See also the critique of (mental) 'representationalism' in Shanon (1993).

These directions of research deserve detailed analysis, which is, however, beyond the scope of this book. I hope to return to this issue in a future publication. As is shown in this section of the book, I recognize the relevance of a proper cognitive analysis, but agree with the discursive psychologists that discourse and interaction play a fundamental role in the acquisition and the structures of 'mental' phenomena, such as knowledge and ideologies. Also, I fully agree with them that most of traditional social psychology and of course most cognitive psychology has ignored the relevance of the influence of social structures in psychological studies.

5 The nature of beliefs and their relation to knowledge continues to be discussed mainly in epistemology, and much less in psychology itself, as is often the case for such fundamental notions. See, for example, Kornblith (1994); Lehrer (1990). We shall later come back to the discussion of belief systems in social and political psychology.

6 For a review of discussions on the nature of emotion, see, for example, Frijda (1987); Ortony et al. (1988).

7 For classical and recent studies that define our current thinking on mind and memory, see (among many other books), Ashcraft (1994); Barsalou (1992); Cohen et al. (1993); Kintsch (1977); Neisser (1982); Solomon et al. (1989); Tulving (1983).

8 Many cognitive approaches to memory and beliefs (see Notes 5 and 7) assume such a network representation, even when they (also) use propositions for practical purposes of description. A more recent, neurologically inspired reformulation of the network idea may be found in connectionist cognitive psychology (McClelland and Rumelhart, 1986; Rumelhart and McClelland, 1986). Here the linear processing metaphor of classical computers is replaced by the parallel processing metaphor of 'neuro-computers'.

9 The question of basic beliefs is here related to that of 'basic acts', which also has been discussed in psychology. See Newtson (1973). For a philosophical analysis of basic actions (using an example similar to the one we used – about the Balkans), see Searle, 1983: 99–100).

10 The nature and structure of such ideological (and other) belief systems have been studied by, for example, Abelson (1973); Carlton (1984); Converse (1964); Little and Smith (1988); Tetlock (1984, 1989); Wegman (1981). For the difference between such approaches and cognitive psychological approaches to beliefs, see Quackenbush (1989).

11 Among the theorists of ideology who reject mere study of belief systems and who plead for a combination with social, interactional, dimensions, is Rosenberg (1988).

12 See, for example, Geertz (1973); Oberschall (1993); Wuthnow (1989).

13 For a discussion of this debate (about the linguistic relativity thesis), see, for example, Lucy (1992).

Chapter 3

1 A classical study of political belief systems is Converse (1964). For current discussions and critique, see, for example, Iyengar and McGuire (1993); Lau and Sears (1986).

2 The limerick opens Salman Rushdie's book *The Jaguar Smile: A Nicaraguan Journey*, London: Pan, 1987.

3 See Tulving (1983) for a classical theory of episodic memory and its distinction from 'semantic' memory.

4 For the 'deeper' neuroscientific approaches to the architecture of the mind and its various constructs, see the notes in the previous chapter.

5 As we shall see in more detail later, part of social memory, namely, knowledge, tends to be studied by cognitive psychologists, whereas other socially shared beliefs (such as attitudes) are the domain of study of social psychology. Social memory is currently studied especially in cognitive social psychology (Devine et al., 1994; Fiske and Taylor, 1991; Forgas, 1981; Resnick et al., 1991). Although most studies of social cognition in the USA are oriented towards cognitive psychology (an 'individualistic bias' criticized by more socially oriented social psychologists), this love is unfortunately hardly returned by the cognitive psychologists, who generally ignore the many forms of 'hot (social) cognition'. This situation is among the

many explanatory factors why much of contemporary psychology (and the same is true for cognitive science) is socially and culturally rather underdeveloped. It is especially under the inspiration of Soviet psychology that the socio-cultural study of cognition has been able to find a small, but important, niche in Western (and especially US) psychology (see, e.g., Hickmann, 1987; Wertsch, 1985; Wertsch et al., 1994).

6 Within the framework of his sociology of knowledge, Mannheim (1936: 2) already emphasized that ideologies cannot be explained in terms of personal beliefs, but have a social nature. In his argument he also uses language for comparison to show that although language may be used individually as 'speech', people use a language as a system that is socially and historically shaped. At the same time, Mannheim warns that the notion of social thought does not imply that there is something like a 'group mind'. Thus, in his words, ideology is the 'style of thought' of (the members) of a group (p. 3). He distinguishes between *particular* (personal, individual) ideologies, for example as distorted views of reality arising from people's life situation, on the one hand, and *inclusive*, *total* conceptions of ideology, which are the ideologies of an age or a group. The latter are widely diverging thought systems, which give rise to totally different modes of experience and interpretation (p. 51).

7 One of the authors writing on ideology who emphasize that ideologies are a group characteristic is Scarbrough (1990).

8 See, for example, the contributions in Lau and Sears (1986) for discussion about whether or not ideologies actually exist as 'belief systems'.

9 The notion of 'factual belief' is of course a theoretical one, not a commonsense notion, given the fact that in everyday language use 'beliefs' are associated with doubtful knowledge or (mere) opinions, so that 'factual beliefs' would be a contradiction. We use the notion in order to emphasize the general notion of 'belief', and in order to be able to differentiate between different kinds of belief. See also the discussion in Chapter 11.

10 For various approaches to the discourse marking of evidentiality, perspective and opinion, see, for example, Biber and Finegan (1989); Mayer, (1990); Schieffelin (1996).

11 This is the approach advocated by discursive psychology. See, for example, Edwards (1996) for detail.

12 For a detailed discussion of the traditional notion of attitude, see Eagly and Chaiken (1993). Note that most traditional approaches to attitude make no clear distinction between social and personal opinions, or specific and general opinions. Jaspars and Fraser (1984) criticized the individualistic approach to attitudes in much of social psychology, and usefully remind us of the fact that the original notion of attitude refers to socially shared beliefs of a group. This will also be my approach, thereby adding that such social attitudes (e.g. about abortion or nuclear energy) are not isolated beliefs, but complex structures). We shall come back to the notion of 'attitude' and its structures in the next chapter.

13 There is now a considerable literature in this kind of discursive, rhetorical and social constructionist psychology. For some key texts in which these claims are formulated, see, for example, Billig (1987, 1991b, 1995b); Billig et al. (1988); Edwards (1997); Edwards and Potter (1992); Harré (1995); Harré and Gillett (1994); Potter (1996); Potter and Wetherell (1987).

14 One theory of 'social representations' is usually associated with the work of Serge Moscovici (Paris) and his followers. See, for instance, Augoustinos and Walker (1995); Breakwell and Canter (1993); Farr and Moscovici (1984). For an account of ideology in terms of social representations, see Aebischer et al. (1992); Augoustinos and Walker (1995). The French theory of social representations, however, is more specific than our general use of the term (as socially shared beliefs), and especially applies to mundane, commonsense uses of scientific knowledge in everyday life, for instance the lay uses of psychoanalysis. There has also been considerable critique of the notion of social representation. See, for example, Jahoda (1988) and the reply by Moscovici (1988).

15 The notion of *habitus* was introduced by French sociologist Pierre Bourdieu. See, among many of his writings, for example, Bourdieu (1985, 1988, 1990). For (sociological) critique, see, for example, Alexander (1995).

16 For another example of a more integrated approach to social cognition, see Augostinos and Walker (1995). For US approaches to social cognition, see, for example, Devine et al. (1994); Fiske and Taylor (1991); Higgins et al. (1981); Wyer and Srull (1984, 1989). For (mostly European) work on social identity, social categorization, social represenations, and intergroup relations, see, for example, Farr and Moscovici (1984); Forgas (1981); Spears et al. (1997); Tajfel (1978, 1981); Turner and Giles (1981). See also the references in Note 4 and the references in the next chapter.

17 There are some (not very detailed) suggestions in the literature that take ideologies as the general organizational basis for attitudes, and that define attitudes as more-specific opinions about issues or social domains. See, for instance, Scarbrough (1984, 1990), who also discusses the relations between ideologies, attitudes and social representations.

18 See especially the relevant work of Foucault about these relationships between (medical) knowledge and power: for example, Foucault (1975, 1980).

Chapter 4

1 As far as I know, there are no detailed general studies of the difference between the 'structural' and the 'dynamic' approach in the humanities and the social sciences. For a discussion of the distinction in psychology, see van Dijk and Kintsch (1983). In sociology, this debate typically sets apart microsociological and ethnomethodological approaches from earler 'structural' or 'functional' sociology. See, among many other studies, Button (1991) and Heritage (1987).

2 Schema-theory in cognitive science essentially goes back to Bartlett (1932), who assumed that knowledge is represented in a schematic fashion. Its most influential formulation in contemporary psychology has been in terms of knowledge 'scripts' as introduced by Schank and Abelson (1977), after earlier notions such as that of 'scenarios' (Charniak, 1972) and 'frames' (Bobrow and Collins, 1975).

3 For discussion, see the recent debate on connectionist, neural and parallel processing: Baumgartner and Payr (1995), Clancey et al. (1994), Rumelhart and McClelland (1986). This work only very recently begins to influence social psychology and the theory of attitudes and social representations (Eiser, 1994).

4 See Schank and Abelson (1977).

5 Such smaller units, sometimes called Memory Organization Packages (MOPS), are for instance discussed in Schank (1982).

6 This is especially the case in the 'social cognition' approach in the USA. See, for example, Fiske and Taylor (1991). For a discussion of the early uses of 'schemata' in social cognition, see Brewer and Nakamura (1984), Higgins et al. (1981). For the use of schemata in political psychology, see Kuklinski et al. (1991).

7 Representations for opinions and attitudes have especially been attempted by Robert Abelson, who may also be credited with the invention of the script-concept (see, e.g., Abelson, 1973, 1976, 1981; and his very early attempt with Rosenberg in Abelson and Rosenberg, 1958). For a survey of other attempts to model attitudes and other evaluative social cognition, see Fiske and Taylor (1991) and Eagly and Chaiken 1993).

8 These natural, but fallible, forms of information processing and social judgement have been extensively studied in psychology. See, for example, Arkes and Hammond (1986); Kahneman et al. (1982); Martin and Tesser (1992); Nisbett and Ross (1980).

9 Although this three-component distinction may be found in many studies of attitudes (for survey, see Eagly and Chaiken, 1993), it was in fact seldom empirically tested (see, however, Breckler, 1984).

10 For classical studies in social psychology on the consistency, balance or cognitive dissonance of opinions, see, for example, Abelson et al. (1968); Heider (1946, 1958); Festinger (1957). More recent approaches are collected in Pratkanis et al. (1989). For a recent survey of classical as well as modern approaches, see Eagly and Chaiken (1993).

Chapter 5

1 As noted several times before, the vast literature on ideologies has seldom been concerned with the detailed internal organization of ideologies. Ideology descriptions, when given at all, tend to be largely impressionistic from this structural point of view, that is, summaries or stories about the beliefs of groups. Since also opinions, attitudes and ideologies are not always distinguished, some proposals for ideological 'structures' are in fact proposals for attitude structures. For some more explicit attempts that speculate about ideological organization, see, for example, Seliger (1979), who organizes ideologies in terms of the nature of the kinds of statements they contain: a circle of descriptions, analysis, implementation and rejections, with moral or technical prescriptions in the centre. See also Roseman (1994).

2 See Abelson (1976) for a script-like approach to attitudes.

3 For a detailed analysis of such opinions about immigration and immigrants, see van Dijk (1984, 1987, 1991, 1993a).

4 The organization of (party) ideologies as a function of the perceived (importance of) problems has been studied by Van Schuur (1984).

5 These narrative structure categories have first been introduced by Labov and Waletzky (1967) and Labov (1972). Later it was also applied in the analysis of our knowledge about such narrative structures, and indeed in the study of story comprehension, although also other structures (for instance in terms of actions, events and goals) have been proposed (see, e.g., Mandler, 1984; van Dijk, 1980).

6 Despite the occasional reference in social cognition research to the notion of 'group schema', no such schemata have ever been described in any detail, as far as I know. There are some research suggestions that groups are represented much like persons, but no structural description is given in that case (Wyer and Gordon, 1984; Fiske and Taylor, 1991: 327). The present schema is derived from my earlier work on the structure of ethnic attitudes on minorities (van Dijk, 1984, 1987).

7 See, however, Billig's work on 'rhetorical thinking', in which thought itself is assumed to be organized in a rhetorical or argumentative way (Billig, 1987, 1991b).

8 One empirical study of two possibly conflicting ideologies is that of Eckhardt et al. (1992), which shows that religious scholars seem to be able to handle coexisting religious and scientific belief systems without much personal conflict.

Chapter 6

1 The literature on values is vast. As is the case for other social representations, however, we know as yet very little about their precise cognitive nature. How, indeed, are they represented in social memory? Probably not just as the word-concepts (such as 'Happiness' or 'Justice') used here as well as in other studies. They may be complex mental representations (indeed, the whole complex 'idea of Justice') that are merely conveniently 'summarized' by such concept-words, so that they can be easily expressed in communication and interaction. For examples of classical and modern studies, see Brewster Smith (1969); Eisenberg et al. (1989); Hechter et al. (1993); Hofstede (1980); Rokeach (1973, 1979). Schwartz and Bilsky (1990) propose an empirical theory of universal content and structure of human values defined as people's conceptions of the goals that serve as guiding principles in their lives, that is, a (small) number of universal motivational concerns (such as hedonism, achievement, power, security, etc.). Even when I assume that values are mentally represented, I would emphasize the socio-cultural nature of such values instead of their individual (motivational) dimension.

Chapter 7

1 The theory of mental models has been developed in psychology, and especially also in the theory of text comprehension, since the early 1980s (Johnson-Laird, 1983; van Dijk and

Kintsch, 1983; van Oostendorp and Zwaan, 1994). Some of its more logical aspects go back to abstract model theories that were designed as semantics for formal languages. Such formal models (or model structures) feature, for example, the set of individuals referred to by the expressions of formal statements. Mental models, although theoretically little developed, should be more 'realistic' in the sense that they must account for the typical types of objects that define possible situations.

2 So far, there is no theoretical work on experience models as such (see van Dijk, 1997). However, most literature on episodic memory, and about 'autobiographic' memory for events, actions, persons, episodes and personal experiences, will provide some elements of such a theory (see, e.g., Neisser and Fivush, 1994; Rubin, 1986; Srull and Wyer, 1993; Tulving, 1983). Our point here is first that the subjective representation of episodes should be framed in terms of models and model structures. Second, we want to emphasize that such models also play a role in the production and understanding of social practices in general and in discourse in particular. We thus want to unify the usual accounts of 'situation models' in the text-processing literature and the work on episodic representations of actions and events as well as on autobiographical memory. In other words, also cognitively (and not only socially) the way we engage in, and understand, text and talk should be made a part of a broader theory of our everyday experiences.

3 Various sociological and psychological theories of social episodes provide suggestions for the inclusion of basic categories into model schemata (see, e.g., Argyle et al., 1981; Forgas, 1979; Furnham and Argyle, 1981).

4 In linguistics, case grammars and other functional approaches to the study of the structure of propositions and their syntactic expressions make use of such basic categories (Dik, 1978, 1989; Fillmore, 1968). At another level some of them also appear, as 'descriptions of episodes', in theories of narrative (see Labov and Waletzky, 1967; Labov, 1972).

5 One of the studies that examines the representation of Self in relation to ideologies and narrative structures, is Gregg (1991).

6 This seems to be the more intuitively 'empirical' way of learning about the world. However, there is evidence that 'learning from experience' through the generalization of episodic models may not (always) be the way we acquire general knowledge. At least fragments of semantic or social knowledge about the world may be acquired 'directly', that is through discourse: for example, by the explanation of words or by generic sentences in stories, arguments or other forms of discourse. At this point, the theory joins the more general theory of knowledge acquisition and learning, a vast field of cognitive, developmental and educational psychology that obviously cannot be discussed here. My point is only to show how personal knowledge (models) about events can be related to socially shared beliefs. Although much is known about processes and conditions of learning and social knowledge acquisition, our insight into the detailed representations involved is as yet rather fragmentary, as we have seen before for the notion of scripts and related concepts. Since much knowledge acquisition and learning takes place on the basis of discourse, much of the relevant literature on text comprehension deals with the same processes. Similarly, also much work in artificial intelligence, dealing with the simulation of knowledge representation and acquisition, is relevant here. Thus, broadly speaking, after the more behaviouristic reduction of learning in terms of conditioning and stimulus generalization, and 'social learning' approaches based on them, most contemporary approaches are clearly cognitive, and formulated in terms of various formats of memory representations for knowledge and beliefs. For various surveys and other studies that use the framework proposed here, see Freedle and Carroll (1972); Glaser (1987); Gonzalvo et al. (1994); Mandl and Levin (1989); Schank (1982); Schank and Abelson (1977); Strube and Wender (1993); van Dijk and Kintsch (1983).

7 Also in relation to what has been said in Note 5, there exists evidence that shows that social representations may sometimes be stronger than personal experiences (e.g. of poverty) as a reason to support (e.g. economic) policies (Lau and Sears, 1981). This suggests either that public arguments are integrated into the model, and thereby influence personal experience, action and discourse, or else that social representations (attitudes) may influence discourse directly, especially when these are communicated by credible elite groups. Of course,

responses to (survey) questions may also show effects of compliance and consensus with what 'everybody thinks', and hesitations to show economic hardship. In sum, models, opinions, social representations and the ways these are expressed or not, mitigated or not, in various discourses and contexts, form a very complex combination, which simplistic results of public opinion surveys cannot possibly begin to make explicit.

8 There are many theories of attitude formation and change, as well as theories of persuasion, that deal with these processes, but seldom in terms of models. This is also because much work on opinions and attitudes does not differentiate between personal, contextual opinions as represented in models, and general, socially shared attitudes. For survey of the more traditional approaches to attitude formation, see Eagly and Chaiken (1993).

9 See van Dijk (1984, 1987) for studies about such forms of biased recall of negative events in racist storytelling and argumentation. For general social psychological work on hypothesis testing and the self-confirmation of social stereotypes, see, e.g., Snyder (1981a, 1981b). Note though that this phenomenon does not exclude that in specific contexts people precisely tend to recall what is *not* consistent with their own group attitudes, e.g., when they (better) recall the statements of their opponents, so as to be able to better refute these.

10 These assumptions may be found both in classical political science (Converse, 1964) and current political cognition (Lau and Sears, 1986; Iyengar and McGuire, 1993), as well as in discursive psychology (Billig et al., 1988).

Chapter 8

1 These assumptions may be found both in classical political science (Converse, 1964) and current political cognition (Lau and Sears, 1986; Iyengar and McGuire, 1993), and presently also, in different guises in discursive and rhetorical psychology (e.g. Billig et al., 1988; Billig, 1991a, 1991b; Potter and Wetherell, 1987). More specifically for ideologies, Seliger (1979) adopts a middle position: He assumes that ideologies are structured, but not fully consistent. Also Rosenberg (1988) emphasizes the structured nature of ideologies. In the literature on political cognition, it is generally assumed that ideological consistency is a function of expertise: Those who know more about politics simply have more consistent political attitudes, and probably a more consistent underlying ideology (see, e.g., Judd and Downing, 1990). Other research suggests that opinions expressed when an ideological schema is activated are more coherent than when no such schema is activated, at least for people who are conscious about their ideological orientation (Milburn, 1987).

2 Such questions have been raised at least since the classical theories of cognitive balance, consistency and dissonance, mostly in social psychology, and often related to the study of attitudes (Abelson, 1973, 1983; Abelson and Rosenberg, 1958; Abelson et al., 1968; Festinger, 1957; Heider, 1946, 1958; Rosenberg, 1960; Rosenberg et al., 1960). However, most of these studies focused on relations between individual beliefs, and did not investigate the overall structure of attitude systems and ideologies. Grofman and Hyman (1974) analyse the systematicity of ideologies in terms of connectedness, consistency and coherence, and conclude that, by these criteria, ideologies are indeed belief systems.

3 Among the many sociological and historical studies that pay attention to these institutional and organizational dimensions of ideology, see, for example, Douglas, 1986; Jones, 1984; Wuthnow, 1989.

4 For cognitive dissonance, see, e.g., the classical study by Festinger (1957). For a more general discussion of this and other aspects of cognitive consistency, see Abelson et al. (1968).

5 See my earlier empirical work on discourse and racism, based on data in several countries and involving people from different socio-economic backgrounds and in different institutional situations (van Dijk, 1984, 1987, 1991, 1993a).

6 For some studies of contemporary ideological change, see, for example, Adams, 1993; Collins, 1992; Larana et al., 1994.

Chapter 9

1 Since this study avoids historical reviews of earlier conceptions of ideology, it is also beyond its scope to examine the history of the notion of 'false consciousness'. For such a historical study, see Lewy, 1982; Pines, 1993. See also Jost and Banaji, 1994; Wood, 1988. See also the classical discussion in Mannheim (1936: 62ff.).

2 See the well-known debate about the 'dominant ideology hypothesis' (Abercrombie et al., 1980, 1990).

3 For studies of the example of class and class consciousness in relation to dominant ideologies, see, for example, Giddens and Held, 1982; Joyce, 1995; Therborn, 1980.

4 Awareness has also been studied in political psychology, for example, in relation to the issue of elites versus public opinion. See, for example, Zaller (1990).

5 For studies of group-consciousness (for example, of gender, class or ethnicity), see, for example, Bell, 1995; Brooks, 1994; Davis and Robinson, 1991; Dillingham, 1981; Edwards, 1994; Graetz, 1986; Gurin and Townsend, 1986; Hall and Allen, 1989; King, 1988; Lockwood, 1966; Rowbotham, 1973; Weakliem, 1993.

6 See, for example, Lau and Sears, 1986.

7 For details, see, for example, Baars, 1988; Davies and Humphreys, 1993; Dennett, 1993; Greenberg and Tobach, 1983; Jackendoff, 1987; Marcel and Bisiach, 1988.

8 For a study of ideological denial, see van Dijk, 1992.

Chapter 10

1 See Gramsci (1971). See also Adamson, 1983; Femia, 1987; Hall et al., 1978.

2 For a discussion of 'common sense' in ethnomethodology, see Eglin, 1979; Elliot, 1974; Sharrock and Anderson, 1991. See also the other contributions in Button, 1991.

3 See, for example, Billig, 1991b; Billig and Sabucedo, 1994; Eagleton, 1991; Lewis, 1992.

4 On common sense and social representations, see Billig and Sabucedo (1994); Purkhardt (1993).

5 For the role of common sense in argumentation and accounts, see, for example, Antaki, 1994; Billig et al. (1988).

6 Furnham (1994) discusses these and several other terminological variations of the concept of common sense, such as 'ordinary', 'lay' or 'folk' beliefs.

7 For the relations between common sense and scientific knowledge, see also Fletcher, 1993; Siegfried, 1994; Van Holthoon and Olson, 1987.

8 For a discussion of common sense in psychology, see Siegfried, 1994; Wegner and Vallacher, 1981.

9 See, for example, Farr and Moscovici, 1984; Augoustinos and Walker, 1995.

10 For the role of common sense in the study of racism, see also Essed, 1987; Lawrence, 1982.

Chapter 11

1 For a discussion of the opposition between knowledge/science and ideology, see most classical studies of ideology (see Note 1 of Chapter 1). See also Althusser, 1984; Aronowitz, 1988; Bailey, 1994; Larrain, 1979; Mannheim, 1936; Mészáros, 1989; Pines, 1993. See also the next chapter.

2 See, for example, Button, 1991.

3 For these philosophical debates about knowledge and its foundations, see, for example, Dancy, 1985; Kornblith, 1994; Kruglanski, 1989; Lehrer, 1990.

4 The study of 'opinions' stretches from philosophy (often in terms of 'beliefs' versus 'knowledge'; see, e.g., Hintikka, 1962), to the study of public opinion in social psychology and

political science (e.g. Glasser and Salmon, 1995). Within his own 'rhetorical' framework, Billig (1991b) discusses opinions in relation to ideology, and stresses the argumentative nature of opinions instead of their cognitive properties. Billig (1989) also shows that there is a difference between expressing weak or strong 'views', where people with strong views show more variability.

5 On the relations of knowledge and power, and the truth-defining nature of institutions, see, for example, Aronowitz (1988); Foucault (1972, 1980).

6 The relations between knowledge and ideologically based attitudes have been explored also in social and political psychology. Thus, if feminist attitudes are important to women, also their knowledge acquisition about gender relations may be deeper and more refined (see, e.g., Berent and Krosnick, 1995).

7 Mannheim (1936: 19) also argues that whether or not worldviews or ideologies may be (objectively) 'false', they may serve to make 'coherent' the fragments of reality as seen by the group members that share such a worldview. Whether beliefs of a group are true or false, it is *their* 'definition of the situation' that counts. Indeed, besides other criteria, group membership for him implies that group members 'see the world' in terms of the meanings of the group. He also emphasizes that for this same reason, more generally, knowledge is by definition related to the viewpoint, position and interests of the group, and hence relative (or rather what he calls 'relationist') (p. 67ff.).

Chapter 12

1 The literature on social identity is vast, and cannot possibly be reviewed here. I limit my discussion to social (group) identity and to the (close) relationship between such group identity and ideology, that is to the question 'Who are *we*?' (related to, but different from the question about the social Self). For details, see, for example, Abrams and Hogg, 1990; Tajfel, 1981; Turner and Giles, 1981. It is remarkable, though, that this literature seldom speaks of ideologies, and more generally it is not always clear in this social psychological literature whether 'social identity' is a property of individual social group members, or a *shared* property of a whole group. On the other hand, there is work on (new) social movements in which the relations between ideology and identity are more clearly established. See, for example, the studies in Laraña et al. (1994).

2 For the notion of 'self-schema', see Markus (1977).

3 On social identity, see, for example, Abrams and Hogg, 1990; Morris and Mueller, 1992.

4 See the discussion on the relations between social movements, social identity, ideology and (mainly referrring to Mannheim's work) 'utopia' in Turner (1994).

5 Melucci's approach to social identity and the self-definition of groups features similar categories (see Melucci, 1996; and, for general discussion, Johnston et al., 1994).

6 This example of the 'transient identity' of the (Dutch) peace movement is discussed by Klandermans (1994).

7 See Billig (1990) for how collective memory (about the Royal Family in the UK) may be managed by ideologies, for example, what is remembered and what is ignored.

8 The relations between social groups and questions of social identity have especially been emphasized for the 'new social movements' (NSMs) of the last decades, such as the peace movement, the ethnic and women's movements, the gay rights movement, and various nationalist movements. For these NSMs the main reasons of their existence were not so much 'structural', socio-economic (as was the case for the 'old' social movements, such as the working-class movement), but especially also a question of identity, human rights or even lifestyle, where individual and social claims may be merged. Especially also, questions of symbolism and culture have been found to be characteristic of NSMs. Contrary to earlier structuralist approaches to social movements, with their focus on socio-economic conditions and opportunities, current analyses of the NSMs thus tend to emphasize the 'shared meanings' involved in the self-definition of movements. For discussion, see, for example, Johnston et al.

(1994); McAdam (1994); Melucci (1989, 1996). For a critical comment on the cognitive 'shared frameworks' concept of Melucci, see Billig (1995b).

9 For a discussion of these discursive dimensions of the construction of social movements, see, for example, Klandermans (1992). My own earlier work on discourse and racism shows how racist and anti-racist groups and institutions are largely also constituted by text and talk (van Dijk, 1984, 1987, 1991, 1993a).

Chapter 13

1 The critique that follows is not directed against individual writers, but to the various traditional and contemporary approaches to ideology we have been referring to in the past chapters. Thus, my critique first addresses the various Marxist or neo-Marxist approaches, which all but ignore psychological dimensions of ideologies (for surveys, see Eagleton, 1991; Larrain, 1979; see also Fairclough, 1995). Second, it addresses some of the more radical tenets of 'discursive psychology', which tend to reduce the mind to discourse (Edwards and Potter, 1992; Harré and Gillett, 1994; Harré and Stearns, 1995; Potter and Wetherell, 1987; Potter et al. 1993; for ideology, see also a less radical position in Billig, 1991b).

2 For some of the critical positions summarized here, see, for example, Himmelweit and Gaskell (1990); Resnick et al. (1991).

Chapter 14

1 See the references in Note 1 of Chapter 1.

2 Such a (unfortunately seldom heeded) plea for a cognitive sociology, has been eloquently made already by Cicourel (1973).

3 This conception of racism has been dealt with in more detail in van Dijk (1984, 1987, 1991, 1993). See also Essed (1991). Among the numerous other studies on racism that have influenced my conception are, for example, Barkan (1992); Barker (1981); Dovidio and Gaertner (1986); Haghighat (1988); Katz and Taylor (1988); Miles (1989); Solomos (1993); Solomos and Wrench (1993); Wellman (1993).

Chapter 15

1 As long ago as 1936, Mannheim (p. 3) emphasized that ideologies are shared by groups, and function as a basis of collective action.

2 A useful survey of the classical and contemporary perspectives on class may be found in Joyce (1995).

3 For these and other criteria of groups and group relations, see especially (mostly European) social-psychological studies on inter-group theory, for example, Billig (1976); Tajfel (1978, 1981); Turner and Giles (1981); Turner et al. (1987).

4 For a similar analysis of the relationship between social identity and sharing representations, see, for example, Moscovici and Hewstone, 1983; Scarbrough, 1990.

5 Social movements and their ideologies are discussed by, for example, Laraña et al. (1994), Melucci (1996) and Oberschall (1993). For the close relation between social identity, ideology and new social movements, see the discussion and the references given in Chapter 12 (see also Note 6).

6 For corporate cultures, see, for example, Hofstede (1980). Business ideologies have been studied by Goll and Zeitz (1991); Mattelart (1979); Mizruchi (1990); Neustadtl and Clawson (1988); Rothman and Lichter (1984).

7 Indirectly and directly, there is a massive literature on the relations between ideology and social group conflict. Most studies mentioned earlier (see Chapter 1, Note 2), especially those reviewing the Marxist tradition, of course emphasize the role of group (class) conflict as a

basis for ideologies. From a psychological perspective (about social dominance), see also Sidanius (1993). More generally, see the following recent studies of social conflict, often also discussed in relation to ideology: Feagin and Feagin (1994); Fisher (1990); Oberschall (1993); Worchel and Simpson (1993). For the expression and enactment of conflict in discourse, see Grimshaw (1990).

8 As with many other sociological issues dealt with in this and other chapters of this section, we cannot go into the complex details of the macro–micro problem (often pseudo-problem) in the social sciences. What, among other issues, is at stake here are analyses of different levels of social reality, which each may require its own theoretical framework, as is the case for microsociological analyses of interaction and conversation on the one hand, and larger social (group) relations and structures on the other hand, with several meso-levels in between. That the problem, on one analysis, is often a pseudo-problem is because in concrete analyses *both* macro- and micro-notions may be required. Thus, to study social power (such as sexism or racism) in conversation, for instance, we obviously need a framework that combines both levels. And as microsociologists often remind us, higher-level societal relations and structures simply manifest themselves only at the level of everyday routines, practices, or interactions of social actors. For further discussion, see, for example, Alexander et al. (1987); Knorr-Cetina and Cicourel (1981); see also van Dijk (1980).

9 Relationships between group ideology and (often conflicting) identities have often been studied, for example, by Garcia (1989); Gregg (1991); Hummon (1990); King (1991); Lipiansky (1991); Oberschall (1993); Rees (1985); Rothstein (1991); Shotter and Gergen (1989). For combined influences of race and class, see McDermott (1994).

10 This example of women and blacks in the media has been examined in several studies. See, for example, Dines and Humez (1995); Mills (1988); Van Zoonen (1994); Wilson (1991).

11 On class in general, see Joyce, 1995. For an analysis of various forms of 'symbolic capital' as constitutive of class, see especially the work by Pierre Bourdieu (e.g. Bourdieu, 1984a, 1989). McDermott (1994) shows how ideologies are often the result of the combined influence of different group memberships, such as those of race and class.

12 Professional ideologies have been the object of much research, especially in the medical and legal professions; see, for example, Byrne (1993); Dickson (1993); Globerman (1990); Greenfeld (1989); Howard (1985); Loewenberg (1984); Shaw (1990); Wuthnow and Shrum (1983).

13 For a discussion of social movement ideologies, see, for example, Laraña et al. (1994); Oberschall (1993); Ryan (1992); Sassoon (1984).

14 Managerial ideologies are studied in Barley and Kunda (1992); Enteman (1993); Grenier and Hogler (1991); Le Goff (1992); Miyajima (1986); Weiss (1986).

15 Feminist ideologies are studied in, for example, Ballaster (1991); Billington (1982); Poole and Zeigler (1981); Ryan (1992); Sharistanian (1986).

16 Not only commonsense conceptions of racism, but also much scholarly work on racism, rather exclusively identifies racism or 'racists' (only) with right-wing, extremist groups, parties or organizations. Despite the fact that racist is usually defined as an inter-group phenomenon (e.g. between white Europeans and Others), white people 'like us' are never racist. See, for example, Able (1995); Blackwell (1994); Landau (1993); Thompson (1994). Indeed, as we have seen before, also most leaders of racist parties will deny that they are racist, but at most 'nationalist'.

17 For the strategies of the denial of racism, see van Dijk (1992).

18 For prototypes, see Rosch and Lloyd (1978).

Chapter 16

1 Many approaches to ideology implicitly or explicitly discuss social (group) relations as the basis for ideology. Thus, in psychology, Social Dominance Theory (SDT) by Jim Sidanius and his associates assumes that 'humans are predisposed to form group-based social hier-

archies'. Moreover, especially people of greater status seem to display a greater tendency to ingroup favouritism (Sidanius, 1993; Sidanius and Ekehammar, 1980, 1983; Sidanius et al., 1994). Although I reject the (innate, natural?) disposition argument about social hierarchies, my work on elite discourse and racism suggests indeed the special role of elites in the reproduction of one type of ingroup favouritism: racism (van Dijk, 1993a; see also Sidanius and Liu, 1992).

2 For details on power, see, for example, Clegg (1989); Lukes (1974, 1986); Oleson and Marger (1993); Wrong (1979).

3 Persuasive power and mind control has been studied in several disciplines and from many perspectives. From a socio-political perspective, namely, that of hegemony, the classical source remains Gramsci (1971). A contemporary, more political orientation to the 'manufacturing of consent' has been presented by Herman and Chomsky (1988). Mind control by the media has been studied in a rich and controversial tradition of media power, 'influence' and the 'effects' of mass communication (among numerous studies, see Altheide (1985); Altschull (1984); Bryant and Zillmann (1986); Curran et al. (1987); Klapper (1960); Schiller (1973). The cognitive and social psychological dimensions of mind control, usually defined as 'persuasion' or more critically as 'manipulation', have been studied by, for example, Bostrom (1983); Bradac (1989); Harris (1989); Margolis and Mauser (1989).

4 See for instance Foucault's work on power (e.g. Foucault, 1980).

5 For discussion about the historical roots of racist ideologies and their relations to the slave system, see, for example, Barker (1978).

Chapter 17

1 About the role of 'ideologues' in the formation of ideologies, see the contributions in Lau and Sears (1986). My use of 'elites' is complementary to the customary use in the social sciences (e.g. Domhoff, 1978; Domhoff and Ballard, 1968; Mills, 1956). It especially emphasizes, within the framework of critical discourse analysis, the special access to, and control over public discourse, by the elites (see, e.g., van Dijk, 1993a, 1995). Lau et al. (1991) provide some empirical evidence about the persuasiveness of policy proposals and of the role of the elites in decision making. Zaller (1990) shows how ordinary citizens use elite cues in order to transform their value orientations into support for specific policies. Jennings (1992), finally, showed that party elites generally have more stable and consistent ideologies than 'mass publics'.

2 For differences of access to public discourse, see van Dijk (1996). Generally it is found that those who have more knowledge or expertise about politics, also have more consistent attitudes and ideologies (see, e.g., Judd and Downing, 1990).

3 On ideologues, see, for example, Langston (1992); Martin (1983); Welch (1984). The role of group leaders and the development of ideology has been studied by, e.g., Blommaert, 1991; Dreier, 1982; Folkertsma, 1988; Gaffney, 1989; Garcia, 1989).

4 For the everyday implications of feminist ideology, see, for example, Flaherty (1982); Krishnan (1991); Redclift and Sinclair (1991); Ryan (1992); Sharistanian (1986); Togeby (1995).

5 For feminist ideologies, see Note 4. For ethnically or 'racially' based ideologies of resistance, see, for example, Fatton (1986); Innis and Feagin (1989); Marable and Mullings (1994); McCarthney (1992); Turner and Wilson (1976). For environmental ideologies, see Buttel and Flinn (1978).

6 For theoretical and empirical studies of elite racism, see van Dijk (1993a); for the way the elites may frame racial issues, see also Kinder and Sanders (1990).

7 There is some experimental evidence on group-based dominance (e.g. of gender or 'race') that seems to support this assumption: For members of high status groups (e.g. whites, males) there is a positive correlation between desire for group dominance and group affiliation (see, e.g., Sidanius et al., 1994).

8 For details on the relations between ideologies, immigration policies and political rhetoric, see, for example, Fitzgerald (1996).

Chapter 18

1 This discussion about dominant ideologies has been sparked especially by Abercrombie et al. (1980, 1990). See also Howe (1994) for a critique of the critique of dominant ideologies and for alternative suggestions to a Marxist concept of ideology, that is, as a 'possibly contradictory set of themes'.

2 About these relations between the media and (other) power elites and their ideologies, see Connell (1978); Dreier (1982); Fletcher (1991); Golding and Murdock (1979); Lichter et al. (1990); Negrine (1989); Paletz and Entman (1981); Rothman and Lichter (1984); Dreier (1982).

3 See Hall (1980, 1982) for such an approach to the overall, ideological influence of the media, which is also defended and illustrated in, for example, Herman and Chomsky (1988); Schiller (1973); van Dijk (1991).

4 This again brings in the discussion of media effects and influence. That media in many domains have power, is beyond dispute, and documented in many studies (see references in Note 2). Whether and how exactly they have a pervasive, and not just a marginal or occasional influence on the basic attitudes and ideologies of the reader, is much harder to prove (or to reject). See for debate, for example, Bryant and Zillman (1986); Graber (1988); Iyengar and Kinder (1987); Liebes and Katz (1993); MacKuen and Coombs (1981); Morley (1986, 1993); Neuman et al. (1992).

5 See Mannheim (1936). Note, though, that for Mannheim, utopias (like the ideologies of dominant groups) are essentially misguided, because they are so 'strongly interested in the descrution and transformation of a given condition of society' that their 'thinking is incapable of correctly diagnosing an existing condition of society' (p. 36). Because, as suggested before, both dominant as well as non-dominant ideologies may be true or false, also ideologies of resistance are not necessarily based on valid analyses of the social order. Nor, however, is the opposite necessarily false. Indeed, as suggested before, whereas dominant groups may have interest in ignoring or denying true relations of domination in order to legitimate or conceal their power, opposition groups should rather have a correct view of the social situation, in order to be better placed to transform it. Thus, it would be quite inappropriate to generally qualify feminist or anti-racist 'utopias' as misguided diagnoses of gender and race domination in society. In other words, the way dominant and oppositional groups understand the social world cannot be the same (or similarly misguided). On the contrary, the ideological basis of their beliefs is itself (also, though not only) a function of their respective social positions and interests, and hence by definition different.

6 On the ideologies and popular success of Thatcherism and Reagonomics, see, for example, Hall (1988); Kiewe and Houck (1991); Krieger (1986); Langston (1992). Yantek (1988). For the New Right, see, for example, Bennett (1990); Levitas (1986); Sunic (1990).

7 On various forms of resistance and dissidence, see, for example, Fisher and Davis (1993); Hall and Jefferson (1976); Luke (1989); Miller et al. (1989); Mullard (1985); Scott (1986); Sivanandan (1982).

Chapter 19

1 Ideological institutions, also defined as 'ideological state apparatuses', and their role in reproduction, have, for example, been discussed in more philosophical terms by Althusser (1984); as well as in several books by Foucault (see, e.g., Foucault, 1972, 1979). From a different perspective, much empirical work has been done on the ideological role of organizations (Alvesson, 1987, 1991; Berezin, 1991; Downey, 1986; Goll and Zeitz, 1991; Hill and Leighley, 1993; Jones, 1984; Mumby, 1988; Sassoon, 1984; Theus, 1991; Weiss,

1986). Douglas (1986) specifically also focuses on organizations or institutions as 'thinking' and hence as instances that develop ideologies, just as they make decisions.

2 The ideological functions of the family have been investigated more generally in much primary socialization research, but also more specifically, for instance with respect to the acquisition of gender roles, the acquisition of prejudices, and so on. See, for example, Aboud (1988); Gittins (1993); Kraut and Lewis (1975); Todd (1985); Walsh (1983).

3 The ideological functions of schooling and formal education have been among the best-studied institutional aspects of ideology. See, among many other publications, the following studies: Apple (1979, 1982); Apple and Weiss (1983); Ekehammar et al. (1987); Giroux (1981); Karabel and Halsey (1977); Rothstein (1991); Sarup (1991); Sharp (1980); Stevens and Wood (1992); Tierney (1991); Watt (1994); Willis (1977); Young (1971). More specifically, Baer and Lambert (1990) found that students of business and the professions tend to support dominant ideologies, and those who studied social sciences tend consequently to support counter-ideologies.

4 The ideological influence of the mass media has been discussed within the broader framework of the power, effects and influence of the media, and has alternatively been emphasized or mitigated, depending on theory and empirical findings. See Barrett et al. (1979); Connell (1978); Downing (1984); Fletcher (1991); Fowler (1991); Golding and Murdock (1979); Hachten (1981); Hall (1982); Hartley and Montgomery (1985); Rothman and Lichter (1985); Schiller (1973); Schiller and Alexandre (1992); Thompson (1990). For the relations between news values and ideologies, see Westerstahl and Johansson (1994).

5 For the role of political parties and organizations in the reproduction of racist ideologies, see, for example, Ben-Tovim et al. (1986); Browning et al. (1990); Feldman (1992); Fitzgerald (1996); Kinder and Sears (1981); Lauren (1988); Layton-Henry (1992); Miles and Phizacklea (1979); Reeves (1983); Sniderman et al. (1993); Solomos (1986, 1993); van Dijk (1993a).

6 For the role of science and scholarship in the reproduction of racism, see, for example, Barkan (1992); Benedict (1982); Chase (1975); Essed (1987); Haghighat (1988); Joseph et al. (1990); Shipman (1994); Tucker (1994); Unesco (1993); van Dijk (1993a).

Chapter 20

1 This does not mean, of course, that there is no earlier work on discourse and ideology. See the references given in Note 4. The problem is that much work on discourse and ideology does not discuss discourse structures in any detail at all, or vaguely identifies discourse with ideology. Though critical of such identification, Purvis and Hunt (1993) simply continue the reduction of discourse to some kind of overall 'order of discourse' without actually analysing it, thus continuing the (usually Marxist or Foucauldian) tradition they criticize. See, for example, Fairclough (1992) for a discourse analytical critique of Foucault.

2 This is the approach especially advocated, in various degrees of orthodoxy, by discursive psychologists in the UK, an approach we have commented on before. See, for example, Potter and Wetherell (1987, 1989); Billig (1991b). For discussion of this approach, see also Augoustinos and Walker (1995).

3 Although crucially relevant for many forms of communication and interaction, we must unfortunately ignore this broader 'semiotic' approach to discourse in this book. For ideological implications of various types of visual communication, see, for example, Austin (1977); Barker (1989); Hall et al. (1980); Hodge and Kress (1988); Kress and Van Leeuwen (1990); Pauly (1993); Reis (1993); Shohat and Stam (1994).

4 Implicitly, many studies of the acquisition or expression of ideology deal with language, discourse or communication. Focused interest in the role of discourse in the acquisition and change of ideologies can be found in the following studies, among many others: Aronowitz (1988); Barley and Kunda (1992); Billig (1991b); Boylan and Foley (1992); Burton and Carlen (1979); Dant (1991); Fairclough (1989, 1995); Fowler (1991); Hodge and Kress (1993); Mumby (1988); Pecheux (1982); Reis (1993); Rossi-Landi (1978); Strassner (1987); van Dijk (1995); Wenden and Schaffner (1994); Wodak (1989, 1996); Wuthnow (1989). However, very

few of these studies provide a detailed and systematic study of the relations between ideological structures and discourse structures.

5 See, for example, Foucault (1981).

6 For this critical approach, critical discourse analysis (CDA), see for instance, van Dijk (1993b). Of course, there is much other work in discourse analysis on ideology (see Note 3), and other directions of CDA. However most of these only bridge the gap between (linguistic and other) approaches to discourse structures on the one hand, and social interaction or social structure, on the other, and neglect the important cognitive 'interface'. Similarly, important work on the cognitive psychology of discourse production and comprehension, usually neglects the social basis of discourse and understanding. One of the few approaches in critical discourse analysis that integrates these different dimensions is the work of Ruth Wodak and her associates (see, e.g., Wodak, 1987, 1989, 1991, 1996). Finally, much of the tradition of critical linguistics in the UK and Australia (such as the work, cited in Note 3, by Fowler, Kress, Van Leeuwen and others), has been formulated in the broader framework of functional, systemic linguistics and semiotics as initiated by Halliday (1973, 1985, 1987).

7 For other approaches to discourse, see the following introductions: Renkema (1993); Schiffrin (1993); van Dijk (1985, 1997).

8 We shall not engage in this debate here, nor detail the many differences between our framework and the more philosophical or postmodern approaches to discourse. For discussion, see, for example, Agger (1990, 1992, 1993); Rojek and Turner (1993); Simons and Billig (1994); see also Fairclough's assessment of the relevance of Foucault for discourse analysis (Fairclough, 1992).

9 See the references given in Note 2.

10 A typical example of more contemporary 'social' semiotic analysis that integrates modern linguistics and discourse analysis, is the work by Hodge and Kress (1988) and Kress and Van Leeuwen (1990).

Chapter 21

1 For analyses of graphical or visual properties of discourse, see, for example, Hodge and Kress (1988); Kress and Van Leeuwen (1990); Mitchell (1994); Rutter (1984); Solso (1994); Saint-Martin (1990).

2 The ideological implications of visual communication have been studied by, for example, Austin (1977); Bristor et al. (1995); Davis and Walton (1983); Doise (1978); Ellsworth and Whatley (1990); ElWarfally (1988); Mitchell (1986); Pauly (1989); Sinclair (1987).

3 For the study of sound structures in discourse, and especially of intonation, see Brazil (1983); Gibbon and Richter (1984); Selting (1995).

4 Of the few studies that relate phonological variables with social or political functions, see Moosmüller (1989); Van Leeuwen (1992). In conversation analysis, special attention is paid to the nature and functions of applause. A politically oriented study of applause is given by Atkinson (1984).

5 An early study of the role of syntax in the expression of ideologically based meanings is Fowler et al. (1979).

6 For the ideologically based expression of agency and responsibility, see, for example, Fowler (1991); Fowler et al. (1979); Sykes (1985); van Dijk (1991); van Leeuwen (1995).

7 For social, political and ideological studies of pronouns, see for instance Brown and Gilman (1960); Carbó (1987); Duranti (1984); Jacquemet (1994); Maitland and Wilson (1987); Urban (1988); van Dijk (1987); Wilson (1990). For experimental evidence about the persuasive role of the use of 'Us' and 'Them' in social categorization, see Perdue et al. (1990).

8 For ideological studies of discourse meanings, see, for example, Luke (1989); Pecheux (1982); van Dijk (1995).

9 For news schemata and their ideological implications, see van Dijk (1988a, 1998b).

10 The ideological implications of the use of rhetorical figures (and especially metaphor) have been studied in much work, such as in Billig (1991b, 1995); Billig and Sabucedo (1994); Chilton (1995); Gale (1994); Kenshur (1993); Lakoff (1987, 1995); Medhurst (1990); Miller and Fredericks (1990); Montgomery et al. (1989); Mumby and Spitzack (1983); Roeh and Nir (1990); van Dijk (1991); Wander (1984).

11 Ideological analysis of conversational structures and strategies is a direction of research that until recently was anathema in most conversation analysis. However, there are now several studies of conversation that focus on social relations that may have an ideological basis, such as those of gender or profession. See, for example, Atkinson (1984); Boden and Zimmerman (1991); Firth (1995); Greatbatch (1992); Heritage (1985); Heritage and Greatbatch (1986); West (1979, 1984, 1990).

Chapter 22

1 Despite the absence of a general theory of context, there have been many writers, especially also in the ethnography of discourse, who have dealt with various aspects of context. See, for example, the well-known SPEAKING model of Dell Hymes, as the first discussion of the parameters of context-of-speaking (Hymes, 1962). See also Auer and Di Luzio (1992); Duranti and Goodwin (1992); Gumperz (1982a, 1982b); van Dijk (1977).

2 The notion of context model has been discussed in somewhat more detail in van Dijk (1996, 1997). See also the general discussion of models in Chapter 7.

3 The theory of experience models is based on various ideas in cognitive and social psychology, for example, mental models in general (Johnson-Laird, 1983; van Dijk and Kintsch, 1983); about episodic memory (Tulving, 1983); about memory for mundane events and the role of the Self (Neisser, 1986; Neisser and Fivush, 1994); about self-schema (Markus, 1977); and about autobiographical memories (Robinson, and Swanson, 1990; Rubin, 1986; Thompson et al., 1996; Trafimow and Wyer, 1993).

4 More generally, genre information regulates the choice of specific topics and their hierachical importance (Tenney, 1989).

5 For a discussion of these various participant roles, see, for example, Goffman (1974).

6 For the influence of (interpretations of) professional roles on discourse, see, for example, Boden and Zimmerman (1991); Drew and Heritage (1992); Fisher and Todd (1986).

7 Op-ed is a US term, meaning 'opposite the editorial page'.

8 The influence of ideologically based group membership in the production of discourse has been examined in many studies, especially in the fields of gender and ethnicity (Balon et al., 1978; Dines and Humez, 1995; Mazingo, 1988; van Dijk, 1991; van Zoonen, 1994; Wilson, 1991; Wodak et al., 1990). Thus, it has been found that black readers will tend to focus more on civil rights issues than whites, and their contextual self-representation will thus also influence the ways news meanings are interpreted as relevant models (Burgoon et al., 1987; Iyengar and Kinder, 1987; see also Johnson, 1987). Similarly, differences of class and education, correlated with that of knowledge also play a role in understanding (Graber, 1988; Wodak, 1987).

9 Relevant for the construction of models of the production context are also the beliefs of speakers or writers about their recipients' beliefs, which may well be erroneous, as has often been demonstrated for journalists' beliefs about their readers (Gans, 1979; Gunter, 1987; Neuman et al., 1992). For experimental evidence about the role of what speakers know about the knowledge of their recipients, see Fussell and Kraus, 1992.

Chapter 23

1 Processes and conditions of social and cultural reproduction have been studied especially by, for example, Apple (1979, 1982); Banerjee (1986); Bourdieu (1973, 1988, 1989); Bourdieu

and Passeron (1977); Chodorow (1978); Corson (1995); Fowler (1987); Liebes et al. (1991); Minnini (1990); Passeron (1986); Rossi-Landi (1978); Thompson (1990).

2 Learning to understand racism from everyday experiences has been described in detail in Essed (1990, 1991). See also Brown (1986).

3 For the various macro–micro relations involved here, see also, for example, Alexander et al. (1987); Knorr-Cetina and Cicourel (1981).

4 These ideological dilemmas and contradictions have been studied by Billig et al. (1988).

5 Differential ingroup and outgroup attribution of negative acts has been found in much of the social psychological literature. See, for example, Fishkin et al. (1993); Hewstone et al. (1989); Simon (1992); Stephan (1977); Weber (1994).

Chapter 24

1 Most work on discourse processing focuses on understanding (Britton and Graesser, 1996; Flammer and Kintsch, 1982; Graesser, 1981; van Dijk and Kintsch, 1983; van Oostendorp and Zwaan, 1994; Weaver et al., 1995). One of the reasons for this bias is that most of this work is experimental, and comprehension processing is easier to control (precisely by experimental texts) than production processes, of which the very 'start' is much less obvious than that of comprehension. However, especially for the psycholinguistics of language production (which, on the other hand, largely ignores discourse structures) see Levelt (1989).

2 For context models and the ways they control discourse production and comprehension, see van Dijk (1997).

3 For the role of topics or macrostructures in discourse processing, see the references given in Note 1, as well as van Dijk (1980).

4 See Levelt (1989).

Chapter 25

1 For 'effects' research in the field of mass communication, see, for example, Bradac (1989); Bryant and Zillman (1986); Klapper (1960); Lowery and DeFleur (1995); Rosengren (1994). In social psychology, persuasion research overlaps with the broader field of attitude change research (see Eagly and Chaiken, 1993), but generally focuses on the role of 'messages' in attitude change. Among a vast literature, see, for example, the following books: Austen and Davie (1991); Bostrom (1993); Cialdini (1993); Jowett and O'Donnell (1992); O'Keefe (1990); Pratkanis and Aronson (1992); Reardon (1991); Shavitt and Brock (1994); Zanna et al. (1987). Work in political cognition, shows, among other things, that the influence of political messages may depend on knowledge about the politician's ideological position and sometimes on the issues themselves, depending under what conditions the discourse is understood and evaluated (see, e.g., Wyer et al., 1991).

2 For agenda-setting research, see, for example, McCombs and Shaw (1972, 1993); Protess and McCombs (1991).

3 For some experimental evidence of this claim, in relation to the interpretation of public policies and debates, see, for example, Lau et al. (1991).

4 That arguments and the definition of 'facts' may be ideologically variable, has been demonstrated for administrative settings (discussions on minorities by boards of trustees of a school) by Corson (1993).

5 The acquisition of opinions and attitudes has been studied in, for example, Aboud and Doyle (1993); Brome (1989); Katz (1976); Sigel (1985, 1989).

Chapter 26

1 For this chapter I am particularly indebted to Luisa Martín Rojo. For further discussion of the relations between discourse and legitimation, see our paper Martín Rojo and van Dijk (1997).

2 Among the many general studies on legitimation and its normative basis, see, for example, Della Fave (1986); Dworkin (1986); Habermas (1975, 1993); Lenski (1966); Rawls (1972); Walker et al. (1986); Wolfe (1977).

3 For earlier studies of the language and discourse of legitimation, see, for example, Goke-Pariola (1993); Mueller (1973).

4 For pragmatic analyses of legitimation, see, for example, De Fornel (1983).

5 Such everyday accounts and explanations have been studied by, for example, Antaki (1981, 1988, 1994b).

6 This combination of power, rhetoric and impression management has often been observed in studies of legitimation. See, for example, Allen, and Caillouet (1994); Anderson (1988).

7 See Dworkin (1986); Finnis (1980); Habermas (1993); Rawls (1972).

8 See for instance the discussion in Della Fave (1980, 1986).

9 For an analysis of the democratic norms, ideologies and legitimation, see, for example, Barnard (1992); Habermas (1993).

10 See van Dijk (1992) for a study of denials of racism.

11 For analyses of the legitimation of racism, see Skutnabb-Kangas (1990); Wetherell and Potter (1992).

12 For empirical evidence about such forms of delegitimation of minorities both in everyday conversation as well as by the elites, see van Dijk (1984, 1987, 1991, 1993a).

13 See Molm (1986).

14 See, for example, Richardson (1985).

15 See the studies on media coverage of industrial disputes by Glasgow University Media Group (1976, 1980).

16 For such forms of limitation of media access of minorities, see van Dijk (1991) and references given there.

17 For the legitimation of opposition, dissidence and revolution, see, for example, Martin et al. (1990).

18 For studies of the role of authority in legitimation, see Heisey and Trebing (1986); Johnson (1994); Raz (1986); Tyler (1990).

19 For analyses of the legitimating authority of knowledge and science, see, for example, Aronowitz (1988); Brown (1989); Foucault (1980).

Chapter 27

1 Despite the vast literature on ideology, and the similarly vast literature on discourse, there is in fact very little explicit and systematic work on those structures of discourse that typically have ideological implications, conditions or consequences. See, from different perspectives, however, the following studies: Billig (1991b); Billig et al. (1988); Chilton (1985, 1988); Dant (1991); Fowler (1991); CCCS (1977); Herman (1992); Herman and Chomsky (1988); Kress (1985); Kress and Hodge (1993); Mumby (1988); Pecheux (1982); Strassner (1987); Tetlock (1983); Thompson (1984, 1990); van Dijk (1995); Verschueren and Blommaert (1992); Wodak (1989, 1996); Wuthnow (1989). However, it should be added that even these studies either do not explicitly theorize about the structures and functions of ideologies, or about those of discourse. Strictly speaking, then, there is no theory of the relations between discourse structures and ideological structures. Hence also the rationale for this book and those that are planned to follow.

2 For references about the discourse structures discussed below, see the notes to Chapter 22.

3 See the references in Chapter 24, Note 1.

4 See van Dijk (1991).

5 The role of causes and explanations in the expression of ethnic prejudice, and hence in the expression of racist ideologies, has been studied in, for example, Schuman et al. (1985).

6 For examples and analyses of disclaimers, and generalization and specification moves in discourse about ethnic affairs, see van Dijk (1984, 1987).

7 For such 'deviations' of normal procedures as constitutive of racist events, see Essed (1991).

8 For the ideological implications of these syntactic variations, see, for example, Fowler (1991); Fowler et al. (1979); van Dijk (1991).

9 Although, initially, conversation analysis ignored typical macro-notions such as power and inequality, later work in this area has uncovered many conversational enactments of such social relations. See, for example, Boden and Zimmerman (1991); Coulthard (1992); Crawford (1994); Drew and Heritage (1992); Holmes (1995); West (1984).

10 On manipulation and mind management in ideological production (e.g. related to US foreign policy), see, for example, Herman (1992); Herman and Chomsky (1988). However, although frequently used, the notion of 'manipulation' has, to my knowledge, never been made explicit in a theory.

11 See Vallas (1991) for a study that shows how hegemonic ideological control by management over the workers may fail when the latter are able to develop a critical consciousness of the employment relation. This study also shows, however, that in this case it is the strength of sexist ideologies among male workers that may override management ideologies. See Martín Rojo and Callejo Gallego (1995) for a related study of executives and 'inhibited' sexism, and the responses of women to forms of dominant discourse.

Chapter 28

1 For 'symbolic' racism and related forms of 'modern', 'everyday,' or 'new' racism, see, for example, Barker (1981); Dovidio and Gaertner (1986); Essed (1991). See also Note 7.

2 For studies of neo-conservatism and the New Right, see Bennett (1990); Kroes (1984); Levitas (1986).

3 See for instance his controversial book *Illiberal Education* (D'Souza, 1992).

4 See, for example, Aufderheide (1992); Berman (1992); Fish (1994); Williams (1995).

5 Similar strategic moves of 'frankness' were also found in many other discourses about minorities, both in everyday conversation as well in institutional talk and text of the elites (van Dijk, 1987, 1993a).

6 See van Dijk (1991).

7 See Chapter 14, Note 3 for references to other studies on racism. For (the permanence of) racism in the USA, see also Bell (1992); Doob (1993); Feagin and Sikes (1994); Feagin and Vera (1995); Powell (1993). For a bibliography, see Weinberg (1990).

References

Abelson, R.P. (1973) 'The structure of belief systems', in R.C. Schank and K.M. Colby (eds), *Computer Models of Thought and Language*. San Francisco: Freeman. pp. 287–340.

Abelson, R.P. (1976) 'Script processing in attitude formation and decision making', in J.S. Carroll and J.W. Payne (eds), *Cognition and Social Behavior*. Hillsdale, NJ: Erlbaum. pp. 33–46.

Abelson, R.P. (1981) 'The psychological status of the script concept', *American Psychologist*, 36: 715–29.

Abelson, R.P. (1983) 'Whatever became of consistency theory?', *Personality and Social Psychology Bulletin*, 9: 37–54.

Abelson, R.P. and Rosenberg, J.J. (1958) 'Symbolic psycho-logic: a model of attitude cognition', *Behavioral Science*, 3: 1–13.

Abelson, R.P., Aronson, E., McGuire, W.J., Newcomb, T.M., Rosenberg, M.J. and Tannenbaum, P.H. (eds) (1968) *Theories of Cognitive Consistency: A Sourcebook*. Chicago: Rand McNally.

Abercrombie, N., Hill, S. and Turner, B.S. (1980) *The Dominant Ideology Thesis*. London: Allen and Unwin.

Abercrombie, N., Hill, S. and Turner, B.S. (eds) (1990) *Dominant Ideologies*. London: Unwin Hyman.

Able, D. (1995) *Hate Groups*. Springfield, NJ: Enslow.

Aboud, F.E. (1988) *Children and Prejudice*. Oxford: Blackwell.

Aboud, F. E. and Doyle, A.B. (1993) 'The early development of ethnic identity and attitudes', in Martha E. Bernal and George P. Knight (eds), *Ethnic Identity: Formation and Transmission among Hispanics and Other Minorities*. (SUNY series, United States Hispanic studies) Albany, NY: State University of New York Press. pp. 47–59.

Abrams, D. and Hogg, M.A. (eds) (1990) *Social Identity Theory: Constructive and Critical Advances*. New York: Harvester-Wheatsheaf.

Adams, I. (1993) *Political Ideology Today*. Manchester: Manchester University Press.

Adamson, W.L. (1983) *Hegemony and Revolution: A Study of Antonio Gramsci's Political and Cultural Theory*. Berkeley, CA: University of California Press.

Aebischer, V., Deconchy, J.P. and Lipiansky, E.M. (1992) *Idéologies et répresentations sociales*. Fribourg: Delval.

Agger, B. (1990) *The Decline of Discourse: Reading, Writing, and Resistance in Postmodern Capitalism*. London: Falmer.

Agger, B. (1991) *A Critical Theory of Public Life: Knowledge, Discourse, and Politics in an Age of Decline*. London: Falmer.

Agger, B. (1992) *The Discourse of Domination: From the Frankfurt School to Postmodernism*. Evanston, IL: Northwestern University Press.

Agger, B. (1993) *Gender, Culture, and Power: Toward a Feminist Postmodern Critical Theory*. New York: Praeger.

Alexander, J.C. (1995) 'The reality of reduction: the failed synthesis of Pierre Bourdieu', in J.C. Alexander, *Fin de Siècle Social Theory: Relativism, Reduction and the Problem of Reason*. London: Verso. pp. 128–217.

Alexander, J.C., Giesen, B., Munch, R. and Smelser, N.J. (eds) (1987) *The Micro–Macro Link*. Berkeley, CA: University of California Press.

Allen, M.W. and Caillouet, R.H. (1994) 'Legitimation endeavors: impression management strategies used by an organization in crisis', *Communication Monographs*, 61 (1): 44–62.

Altheide, D.L. (1985) *Media Power*. Beverly Hills, CA: Sage.

Althusser, L. (1984) *Essays on Ideology*. London: Verso.

Altschull, J.H. (1984) *Agents of Power: The Role of the News Media in Human Affairs*. New York: Longman.

Alvesson, M. (1987) *Organization Theory and Technocratic Consciousness: Rationality, Ideology, and Quality of Work*. Berlin: De Gruyter.

Alvesson, M. (1991) 'Organizational symbolism and ideology', *Journal of Management Studies*, 28 (3): 207–25.

Anderson, D.G. (1988) 'Power, rhetoric, and the state: a theory of presidential legitimacy', *Review of Politics*, 50 (2): 198–214.

Antaki, C. (ed.) (1981) *The Psychology of Ordinary Explanations of Social Behaviour*. London: Academic Press.

Antaki, C. (ed.) (1988) *Analysing Everyday Explanation: A Casebook of Methods*. London: Sage.

Antaki, C. (1994a) 'Commonsense reasoning: arriving at conclusions or traveling towards them?', in Jürg Siegfried (ed.), *The Status of Common Sense in Psychology*. Norwood, NJ: Ablex. pp. 169–82.

Antaki, C. (1994b) *Explaining and Arguing: The Social Organization of Accounts*. London: Sage.

Apple, M.W. (1979) *Ideology and Curriculum*. London: Routledge and Kegan Paul.

Apple, M.W. (ed.) (1982) *Cultural and Economic Reproduction in Education: Essays on Class, Ideology, and the State*. London: Routledge and Kegan Paul.

Apple, M.W. and Weis, L. (eds) (1983) *Ideology and Practice in Schooling*. Philadelphia: Temple University Press.

Argyle, M., Furnham, A. and Graham, J.A. (1981) *Social Situations*. Cambridge: Cambridge University Press.

Arkes, H.R. and Hammond, K.R. (eds) (1986) *Judgement and Decision Making: An Interdisciplinary Reader*. Cambridge: Cambridge University Press.

Aronowitz, S. (1988) *Science as Power: Discourse and Ideology in Modern Society*. Minneapolis, MN: University of Minnesota Press.

Ashcraft, M.H. (1994) *Human Memory and Cognition*. New York: HarperCollins.

Atkinson, J.M. (1984) *Our Masters' Voices: The Language and Body Language of Politics*. London: Methuen.

Aufderheide, P. (ed.) (1992) *Beyond PC: Toward a Politics of Understanding*. Saint Paul, MN: Graywolf Press.

Auer, P. and Di Luzio, A. (eds) (1992) *The Contextualization of Language*. Amsterdam: Benjamins.

Augoustinos, M. and Walker, I. (1995) *Social Cognition: An Integrated Introduction*. London: Sage.

Austen, J. and Davie, J. (eds) (1991) *Persuasion*. New York: Oxford University Press.

Austin, L. (1977) 'Visual symbols, political ideology, and culture', *Ethos*, 5 (3): 306–25.

Baars, B.J. (1988) *A Cognitive Theory of Consciousness*. Cambridge: Cambridge University Press.

Baer, D.E. and Lambert, R.D. (1990) 'Socialization into dominant vs. counter ideology among university-educated Canadians', *Canadian Review of Sociology and Anthropology*, 27 (4): 487–504.

Bailey, L. (1994) *Critical Theory and the Sociology of Knowledge. A Comparative Study in the Theory of Ideology*. New York: Lang.

Ballaster, R (1991) *Women's Worlds: Ideology, Femininity and the Woman's Magazine*. New York: Macmillan.

Balon, R.E., et al. (1978) 'How sex and race affect perceptions of newscasters', *Journalism Quarterly*, 55: 160–3.

Banerjee, S. (ed.) (1986) *Culture and Communication*. Patriot.

Barkan, E. (1992) *The Retreat of Scientific Racism: Changing Concepts of Race in Britain and the United States between the World Wars*. Cambridge: Cambridge University Press.

Barker, A.J. (1978) *The African Link: British Attitudes to the Negro in the Era of the Atlantic Slave Trade, 1550–1807*. London: Frank Cass.

Barker, M. (1981) *The New Racism*. London: Junction Books.

Barker, M. (1989) *Comics: Ideology, Power and the Critics*. Manchester: Manchester University Press.

Barley, S.R. and Kunda, G. (1992) 'Design and devotion: surges of rational and normative ideologies of control in managerial discourse', *Administrative Science Quarterly*, 37 (3): 363–99.

Barnard, F.M. (1992) 'Norms, procedures, and democratic legitimacy', *Political Studies*, 40 (4): 659–78.

Barrett, M., Corrigan, P., Kuhn, A. and Wolff, J. (1979) 'Representation and cultural production', in M. Barrett, P. Corrrigan, A. Kuhn and J. Wolff (eds), *Ideology and Cultural Production*. London: Croom Helm.

Barsalou, L.W. (1992) *Cognitive Psychology: An Overview for Cognitive Scientists*. Hillsdale, NJ: Erlbaum.

Bartlett, F.C. (1932) *Remembering: An Experimental and Social Study*. Cambridge: Cambridge University Press.

Baumgartner, P. and Payr, S. (1995) *Speaking Minds: Interviews with Twenty Eminent Cognitive Scientists*. Princeton, NJ: Princeton University Press.

Bell, A. (1995) 'Language and the media', *Annual Review of Applied Linguistics*, 15: 23–41.

Bell, D. (1960) *The End of Ideology: On the Exhaustion of Political Ideas in the Fifties*. New York: Free Press.

Bell, D.A. (1992) *Faces at the Bottom of the Well: The Permanence of Racism*. New York: Basic Books.

Benedict, R. (1982) *Race: Science and Politics: With the Races of Mankind*. Westport, CN: Greenwood Press.

Bennett, D.H. (1990) *The Party of Fear: From Nativist Movements to the New Right in American History*. New York: Vintage Books.

Ben-Tovim, G., Gabriel, J., Law, I. and Stredder, K. (1986) *The Local Politics of Race*. London: Macmillan.

Berent, M.K. and Krosnick, J.K. (1995) 'The relation between political attitude importance and knowledge structure', in Milton Lodge and Kathleen M. McGraw (eds), *Political Judgment: Structure and Process*. Ann Arbor, MI: University of Michigan Press. pp. 91–109.

Berezin, M. (1991) 'The organization of political-ideology: culture, state, and theater in Fascist Italy', *American Sociological Review*, 56 (5): 639–51.

Berman, P. (ed.) (1992) *Debating P.C.: The Controversy over Political Correctness on College Campuses*. New York: Dell.

Biber, D. and Finegan, E. (1989) 'Styles of stance in English: lexical and grammatical marking of evidentiality and affect', *Text*, 9 (1): 93–124.

Billig, M. (ed.) (1976) *Social Psychology and Intergroup Relations*. London: Academic Press.

Billig, M. (1982) *Ideology and Social Psychology*. Oxford: Blackwell.

Billig, M. (1987) *Arguing and Thinking: A Rhetorical Approach to Social Psychology*. Cambridge: Cambridge University Press.

Billig, M. (1989) 'The argumentative nature of holding strong views: a case study', *European Journal of Social Psychology*, 19: 203–22.

Billig, M. (1990) 'Collective memory, ideology and the British Royal Family', in D. Middleton and D. Edwards (eds), *Collective Remembering*. Sage: London. pp. 60–80.

Billig, M. (1991a) 'Consistency and group ideology: towards a rhetorical approach to the study of justice', in R. Vermunt and H. Steensma (eds), *Social Justice in Human Relations*. New York: Plenum.

Billig, M. (1991b) *Ideology and Opinions: Studies in Rhetorical Psychology*. London: Sage.

Billig, M. (1995a) *Banal Nationalism*. London: Sage.

Billig, M. (1995b) 'Rhetorical psychology, ideological thinking and imagining nationhood', in H. Johnston and B. Klandermans (eds), *Culture and Social Movements*. Minneapolis, MN: University of Minnesota Press.

Billig, M. and Sabucedo, J.M. (1994) 'Rhetorical and ideological dimensions of common sense', in Jürg Siegfried (ed.), *The Status of Common Sense in Psychology*. Norwood, NJ: Ablex. pp. 121–45.

Billig, M., Condor, S., Edwards, D., Gane, M., Middleton, D. and Radley, A.R. (1988) *Ideological Dilemmas: A Social Psychology of Everyday Thinking*. London: Sage.

Billington, R. (1982) 'Ideology and feminism: why the suffragettes were "wild women"', *Women's Studies International Forum*, 5 (6): 663–74.

Blackwell, D. (1994) 'The emergence of racism in group analysis', *Group Analysis*, 27 (2): 197–210.

Blommaert, J.M.E. (1991) 'Nation-building, democracy, and pragmatic leadership in Kenya Nyayo ideology', *Communication and Cognition*, 24 (2): 181–94.

Bobrow, D.G. and Collins, A. (1975) *Representation and Understanding: Studies in Cognitive Science*. New York: Academic Press.

Boden, D. and Zimmerman, D.H. (eds) (1991) *Talk and Social Structure: Studies in Ethnomethodology and Conversation Analysis*. Cambridge: Polity.

Bostrom, R.N. (1983) *Persuasion*. Englewood Cliffs, NJ: Prentice-Hall.

Bourdieu, P. (1973) 'Cultural reproduction and social reproduction', in R. Brown (ed.), *Knowledge, Education, and Cultural Change: Papers in the Sociology of Education*. London: Tavistock. pp. 71–112.

Bourdieu, P. (1984) *Distinction: A Social Critique of the Judgment of Taste*. Cambridge, MA: Harvard University Press.

Bourdieu, P. (1984) *Homo Academicus*. Paris: Minuit.

Bourdieu, P. (1985) 'The genesis of the concepts of "Habitus" and "Field"', *Sociocriticism*, 2 (2): 11–24.

Bourdieu, P. (1988) *Language and Symbolic Power*. Cambridge: Polity.

Bourdieu, P. (1989) *La noblesse d'état: grandes écoles et esprit de corps*. Paris: Minuit.

Bourdieu, P. (1990) *The Logic of Practice*. Stanford, CA: Stanford University Press.

Bourdieu, P. and Passeron, J.C. (1977) *Reproduction: In Education, Society and Culture*. London: Sage.

Boylan, T.A. and Foley, T.P. (1992) *Political Economy and Colonial Ireland: The Propagation and Ideological Function of Economic Discourse in the Nineteenth Century*. London: Routledge.

Bradac, J.J. (1989) *Message Effects in Communication Science*. London: Sage.

Brazil, D. (1983) 'Intonation and discourse: some principles and procedures', *Text*, 3 (1): 39–70.

Breakwell, G.M., and Canter, D.V. (eds) (1993) *Empirical Approaches to Social Representations*. Oxford: Clarendon.

Breckler, S.J. (1984) 'Empirical validation of affect, behavior, and cognition as distinct components of attitude', *Journal of Personality and Social Psychology*, 47: 1191–1205.

Brewer, W.F. and Nakamura, G.V. (1984) 'The nature and functions of schemas', in R.S. Wyer and T.K. Srull (eds), *Handbook of Social Cognition*, (vol. 1). Hillsdale, NJ: Erlbaum. pp. 119–60.

Brewster Smith, M. (1969) *Social Psychology and Human Values*. Chicago: Aldine.

Bristor, J.M., Lee, R.G. and Hunt, M.R. (1995) 'Race and ideology: African-American images in television advertising', *Journal of Public Policy and Marketing*, 14 (1): 48–59.

Britton, B.K. and Graesser, A.C. (eds) (1996) *Models of Understanding Text*. Mahwah, NJ: Erlbaum.

Brome, D.R. (1989) 'A developmental analysis of Black children's others concept', *Journal of Black Psychology*, 15 (2): 149–62.

Brooks, C. (1994) 'Class consciousness and politics in comparative perspective', *Social Science Research*, 23 (2): 167–95.

Brown, R.H. (1989) *Social Science as Civic Discourse: Essays on the Invention, Legitimation, and Uses of Social Theory.* Chicago, IL: University of Chicago Press.

Brown, R. and Gilman, A. (1960) 'The pronouns of power and solidarity', in T.A. Sebeok (ed.), *Style in Language.* Cambridge, MA: MIT Press. pp. 253–77.

Browning, R.P., Marshall, D.R. and Tabb, D.H. (eds) (1990) *Racial Politics in American Cities.* New York: Longman.

Bryant, J. and Zillmann, D. (eds) (1986) *Perspectives on Media Effects.* Hillsdale, NJ: Erlbaum.

Burgoon, M., Burgoon, J.K. and Shatzer, M.J. (1987) 'Ethnic differences in the evaluation of newspaper image', *International Journal of Intercultural Relations*, 11 (1): 49–64.

Burton, F. and Carlen, P. (1979) *Official Discourse: On Discourse Analysis, Government Publications, Ideology and the State.* London: Routledge and Kegan Paul.

Buttel, F.H. and Flinn, W.L. (1978) 'The politics of environmental concern: the impacts of party identification and political ideology on environmental attitudes', *Environment and Behavior*, 10 (1): 17–36.

Button, G. (ed.) (1991) *Ethnomethodology and the Human Sciences.* Cambridge: Cambridge University Press.

Byrne, J.P. (1993) 'Academic-freedom and political neutrality in law-schools: an essay on structure and ideology in professional-education', *Journal of Legal Education*, 43 (3): 315–39.

Carbó, T. (1987) 'Identité et difference dans le discours parlementaire mexicaine' (Identity and difference in Mexican parliamentary discourse), *Langage et Société*, 39: 31–44.

Carlton, E. (1984) 'Ideologies as belief systems', *International Journal of Sociology and Social Policy*, 4 (2): 17–29.

CCCS (Centre for Contemporary Cultural Studies) (1978) *On Ideology.* London: Hutchinson.

Charniak, E. (1972) 'Toward a model of children's story comprehension', PhD dissertation, Massachusetts Institute of Technology.

Chase, A. (1975) *The Legacy of Malthus: The Social Costs of the New Scientific Racism.* Urbana, IL: University of Illinois Press.

Chilton, P. (ed.) (1985) *Language and the Nuclear Arms Debate: Nukespeak Today.* London and Dover, NH: Frances Pinter.

Chilton, P. (1988) *Orwellian Language and the Media.* London: Pluto Press.

Chilton, P. (1995) *Security Metaphors: Cold War Discourse from Containment to Common House.* New York: Lang.

Chodorow, N. (1978) *The Reproduction of Mothering.* Berkeley, CA: University of California Press.

Cialdini, R.B. (1993) *Influence: The New Psychology of Persuasion.* New York: William Morrow.

Cicourel, A.V. (1973) *Cognitive Sociology: Language and Meaning in Social Interaction.* Harmondsworth: Penguin.

Clancey, W.J., Smoliar, S.W. and Stefik, M.J. (eds) (1994) *Contemplating Mind: A Forum for Artificial Intelligence.* Cambridge, MA: MIT Press.

Clegg, S.R. (1989) *Frameworks of Power.* London: Sage.

Cohen, G., Kiss, G. and Le Voi, M.E. (1993) *Memory: Current Issues.* Milton Keynes: Open University Press.

Collins, H. (1992) *Equality Matters: Equal Opportunities in the 90's – Background and Current Issues.* London: Library Association.

Connell, I. (1978) 'Monopoly capitalism and the media', in S. Hibbin (ed.), *Politics, Ideology and the State.* London: Lawrence and Wishart. pp. 69–98.

Converse, P.E. (1964) 'The nature of belief systems in mass publics', *International Yearbook of Political Behavior Research*, 5: 206–62.

Corson, D. (1995) 'World view, cultural values and discourse norms: the cycle of cultural reproduction', *International Journal of Intercultural Relations*, 19 (2): 183–95.

Coulter, J. (1979) *Social Construction of Mind: Studies in Ethnomethodology and Linguistic Philosophy*. London: Macmillan.

Coulter, J. (1983) *Rethinking Cognitive Theory*. New York: St Martin's Press.

Coulter, J. (1989) *Mind in Action*. Cambridge: Polity.

Coulthard, R.M. (ed.) (1992) *Advances in Spoken Discourse Analysis*. London: Routledge.

Crawford, M. (1994) *Talking Difference: On Gender and Language*. London: Sage.

Curran, J., Smith, A. and Wingate, P. (eds) (1987) *Acton Society Impacts and Influences: Essays on Media Power in the Twentieth Century*. New York: Methuen.

Dancy, J. (1985) *Introduction to Contemporary Epistemology*. Oxford: Blackwell.

Dant, T. (1991) *Knowledge, Ideology, and Discourse: A Sociological Perspective*. London: Routledge.

Davies, M. and Humphreys, G.W. (eds) (1993) *Consciousness: Psychological and Philosophical Essays*, (Readings in Mind and Language, vol. 2). Oxford: Blackwell.

Davis, N.J. and Robinson, R.V. (1991) 'Men's and women's consciousness of gender inequality: Austria, West-Germany, Great-Britain, and the United- States', *American Sociological Review*, 56 (1): 72–84.

Davis, H. and Walton, P. (eds) (1983) *Language, Image, Media*. Oxford: Blackwell.

De Fornel, M. (1983) 'Legitimité et actes de langage' (Legitimacy and speech acts), *Actes de la recherche en sciences sociales*, 46: 31–8.

Della Fave, L.R. (1980) 'The meek shall not inherit the earth: self evaluation and the legitimacy of stratification', *American Sociological Review*, 45: 955–72.

Della Fave, L.R. (1986) 'Toward an explication of the legitimation process', *Social Forces*, 65 (2): 476–500.

Denhière, G. and Baudet, S. (1992) *Lecture, compréhension de texte et science cognitive*. Paris: Presses Universitaires de France.

Dennett, D.C. (1993) *Consciousness Explained*. London: Penguin.

Devine, P.G., Hamilton, D.L. and Ostrom, T.M. (eds) (1994) *Social Cognition: Impact on Social Psychology*. London: Academic Press.

Dickson, G.L. (1993) 'The unintended consequences of a male professional ideology for the development of nursing-education', *Advances in Nursing Science*, 15 (3): 67–83.

Dik, S.C. (1978) *Functional Grammar*. Amsterdam: North Holland.

Dik, S.C. (1989) *The Theory of Functional Grammar, Part I: The Structure of the Clause*. Dordrecht: Foris.

Dillingham, G. (1981) 'The emerging black middle class: class conscious or race conscious?', *Ethnic and Racial Studies*, 4: 432–47.

Dines, G. and Humez, J.M.M. (eds) (1995) *Gender, Race, and Class in Media: A Text-Reader*. London: Sage.

Doise, W. (1978) 'Images, representations, ideologies and psychosociological experimentation', *Social Science Information*, 17 (1): 41–69.

Domhoff, G.W. (1978) *The Powers that Be: Processes of Ruling Class Domination in America*. New York: Random House.

Domhoff, G.W. and Ballard, H.B. (eds) (1968) *C. Wright Mills and the Power Elite*. Boston: Beacon.

Doob, C.B. (1993) *Racism: An American Cauldron*. New York: HarperCollins.

Douglas, M. (1986) *How Institutions Think*. Syracuse, NY: Syracuse University Press.

Dovidio, J.F. and Gaertner, S.L. (eds) (1986) *Prejudice, Discrimination, and Racism*. Orlando, FL: Academic Press.

Downey, G.L. (1986) 'Ideology and the clamshell identity: organizational dilemmas in the anti-nuclear power movement', *Social Problems*, 33 (5): 357–73.

Downing, J. (1984) *Radical Media: The Political Experience of Alternative Communication*. Boston: South End Press.

Dreier, P. (1982) 'Capitalists vs. the media: an analysis of an ideological mobilization amongst business leaders', *Media, Culture and Society*, 4: 111–32.

Drew, P. and Heritage, J. (eds) (1992) *Talk at Work: Interaction in Institutional Settings*. Cambridge: Cambridge University Press.

D'Souza, D. (1992) *Illiberal Education: The Politics of Sex and Race on Campus.* New York: Vintage Books.

D'Souza, D. (1995) *The End of Racism: Principles for a Multiracial Society.* New York: Free Press.

Duranti, A. (1984) 'The social meaning of subject pronouns in Italian conversation', *Text,* 4 (4): 277–311.

Duranti, A. and Goodwin, C. (eds) (1992) *Rethinking Context: Language as an Interactive Phenomenon.* Cambridge: Cambridge University Press.

Dworkin, R. (1986) *Law's Empire.* London: Fontana.

Eagleton, T. (1991) *Ideology: An Introduction.* London: Verso.

Eagly, A.H. and Chaiken, S. (1993) *The Psychology of Attitudes.* Orlando, FL: Harcourt Brace Jovanovich.

Eckhardt, C.I., Kassinove, H. and Edwards, L. (1992) 'Religious beliefs and scientific ideology in psychologists: conflicting or coexisting systems?', *Psychological Reports,* 71 (1): 131–45.

Edwards, D. (1994) 'Script formulations: an analysis of event descriptions in conversation', *Journal of Language and Social Psychology,* 13 (3): 211–47.

Edwards, D. (1996) *Discourse and Cognition.* London: Sage.

Edwards, J. (1994) 'Group rights v. individual rights: the case of race-conscious policies', *Journal of Social Policy,* 23 (January): 55–70.

Edwards, D. and Potter, J. (1992) *Discursive Psychology.* London: Sage.

Eglin, P. (1979) 'How conversational analysis elucidates Schutz's commonsense concept of rationality', *Sociolinguistics Newsletter,* 10 (2): 11–17.

Eisenberg, N., Reykowski, J. and Staub, E. (eds) (1989) *Social and Moral Values: Individual and Societal Perspectives.* Hillsdale, NJ: Erlbaum.

Eiser, J.R. (1994) *Attitudes, Chaos and the Connectionist Mind.* Oxford: Blackwell.

Ekehammar, B., Nilsson, I. and Sidanius, J. (1987) 'Education and ideology: basic aspects of education related to adolescents sociopolitical attitudes', *Political Psychology,* 8: 395–410.

Elliot, H.C. (1974) 'Similarities and differences between science and common sense', in R. Turner (ed.), *Ethnomethodology.* Baltimore, MD: Penguin. pp. 21–6.

Ellsworth, E.A. and Whatley, M.H. (eds) (1990) *The Ideology of Images in Educational Media: Hidden Curriculums in the Classroom.* New York: Teachers College Press.

El Warfally, M.G. (1988) *Imagery and Ideology in U.S. Policy Toward Libya, 1969–1982.* Pittsburgh, PA: University of Pittsburgh Press.

Enteman, W.F. (1993) *Managerialism: The Emergence of a New Ideology.* Madison, WI: University of Wisconsin Press.

Essed, P.J.M. (1987) *Academic Racism: Common Sense in the Social Sciences.* Amsterdam: University of Amsterdam, Centre for Ethnic Studies. CRES Publications, No. 5.

Essed, P.J.M. (1990) *Everyday Racism.* Claremont, CA: Hunter House.

Essed, P.J.M. (1991) *Understanding Everyday Racism: An Interdisciplinary Theory.* Newbury Park, CA: Sage.

Fairclough, N.L. (1989) *Language and Power.* London: Longman.

Fairclough, N.L. (1992) 'Michel Foucault and the analysis of discourse', in N.L. Fairclough, *Discourse and Social Change.* Cambridge: Polity. pp. 37–61.

Fairclough, N.L. (1995) *Critical Discourse Analysis: The Critical Study of Language.* Harlow: Longman.

Farr, R.M. and Moscovici, S. (eds) (1984) *Social Representations.* Cambridge: Cambridge University Press.

Fatton, R. (1986) *Black Consciousness in South Africa: The Dialectics of Ideological Resistance to White Supremacy.* Albany, NY: State University of New York Press.

Feagin, J.R. and Feagin, C.B. (1994) *Social Problems: A Critical, Power-conflict Perspective.* Englewood Cliffs, NJ: Prentice-Hall.

Feagin, J. R. and Sikes, M.P. (1994) *Living with Racism: The Black Middle-class Experience.* Boston, MA: Beacon.

Feagin, J. and Vera, H. (1995) *White Racism.* London: Routledge.

Feldman, S.M. (1992) 'Whose common good: racism in the political community', *Georgetown Law Journal*, 80 (5): 1835–77.

Femia, J.V. (1987) *Gramsci's Political Thought: Hegemony, Consciousness and the Revolutionary Process*. Oxford: Clarendon.

Festinger, L. (1957) *A Theory of Cognitive Dissonance*. Stanford, CA: Stanford University Press.

Fillmore, C.J. (1968) 'The case for case', in E. Bach and R.T. Harms (eds), *Universals in Linguistic Theory*. New York: Holt, Rinehart and Winston. pp. 1–88.

Finnis, J. (ed.) (1980) *Natural Law and Natural Rights*. Oxford: Clarendon.

Firth, A. (ed.) (1995) *The Discourse of Negotiation: Studies of Language in the Workplace*. Oxford: Pergamon.

Fish, S.E. (1994) *There's No Such Thing as Free Speech . . . And It's a Good Thing Too*. New York: Oxford University Press.

Fisher, R.J. (1990) *The Social Psychology of Intergroup and International Conflict Resolution*. New York: Springer.

Fisher, S. and Davis, K. (eds) (1993) *Negotiating at the Margins: The Gendered Discourse of Power and Resistance*. New Brunswick, NJ: Rutgers University Press.

Fisher, S. and Todd, A.D. (eds) (1986) *Discourse and Institutional Authority: Medicine, Education, and Law*. Norwood, NJ: Ablex.

Fishkin, S.A., Sussman, S., Stacy, A.W., Dent, C.W., Burton, D. and Flay, B.R. (1993) 'Ingroup versus outgroup perceptions of the characteristics of high-risk youth: negative stereotyping', *Journal of Applied Social Psychology*, 23 (13): 1051–68.

Fiske, S.T. and Taylor, S.E. (1991) *Social Cognition*, (2nd edn). New York: McGraw-Hill.

Fitzgerald, K. (1996) *The Face of the Nation: Immigration, the State and the National Identity*. Stanford, CA: Stanford University Press.

Flaherty, L.T. (1982) 'To love and/or to work: the ideological dilemma of young women', *Adolescent Psychiatry*, 10: 41–51.

Flammer, A. and Kintsch, W. (eds) (1982) *Discourse Processing*. Amsterdam: North Holland.

Fletcher, G.J.O. (1993) 'The scientific credibility of commonsense psychology', in Kenneth H. Craik, Robert Hogan and Raymond N. Wolfe (eds), *Fifty Years of Personality Psychology: Perspectives on Individual Differences*. New York: Plenum. pp. 251–68.

Fletcher, R. (1991) *Science, Ideology, and the Media: The Cyril Burt Scandal*. New Brunswick, NJ: Transaction.

Folkertsma, M.J. (1988) *Ideology and Leadership*. Englewood Cliffs, NJ: Prentice-Hall.

Forgas, J. P. (1979) *Social Episodes*. London: Academic Press.

Forgas, J.P. (ed.). (1981) *Social Cognition: Perspectives on Everyday Understanding*. London: Academic Press.

Foucault, M. (1972) *The Archaeology of Knowledge and the Discourse on Language*. New York: Harper and Row (Harper Colophon).

Foucault, M. (1975) *The Birth of the Clinic: An Archaeology of Medical Perception*. New York: Random House.

Foucault, M. (1979) *Discipline and Punish: The Birth of the Prison*. Harmondsworth: Penguin.

Foucault, M. (1980) *Power/Knowledge: Selected Interviews and Other Writings, 1972–1977*. New York: Pantheon Books.

Foucault, M. (1981) 'The order of discourse', in Robert Young (ed.), *Untying the Text: A Post-Structuralist Reader*. London: Routledge and Kegan Paul. pp. 48–78.

Fowler, R. (1987). 'The intervention of the media in the reproduction of power', in I.M. Zavala, T.A. van Dijk and D.M. Diaz (eds), *Approaches to Discourse, Poetics and Psychiatry*. Amsterdam: Benjamins. pp. 67–80.

Fowler, R. (1991) *Language in the News: Discourse and Ideology in the Press*. London: Routledge.

Fowler, R., Hodge, B., Kress, G. and Trew, T. (1979) *Language and Control*. London: Routledge and Kegan Paul.

Freeden, M. (1996) *Ideologies and Political Theory: A Conceptual Approach.* Oxford: Clarendon.

Freedle, R.O. and Carroll, J.B. (eds) (1972) *Language Comprehension and the Acquisition of Knowledge.* New York: Winston.

Frijda, N. (1987) *The Emotions.* Cambridge: Cambridge University Press.

Furnham, A. (1994) 'The psychology of common sense', in J. Siegfried (ed.), *The Status of Common Sense in Psychology.* Norwood, NJ: Ablex. pp. 259–78.

Furnham, A. and Argyle, M. (eds) (1981) *The Psychology of Social Situations.* Oxford: Pergamon.

Fussell, S.R. and Krauss, R.M. (1992) 'Coordination of knowledge in communication: effects of speakers' assumptions about what others know', *Journal of Personality and Social Psychology*, 62 (3): 378–91.

Gaffney, J. (ed.) (1989) *The French Presidential Elections of 1988: Ideology and Leadership in Contemporary France.* Aldershot: Gower.

Gale, F.G. (1994) *Political Literacy: Rhetoric, Ideology, and the Possibility of Justice.* Albany, NY: State University of New York Press.

Gans, H. (1979) *Deciding What's News.* New York: Pantheon Books.

Garcia, M.T. (1989) *Mexican Americans: Leadership, Ideology, and Identity, 1930–1960.* New Haven, CT: Yale University Press.

Garner, R. (1996) *Contemporary Movements and Ideologies.* New York: McGraw-Hill.

Geertz, C. (1973a) 'Ideology as a cultural system', in C. Geertz, *The Interpretation of Cultures.* New York: Basic Books. pp. 193–233.

Geertz, C. (1973b) *The Interpretation of Cultures.* New York: Basic Books.

Gibbon, D. and Richter, H. (eds) (1984) *Intonation, Accent, and Rhythm: Studies in Discourse Phonology.* Berlin: De Gruyter.

Giddens, A. and Held, D. (eds) (1982) *Classes, Power, and Conflict: Classical and Contemporary Debates.* Berkeley, CA: University of California Press.

Giroux, H. (1981) *Ideology, Culture and the Process of Schooling.* London: Falmer.

Gittins, D. (1993) *The Family in Question: Changing Households and Familiar Ideologies.* New York: Macmillan.

Glasgow University Media Group (1976) *Bad News.* London: Routledge and Kegan Paul.

Glasgow University Media Group (1980) *More Bad News.* London: Routledge and Kegan Paul.

Glaser, R. (1987) 'Learning theory and theories of knowledge', in Erik De Corte, Hans Lodewijks and Roger Parmentier (eds), *Learning and Instruction: European Research in an International Context*, (vol. 1). Oxford: Pergamon Press. pp. 397–414.

Glasser, T.L. and Salmon, C.T. (eds) (1995) *Public Opinion and the Communication of Consent.* New York: Guilford Press.

Globerman, J. (1990) 'Free enterprise, professional ideology, and self-interest: an analysis of resistance by Canadian physicians to universal health-insurance', *Journal of Health and Social Behavior*, 31 (1): 11–27.

Goffman, E. (1974) *Frame Analysis.* New York: Harper and Row.

Goke-Pariola, A. (1993) *The Role of Language in the Struggle for Power and Legitimacy in Africa.* Lampeter: Mellen Press.

Golding, P. and Murdock, G. (1979) 'Ideology and the mass media: the question of determination', in M. Barrett, P. Corrigan, A. Kuhn and J. Wolff (eds), *Ideology and Cultural Production.* London: Croom Helm. pp. 198–224.

Goll, I. and Zeitz, G. (1991) 'Conceptualizing and measuring corporate ideology', *Organization Studies*, 12 (2): 191–207.

Gonzalvo, P., Canas, J.J. and Bajo, M.T. (1994) 'Structural representations in knowledge acquisition', *Journal of Educational Psychology*, 86 (4): 601–16.

Graber, D.A. (1988) *Processing the News*, (2nd edn). New York: Longman.

Graesser, A.C. (1981) *Prose Comprehension Beyond the Word.* New York: Springer.

Graetz, B. (1986) 'Social structure and class consciousness: facts, fictions and fantasies', *Australian and New Zealand Journal of Sociology*, 22 (1): 46–64.

Gramsci, A. (1971) *Prison Notebooks*. New York: International Publishers.

Greatbatch, D. (1992) 'On the management of disagreement between news interviewees', in P. Drew and J. Heritage (eds), *Talk at Work: Interaction in Institutional Settings*. Cambridge: Cambridge University Press. pp. 268–310.

Greenberg, G. and Tobach, E. (eds) (1983) *Cognition, Language and Consciousness: Integrative Levels*. Hillsdale, NJ: Erlbaum.

Greenfeld, L. (1988) 'Professional ideologies and patterns of gatekeeping: evaluation and judgment within 2 art worlds', *Social Forces*, 66 (4): 903–25.

Gregg, G.S. (1991) *Self-representation: Life Narrative Studies in Identity and Ideology*. New York: Greenwood.

Grenier, G. and Hogler, R.L. (1991) 'Labor law and managerial ideology: employee participation as a social control system', *Work and Occupations*, 18 (3): 313–33.

Grimshaw, A.D. (ed.) (1990) *Conflict Talk: Sociolinguistic Investigations of Arguments in Conversations*. Cambridge: Cambridge University Press.

Grofman, B. and Hyman, G. (1974) 'The logical foundations of ideology', *Behavioral Science*, 19 (4): 225–37.

Gumperz, J.J. (1982a) *Discourse Strategies*. Cambridge: Cambridge University Press.

Gumperz, J.J. (ed.) (1982b) *Language and Social Identity*. Cambridge: Cambridge University Press.

Gunter, B. (1987) *Poor Reception: Misunderstanding and Forgetting Broadcast News*. Hillsdale, NJ: Erlbaum.

Gurin, P. and Townsend, A. (1986) 'Properties of gender identity and their implications for gender consciousness', *British Journal of Social Psychology*, 25 (2): 139–48.

Habermas, J. (1975) *Legitimation Crisis*. Boston: Beacon.

Habermas, J. (1993) *Justification and Application: Remarks on Discourse Ethics*. Oxford: Polity.

Hachten, W. (1981) *The Worlds News Prism: Changing Media, Clashing Ideologies*. Ames, IA: Iowa State University Press.

Haghighat, C. (1988) *Racisme 'scientifique': offensive contre l'égalité sociale*. Paris: L'Harmattan.

Hall, S. (1980) 'Introduction to media studies at the Centre', in S. Hall et al. (eds), *Culture, Media, Language*. London: Hutchinson. pp. 117–21

Hall, S. (1982) 'The rediscovery of "ideology": return of the repressed in media studies', in M. Gurevitch, T. Bennett, J. Curran and J. Woollacott (eds), *Culture, Society and the Media*. London and New York: Methuen. pp. 56–90.

Hall, S. (1988) *The Hard Road to Renewal: Thatcherism and the Crisis of the Left*. London: Verso.

Hall, S. (1996) 'The problem of ideology: Marxism without guarantees', in D. Morley and K.H. Chen (eds), *Stuart Hall: Critical Dialogues in Cultural Studies*. London: Routledge. pp. 25–46. (Earlier published in B. Matthews (ed.) (1983) *Marx: 100 Years On*. London: Lawrence and Wishart. pp. 57–84.)

Hall, M.L. and Allen, W.R. (1989) 'Race consciousness among African-American college students', in Gordon LaVern Berry and Joy Keiko Asamen (eds), *Black Students: Psychosocial Issues and Academic Achievement*, (Sage focus editions, vol. 109). Newbury Park, CA: Sage Publications. pp. 172–97.

Hall, S. and Jefferson, T. (eds) (1976) *Resistance through Rituals*. London: Hutchinson.

Hall, S., Lumley, B. and McLennan, G. (1978) 'Politics and ideology: Gramsci', in CCCS (ed.), *On Ideology*. London: Hutchinson. pp. 45–76.

Hall, S., Hobson, D., Lowe, A. and Willis, P. (eds) (1980) *Culture, Media, Language*. London: Hutchinson.

Halliday, M.A.K. (1973) *Explorations in the Functions of Language*. London: Edward Arnold.

Halliday, M.A.K. (1985) *A Short Introduction to Functional Grammar*. London: Edward Arnold.

Halliday, M.A.K. (ed.) (1987) *New Developments in Systemic Linguistics*. London: Pinter.

Harré, R. (1995) 'Discursive psychology', in J.A. Smith, R.Harré and L. van Langenhove (eds), *Rethinking Psychology*. London: Sage. pp. 143–59.

Harré, R. and Gillett, G. (1994) *The Discursive Mind*. London: Sage.

Harré, R. and Stearns, P. (eds) (1995) *Discursive Psychology in Practice*. London: Sage.

Harris, R.J. (1989) *A Cognitive Psychology of Mass Communication*. Hillsdale, NJ: Erlbaum.

Hartley, J. and Montgomery, M. (1985) 'Representations and relations: ideology and power in press and TV news', in T.A. van Dijk (ed.), *Discourse and Communication: New Approaches to the Analysis of Mass Media Discourse and Communication*. Berlin: de Gruyter. pp. 233–69.

Hechter, M., Nadel, L. and Michod, R.E. (eds) (1993) *The Origin of Values*. New York: de Gruyter.

Heider, F. (1946) 'Attitudes and cognitive organization', *Journal of Psychology*, 21: 107–12.

Heider, F. (1958) *The Psychology of Interpersonal Relations*. New York: Wiley.

Heisey, D.R. and Trebing, J.D. (1986) 'Authority and legitimacy: a rhetorical case-study of the Iranian revolution', *Communication Monographs*, 53: 295–310.

Heritage, J. C. (1985) 'Analyzing news interviews: aspects of the production of talk for an overhearing audience', in T.A. van Dijk (ed.), *Handbook of Discourse Analysis* (vol. 3). New York: Academic Press. pp. 95–119.

Heritage, J. C. (1987) 'Ethnomethodology', in A. Giddens and J. Turner (eds), *Social Theory Today*. Cambridge: Polity. pp. 224–72.

Heritage, J.C. and Greatbatch, D. (1986) 'Generating applause: a study of rhetoric and response at party political conferences', *American Journal of Sociology*, 92 (1): 110–57.

Herman, E.S. (1992) *Beyond Hypocrisy: Decoding the News in an Age of Propaganda: Including a Doublespeak Dictionary for the 1990s*, (Illustrations by Matt Wuerker). Boston: South End Press.

Herman, E.S. and Chomsky, N. (1988) *Manufacturing Consent: The Political Economy of the Mass Media*. New York: Pantheon Books.

Hewstone, M., Machleit, U. and Wagner, U. (1989) 'Selfgroup, ingroup, and outgroup achievement attributions of German and Turkish pupils', *Journal of Social Psychology*, 129 (4): 459–70.

Hickmann, M. (ed.) (1987) *Social and Functional Approaches to Language and Thought*. London: Academic Press.

Higgins, E.T., Herman, C.P. and Zanna, M.P. (eds) (1981) *Social Cognition: The Ontario Symposium*, (vol. 1). Hillsdale, NJ: Erlbaum.

Hill, K.Q. and Leighley, J.E. (1993) 'Party ideology, organization, and competitiveness as mobilizing forces in gubernatorial elections', *American Journal of Political Science*, 37 (4): 1158–78.

Himmelweit, H.T. and Gaskell, G. (eds) (1990) *Societal Psychology*. London: Sage.

Hintikka, J. (1962) *Knowledge and Belief: An Introduction to the Logic of the Two Notions*. Ithaca, NY: Cornell University Press.

Hodge, R. and Kress, G.R. (1988) *Social Semiotics*. London: Polity.

Hodge, R. and Kress, G.R. (1993) *Language as Ideology*. London: Routledge.

Hofstede, G. (1980) *Culture's Consequences*. Beverly Hills, CA: Sage.

Hofstede, G. (1991) *Cultures and Organizations: Software of the Mind*. London: McGraw-Hill.

Holmes, J. (1995) *Women, Men and Politeness*. New York: Longman.

Howard, T.U. (1985) 'Moral reasoning and professional value commitments: a study of social work students' ideology', *Journal of Applied Social Sciences*, 9 (2): 203–21.

Hummon, D.M. (1990) *Commonplaces: Community Ideology and Identity in American Culture*. Albany, NY: State University of New York Press.

Husserl, E. (1962) *Ideas: General Introduction to Pure Phenomenology*. New York: Collier.

Hymes, D. (1962) 'The ethnography of speaking', in T. Gladwin and W.C. Sturtevant (eds), *Anthropology and Human Behavior*. Washington, DC: Anthropological Society of Washington. pp. 13–53.

Ibañez, T. and Iñiguez, L. (eds) (1997) *Critical Social Psychology*. London: Sage.

Inniss, L. and Feagin, J.R. (1989) 'The black underclass ideology in race-relations analysis', *Social Justice – A Journal of Crime Conflict and World Order*, 16 (4): 13–34.

Iyengar, S. and Kinder, D.R. (1987) *News that Matters: Television and American Opinion*. Chicago: University of Chicago Press.

Iyengar, S. and McGuire, W.J. (eds) (1993) *Explorations in Political Psychology* (Duke studies in political psychology). Durham, NC: Duke University Press.

Jackendoff, R. (1987) *Consciousness and the Computational Mind*. Cambridge, MA: MIT Press.

Jacquemet, M. (1994) 'T-Offenses and metapragmatic attacks: strategies of interactional dominance', *Discourse and Society*, 5 (3): 297–319.

Jahoda, G. (1988) 'Critical notes and reflections on social representations', *European Journal of Social Psychology*, 18: 195–209.

Jaspars, J. and Fraser, C. (1984) 'Attitudes and social representations', in R.M. Farr and S. Moscovici (eds), *Social Representations*. Cambridge: Cambridge University Press. pp. 101–24.

Jennings, M.K. (1992) 'Ideological thinking among mass publics and political elites', *Public Opinion Quarterly*, 56 (4): 419–41.

Johnson, C. (1994) 'Gender, legitimate authority, and leader–subordinate conversations', *American Sociological Review*, 59 (1): 122–35.

Johnson, E. (1987) 'Believability of newscasters to Black television viewers', *Western Journal of Black Studies*, 11 (2): 64–68.

Johnson-Laird, P.N. (1983) *Mental Models*. Cambridge: Cambridge University Press.

Johnston, H., Laraña, E. and Gusfield, J.R. (1994) 'Identities, grievances, and new social meovements', in E. Laraña, H. Johnston and J.R. Gusfield (eds), *New Social Movements: From Ideology to Identity*. Philadelphia, PA: Temple University Press. pp. 3–35.

Jones, R.K. (1984) *Ideological Groups: Similarities of Structure and Organisation*. London: Gower.

Joseph, G.G., Reddy, V. and Searle-Chatterjee, M. (1990) 'Eurocentrism in the social-sciences', *Race and Class*, 31 (4): 1–26.

Jost, J.T. and Banaji, M.R. (1994) 'The role of stereotyping in system-justification and the production of false consciousness', Special Issue: 'Stereotypes: Structure, function and process', *British Journal of Social Psychology*, 33 (1): 1–27.

Jowett, G. and O'Donnell, V. (1992) *Propaganda and Persuasion*. London: Sage.

Joyce, P. (ed.) (1995) *Class*. Oxford: Oxford University Press.

Judd, C.M. and Downing, J.W. (1990) 'Political expertise and the development of attitude consistency', *Social Cognition*, 8 (1): 104–24.

Kahneman, D., Slovic, P. and Tversky, A. (eds) (1982) *Judgment under Uncertainty: Heuristics and Biases*. New York: Cambridge University Press.

Karabel, J. and Halsey, A.H. (eds) (1977) *Power and Ideology in Education*. Oxford: Oxford University Press.

Katz, P.A. (1976) 'The acquisition of racial attitudes in children', in Katz, P.A. (ed.), *Towards the Elimination of Racism*. New York: Pergamon. pp. 125–54.

Katz, P.A. and Taylor, D.A. (eds) (1988) *Eliminating Racism: Profiles in Controversy*. New York: Plenum.

Kenshur, O. (1993) *Dilemmas of Enlightenment: Studies in the Rhetoric and Logic of Ideology*. Berkeley, CA: University of California Press.

Kiewe, A. and Houck, D.W. (1991) *A Shining City on a Hill: Ronald Reagan's Economic Rhetoric, 1951–1989*. New York: Praeger.

Kinder, D.R. and Sanders, L.M. (1990) 'Mimicking political debate with survey questions: the case of white opinion on affirmative-action for blacks', *Social Cognition*, 8 (1): 73–103.

Kinder, D.R. and Sears, D.O. (1981) 'Prejudice and politics: symbolic racism versus racial threats to the good life', *Journal of Personality and Social Psychology*, 40: 414–31.

King, D.K. (1988) 'Multiple jeopardy, multiple consciousness: the context of a black feminist ideology', *Signs*, 14 (1): 42–72.

King, J.E. (1991) 'Dysconscious racism: ideology, identity, and the miseducation of teachers', *Journal of Negro Education*, 60 (2): 133–46.

Kinloch, G.C. (1981) *Ideology and Contemporary Sociological Theory*. Englewood Cliffs, NJ: Prentice Hall.

Kintsch, W. (1977) *Memory and Cognition*. New York: Wiley.

Klandermans, B. (1992) 'The social construction of protest and multiorganizational fields', in A.D. Morris and C.M. Mueller (eds), *Frontiers in Social Movement Theory*. New Haven, CT: Yale University Press.

Klandermans, B. (1994) 'Transient identities? Membership patterns of the Dutch peace movement', in E. Laraña, H. Johnston and J. R. Gusfield (eds), *New Social Movements: From Ideology to Identity*. Philadelphia, PA: Temple University Press. pp. 168–84.

Klapper, J.T. (1960) *The Effects of Mass Communications*. Glencoe, IL: Free Press.

Knorr-Cetina, K. and Cicourel, A.V. (eds) (1981) *Advances in Social Theory and Methodology: Towards an Integration of Micro- and Macrosociologies*. London: Routledge and Kegan Paul.

Kornblith, H. (ed.) (1994) *Naturalizing Epistemology*, (2nd edn). Cambridge, MA: MIT Press.

Kosslyn, S.M. and Koenig, O. (1992) *Wet Mind: The New Cognitive Neuroscience*. New York: Free Press.

Kraut, R.E. and Lewis, S.H. (1975) 'Alternate models of family influence on student political ideology', *Journal of Personality and Social Psychology*, 31 (5): 791–800.

Kress, G. (1985) 'Ideological structures in discourse', in T.A. van Dijk (ed.), *Handbook of Discourse Analysis*, (vol. 4: *Discourse Analysis in Society*). London: Academic Press. pp. 27–42.

Kress, G. and van Leeuwen, T. (1990) *Reading Images*. Victoria, Australia: Deakin University Press.

Krieger, J. (1986) *Reagan, Thatcher, and the Politics of Decline*. Cambridge: Polity.

Krishnan, V. (1991) 'Abortion in Canada: religious and ideological dimensions of women's attitudes', *Social Biology*, 38 (3–4): 249–57.

Kroes, R. (1984) *Neo-conservatism, its Emergence in the USA and Europe*. Amsterdam: Free University Press.

Kruglanski, A. W. (1989) *Lay Epistemics and Human Knowledge*. New York: Plenum.

Kuklinski, J.H., Luskin, R.C. and Bolland, J. (1991) 'Where is the schema: going beyond the S-word in political psychology', *American Political Science Review*, 85 (4): 1341–56.

Labov, W. (1972) *Language in the Inner City*. Philadelphia: University of Pennsylvania Press.

Labov, W. and Waletzky, J. (1967) 'Narrative analysis: oral versions of personal experience', in J. Helm (ed.), *Essays on the Verbal and Visual Arts*. Seattle: University of Washington Press. pp. 12–44.

Lakoff, G. (1987) *Women, Fire and Dangerous Things: What Categories Reveal about the Mind*. Chicago: University of Chicago Press.

Lakoff, G. (1995) 'Metaphor, morality, and politics, or, why conservatives have left liberals in the dust', *Social Research*, 62 (2): 177–213.

Landau, E. (1993) *The White Power Movement: America's Racist Hate Groups*. Brookfield, CN: Millbrook Press.

Langston, T.S. (1992) *Ideologues and Presidents: From the New Deal to the Reagan Revolution*. Baltimore, MD: Johns Hopkins University Press.

Laraña, E., Johnston, H. and Gusfield, J. R. (eds) (1994) *New Social Movements: From Ideology to Identity*. Philadelphia: Temple University Press.

Larrain, J. (1979) *The Concept of Ideology*. London: Hutchinson.

Larrain, J. (1994) 'The postmodern critique of ideology', *Sociological Review*, 42 (2): 289–314.

Lau, R.R. and Sears, D.O. (1981) 'Cognitive links between economic greavances and political responses', *Political Behavior*, 3 (4): 279–302.

Lau, R.R. and Sears, D.O. (eds) (1986) *Political Cognition*. Hillsdale, NJ: Erlbaum.

Lau, R.R., Smith, R.A. and Fiske, S.T. (1991) 'Political beliefs, policy interpretations, and political persuasion', *Journal of Politics*, 53 (3): 644–75.

Lauren, P.G. (1988) *Power and Prejudice: The Politics and Diplomacy of Racial Discrimination.* Boulder, CO: Westview Press.

Lawrence, E. (1982) 'Just plain common sense: the roots of "racism" ', in CCCS (ed.), *The Empire Strikes Back: Race and Racism in 70s Britain.* London: Hutchinson. pp. 47–94.

Layton-Henry, Z. (1992) *The Politics of Immigration: Immigration, 'Race' and 'Race' Relations in Post-war Britain.* Oxford: Blackwell.

Le Goff, J.P. (1992) *Le mythe de l'entreprise: critique de l'idéologie managériale.* Paris: Éditions la Decouverte.

Lehrer, K. (1990) *Theory of Knowledge.* London: Routledge.

Lenski, G. (1966) *Power and Privilege.* New York: McGraw-Hill.

Lerner, M. (1991) *Ideas are Weapons: The History and Uses of Ideas*, (with an introductiona and an afterword by the author). New Brunswick, NJ: Transaction.

Levelt, W.J.M. (1989) *Speaking: From Intention to Articulation.* Cambridge, MA: MIT Press.

Levitas, R. (ed.) (1986) *The Ideology of the New Right.* Cambridge: Polity.

Lewis, C. (1992) 'Making sense of common-sense: a framework for tracking hegemony', *Critical Studies in Mass Communication*, 9 (3): 277–92.

Lewy, G. (1982) *False Consciousness: An Essay on Mystification.* New Brunswick, NJ: Transaction Books.

Lichter, S.R., Rothman, S. and Lichter, L. (1990) *The Media Elite: America's New Power-brokers.* New York: Hastings House.

Liebes, T. and Katz, E. (1990) *The Export of Meaning: Cross-cultural Readings of 'Dallas'.* New York: Oxford University Press.

Liebes, T., Katz, E. and Ribak, R. (1991) 'Ideological reproduction', *Political Behavior*, 13 (3): 237–52.

Lipiansky, E.M. (1991) *L'identité française: représentations, mythes, idéologies.* Paris: Editions de l'Espace Européen.

Lipset, S.M. (1960) *Political Man.* New York: Doubleday.

Lipset, S.M. (1972) 'Ideology and no end: the controversy till now', *Encounter 89*.

Little, R. and Smith, S.M. (eds) (1988) *Belief Systems and International Relations.* Oxford: Blackwell.

Lockwood, D. (1966) *The Blackcoated Worker: A Study in Class Consciousness.* London: Unwin.

Loewenberg, F.M. (1984) 'Professional ideology, middle range theories and knowledge building for social work practice', *British Journal of Social Work*, 14 (4): 309–22.

Lowery, S. and DeFleur, M.L. (1995) *Milestones in Mass Communication Research: Media Effects.* London: Longman.

Lucy, J.A. (1992) *Language Diversity and Thought: A Reformulation of the Linguistic Relativity Hypothesis.* Cambridge: Cambridge University Press.

Luke, T.W. (1989) *Screens of Power: Ideology, Domination, and Resistance in Informational Society.* Urbana, IL: University of Illinois Press.

Lukes, S. (1974) *Power: A Radical View.* London: Macmillan.

Lukes, S. (ed.) (1986) *Power.* Oxford: Blackwell.

McAdam, D. (1994) 'Culture and social movements', in E. Laraña, H. Johnston and J.R. Gusfield (eds), *New Social Movements: From Ideology to Identity.* Philadelphia: Temple University Press. pp. 36–57.

McCarthy, E.D. (1994) 'The uncertain future of ideology: rereading Marx', *Sociological Quarterly*, 35 (3): 415–29.

McCartney, J.T. (1992) *Black Power Ideologies: An Essay in African-American Political Thought.* Philadelphia: Temple University Press.

McClelland, J.L. and Rumelhart, D.E. (1986) *Parallel Distributed Processing: Explorations in the Microstructure of Cognition* (vol. 2: Psychological and Biological Models). Cambridge, MA: MIT Press.

McClelland, J.L. and Rumelhart, D.E. (1988) *Explorations in Parallel Distributed Processing: A Handbook of Models, Programs and Exercise*. Cambridge, MA: MIT Press.

McCombs, M.E. and Shaw, D.L. (1972) 'The agenda-setting function of the press', *Public Opinion Quarterly*, 36, 176–87.

McCombs, M.E. and Shaw, D.L. (1993) 'The evolution of agenda-setting research: 25 years in the marketplace of ideas', *Journal of Communication*, 43 (2): 58–67.

McDermott, M. (1994) 'Race/class interactions in the formation of political ideology', *Sociological Quarterly*, 35 (2): 347–66.

MacKuen, M. and Coombs, S. (1981) *More than News: Media Power in Public Affairs*. Newbury Park, CA: Sage.

Maitland, K. and Wilson, J. (1987) 'Pronominal selection and ideological conflict', *Journal of Pragmatics*, 11 (4): 495–512.

Mandl, H. and Levin, J.R. (eds) (1989) *Knowledge Acquisition from Text and Pictures*, (Advances in psychology, 58). Amsterdam: North-Holland.

Mandler, J.M. (1984) *Stories, Scripts, and Scenes: Aspects of Schema Theory*. Hillsdale, NJ: Erlbaum.

Mannheim, K. (1936) *Ideology and Utopia: An Introduction to the Sociology of Knowledge*. New York: Harcourt, Brace and World (Harvest).

Manning, D.J. (ed.) (1980) *The Form of Ideology*. London: George, Allen and Unwin.

Marable, M. and Mullings, L. (1994) 'The divided mind of black-America: race, ideology and politics in the post civil-rights era', *Race and Class*, 36 (1): 61–72.

Marcel, A.J. and Bisiach, E. (eds) (1988) *Consciousness in Contemporary Science*. Oxford: Clarendon.

Margolis, M. and Mauser, G.A. (eds) (1989) *Manipulating Public Opinion: Essays on Public Opinion as a Dependent Variable*. Pacific Grove, CA: Brooks/Cole.

Markus, M. (1977) 'Self-schemata and processing information about the self', *Journal of Personality and Social Psychology*, 35: 63–78.

Martin, M.A. (1983) 'Ideologues, ideographs, and "The Best Men": from Carter to Reagan', *Southern Speech Communication Journal*, 49: 12–25.

Martin, L.L. and Tesser, A. (eds) (1992) *The Construction of Social Judgments*. Hillsdale, NJ: Erlbaum.

Martin, J., Scully, M. and Levitt, B. (1990) 'Injustice and the legitimation of revolution: damning the past, excusing the present, and neglecting the future', *Journal of Personality and Social Psychology*, 59 (2): 281–90.

Martín Rojo, L. (1994) 'Jargon of delinquents and the study of conversational dynamics', *Journal of Pragmatics*, 21 (3): 243–89.

Martín Rojo, L. (1995) 'Division and rejection: from the personification of the Gulf conflict to the demonisation of Saddam Hussein', *Discourse and Society*, 6 (1): 49–79.

Martín Rojo, L. and Callego Gallego, J. (1995) 'Argumentation and inhibition: sexism in the discourse of Spanish executives', *Pragmatics* 5 (4): 455–84.

Martín Rojo, L. and van Dijk, T.A. (1997) '"There was a problem, and it was solved!" Legitimating the expulsion of "illegal" immigrants in Spanish parliamentary discourse', *Discourse and Society*, 8 (4): 523–67.

Martín Rojo, L., Gómez Esteban, C., Arranz, F. and Gabilondo, A. (eds) (1994) *Hablar y Dejar Hablar: Sobre Racismo y Xenofobia* (To speak and to let speak: on racism and xenophobia). Madrid: Universidad Autónoma de Madrid.

Marx, K. and Engels, F. (1974) *The German Ideology*. London: Arthur.

Mattelart, A. (1979) *Multinational Corporations and the Control of Culture: The Ideological Apparatuses of Imperialism*. Atlantic Highlands, NJ: Humanities Press.

Mayer, R. (1990) 'Abstraction, context, and perspectivization-evidentials in discourse semantics', *Theoretical Linguistics*, 16 (2–3): 101–63.

Mazingo, S. (1988) 'Minorities and social control in the newsroom: thirty years after Breed', in G. Smitherman-Donaldson and T.A. van Dijk (eds), *Discourse and Discrimination*. Detroit, MI: Wayne State University Press. pp. 93–130.

Medhurst, M.J. (1990) *Cold War Rhetoric: Strategy, Metaphor, and Ideology*. Westport, CT: Greenwood.

Melucci, A. (1989) *Nomads of the Present: Social Movements and Individual Needs in Contemporary Society*. Philadelphia: Temple University Press.

Melucci, A. (1996) *Challenging Codes: Collective Action in the Information Age*. Philadelphia: Temple University Press.

Meszaros, I. (1989) *The Power of Ideology*. New York: New York University Press.

Milburn, M.A. (1987) 'Ideological self-schemata and schematically induced attitude consistency', *Journal of Experimental Social Psychology*, 23 (5): 383–98.

Miles, R. (1989) *Racism*. London: Routledge.

Miles, R. and Phizacklea, A. (eds) (1979) *Racism and Political Action in Britain*. London: Routledge and Kegan Paul.

Miller, S. I. and Fredericks, M. (1990) 'Perceptions of the crisis in American public-education: the relationship of metaphors to ideology', *Metaphor and Symbolic Activity*, 5 (2): 67–81.

Miller, D., Rowlands, M. and Tilley, C.Y. (eds) (1989) *Domination and Resistance*. Boston, MA: Unwin Hyman.

Mills, C.W. (1956) *The Power Elite*. London: Oxford University Press.

Mills, K. (1988) *A Place in the News: From the Women's Pages to the Front Page*. New York: Dodd, Mead.

Minnini, G. (1990) 'Common speech as pragmatic form of social reproduction', *Journal of Pragmatics*, XIV: 125–35.

Mitchell, W.J.T. (1986) *Iconology: Image, Text, Ideology*. Chicago: University of Chicago Press.

Mitchell, W.J.T. (1994) *Picture Theory: Essays on Verbal and Visual Representation*. Chicago: University of Chicago Press.

Miyajima, R. (1986) 'Organization ideology of Japanese managers', *Management International Review*, 26 (1): 73–6.

Mizruchi, M.S. (1990) 'Similarity of ideology and party preference among large American corporations: a study of political-action committee contributions', *Sociological Forum*, 5 (2): 213–40.

Molm, L.D. (1986) 'Gender, power, and legitimation: a test of 3 theories', *American Journal of Sociology*, 91: 1356–86.

Montgomery, M., Tolson, A. and Garton, G. (1989) 'Media discourse in the 1987 general election: ideology, scripts and metaphors', *ELR Journal*, 3: 173–204.

Moosmuller, S. (1989) 'Phonological variation in parliamentary discussions', in R. Wodak (ed.), *Language, Power and Ideology*. Amsterdam: Benjamins. pp. 165–80.

Morin, E. (1991) *La méthode. 4. Les idées: leur habitat, leur vie, leurs moeurs, leur organisation*. Paris: Seuil.

Morley, D. (1986) *Family Television: Cultural Power and Domestic Leisure*. London: Comedia.

Morley, D. (1993) 'Active audience theory: pendulums and pitfalls', *Journal of Communication*, 43 (4): 13–19.

Morley, D. and Chen, K.H. (eds) (1996) *Stuart Hall: Critical Dialogues in Cultural Studies*. London: Routledge.

Morris, A.D. and Mueller, C.M. (eds) (1992) *Frontiers in Social Movement Theory*. New Haven, CT: Yale University Press.

Moscovici, S. (1988) 'Notes towards a description of social representations', *European Journal of Social Psychology*, 18: 211–50.

Moscovici, S. and Hewstone, M. (1983) 'Social representations and social explanations: from the "naive" to the "amateur" scientist', in M. Hewstone (ed.), *Attribution Theory*. Oxford: Blackwell. pp. 98–125.

Mueller, C. (1973) *The Politics of Communication: A Study in the Political Sociology of Language, Socialization and Legitimation*. New York: Oxford University Press.

Mullard, C. (1985) *Race, Class and Ideology*. London: Routledge and Kegan Paul.

Mumby, D.K. (1988) *Communication and Power in Organizations: Discourse, Ideology, and Domination.* Norwood, NJ: Ablex.

Mumby, D.K. and Spitzack, C. (1983) 'Ideology and television news: a metaphoric analysis of political stories', *Central States Speech Journal*, 34: 162–71.

Negrine, R.M. (1989) *Politics and the Mass Media in Britain.* London: Routledge.

Neisser, U. (ed.) (1982) *Memory Observed: Remembering in Natural Contexts.* San Francisco: Freeman.

Neisser, U. (1986) 'Nested structure in autobiographical memory', in D.C. Rubin (ed.), *Autobiographical Memory.* Cambridge: Cambridge University Press. pp. 71–81.

Neisser, U. and Fivush, R. (eds) (1994) *The Remembering Self: Construction and Accuracy in the Self-narrative.* Cambridge: Cambridge University Press.

Neuman, W.R., Just, M.R. and Crigler, A.N. (1992) *Common Knowledge: News and the Construction of Political Meaning.* Chicago, IL: University of Chicago Press.

Neustadtl, A. and Clawson, D. (1988) 'Corporate political groupings: does ideology unify business political-behavior', *American Sociological Review*, 53 (2): 172–90.

Newtson, D. (1973) 'Attribution and the unit of perception of ongoing behavior', *Journal of Personality and Social Psychology*, 28: 28–38.

Nisbett, R.E. and Ross, L. (1980) *Human Inference: Strategies and Shortcomings of Social Judgment.* Englewood Cliffs, NJ: Prentice-Hall.

O'Keefe, D.J. (1990) *Persuasion: Theory and Research.* London: Sage.

Oberschall, A. (1993) *Social Movements: Ideologies, Interests, and Identities.* New Brunswick, NJ: Transaction.

Olsen, M.E. and Marger, M.N. (eds) (1993) *Power in Modern Societies.* Boulder, CO: Westview.

Ortony, A., Clore, C.L. and Collins, A.M. (1988) *The Cognitive Structure of Emotions.* New York: Cambridge University Press.

Paletz, D.L. and Entman, R.M. (1981) *Media, Power, Politics.* New York: Free Press.

Passeron, J.C. (1986) 'Theories of socio-cultural reproduction', *International Social Science Journal*, 38 (4): 619–29.

Pauly, R.M. (1993) *The Transparent Illusion: Image and Ideology in French Text and Film.* New York: Lang.

Pêcheux, M. (1982) *Language, Semantics and Ideology.* New York: St Martin's Press.

Perdue, C.W., Gurtman, M.B., Dovidio, J.F. and Tyler, R.B. (1990) 'Us and them: social categorization and the process of intergroup bias', *Journal of Personality and Social Psychology*, 59 (3): 475–86.

Pines, C.L. (1993) *Ideology and False Consciousness: Marx and his Historical Progenitors.* Albany, NY: State University of New York Press.

Pinker, S. (1994) *The Language Instinct: The New Science of Language and Mind.* New York: Morrow.

Poole, K.T. and Zeigler, L.H. (1981) 'The diffusion of feminist ideology', *Political Behavior*, 3 (3): 229–56.

Potter, J. (1996) *Representing Reality: Discourse, Rhetoric and Social Construction.* London: Sage.

Potter, J. and Wetherell, M. (1987) *Discourse and Social Psychology: Beyond Attitudes and Behavior.* Beverly Hills, CA: Sage.

Potter, J. and Wetherell, M. (1989) 'Fragmentated ideologies: accounts of educational failure and positive discrimination', *Text*, 9: 175–90.

Potter, J., Edwards, D. and Wetherell, M. (1993) 'A model of discourse in action', *American Behavioral Scientist*, 36 (3): 383–401.

Powell, T. (1993) *The Persistence of Racism in America.* Paterson, NJ: Littlefield Adams Quality Paperbacks.

Pratkanis, A.R. and Aronson, E. (1992) *Age of Propaganda: The Everyday Use and Abuse of Persuasion.* San Francisco, CA: Freeman.

Pratkanis, A.R., Breckler, S.J. and Greenwald, A.G. (eds) (1989) *Attitude Structure and Function.* Hillsdale, NJ: Erlbaum.

Protess, D.L. and McCombs, M.E. (eds) (1991) *Agenda Setting: Readings on Media, Public Opinion, and Policymaking*, (Communication textbook series). Hillsdale, NJ: Erlbaum.

Purkhardt, S.C. (1993) *Transforming Social Representations: A Social Psychology of Common Sense and Science*. London: Routledge.

Purvis, T. and Hunt, A. (1993) 'Discourse, ideology, discourse, ideology, discourse, ideology', *British Journal of Sociology*, 44 (3): 473–99.

Quackenbush, R.L. (1989) 'Comparison and contrast between belief system-theory and cognitive theory', *Journal of Psychology*, 123 (4): 315–28.

Rasmussen, D.M. (ed.) (1996) *The Handbook of Critical Theory*. Oxford: Blackwell.

Rawls, J. (1972) *A Theory of Justice*. Oxford: Oxford University Press.

Raz, J. (1986) *The Morality of Freedom*. Oxford: Clarendon.

Reardon, K.K. (1991) *Persuasion in Practice*. Newbury Park, CA: Sage.

Redclift, N. and Sinclair, M.T. (eds) (1991) *Working Women: International Perspectives on Labour and Gender Ideology*. London: Routledge.

Rees, G. (ed.) (1985) *Political Action and Social Identity: Class, Locality and Ideology*. New York: Macmillan.

Reeves, F. (1983) *British Racial Discourse*. Cambridge: Cambridge University Press.

Reis, C.A.A. (1993) *Towards a Semiotics of Ideology*. Berlin: de Gruyter.

Renkema, J. (1993) *Discourse Studies: An Introductory Textbook*. Amsterdam: Benjamins.

Resnick, L.B., Levine, J.M. and Teasley, S.D. (eds) (1991) *Perspectives on Socially Shared Cognition*. American Psychological Association.

Richardson, K. (1985) 'Pragmatics of speeches against the peace movement in Britain: a case study', in P. Chilton (ed.), *Language and the Nuclear Arms Debate: Nukespeak Today*. London: Pinter. pp. 23–44.

Robinson, J.A. and Swanson, K.L. (1990) 'Autobiographical memory: the next phase', *Applied Cognitive Psychology*, 4 (4): 321–35.

Roeh, I. and Nir, R. (1990) 'Speech presentation in the Israel radio news: ideological constraints and rhetorical strategies', *Text*, 10 (3): 225–44.

Rojek, C. and Turner, B.S. (eds) (1993) *Forget Baudrillard?* London: Routledge.

Rokeach, M. (1973) *The Nature of Human Values*. New York: Free Press.

Rokeach, M. (1979) *Understanding Human Values: Individual and Societal*. New York: Free Press.

Rosch, E. and Lloyd, B.B. (eds) (1978) *Cognition and Categorization*. Hillsdale, NJ: Erlbaum.

Roseman, I.J. (1994) 'The psychology of strongly held beliefs: theories of ideological structure and individual attachment', in Roger C. Schank and Ellen Langer (eds), *Beliefs, Reasoning, and Decision Making: Psycho-logic in Honor of Bob Abelson*. Hillsdale, NJ: Erlbaum. pp. 175–208.

Rosenberg, M.J. (1960) 'An analysis of affective-cognitive consistency', in C.I. Hovland and M.J. Rosenberg (eds), *Attitude Organization and Change*. New Haven, CT: Yale University Press.

Rosenberg, S.W. (1988) *Reason, Ideology and Politics*. Princeton, NJ: Princeton University Press.

Rosenberg, M.J., Hovland, C.I., McGuire, W.J., Abelson, R.P. and Brehm, J.W. (1960) *Attitude Organization and Change: An Analysis of Consistency among Attitude Components*. New Haven, CT: Yale University Press.

Rosengren, K.E. (ed.) (1994) *Media Effects and Beyond: Culture, Socialization and Lifestyles*. London: Routledge.

Rossi-Landi, F. (1978) *Ideologia*. Milan: ISEDI.

Rothman, S. and Lichter, S.R. (1984) 'Personality, ideology and worldview: a comparison of media and business elites', *British Journal fo Political Science*, 15: 29–49.

Rothstein, S.W. (1991) *Identity and Ideology: Sociocultural Theories of Schooling*. Westport, CT: Greenwood.

Rowbotham, S. (1973) *Women's Consciousness, Man's World*. Harmondsworth: Penguin.

Rubin, D.S. (ed.) (1986) *Autobiographical Memory*. New York: Cambridge University Press.

Rumelhart, D.E. and McClelland, J.L. (1986) *Parallel Distributed Processing: Explorations in the Microstructure of Cognition*, (vol. 1: Foundations). Cambridge, MA: MIT Press.

Rumelhart, D.E. and McClelland, J.L. (1988) *Explorations in Parallel Distributed Processing: A Handbook of Models, Programs, and Exercises*. Cambridge, MA: MIT Press.

Rutter, D.R. (1984) *Looking and Seeing: The Role of Visual Communication in Social Interaction*. Chichester: Wiley.

Ryan, B. (1992) *Feminism and the Women's Movement: Dynamics of Change in Social Movement Ideology, and Activism*. London: Routledge.

Saint-Martin, F. (1990) *Semiotics of Visual Language*. Bloomington, IN: Indiana University Press.

Sartori, G. (1966) 'European political parties', in J. LaPalombara and M. Weiner (eds), *Political Parties and Political Development*. Princeton: Princeton University Press.

Sartori, G. (1969) 'Politics, ideology and belief systems', *American Political Science Review* 63 (2).

Sarup, M. (1991) *Education and the Ideologies of Racism*. Stoke-on-Trent: Trentham.

Sassoon, J. (1984) 'Ideology, symbolic action and rituality in social movements: the effects on organizational forms', *Social Science Information*, 23 (4–5): 861–73.

Scarbrough, E. (1984) *Political Ideology and Voting: An Exploratory Study*. Oxford: Clarendon.

Scarbrough, E. (1990) 'Attitudes, social representations, and ideology', in Colin Fraser and George Gaskell (eds), *The Social Psychological Study of Widespread Beliefs*. New York: Clarendon. pp. 99–117.

Schank, R.C. (1982) *Dynamic Memory: A Theory of Reminding in Computers and People*. Cambridge: Cambridge University Press.

Schank, R.C. and Abelson, R.P. (1977) *Scripts, Plans, Goals, and Understanding: An Inquiry into Human Knowledge Structures*. Hillsdale, NJ: Erlbaum.

Schieffelin, B.B. (1996) 'Creating evidence: making sense of written words in Bosavi', in E. Ochs, E.A. Schefloff and S.A. Thompson (eds), *Interaction and Grammar*. Cambridge: Cambridge University Press. pp. 435–60.

Schiffrin, D. (1993) *Approaches to Discourse*. Oxford: Blackwell.

Schiller, H.I. (1973) *The Mind Managers*. Boston: Beacon Press.

Schiller, H.I. and Alexandre, L. (ed.) (1992) *The Ideology of International Communications*. New York: Institute for Media Analysis.

Schuman, H, Steeh, C. and Bobo, L. (1985) *Racial Attitudes in America: Trends and Interpretations*. Cambridge, MA: Harvard University Press.

Schwartz, S.H. and Bilsky, W. (1990) 'Toward a theory of the universal content and structure of values: extensions and cross-cultural replications', *Journal of Personality and Social Psychology*, 58 (5): 878–91.

Scott, J.C. (1986) *Weapons of the Weak: Everyday Forms of Peasant Resistance*. New Haven, CT: Yale University Press.

Searle, J.R. (1983) *Intentionality*. Cambridge: Cambridge University Press.

Searle, J.R. (1992) *The Rediscovery of the Mind*. Cambridge, MA: MIT Press.

Searle, J.R. (1995) *The Construction of Social Reality*. London: Penguin.

Seliger, M. (1976) *Ideology and Politics*. New York: Free Press.

Seliger, M. (1979) *The Marxist Conception of Ideology: A Critical Essay*. Cambridge: Cambridge University Press.

Selting, M. (1995) *Prosodie im Gespräch: Aspekte einer interaktionalen Phonologie der Konversation* (Prosody in conversation: aspects of an interactional phonology of conversation). Tübingen: Niemeyer.

Shanon, B. (1993) *The Representational and the Presentational: An Essay on Cognition and the Study of Mind*. New York: Harvester-Wheatsheaf.

Sharistanian, J. (ed.) (1986) *Gender, Ideology, and Action: Historical Perspectives on Women's Public Lives*. Westport, CT: Greenwood.

Sharp, R. (1980) *Knowledge, Ideology and the Politics of Schooling*. London: Routledge and Kegan Paul.

Sharrock, W.W. and Anderson, B. (1991) 'Epistemology: professional scepticism', in G. Button (ed.), *Ethnomethodology and the Human Sciences*. Cambridge: Cambridge University Press. pp. 51–76.

Shavitt, S. and Brock, T.C. (eds) (1994) *Persuasion: Psychological Insights and Perspectives*. London: Allyn and Bacon.

Shaw, K.E. (1990) 'Ideology, control and the teaching profession', *Policy and Politics*, 18 (4): 269–78.

Shils, E.A. (1958) 'Ideology and civility: on the politics of the intellectual', *Sewanee Review* 66 (3).

Shipman, P. (1994) *The Evolution of Racism: Human Differences and the Use and Abuse of Science*. New York: Simon and Schuster.

Shohat, E. and Stam, R. (1994) *Unthinking Eurocentrism: Multiculturalism and the Media*. London: Routledge.

Shotter, J. and Gergen, K.J. (eds) (1989) *Texts of Identity*. London: Sage.

Sidanius, J. (1993) 'The psychology of group conflict and the dynamics of oppression: a social dominance perspective', in Shanto Iyengar and William James McGuire (eds), *Explorations in Political Psychology*, (Duke Studies in Political Psychology). Durham, NC: Duke University Press. pp. 183–219.

Sidanius, J. and Ekehammar, B. (1980) 'Sex-related differences in socio-political ideology', *Scandinavian Journal of Psychology*, 21 (1): 17–26.

Sidanius, J. and Ekehammar, B. (1983) 'Sex, political party preference, and higher-order dimensions of sociopolitical ideology', *Journal of Psychology*, 115 (2): 233–9.

Sidanius, J. and Liu, J.H. (1992) 'The Gulf War and the Rodney King beating: implications of the general conservatism and social dominance perspectives', *Journal of Social Psychology*, 132 (6): 685–700.

Sidanius, J., Pratto, F. and Rabinowitz, J.L. (1994) 'Gender, ethnic status, and ideological asymmetry: a social dominance interpretation', *Journal of Cross Cultural Psychology*, 25 (2): 194–216.

Siegfried, J. (ed.) (1994) *The Status of Common Sense in Psychology*. Norwood, NJ: Ablex.

Sigel, I.E. (ed.) (1985) *Parental Belief Systems: The Psychological Consequences for Children*. Hillsdale, NJ: Erlbaum.

Sigel, R.S. (ed.) (1989) *Political Learning in Adulthood: A Sourcebook of Theory and Research*. Chicago: University of Chicago Press.

Simon, B. (1992) 'Intragroup differentiation in terms of ingroup and outgroup attributes', *European Journal of Social Psychology*, 22 (4): 407–13.

Simons, H.W. and Billig, M. (eds) (1994) *After Postmodernism: Reconstructing Ideology Critique*. Newbury Park, CA: Sage.

Sinclair, J. (1987) *Images Incorporated: Advertising as Industry and Ideology*. London: Croom Helm.

Sivanandan, A. (1982) *A Different Hunger: Writings on Black Resistance*. London: Pluto.

Skidmore, M.J. (1993) *Ideologies: Politics in Action*. Orlando, FL: Harcourt Brace Jovanovich.

Skutnabb-Kangas, T. (1990) 'Legitimating or delegitimating new forms of racism: the role of researchers', *Journal of Multilingual and Multicultural Development*, 11 (1–2): 77–100.

Sniderman, P.M., Tetlock, P.E. and Carmines, E.G. (eds) (1993) *Prejudice, Politics, and the American Dilemma*. Stanford, CA: Stanford University Press.

Snyder, M.L. (1981) 'On the self-perpetuating nature of social stereotypes', in D.L. Hamilton (ed.), *Cognitive Processes in Stereotyping and Intergroup Behavior*. Hillsdale, NJ: Erlbaum. pp. 183–212.

Snyder, M.L. (1981) 'Seek and ye shall find: testing hypotheses about other people', in E.T. Higgins, C.P. Herman and M.P. Zanna (eds), *Social Cognition: The Ontario Symposium*, vol. 1. Hillsdale, NJ: Erlbaum. pp. 277–304.

Solomon, P.R., Goethals, G.R., Kelley, C.M. and Stephens, B.R. (1989) *Memory: Interdisciplinary Approaches*. New York: Springer.

Solomos, J. (1986) 'Trends in the political-analysis of racism', *Political Studies*, 34 (2): 313–24.

Solomos, J. (1993) *Race and Racism in Britain*. New York: St Martin's Press.

Solomos, J. and Wrench, J. (1993) *Racism and Migration in Western Europe*. Oxford: Berg.

Solso, R.L. (1994) *Cognition and the Visual Arts*. Cambridge, MA: MIT Press.

Spears, R., Oakes, P.J., Ellemers, N. and Haslam, S.A. (eds) (1997) *The Social Psychology of Stereotyping and Group Life*. Cambridge: Blackwell.

Srull, T.K. and Wyer, R.S. (eds) (1993) *The Mental Representation of Trait and Autobiographical Knowledge about the Self*, (Advances in Social Cognition, vol. 5). Hillsdale, NJ: Erlbaum.

Stephan, W.G. (1977) 'Stereotyping: the role of ingroup-outgroup differences in causal attribution for behavior', *The Journal of Social Psychology*, 101: 255–66.

Stevens, E. and Wood, G.H. (1992) *Justice, Ideology, and Education: An Introduction to the Social Foundations of Education*. New York: McGraw-Hill.

Strassner, E. (1987) *Ideologie – Sprache – Politik: Grundfragen ihres Zusammenhangs* (Ideology, language, politics: basic questions about their relationship). Tübingen: Niemeyer.

Strube, G. and Wender, K.F. (eds) (1993) *The Cognitive Psychology of Knowledge*. Amsterdam: North-Holland / Elsevier Science.

Sunic, T. (1990) *Against Democracy and Equality: The European New Right*. New York: Lang.

Sykes, M. (1985) 'Discrimination in discourse', in T.A. van Dijk (ed.), *Handbook of Discourse Analysis*, (vol. 4: *Discourse Analysis in Society*). London: Academic Press. pp. 83–101.

Tajfel, H. (ed.) (1978) *Differentiation between Social Groups: Studies in the Social Psychology of Intergroup Relations*. London: Academic Press.

Tajfel, H. (1981) *Human Groups and Social Categories*. Cambridge: Cambridge University Press.

Tenney, Y.J. (1989) 'Predicting conversational reports of a personal event', *Cognitive Science*, 13 (2): 213–33.

Tetlock, P.E. (1983) 'Cognitive style and political ideology', *Journal of Personality and Social Psychology*, 45 (1): 118–26.

Tetlock, P.E. (1984) 'Cognitive style and political belief systems in the British House of Commons', *Journal of Personality and Social Psychology*, 46: 365–75.

Tetlock, P.E. (1989) 'Structure and function in political belief systems', in Anthony R. Pratkanis, Steven J. Breckler and Anthony G. Greenwald (eds), *Attitude Structure and Function: The Third Ohio State University Volume on Attitudes and Persuasion*. Hillsdale, NJ: Erlbaum. pp. 129–51.

Therborn, G. (1980) *The Ideology of Power and the Power of Ideology*. London: Verso.

Theus, K.T. (1991) 'Organizational ideology, structure, and communication efficacy: a causal analysis', in Larissa A. Grunig and James E. Grunig (eds), *Public Relations Research Annual*, vol. 3. Hillsdale, NJ: Erlbaum. pp. 133–49.

Thompson, J.B. (1984) *Studies in the Theory of Ideology*. Berkeley, CA: University of California Press.

Thompson, J.B. (1990) *Ideology and Modern Culture: Critical Social Theory in the Era of Mass Communication*. Stanford, CA: Stanford University Press.

Thompson, S.E. (1994) *Hate Groups*. San Diego, CA: Lucent Books.

Thompson, C.P., Skowronski, J.J., Larsem S.F. and Betz, A.L. (1996) *Autobiographical Memory: Remembering What and Remembering When*. Mahwah, NJ: Erlbaum.

Tierney, W.G. (ed.) (1991) *Culture and Ideology in Higher Education: Advancing a Critical Agenda*. New York: Praeger.

Todd, E. (1985) *The Explanation of Ideology: Family Structures and Social Systems*. Oxford: Blackwell.

Togeby, L. (1995) 'Feminist attitudes: social interests or political-ideology', *Women and Politics*, 15 (4): 39–61.

Trafimow, D. and Wyer, R.S. (1993) 'Cognitive representation of mundane social events', *Journal of Personality and Social Psychology*, 64 (3): 365–76.

Tucker, W.H. (1994) *The Science and Politics of Racial Research*. Urbana, IL: University of Illinois Press.

Tulving, E. (1983) *Elements of Episodic Memory*. Oxford: Oxford University Press.

Turner, B.S. (1992) 'Ideology and utopia in the formation of an intelligentsia: reflections on the English cultural conduit', *Theory Culture & Society*, 9 (1): 183–210.

Turner, J.H. (1994) *Sociology: Concepts and Uses*. New York: McGraw-Hill.

Turner, R.H. (1994) 'Ideology and utopia after scoialism', in E. Laraña, H. Johnston and J.R. Gusfield (eds), *New Social Movements: From Ideology to Identity*. Philadelphia, PA: Temple University Press. pp. 79–100.

Turner, J.C. and Giles, H. (eds) (1981) *Intergroup Behaviour*. Oxford: Blackwell.

Turner, C.B. and Wilson, W.J. (1976) 'Dimensions of racial ideology: a study of urban Black attitudes', *Journal of Social Issues*, 32 (2): 139–52.

Turner, J.C., Hogg, M.A., Oakes, P.J., Reicher, S.D. and Wetherell, M.S. (1987) *Rediscovering the Social Group: A Self-categorization Theory*. Oxford: Blackwell.

Tyler, T.R. (1990) 'Justice, self-interest, and the legitimacy of legal and political authority', in Jane J. Mansbridge (ed.), *Beyond Self-interest*. Chicago: University of Chicago Press. pp. 171–9.

Urban, G. (1988) 'The pronominal pragmatics of nuclear war discourse', *Multilingua*, 7 (1–2): 67–93.

Vallas, S.P. (1991) 'Workers, firms, and the dominant ideology: hegemony and consciousness in the monopoly core', *Sociological Quarterly*, 32 (1): 61–83.

van Dijk, T.A. (1977) *Text and Context: Explorations in the Semantics and Pragmatics of Discourse*. London: Longman.

van Dijk, T.A. (1980) *Macrostructures: An Interdisciplinary Study of Global Structures in Discourse, Interaction, and Cognition*. Hillsdale, NJ: Erlbaum.

van Dijk, T.A. (1984) *Prejudice in Discourse*. Amsterdam: Benjamins.

van Dijk, T.A. (ed.) (1985) *Handbook of Discourse Analysis* (4 vols). London: Academic Press.

van Dijk, T.A. (1987) *Communicating Racism: Ethnic Prejudice in Thought and Talk*. Newbury Park, CA: Sage.

van Dijk, T.A. (1988) *News Analysis: Case Studies of International and National News in the Press*. Hillsdale, NJ: Erlbaum.

van Dijk, T.A. (1988) *News as Discourse*. Hillsdale, NJ: Erlbaum.

van Dijk, T.A. (1991) *Racism and the Press*. London: Routledge.

van Dijk, T.A. (1992) 'Discourse and the denial of racism', *Discourse and Society*, 3 (1): 87–118.

van Dijk, T.A. (1993a) *Elite Discourse and Racism*. Newbury Park, CA: Sage.

van Dijk, T.A. (1993b) 'Principles of critical discourse analysis', *Discourse and Society*, 4 (2): 249–83.

van Dijk, T.A. (1995) 'Discourse semantics and ideology', *Discourse and Society*, 6 (2): 243–89.

van Dijk, T.A. (1996) 'Discourse, power and access', in C.R. Caldas-Coulthard and M. Coulthard (eds), *Texts and Practices: Readings in Critical Discourse Analysis*. London: Routledge. pp. 84–104.

van Dijk, T.A. (1997) 'Context models and text processing', in M. Stamenow (ed.), *Language Structure, Discourse and the Access to Consciousness*. Amsterdam: Benjamins. pp. 189–226.

van Dijk, T.A. (ed.) (1997) *Discourse Studies: A Multidisciplinary Study*, (2 vols). London: Sage.

van Dijk, T.A. (1998) 'Towards a theory of context and experience models in discourse processing', in H. van Oostendorp and S. Goldman (eds), *The Construction of Mental Models during Reading*. Hillsdale, NJ: Erlbaum.

van Dijk, T.A. and Kintsch, W. (1983) *Strategies of Discourse Comprehension*. New York: Academic Press.

van Holthoon, F. and Olson, D.R. (eds) (1987) *Common Sense: The Foundations for Social Science*. Lanham, MD: University Press of America.

van Leeuwen, T.J. (1992) 'Rhythm and social context', in P. Tench (ed.), *Studies in Systemic Phonology*. London: Pinter.

van Leeuwen, T.J. (1995) 'Representing social-action', *Discourse and Society*, 6 (1): 81–106.

van Oostendorp, H. and Zwaan, R.A. (eds) (1994) *Naturalistic Text Comprehension*. Norwood, NJ: Ablex.

van Schuur, H. (1984) 'Structure in political beliefs: a new model for stochastic unfolding with application to European party activists', Doctoral dissertation, University of Groningen, the Netherlands.

van Zoonen, L. (1994) *Feminist Media Studies*. London: Sage.

Verschueren, J. and Blommaert, J. (1992) 'The role of language in European nationalist ideologies', *Pragmatics: Quarterly Publication of the International Pragmatics Association*, 2 (3): 355–75.

Walker, H.A., Thomas, G.M. and Zelditch, M. (1986) 'Legitimation, endorsement, and stability', *Social Forces*, 64 (3): 620–43.

Walsh, F. (1983) 'Normal family ideologies: myths and realities', *Family Therapy Collections*, 6: 1–14.

Wander, P. (1984) 'The 3rd persona: an ideological turn in thetorical theory', *Central States Speech Journal*, 35 (4): 197–216.

Warner, R. and Szubka, T. (eds) (1994) *The Mind–Body Problem: A Guide to the Current Debate*. Oxford: Blackwell.

Watt, J. (1994) *Ideology, objectivity, and education*. New York: Teachers College Press.

Weakliem, D. (1993) 'Class-consciousness and political-change: voting and political-attitudes in the British working-class, 1964 to 1970', *American Sociological Review*, 58 (3): 382–97.

Weaver, C.A., Mannes, S. and Fletcher, C.R. (eds) (1995) *Discourse Comprehension: Essays in Honor of Walter Kintsch*. Hillsdale, NJ: Erlbaum.

Weber, J.G. (1994) 'The nature of ethnocentric attribution bias: ingroup protection or enhancement?', *Journal of Experimental Social Psychology*, 30 (5): 482–504.

Wegman, C. (1981) 'Conceptual representations of belief systems', *Journal for the Theory of Social Behavior*, 11: 279–305.

Wegner, D.M. and Vallacher, R.R. (1981) 'Common-sense psychology', in J. Forgas (ed.), *Social Cognition: Perspectives on Everyday Understanding*. New York: Academic Press.

Weinberg, M. (1990) *Racism in the United States: A Comprehensive Classified Bibliography*. New York: Greenwood.

Weiss, R.M. (1986) *Managerial Ideology and the Social Control of Deviance in Organizations*. New York: Praeger.

Welch, C. (1984) *Liberty and Utility: The French Ideologues and the Transformation of Liberalism*. New York: Columbia University Press.

Wellman, D.T. (1993) *Portraits of White Racism*, (2nd edn). Cambridge: Cambridge University Press.

Wenden, A.L. and Schaffner, C. (eds) (1994) *Language and Peace*. Aldershot: Dartmouth.

Wertsch, J.V. (1985) *Vygotsky and the Social Formation of Mind*. Cambridge, MA: Harvard University Press.

Wertsch, J.V., Del Rio, P. and Alvarez, A. (eds) (1994) *Sociocultural Studies of Mind*. New York: Cambridge University Press.

West, C. (1979) ' "Against our will": male interruptions of females in cross-sex conversation', *Annals of the New York Academy of Sciences*, 327: 81–97.

West, C. (1984) *Routine Complications: Troubles with Talk between Doctors and Patients*. Bloomington, IN: Indiana University Press.

West, C. (1990) 'Not just "doctors' orders": directive-response sequences in patients' visits to women and men physicians', *Discourse and Society*, 1 (1): 85–112.

Westerstahl, J. and Johansson, F. (1994) 'Foreign news: news values and ideologies', *European Journal of Communication*, 9 (1): 71–89.

Wetherell, M. and Potter, J. (1992) *Mapping the Language of Racism: Discourse and the Legitimation of Exploitation*. New York: Harvester-Wheatsheaf.

Williams, J. (ed.) (1995) *PC Wars: Politics and Theory in the Academy*. New York: Routledge.

Willis, P. (1977) *Learning to Labour: How Working Class Kids Get Working Class Jobs*. London: Saxon House.

Wilson, J. (1990) *Politically Speaking*. Oxford: Blackwell.

Wilson, C.C. (1991) *Black Journalists in Paradox: Historical Perspective and Current Dilemmas*. New York: Greenwood.

Wodak, R. (1987) '"And Where Is the Lebanon?" A socio-psycholinguistic investigation of comprehension and intelligibility of News', *Text*, 7 (4): 377–410.

Wodak, R. (ed.) (1989) *Language, Power and Ideology: Studies in Political Discourse*. Amsterdam: Bejamins.

Wodak, R. (1991) 'Turning the tables: anti-semitic discourse in post-war Austria', *Discourse and Society*, 2: 65–84.

Wodak, R. (1996) *Disorders of Discourse*. London: Longman.

Wodak, R., Nowak, P., Pelikan, J., Gruber, H., de Cillia, R. and Mitten, R. (1990) ' "Wir sind alle unschuldige Täter": Diskurshistorische Studien zum Nachkriegsantisemitismus' (' "We are all innocent perpetrators": discourse historic studies in post war anti-semitism). Frankfurt-on-Main: Suhrkamp.

Wolfe, A. (1977) *The Limits of Legitimacy: Political Contradictions of Contemporary Capitalism*. New York: Free Press.

Wood, A.W. (1988) 'Ideology, false consciousness, and social illusion', in Brian P. McLaughlin and Amelie Oksenberg Rorty (eds), *Perspectives on Self-deception: Topics in Philosophy*, (vol. 6). Berkeley, CA: University of California Press. pp. 345–63.

Worchel, S. and Simpson, J.A. (eds) (1993) *Conflict between People and Groups: Causes, Processes, and Resolutions*, (Nelson-Hall series in psychology). Chicago: Nelson-Hall.

Wrong, D.H. (1979) *Power: Its Forms, Bases and Uses*. Oxford: Blackwell.

Wuthnow, R. (1987) *Meaning and Moral Order: Explorations in Cultural Analysis*. Berkeley, CA: University of California Press.

Wuthnow, R. (1989) *Communities of Discourse: Ideology and Social Structure in the Reformation, the Enlightenment, and European Socialism*. Cambridge, MA: Harvard University Press.

Wuthnow, R. (1992) 'Infrastructure and superstructure: revisions in Marxist sociology of culture', in R. Munch and N.J. Smelser (eds), *Theory of Culture*. Berkeley, CA: University of California Press. pp. 145–70.

Wuthnow, R. and Shrum, W. (1983) 'Knowledge workers as a "new class": structural and ideological convergence among professional-technical workers and managers', *Work and Occupations*, 10 (4): 471–87.

Wyer, R.S. and Gordon, S.E. (1984) 'The cognitive representation of social information', in R.S. Wyer and T.K. Srull (eds), *Handbook of Social Cognition*, (vol. 2). Hillsdale, NJ: Erlbaum. pp. 72–150.

Wyer, R.S. and Srull, T.K. (eds) (1984) *Handbook of Social Cognition*, (3 vols). Hillsdale, NJ: Erlbaum.

Wyer, R.S., Budesheim, T.L., Shavitt, S. and Riggle, E.D. et al. (1991) 'Image, issues, and ideology: the processing of information about political candidates', *Journal of Personality and Social Psychology*, 61 (4): 533–45.

Wyer, R.S. and Srull, T.K. (1989) *Memory and Cognition in its Social Context*. Hillsdale, NJ: Erlbaum.

Yantek, T. (1988) 'Polity and economy under extreme economic-conditions: a comparative study of the Reagan and Thatcher experiences', *American Journal of Political Science*, 32: 196–216.

Young, M.F.D. (ed.) (1971) *Knowledge and Control: New Directions for the Sociology of Education*. London: Collier-Macmillan.

Zaller, J.R. (1990) 'Political awareness, elite opinion leadership, and the mass survey response', *Social Cognition*, 8 (1): 125–53.

Zanna, M.P., Olson, J. M. and Herman, C.P. (eds) (1987) *Social Influence: The Ontario Symposium*, (vol. 5). Hillsdale, NJ: Erlbaum.

Zeitlin, I.M. (1994) *Ideology and the Development of Sociological Theory*. Englewood Cliffs, NJ: Prentice-Hall.

Index